FLYWHEEL,
SHYSTER,
FLYWHEEL

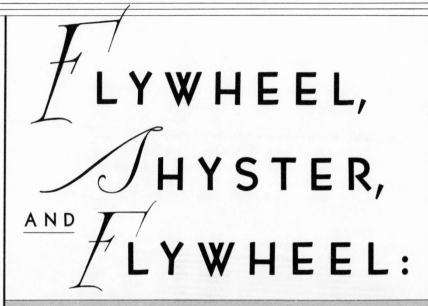

FLYWHEEL, SHYSTER, AND FLYWHEEL:

THE MARX BROTHERS' LOST RADIO SHOW

Edited by Michael Barson

Pantheon Books New York

Library of Congress Cataloging-in-Publication Data

Flywheel, Shyster, and Flywheel.

1. Flywheel, Shyster, and Flywheel (Radio program)
I. Barson, Michael.   II. Marx Brothers.
PN1991.77.F59   1988   791.45′72   88-42616
ISBN 0-679-72036-7 (pbk.)

Book design by Guenet Abraham
Manufactured in the United States of America
First Edition

CONTENTS

TO JEANETTE

HELLO, WE MUST BE GOING:
The Short, Happy Life of the Marx Brothers on Radio

"There were more than three hundred and forty radio programs during 1932. Most of them were hardly fit for human consumption."

So complained *Forum* magazine's radio critic, Cyrus Fisher, in the March 1933 issue. Fit or not, these shows *were* consumed by an avid audience that owned some seventeen million radio sets and offered more than fifty million pairs of ears for the blandishments of radio sponsors. Advertisers were delighted to have their products associated with the likes of Al Jolson, Eddie Cantor, Will Rogers, Bing Crosby, and George Burns and Gracie Allen—just a few of the big names from film and vaudeville who had been lured to radio by salaries that could reach $5,000 a week.

It was a sweet deal from the stars' standpoint. Where else could they have earned such sums in the midst of the Depression for half an hour's work? Radio scripts required no memorization—a few light rehearsals could suffice—and only a few minutes had to be spent extolling the virtues of toothpaste, hand lotion, hair tonic, and the like. By contrast, Garbo's $6,500 weekly salary was earned at hard labor, as MGM's cameras ground on through forty- and fifty-hour weeks.

Such was the climate in the fall of 1932 when the Standard Oil companies combined forces with Colonial Beacon Oil to sponsor a radio series that would promote Esso gasoline and Essolube motor oil. Since archrival Texaco was enjoying vast success with its new *Texaco Fire Chief Program*, starring vaudeville comic Ed Wynn, the Standard Oil companies were naturally interested in carving out their own territory over the airwaves. They turned to their advertising agency, McCann-Erickson, to create a suitable vehicle. The result was *Five Star Theatre*, a variety series that offered a different program each night of the week, Monday through Friday, all to dramatize Esso gasoline's five unique properties, including something called "hydrofining."

The shows ranged from *Charlie Chan* to light opera, but the jewel of the enterprise was Monday night's entry, *Beagle, Shyster, and Beagle, Attorneys at Law*, a series about a malpracticing lawyer and his bungling assistant. The program was created to showcase the talents of Groucho and Chico Marx, half of the Four Marx Brothers. Already veterans of four films—*The Cocoanuts, Animal Crackers, Monkey Business*, and *Horse Feathers*—the Marxes in 1932 were one of Hollywood's brightest comedy teams. As the talents of silent Harpo and bland Zeppo could not be utilized on radio, Groucho and Chico were signed to share $6,500 a week, one of the highest salaries of the day, to portray Waldorf T. Beagle and Emmanuel Ravelli, his incompetent man Friday. The show was broadcast each Monday evening from seven-thirty to eight over the NBC Blue Network—NBC also had a Red Network with separate programming—to thirteen affiliates in nine states throughout the East and South, originating from NBC's flagship station, WJZ in New York.

The task of developing the show fell to Nat Perrin and Arthur Sheekman, young writers who had recently polished the scripts for *Monkey Business* and *Horse Feathers*. And while *Beagle, Shyster, and Beagle* would require that Groucho, Chico, Perrin, and Sheekman travel cross-country to brave New York's chillier climes, the offer must have sounded like a paid vacation, at least to the Marxes. A few years earlier they had been presenting four shows daily in vaudeville; more recently, it had been seven performances a week on Broadway. They were now being paid a princely sum to stand before a microphone each week for half an hour (less really, minus the musical interludes and announcer spots) to read from a script that they had barely bothered rehearsing. True, the brothers did have to cap each skit with a brief paean to the wonders of Essolube—but if Walter Winchell could sell Jergen's Lotion and Rudy Vallee could warble for Fleischmann's yeast, then the Marx Brothers could spend sixty seconds hawking gasoline for Standard Oil. (Luckily for them, Rin-Tin-Tin already had the Ken-L-Ration account sewn up.)

Alert readers have undoubtedly noticed that the book they are holding is *not* titled *Beagle, Shyster, and Beagle*. And thereby hangs a tale, courtesy of Mr. Perrin: An irate attorney by the name of Beagle called the station after the first show had aired and threatened a libel suit if the name of the program was not changed. With the fourth episode, it was. Apparently no Flywheels had entered the legal profession by that time, so *Flywheel, Shyster, and Flywheel* it remained through the twenty-sixth and final episode.

The first installment of the show aired on November 28, 1932. The response of the general public is lost to the ages, but *Variety*'s critic, for one, was not impressed. Describing the episode's infidelity plot, *Variety* complained:

> That's fine stuff for children! Chances are that if the Marxes proceed with their law office continuity along lines like this they will never be able to hold a kid listener. Firstly, because parents don't want their children to hear about bad wives and divorces, and this isn't an agreeable theme to the kids. Which means that if the Marxes don't

look out, whatever kid following they have on the screen will be totally lost to them on the air. . . . It's quite likely the Marxes can make themselves on the air. But they will have to use more headwork than their first effort displayed.

Of course, this impassioned attack is ridiculous. Any kids who'd attended *Monkey Business* and *Horse Feathers* and become fans were well aware of the Marxes' fondness for skits involving adultery and could hardly have been shocked by anything that took place on *Flywheel*.

For the first two months, *Flywheel* originated from WJZ in New York. In January, the Marxes took the then-unprecedented step of moving the broadcasts to the West Coast. After all, if thirty minutes' work a week was appealing during a New York City winter, it had to be that much better out in sunny Los Angeles. There was just one problem: NBC had not established a West Coast studio by 1933. But as necessity is the mother of invention, an empty soundstage at Radio Pictures (RKO) was commandeered for the next thirteen broadcasts (Episodes 10 through 22). How the brothers must have groaned when they (and their writers) had to haul themselves back east for the final four shows of the season. After the May 22 broadcast, *Flywheel, Shyster, and Flywheel* went off the air for the summer. It never returned.

There are a number of possible reasons why *Flywheel* was not renewed for the fall season. As Groucho recalls in his book *The Secret Word Is Groucho:*

> Company sales, as a result of our show, had risen precipitously. Profits doubled in that brief time, and Esso felt guilty taking the money. So Esso dropped us after twenty-six weeks. Those were the days of guilt-edged securities, which don't exist today.

A more likely explanation is that Groucho and Chico were ready to return to films. Or perhaps it was the high cost of retaining Groucho and Chico's services. But the most obvious reason that *Flywheel* did not continue was the indifferent ratings it earned. Not that the 22.1 CAB (or Crossley) rating for show was an embarrassment; in fact, such well-known programs as *The Shadow*, *The Adventures of Sherlock Holmes*, Al Jolson's show for Chevrolet, *Morton Downey*, and *Kate Smith and Her Swanee Music* did not score as high. But *Flywheel* faced a major disadvantage with its 7:30 time slot. According to an article on radio advertising published in the September 1932 issue of *Fortune* magazine, only 40 percent of radio owners tuned in at seven o'clock; by nine the numbers increased to a high of 60 percent. Most of the season's top-rated shows— *The Chase and Sanborn Hour* with Eddie Cantor, *The Robert Burns Program* with Burns and Allen, and Jack Pearl's *Baron Munchausen* show— aired later in the evening. Given *Flywheel's* less-than-ideal scheduling, it actually performed moderately well.

The only rating that really mattered to Standard Oil, however, was the whopping 44.8 earned by the *Texaco Fire Chief Program* in its more favorable 9:30 p.m. time slot. Soundly licked in the arena of oil-cartel comedy, it is not surprising that Standard Oil gave up on *Flywheel*. Had the show been broadcast at 9:00 p.m., perhaps the careers of the Marx Brothers might have taken a different turn.

While decisions about *Five Star Theatre* were being made in New York, the Marxes were taking yet another crosscountry train ride to Hollywood with Perrin and Sheekman. *Duck Soup* was already in the works, and Perrin and Sheekman were needed to add material to the script submitted by Bert Kalmar and Harry Ruby for director Leo McCarey.

Released in November 1933 to mediocre box office, *Duck Soup* proved to be the Marxes' swan song for Paramount. The movie is now considered by many fans to be the Marx Brothers' best. Another, equally vocal, camp —which included Groucho—feels that *A Night at the Opera*, their first film for MGM, is superior. It's interesting that the argument traditionally has centered on whether or not *Duck Soup's* improvisational approach worked better than *Night's* carefully rehearsed routines. (MGM's Thalberg had the Boys roadtest the skits in Seattle for several weeks before filming began.) Looking back, *Duck Soup* was not as anarchic as legend would have it. No fewer than fifteen routines from *Flywheel* were transplanted into *Duck Soup*, on which Perrin and Sheekman, not incidentally, received an "additional dialogue" credit.

The "lifts"—some word for word, others modified for different characters—range from brief bits such as Groucho's "Go, and never darken my office towels again" (Episode 3) and "Oh, Mrs. Brittenhouse . . . would you give me a lock of your hair? . . . I'm letting you off easy—I was going to ask you for the whole wig" (Episode 4), to elaborate routines such as the trial of Joe Crookley (Episode 12), in which Groucho's sudden reversal from prosecutor to defense lawyer presages the nearly identical moment in *Duck Soup* when Groucho, during Chico's trial for treason, leaps from behind his bench after Chico explains that no one would accept his last eighteen dollars to defend him. The memorable exchange between Chico and the leader of Sylvania in *Duck Soup*, wherein Chico is reporting his and Harpo's lack of success in shadowing Groucho, comes directly from the very first NBC episode, in which Chico explains to a hapless client the troubles he has had shadowing his wife ("Tuesday I go to the ball game—she don't show up. Wednesday she go to the ball game —I don't show up. Thursday was a doubleheader. We both no show up."). Even the name of Groucho's character in *Duck Soup*, Rufus T. Firefly, is redolent of the "Waldorf T. Flywheel" he assumes with the fourth episode of the radio series. Fans of *Duck Soup* can thus thank Esso gasoline—not to mention Nat Perrin and Arthur Sheekman—for many of their favorite puns, put-downs, and sketches. (Perrin can also be cited for spinning off the department-store setting of Episode 15 in the 1941 film, *The Big Store*, with Groucho as Wolf J. Flywheel, Private Detective, and Chico as Ravelli.)

Flywheel gaveth, but *Flywheel* also tooketh away. Chico's character was taken from *Animal Crackers*. The seventeeth episode is composed almost entirely of recycled crumbs from *Animal Crackers*, from the plot device of the stolen painting (a "Beaugard" in *Crackers*, a Rembrandt in *Flywheel*) to the extended dictation scene (played between Groucho and Zeppo in the film) to the marvelous "house-building" sequence between Groucho and Chico. *Animal Crackers* also "donates" several other bits to the twenty-third episode: its plot—this time, a stolen diamond—and several skits, including Groucho's discourse on the need for a seven-cent nickel. At least two sequences from *Monkey Business* show up in Episode 25, while *The Cocoanuts* is almost entirely responsible for Number 19, from the Florida-hotel setting to the now classic "Why a Duck?" routine.

The decision to use existing skits may have come from the Marxes themselves, or from Perrin and Sheekman, or perhaps from the two writers who joined the series midway through its run, George Oppenheimer (who later received a scripting credit on *A Day at the Races* in 1937) and Tom McKnight. Advanced Marxists should have a field day tracing *Flywheel* routines forwards and backwards through the brothers' film history.

While *Flywheel, Shyster, and Flywheel* may not have set the entertainment world abuzz, it was more successful than the Marx Brothers' subsequent efforts over the airwaves. In the spring of 1934, while the Marxes were between film studios, Groucho and Chico hooked up with the American Oil Company to do a show satirizing the news of the world. Groucho played Ulysses H. Drivel, "eagle-eyed news hound," and Chico was the "doughty Penelli." The short-lived series was broadcast on Sunday nights at seven p.m. from the CBS studios in New York City. Guest stints on shows such as Campbell Soup's *Hollywood Hotel* and Pepsodent's *Bob Hope* followed in 1937 and 1938. Groucho was then signed as one of many star headliners in Kellogg's variety program, *The Circle*, which aired on NBC's Red Network in 1939. Its erudite approach might have played well in New York, but the abysmal national ratings ensured a speedy cancel-

Groucho and sidekick George Fenneman ponder the overnight success of their radio series, *You Bet Your Life*. NBC broadcast the show after its 1947 debut season on ABC, the "junior" network. In 1950, Groucho and George traded in their radio mikes when the show moved to television, where it remained through 1962–63.

lation. Groucho simply could not find his métier in radio—he even passed up the chance to star in *The Life of Riley*, which he had helped create—until his quiz show, *You Bet Your Life*, became an instant success over the "junior" network, ABC, in 1947. The program debuted on television in the fall of 1950 and stayed on the air until 1962, reaching the top ten several times. Ultimately, *You Bet Your Life* was the show with which Groucho was most closely associated outside of his film work.

Most of these adventures in radio were recorded at the time of broadcast and still exist, at least in representative segments. The exception, alas, is *Flywheel, Shyster, and Flywheel*, which may not even have been recorded—shows rarely were in a period when any radio program not aired live was considered anathema to sponsors and audiences alike. Fortunately, the scripts for all of the *Flywheel* episodes except the twenty-first were submitted to the copyright office of the Library of Congress, where they were eventually put in deep storage. Now, through the fanatical efforts of your correspondent, they have been unearthed, making the world safe once again for the forces of Marxian chaos.

Fortunately, this March I was able to talk with Nat Perrin, one of the show's head writers, about his days working on the *Flywheel* program. Our conversation appears in this collection, as does Groucho's hilarious piece on how he invented radio, reprinted from the July 1934 issue of *Tower Radio* magazine.

A word about the editing we have visited upon these scripts: The episodes that follow appear virtually as they were transcribed for the Library of Congress copyright registry, with a few exceptions. Although the opening episode is presented in its entirety to give the flavor of a complete broadcast, thereafter we have excised the sponsor's opening and closing announcements as well as the references to musical interludes. We've kept additional information when it seemed of particular interest (as with the move to Hollywood) or when it went beyond the announcer's standard weekly patter. Because these scripts were written to be read aloud, and were written by different people, no one worried about minor inconsistencies in character names and sound cues. Buck on one page becomes Bill on another; Miss Dimple appears as Stenographer in some episodes; and sound-effect cues vary widely in form. We've regularized these names and cues, and have also tried to follow a uniform style in the use and spelling of dialect spoken by some of the characters, notably Chico. The rest we leave to your imagination.

Very special thanks to J. Fred MacDonald and Nat Perrin, who provided *very* special help. Thanks are also due to these good soldiers for contributing time and effort to the cause: Jean Behrend, David Feldman, Ron Goulart, Arthur Marx, Brian Rose, Patricia Sheinwold, and, of course, my editor, Ginny Read. (I *told* you it would be easy, didn't I?)

M.B.
APRIL 1988

A Conversation with Nat Perrin

In March 1988, I visited Nat Perrin at his home in Los Angeles and spoke to him about his experiences writing for the Flywheel *show. The following is taken from our conversation.* —M.B.

I'm not sure whether I was invited to work on *Flywheel* by Groucho or by Arthur Sheekman, my writing partner. But I do recall writing the first episode with Arthur, Groucho, and Chico on the train coming East. Later the show would be done on the West Coast, so this was just the first of many train rides back and forth from Hollywood to New York. One thing about those rides: They increased my appreciation for California. I can't remember anything as wonderful as getting off that train, after three or four dusty days, onto the outdoor platform at the Pasadena station at five o'clock in the afternoon. You could smell the orange blossoms. After being in New York it was like stepping into heaven.

The original name of the radio show was *Beagle, Shyster, and Dismal;* by the time it went on the air, it was *Beagle, Shyster, and Beagle.* But we had to change the name after a lawyer from New York named Beagle called us after the first broadcast. As is always the case, the studio panicked when they heard the word "lawsuit," so the name was changed to *Flywheel, Shyster, and Flywheel.* Years later I used the Flywheel name for Groucho in *The Big Store.*

We only had a couple of rehearsals for *Flywheel* on the day it was broadcast—everything was done live at the time—but Chico had trouble making even those. He'd always be late, and usually I'd have to stand in for him on the read-throughs. When he finally *did* show up, he'd be reading Ravelli's lines and Groucho would tell him to stop. "Deacon," he'd say to me—he always said I looked like a crooked deacon because of the steel-rimmed glasses I wore—"show him how the line should be read." My Italian accent was better than Chico's, you see. But Chico didn't care. All he really cared about was the horses and cards, especially bridge. He was a very undisciplined guy, but he negotiated all their deals, and he was the one who mingled with the movers and shakers.

About half the shows were done from Hollywood. It was a pretty primitive setup, because NBC didn't have a real studio there, and it was up to John Swallow, who *was* NBC on the West Coast, to find us an empty soundstage at RKO to broadcast from. The poor guy only had a cubbyhole office himself. But we'd round up thirty or forty people to become an audience—they'd sit on folding chairs—and do the show in front of them. The boys liked playing to a live crowd, being from vaudeville. Once we finished the performance, the stagehands would come right in and start clearing the stage for whatever film needed it.

Doing a weekly radio program was pretty easy for Groucho and Chico, but Arthur and I had our hands full turning out a script each week. Somewhere along the line we did pick up two new writers, Tom McKnight and George Oppenheimer. The way we came up with McKnight was a classic. Groucho was in the men's room during a break, and he was complaining to the guy standing next to him, "Geez, I wish we could find another writer or two to make life easier." Suddenly there's a voice from one of the stalls: "I've got just the guy for you!" And having Tom and George *did* make life easier, although Arthur and I went over their scripts for a light polishing.

I'm not really sure why *Flywheel* went off the air—maybe expectations were too high—but none of us really minded. For one thing, we had *Duck Soup* ready to go back in Hollywood, and for another, we all liked living in California very much indeed. So much for growing up in New York!

We never did get any official bylines on radio the way screenwriters did, which is one reason I preferred working in films and, later, television. In fact, *Flywheel* was my only experience with radio. Movies were considered to be on a higher plane than radio; your name got around more. Of course, my brother Sam spent many, many years as head writer on Jack Benny's radio show, and later the TV show, so the billing wasn't as important to everyone, I suppose.

Arthur and I did get a screen credit for *Duck Soup*, but the picture didn't do very well. Paramount let the boys go, and Arthur and I went on to Goldwyn's studios to work on the new Eddie Cantor film. Eventually the Marxes landed at MGM, and it was a good move for them. Thalberg insisted that their pictures take a new approach: They had to have a plot to hang the comedy on. *Duck Soup* had been comedy built on comedy, and Thalberg didn't like it. Personally, I agree with him. Even though I broke into the business working on their Paramount films, the Marxes made better movies at MGM. *Duck Soup* was so crazy—that was Leo McCarey's approach, and the boys loved working with him. But, to me, *Night at the Opera* is a far better film. Of course, plenty of people disagree with me.

I did have a hand in two other Marx Brothers movies. I was asked to fly out to Detroit to help with the script of *Go West* while they were road-testing it—that was another Thalberg idea—and of course *The Big Store* was developed from my original story. We didn't work together again professionally, but we remained friends for the rest of their lives.

GROUCHO

Groucho's brother, Chico, as the faithful lieutenant, Penelli.

HERE I sit, all hot and bothered, in the luxurious privacy of the West Forty-second Street Turkish Baths, dictating for the first time the memoirs of my radio career to Thursday, my man Friday, while a Swedish masseur is giving me a Russian rubdown.

Through the revolving doors are wafted the strains of an orchestra bearing my name (Perlman's Playboys). A radio on the wall is bellowing forth a transcription of my famous serial, the Adventures of Amos Marx and Andy Marx. In the steam room, the attendants are singing the chorus of my song which is on everyone's lips, "I'm Just a Vagabond Rubber."

Yet it only seems like yesterday—well, day before yesterday—all right, have it your way—it only seems like three weeks ago Tuesday that I was but a humble weaver of dreams working at my loom and a microphone to me was just a musical instrument you played on with drumsticks.

The old-fashioned horse had just been supplanted by the telephone (later called Marx's folly—see any current market report.) The Spanish-American War had played three weeks in the Philippines and folded on the road. Robert Hudson was just steaming up the Fulton and I was getting steamed up over radio.

RADIO was just a child's plaything then. (I used to take the tubes out and throw them against the wall to hear them pop.) Now look at it! O tempora! O Morris! (Morris was the elevator boy at station WHEW where I got my start.) Well, I hardly know where to begin. I don't know when to stop, either. Just give me a couple of drinks and see for yourself.

I suppose I ought to begin with Marconi. I seld do begin with Marconi, though. I prefer to sta with antipasto, follow that with a plate of Minestro and work up to Marconi gradually. Which remir me, I must brush up on my Italian. Goodness kno Penelli has brushed up on me often enough, and tu about is only fair play.

Marconi, DeForest and I were all sophomores gether at old Gorgonzola for six years. I was alwa inventing things for which those boys got the cred But I'm wiser now. I get credit everywhere.

We worked as one man. (Two of us were alwa loafing.) But we had trouble with DeForest. wanted to build a harmony act in every set. It g so bad after a while that we couldn't see DeForest f the trios.

But to get back. One night Marconi was up night tinkering (he was a deep tinker) and in t morning he announced proudly:

"Last night I got Chile!"

"Marconi, you dope!" I chided. "Why didn't you g an ulster?"

That touched his pride and he went right on until got Siam, the Straits of Penang, Upper Mongolia, Nagasaki, Kankakee, Kamchatka and German Measles. After that it was plain sailing.

Leaving college, I tried the theater, supporting my three brothers in an acrobatic act. But all the work fell on my shoulders. So I gave it up. The boys were lost without my support. In fact they haven't been able to earn a dollar for themselves from that day to this.

I felt that the world had no place for them then. I was a misfit in a two-pants suit, a monkey-wrench in the machinery of life. I couldn't even look myself in the face. I didn't have money enough to buy a mirror.

One day with my grind organ—I was doubling for an Italian street

Do you really know the versatile Groucho? Do you realize that he has succeeded under the names of Rudy Vallee, Roxy and Ed Hill?

By
GROUCHO MARX
as told to
EDWARD R. SAMMIS

MARX *tells all*

nist—I wandered idle and ill at ease. Suddenly a sign
ght my eye—a nasty crack. I stepped back and read:
INSBERG'S BOWLING ALLEYS, pin-setter wanted."
hesitated about going in and applying, for I hadn't
en for three days and I was a little shaky on my pins.

T last I mustered up my courage and fell through the
-revolving doors. I found myself inside a radio station.
ll numb with surprise, or just numb, I said to the
uncer, "Where may I find Ginsberg's Bowling Alleys?"
replied: "This is a radio studio, young mugg. That
s only a blind ad. We're looking for a crooner."
I snapped out: "I just saw him going around the cor-
r as I came in."
That floored him and before he came back at the count
nine, I had installed myself as manager and fired the
ole crew.
I didn't want my folks to

Groucho

SAYS:

"It only seems like yesterday—well,
day before yesterday—that the microphone to me was just a musical instrument you played on with drumsticks. Robert Hudson had just
steamed up the Fulton and I was
getting steamed up over radio."

*Radio started, affirms Groucho, when he was a sopho-
more at Gorgonzola with Marconi and DeForest.*

know I had gone into radio. I had always promised them I would make an honest living. So I hid my identity under the pseudonym of Roxy. As Roxy I came to be a famous showman and made quite a name for myself out of discarded electric light bulbs.

But still I wasn't satisfied.

I had seen Kate Smith, Crosby, Morton Downey all rise to glory under my management. And what had I got out of it? A mere eighty per cent!

I wanted to go on the air in person. The owner of the station where I drew my miserly four grand a week—it was still located in Ginsberg's Bowling Alley—promised time after time to put me in radio. At least three times a day he'd say to me, "Groucho, you abysmal cluck, if you do that once more, I'll give you the air!"

But at last my chance came. Our chief crooner also swept out the elevator shaft, and one day he fell down on the job. There was no one to go on in his place. So I stepped into the brooch. Instead of doing my interpretation of Hamlet, as everyone had expected, I did Hamlet's interpretation of those Four Hawaiians, the Marx Brothers.

I was about to go into a rhumba after finishing my nhumba when Ginsberg rushed out and shouted: "Good gracious, Groucho! You've done it all in pantomime!"

I brushed off my coat, rolled up my shirt sleeves and observed with Dignity (he had just come in) "Are you trying to tell me *my* business?"

But posterity (it was at that time just around the corner) proved that I was right. The letters poured in—in fact they are still pouring in—declaring that the Marx silent hour was the finest thing that had ever been heard on Station WHEW.

I became known then and there as the Silent Marx Brother. I later sold out my title to my Brother Harpo, (a famous harpist of whom you may have heard who was then in a dither over a zither for a pretty fancy figure. As no one had either seen me or heard me at that time, it was comparatively easy, except that Harpo wanted to settle for half.

So there I was, at a tender age, my name already established in radio as something which mothers used to frighten their kiddies, heart whole and fancy figure (in fact, a neat thiry-six.)

CASTING about at Random, my summer estate on the Hudson, I decided to become a maestro. I would have become a maestro of ceremonies, but I never stand on ceremony.

I gathered about me a bassoon player, a man who played the viola under the impression that it was a horse and three bass drummers. I then arranged to go on the air as Maestro Marx and his Mad Musclemen of Melody.

Will I ever forget that opening night on station WHEW! I hope so. I've been trying to for years. It was indeed a gala night. The roses, the tulips, the confetti! All the critics were there. In fact, thinking it over later, it seemed to me that every one there was a critic.

I tried to lead with my saxophone. That was where I made my first mistake. Professor McGinsberg, my boxing instructor, told me always to lead with my right. During that premiere broadcast a slight error occurred. The applause went to my head. I became confused. Instead of playing the saxophone before the microphone, I played the microphone before the saxophone.

Shortly afterwards I changed my name to Rudy Vallee for reasons which I do not care to mention here, and I may say with all modesty that my orchestral efforts under that name have been crowned with some success.

I might never have become a crooner had it not been for the sheerest accident. I was having tea one afternoon with Madame Alto-Contralto, the distinguished opera singer, when I chanced to look out the window and observing a goat on a bock-beer sign, I thought for the moment that I was back at the Chalet Marx in dear old Switzerland and broke into a yodel.

Mme. Alto-Contralto laid down her knife and fixed me with those piercing black eyes of hers. "My dear bhoy—" ahoy—ahoy—" she yodelled, falling right in with me, "I never knew that you had such a golden verce—eet ees a gift!"

"The heck it is!" I shot back at her. "It cost me ten payments at a correspondence school!"

Mme. Alto-Contralto was almost instantaneously on the phone, calling none other than the renowned Professor Ginsbergsky. It seemed that the professor was now away up town. Station WHEW had become station WOWW. The professor was in the money. She told the professor in no uncertain terms (the terms, to be exact, were a dollar down and a dollar a week) that she had a new discovery for him, a crooner.

"SEND him right over," I heard the professor reply, "only send him prepaid!" Dear old professor! He hadn't changed!

To make a long story unbearable, I got the job. I signed a contract with the professor to do all the singing on his station. I was a quartet, three trios, and a piccolo player, and the Four Eton Boys.

I thought all was beer and skittles. Then I awoke one morning to make a horrible discovery. My voice had changed. I couldn't speak above a bass.

From that day on I found all doors in radio closed to me. Those that weren't closed were manned by bouncers instructed to throw me out.

There was nothing left for me to do but go into Grand Opera. Again I deemed it advisable to change my cognomen. Few people realize that Chaliapin, the name which I use when angling before the Golden Horseshoe (not to mention a lot of old rusty ones), is simply Groucho Marx spelled backwards.

Ambition still burned fiercely within me, although for a long time I was under the impression that it was just my old heartburn.

Today, as a result, I am the five leading news commentators. You hear me as Edwin C. Hill, Boake Carter, and Lowell Thomas, also H. V. Kaltenborn and Frederic William Wile.

I am happy at last. I feel I have found my *metier,* which is to interpret the news so no one can understand it. I am always last on the scene where things are happening, so I get the latest news.

I feel there are too many things in the world which people can understand. Thus if you give them the news so that they can't understand it, they'll have something to think about.

And if thinking will keep them out of pool halls, then I'm satisfied. It's what I had in mind when I first explained radio to Marconi.

FIVE STAR THEATER
PRESENTS

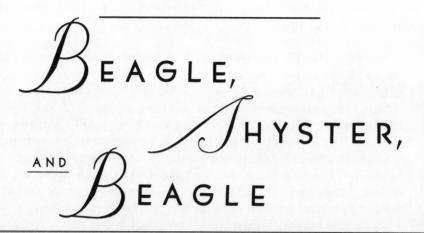

BEAGLE, SHYSTER, AND BEAGLE

EPISODE NO. 1   NOVEMBER 28, 1932

CAST

Groucho Marx as Waldorf T. Beagle, attorney at law
Chico Marx as Emmanuel Ravelli, his assistant
Miss Dimple, stenographer
Mr. Jones, client

(*Fanfare of Trumpets, etc.*)

ANNOUNCER: The Five Star Theatre presents Groucho and Chico Marx, first time on the air.

(*Signature music.*)

The Five Star Theatre makes its bow tonight before the radio audience with the first of a series of radio presentations of a scope, magnitude, and variety never before assembled under any one banner.

Under the patronage of the Standard Oil Companies of New Jersey, Pennsylvania, Louisiana, and the Colonial Beacon Oil Company, the Five Star Theatre will present a brand-new radio attraction every night in the week except Saturday and Sunday. Five stellar productions each week. Every night a first night. With the world's greatest singers, musicians, actors, writers, and speakers collaborating in a gigantic entertainment program for your enjoyment. This, in a word, is the Five Star Theatre, and here is the first week's program:

Tonight the inimitable Marx Brothers, Groucho and Chico, in a series of comedies called "Beagle, Shyster, and Beagle, Attorneys at Law."

Tuesday night at ten p.m., Josef Bonime's Symphony Orchestra, with John Charles Thomas as guest soloist.

Wednesday night at seven-thirty p.m., a dramatization of Rex Beach's story "Cool Waters," with Mr. Rex Beach as guest speaker.

Thursday night at ten p.m., the Aborn Opera Company, in Franz Lehár's opera *The Merry Widow*, broadcast by special arrangement with Tams-Witmark.

Friday night at seven-thirty p.m., that beloved detective of fiction "Charlie Chan," in a dramatization of "The Black Camel," by Earl Derr Biggers.

As these programs will be given on different radio stations, be sure to look in your local paper each night for the Five Star production of the evening.

And now for tonight's feature. Groucho Marx is here, ready for his radio debut—black mustache, horn-rimmed spectacles and all. There's Chico, too, looking just the way he does in the pictures. Yes, he has his Italian accent with him, also.

The studio is filled with distinguished first-night guests. Count Felix Von Luckner, famous sea raider, has just come in—you are going to hear from him later in the evening.

The orchestra is tuning up, the overture is in and the show is about to begin.

(*Overture number by the band.*)

. . .

ANNOUNCER: The curtain is rising on the offices of Beagle, Shyster, and Beagle, Attorneys at Law. That's Miss Dimple on the switchboard, and you'll hear Groucho Marx in the part of the senior Mr. Beagle. *(Phone rings.)*

MISS DIMPLE: Law offices of Beagle, Shyster, and Beagle . . . No, Mr. Beagle isn't in yet . . . He's in court . . . Thank you. *(She hangs up receiver.)*

(Phone rings again.)

MISS DIMPLE: Beagle, Shyster, and Beagle . . . No, Mr. Beagle's in court . . . I expect him any minute . . . Okay. *(She hangs up receiver.)*

(Door opens; footsteps heard.)

MISS DIMPLE: Good morning, Mr. Beagle.

GROUCHO: Never mind that. Get President Hoover on the phone. There's a picture of me in the police station and it doesn't do me justice. It makes me look like my father. In fact, it *is* my father. Never mind calling the president. Just find out what the reward is.

MISS DIMPLE: Mr. Beagle, I've got some letters for you to sign.

GROUCHO *(irritated):*   Not now, not now! I've had a big day in court.

MISS DIMPLE: What was the case?

GROUCHO: Disorderly conduct, but I think I'll get off. Why shouldn't I? She hit me first.

MISS DIMPLE: Mr. Beagle! You hit a woman?

GROUCHO: Well, she was my size. Even smaller. Besides, if it weren't for my own arrests, I'd never get a case. Any calls?

MISS DIMPLE: Yes, your creditors have been calling all morning. They said they're tired of phoning and that something will have to be done.

GROUCHO: All right. We'll do something. We'll have the phone taken out.

MISS DIMPLE: Okay.

GROUCHO: There's a good girl. Your salary is raised ten dollars.

MISS DIMPLE: Thank you, Mr. Beagle.

GROUCHO: It's nothing at all. Say, how about lending me that ten till payday?

MISS DIMPLE: But Mr. Beagle, I haven't been paid in weeks. Besides, you overlook the fact—

GROUCHO: I've overlooked plenty around here. A fine stenographer you are! What do you do with your time? The floors aren't washed, the windows aren't cleaned, and my *pants* aren't even pressed.

MISS DIMPLE: But Mr. Beagle—

GROUCHO: Enough of this small talk. Where's that ten dollars?

MISS DIMPLE: I haven't a penny.

GROUCHO: Who's asking for a penny? If I wanted a penny I could go to my baby's bank—if I had a baby. I'm going into my office now. If the phone rings, don't answer it. It may be a wrong number.
(Footsteps; door closes; knock on door.)

MISS DIMPLE: Come in.

CHICO: Hullo! My name's Emmanuel Ravelli. Is da boss in?

MISS DIMPLE: He's busy. Have you got a card?

CHICO: Sure, but I take another one. I wanna see da boss.

MISS DIMPLE: What do you want to see him about?

CHICO: Well you see I wanna get a divorce.

MISS DIMPLE: Mr. Beagle's a very busy man. I'll have to fill out a report. You want a divorce . . . let's see. Any children?

CHICO: Sure, six, maybe seven. I no see very good. Wait—let me see. There'sa Tony, there'sa Josie, there'sa Pasquale, there'sa Angelino, there'sa Jake—aw, no Jake, no Jake. Jake, that's the kid next door. You see, I got 'em all mixed up. And then we gotta the new littla baby.

MISS DIMPLE: A new little baby? Is it a boy or a girl?

CHICO: I don't know. He no speak yet.

MISS DIMPLE: How long have you been married?

CHICO: Oh, lady, I'm not married. My brother, he is married.

MISS DIMPLE: Oh, *he* wants the divorce.

CHICO: Oh, no, he no wanna divorce. He likes his wife. He's happy, but I think he's a little bit crazy.

MISS DIMPLE *(astonished):* You mean you want him to divorce his wife just because you don't like her?

CHICO: No lady, I like her, she'sa nicea gal, but she'sa not very good cook.

MISS DIMPLE: Does your brother complain?

CHICO: No, he's no complain. He's satisfied. He eats out.

MISS DIMPLE: Why don't you eat out?

CHICO: Well, you see, I can't afford it. I no gotta job.

MISS DIMPLE: Why don't you get a job?

CHICO: Awright, awright, never mind the divorce. I take a job.

MISS DIMPLE: I'll have to speak to Mr. Beagle. Where can I get a hold of you?

CHICO: I don't know, lady. You see, I'm very ticklish.

MISS DIMPLE: I mean, where do you live?

CHICO: I live with my brother.

MISS DIMPLE *(impatient):* Just take a seat. I'll call Mr. Beagle. *(Knocks on door.)* Mr. Beagle!

GROUCHO *(away):* Well, did you get that ten bucks?

MISS DIMPLE: No, there's a man out here wants to talk to you about a job.

(Footsteps approach.)

GROUCHO: Tell him I'll take it. But I won't work for less than twenty dollars a week.

MISS DIMPLE: You misunderstand. He wants a job here.

GROUCHO: Oh, *he* wants a job. I think I can put him to work.

CHICO: I don't wanna work. I just wanna job.

GROUCHO: How about references?

CHICO: Aw, that's awright. You don't need no references. I like your face.

GROUCHO *(coyly):* And I like *your* face—if it *is* a face. Say, you look exactly like a fellow I used to know, by the name of Emmanuel Ravelli. Are you his brother?

CHICO: I *am* Emmanuel Ravelli.

GROUCHO: You're Emmanuel Ravelli?

CHICO: I'm Emmanuel Ravelli.

GROUCHO: No wonder you look like him. But I still insist there's a resemblance.

CHICO: Hey! We no speak about money.

GROUCHO: That suits me fine. If you promise not to say anything about it, I won't mention it either.

CHICO: Awright, but I gotta have more money.

GROUCHO: I'll tell you what I'll do. I'll give you six dollars a week and you can bring your own lunches.

CHICO: Well . . .

GROUCHO: I'll go even *further* than that. I'll give you six dollars a week and you can bring lunch for me too.

CHICO: Six dollars a week . . . six . . . Hey, boss, I can't live on six dollars a week.

GROUCHO: You can't live on six dollars a week. That will make me very happy. You're hired.

CHICO: When do I start?

GROUCHO: Well, it's one o'clock now. If you start now you can be back here at three with the lunch. You can bring me a tomato sandwich on white bread.

CHICO: I no gotta white bread, but I can give you rye.

GROUCHO: All right, then I'll take a quart of rye.

CHICO: I'm sorry, but I'm wearing 'em.

GROUCHO: You're wearing a quart of rye?

CHICO: Yes, my quardorye pants.

GROUCHO: Say, why don't you get double pneumonia?

CHICO: I don't need it. I'm a single man. Besides, I gotta have more money.

GROUCHO: Have you had any experience?

CHICO: You bet. For fifteen years I'm a musician.

GROUCHO: What do you get an hour?

CHICO: Well, for playing I get ten dollars an hour.

GROUCHO: What do you get for not playing?

CHICO: Twelve dollars an hour.

GROUCHO: That's more like it.

CHICO: Now for rehearsing I make a special rate—fifteen dollars an hour.

GROUCHO: What do you get for not rehearsing?

CHICO: Oh, you couldn't afford it. You see, if I no rehearse I no play. And if I no play, that runs into money.

GROUCHO: What would you want to run into an open manhole?

CHICO: Just the cover charge.

GROUCHO: Well, drop in some time.

CHICO: Sewer.

GROUCHO: I guess we've cleaned *that* up.

CHICO: No, we no clean that up. Now, let's see how we stand. Yesterday I didn't come—that cost you fifteen dollars. Today I did come—

GROUCHO: That's twenty dollars you owe me.

CHICO: Tomorrow I leave. That's worth about—

GROUCHO: A million dollars. But let's not quibble over money. I offered you six dollars. I'll raise you two.

CHICO: You raise me two, I raise you three.

GROUCHO: I call you. Whata you got?

CHICO: I got aces up. Whata you got?

GROUCHO: I've got a notion to throw you out of the office.

CHICO: Awright, I take it.

(*Music in strong.*)

MISS DIMPLE: Beagle, Shyster, and Beagle . . . Oh hello, Charlie. Call me back. There's someone coming in.

JONES: My name is Edgar T. Jones. I want to see Mr. Beagle.

MISS DIMPLE: He's in his office. Walk right in.

JONES: Thank you. (*Door opens; footsteps.*) Ah . . . ah . . . How do you do, Mr. Beagle. A friend of mine told me you were a good lawyer.

GROUCHO: You just *think* he's a friend of yours. Sit down. Have you got a couple of cigars?

JONES: Ah . . . no, I'm sorry.

GROUCHO: Well, why don't you send out for some? If you've got a quarter, I'll go myself.

JONES: Oh, no, no, Mr. Beagle.

GROUCHO *(indignantly):* What's the matter? Don't you trust me?

JONES *(disturbed):* Why—I'd like to talk to you. I'm having trouble with my wife.

GROUCHO *(indignant):* You are! Well, I'm having trouble with my wife, too, but I don't go around bragging about it. *(Sneers.)* Hmm. You oughta be ashamed of yourself. *(Calling outside:)* Miss Dimple, show this gentleman the door. On second thought, never mind the door. He saw it when he came in.

JONES: But, Mr. Beagle—I came to you for advice. Let me tell you a story. My wife is in love with two men, and—

GROUCHO *(laughing uproariously):* Ha, ha, ha! Not a bad story. The boys are all repeating it around the club. Now let me tell *you* one. There were two traveling men named Pat and Mike—

JONES: No, no, Mr. Beagle. I came here with a problem.

GROUCHO: Well, why didn't you bring her in?

JONES: You don't understand. I'm looking for evidence against my wife.

GROUCHO: Well, why didn't you say so? Let me look at my law book . . . Here we are . . . *(turning pages)* . . . here it is . . . er . . . the case of Emory T. Gribble against the Lehigh and Western Railroad. Of course, the Lehigh is just a short road. It's only Lehigh to a grasshopper.

JONES: But, Mr. Beagle, that's a *railroad* law book.

GROUCHO: Well, what's wrong with it? It's got eight hundred pages and it's clean as a whistle. If I had a whistle I'd show you.

JONES: But I'm suing my wife.

GROUCHO: Is *that* any reason why I should have to buy another law book? Why don't you sue a railroad? A railroad's got more money than your wife. Besides, the railroad won't ask for alimony.

JONES: *Please*, Mr. Beagle, I don't want to argue. I'm tired, nervous, run down—

GROUCHO: Run down? Say, now we've got a case. Were you run down by a railroad?

JONES: Mr. Beagle, you try my patience.

GROUCHO: I don't mind if I do. You must come over and try mine some day. I'm putting up a new batch.

JONES: Batch? *What* batch?

GROUCHO: The batch on my pants. Some joke, eh? But that's a mere trifle. As I understand it, what you really want is someone to shadow your wife. I've got just the man for you—my new assistant, Emmanuel Ravelli. He looks like an idiot and talks like an idiot. But don't let that fool you. He really *is* an idiot. You and Ravelli will have a lot in common.

JONES: Mr. Beagle, my time is valuable. Let me give you the facts. I married my wife secretly.

GROUCHO: You married her secretly? You mean you haven't told her about it? No wonder she runs around with other men.

JONES: Mr. Beagle, we must get this divorce—I want your assistant, Mr. Ravelli, to follow my wife.

GROUCHO: One thing at a time. Let's get the divorce first and then we can *all* follow your wife.

JONES *(confused):* I . . . I don't quite understand the proceedings, Mr. Beagle, but I leave everything in your hands. You're the doctor.

GROUCHO: I'm the doctor? Good! I'll take your tonsils out on Monday. I'll take your wife out on Tuesday. On Wednesday—

JONES: Just a minute, Beagle!

GROUCHO: *Doctor* Beagle to you. Stick your tongue out and come back next Wednesday.

JONES: Please, please get your assistant. I want to give him a description of my wife.

GROUCHO *(indignantly):* Very well, Mr. Jones. If that's the way you feel about it, I'll call him. Ravelli. Ravelli! . . . Miss Dimple, wake up Ravelli . . . *Miss Dimple,* will you wake up Ravelli? . . . Mr. Jones, will you go in and wake up Miss Dimple and leave a call for me at nine?

CHICO: Here I am, boss. You callin Ravelli?

GROUCHO: See here. I don't like your sleeping on the company's time.

CHICO: I don't like sleeping on it it, either. Why don't you buy me a bed?

GROUCHO: Ravelli, I want you to meet Mr. Jones.

CHICO: Awright, where should I meet him?

JONES: Mr. Ravelli, I'm very happy to make your acquaintance.

CHICO: I don't know what he's talkin about.

GROUCHO: He means he's very happy to know you, but he's probably crazy.

JONES: Mr. Ravelli, I've just been telling Mr. Beagle that, much as I regret to say it, my wife is not all that she should be. She's going around with other men.

CHICO: She's going around with other men? At'sa fine. Hey! You think she like me?

GROUCHO: I can see that you two boys have a lot to talk over. Besides, I have a director's meeting across the street in the poolroom. So, if you'll excuse me, I'll scram.

JONES *(astonished):* Poolroom! Mr. Beagle, it strikes me that things aren't done in a very businesslike way around here. In the middle of a conference, you go out and play pool.

GROUCHO: I've *got* to go out. I can't play pool in *here*—there's no table. Good day, gentlemen.

(Door closes.)

JONES: Well, Mr. Ravelli, as long as you're going to trail my wife, I think I ought to describe her to you. She's of medium height and . . . but never mind, I've got a photograph of my wife with me. Ah, there you are, Mr. Ravelli.

CHICO: Hey, at'sa fine. Awright, I'll take a dozen.

JONES: I'm not *selling* them.

CHICO: You mean, I get it for nothing?

JONES: Of course.

CHICO: Awright. Then I take *two* dozen.

JONES *(irritated):*   *One* picture ought to be enough for the present. Now, Mr. Ravelli, there is one man my wife has been paying particular attention to. I'm counting on you to find out who he is. Do you think you can do it?

CHICO: Sure, you leave 'im to me. I find out who the man was with your wife. And I find out quick.

JONES: Really? How you going to do it?

CHICO: Well, first I put on a disguise . . .

JONES: Yes . . .

CHICO: Then I get a bloodhound . . .

JONES: Yes . . .

CHICO: Then I go to your house . . .

JONES *(increasing interest):*   Yes . . .

CHICO: Then I ask your wife.

(Music in strong.)

(Sounds of typing; phone rings.)

MISS DIMPLE: Law offices of Beagle, Shyster, and Beagle . . . No, Mr. Beagle isn't in yet. But I expect him any moment . . . *(Surprised.)* Oh, *hello*, Mr. Jones. I didn't recognize your voice . . . Yes, Mr. Ravelli is still trailing your wife . . . but it hasn't been long . . . just two weeks. We expect Mr. Ravelli in the office this morning. He says he has some news . . . Okay, I'll tell Mr. Beagle you'll be in . . . Goodbye.

(Typing resumes; door opens.)

MISS DIMPLE: Good morning, Mr. Beagle—

GROUCHO: Quick! Get Warburton, McAllister, Throckmorton and Bruce on the phone and ask for Mr. Schwartz. Tell him I want to borrow a pair of socks.

MISS DIMPLE: Borrow a pair of *socks?*

GROUCHO: Why not? When he came to me, I gave him the very shirt off my back. Of course, it happened to be his shirt. But the cuffs were mine. Any new clients, Miss Dimple?

MISS DIMPLE: No sir.

GROUCHO: Hmm. No clients. Whenever I leave you in charge, there's no business. Yesterday I stuck around and what happened? We had a big day.

MISS DIMPLE: Yesterday was a big day?

GROUCHO: Certainly. Didn't I sell the carpet?

MISS DIMPLE: Why, ah . . .

GROUCHO: And, Miss Dimple, before I forget—call Ravelli and tell him to be sure and oversleep.

MISS DIMPLE: But he phoned and said he was coming right in.

GROUCHO: In that case, I'm going right back to the poolroom. *(Opens door.)*

MISS DIMPLE: But Mr. Jones is on his way here to talk to you about his divorce.

GROUCHO: That's all he *ever* talks to me about. I'm getting pretty sick of it, too.

MISS DIMPLE: But Mr. Beagle, that's your *business.*

GROUCHO: Well, I wish he'd keep his nose *out* of my business.

MISS DIMPLE: Shh! Someone's coming in. I think it's Mr. Jones.
(Door opens.)

MISS DIMPLE: How do you do, Mr. Jones?

JONES: How do you do, Miss Dimple? Morning, Mr. Beagle. About my divorce—

GROUCHO: Divorce! You going to start that again? Listen, Jones, can I sell you a ticket to the Firemen's Ball? It's a five-dollar ticket, and it's yours for a buck and a half.

JONES: Why, ah . . . ah . . . this is *last* year's ticket.

GROUCHO: I know it is, but they had a better show last year.

JONES *(his patience exhausted):* Mr. Beagle, *when* will I find out about my divorce case?

GROUCHO: See here, Jones, don't change the subject. What about that ticket?

JONES: I don't like to appear impatient, Mr. Beagle, but your assistant was supposed to bring in some evidence against my wife. Where *is* Mr. Ravelli?

CHICO *(opens door):* Hey! Who'sa calling Ravelli? Here I am.

JONES: Ah, Mr. Ravelli, I'd like to get the results of your investigation. Have you been trailing my wife?

CHICO: Sure, joosta like a bloodhound. Hey, you remember when you giva me that picture of your wife?

JONES: Yes.

CHICO: Well, I start right out. Joosta like a bloodhound, I tell you. And in one hour, even *less* than one hour—

JONES *(anxiously):*   Yes . . .

CHICO: I losa da picsh.

GROUCHO: There you are, Jones. He did *all that* in only one hour.

JONES: Ravelli, then you *didn't* shadow my wife?

CHICO: Sure, I shadow her all day.

JONES: What day was that?

CHICO: That was Shadowday. I went right to your house—

JONES *(anxiously):*   What did you find out?

CHICO: I find your wife out.

JONES: Then you wasted the entire two weeks?

CHICO: Aw no. Monday I shadow your wife. Tuesday I go to the ball game—she don't show up. Wednesday she go to the ball game—I don't show up. Thursday was a doubleheader. We both no show up. Friday it rain all day—there'sa no ball game, so I go fishing.

JONES: Well, what's that got to do with my wife?

CHICO: Well, I no catcha no fish, but I catch your wife.

JONES: You caught my wife—with a man?

CHICO: Sure.

JONES: Who was he?

CHICO: I don't wanna say.

JONES: I insist that you tell me the man's name.

CHICO: I don't wanna tell.

GROUCHO: Listen, Jones, my assistant isn't the type of fellow who'd bandy a man's good name in public—

JONES: For the last time, gentlemen—*who was the man?*

GROUCHO: Come clean, Ravelli, who was the man with his wife?

CHICO: Awright, awright. You maka me tell, I tell you. Mr. Jones, the man with your wife was my boss, Mr. Beagle.

JONES: This is an outrage. My attorney going out with my wife!

GROUCHO: What do you mean, outrage? Don't you think I'm good enough for her?

JONES: I'm going to get a new attorney.

GROUCHO: Hmm! I suppose you think we can't get a new client?

JONES *(indignant):*   Good *day!*
   (Door slams.)

GROUCHO: Ravelli, you did noble work. You can have the rest of the year off. And if you never come back, I'll give you a bonus.

CHICO: Well, boss, there's something I wanna tell you.

GROUCHO: Go right ahead. I'm not listening.

Chicolini (Chico) and Brownie (Harpo) report to Sylvanian Ambassador Trentino in *Duck Soup:* "Monday we watch Firefly's house but he no come out—he wasn't home. Tuesday we go to a ball game but he fool us—he no show up. Wednesday he go to the ball game and we fool *him*—*we* no show up. Thursday's a doubleheader—nobody show up."

CHICO: You want I should never come back?

GROUCHO: In a word, yes.

CHICO: Awright, boss, I make you a proposition. If you want I should never come back, I gotta have more money.

GROUCHO: Ravelli, it's worth it.

(*Applause.*)

CLOSING ANNOUNCEMENT

ANNOUNCER: The crowd in the studio tonight is giving the Marx Brothers a great ovation. We hope you in the radio audience enjoyed them as much as we did. Groucho and Chico will be back again next Monday at this same time.

Now Count Luckner is going to say a few words to you. He's the famous German war hero, he's an honorary citizen of Great Britain, he's a resident of New York. Count Luckner . . .

(*Applause.*)

LUCKNER: Thank you, everybody. By Joe, I am happy to be with the Five Star Theatre, and if tonight is a good sample, I hope I am not going to miss any of it.

I suppose you are wondering why I am in this show. Well, by Joe, I will tell you. I am here in your great country on a mission of good will, and I am delighted to speak to you all on this program, because it is a real example of the fine way American business interests have cooperated with Europe, to bring together the greatest minds of German and American chemistry, and have created for you a new and better lubricating oil. But—by Joe, I am getting ahead of myself. Tonight I wanted to tell you about my Sea Raider and my adventures during the war when I broke through the British blockade.

Sixteen years ago, I was sailing my Raider on the ocean. This was back in 1916, when the British blockade had cut off Germany from many important supplies. We needed nitrate, to make powder out of, and we needed oil. By Joe, we were in a tight fix. And so all the chemists in Germany got together with their test tubes and began experimenting. And what do you think they did? They finally were able to take nitrate out of the air and oil out of coal.

And so we kept the Allies guessing all right. They did not know from where we were getting our oil. They did not know that our chemists had found out our new secret processes whereby they added hydrogen to coal and that way were able to make petroleum and oil. It was this new German petroleum and oil I used for my one-thousand horsepower motor, when I broke through the British blockade.

When the war was over, the Standard Oil Company of New Jersey found out from where we had gotten our oil and they said, "Those chemists have done something wonderful. The war is over, let us get together." And so the rights to the secret German process were brought over here and your best American chemists continued to work on this process. They developed an entirely new process called hydrofining, by which natural petroleum oil is made into better oil for automobiles. And, by Joe, this new perfected lubricating oil is the Essolube. For sixteen years I have known about this great process being developed, and I always thought that some day your American chemists would find this hydrofining process. And now, by Joe, it is here and every automobile driver can get this new Essolube for his car.

ANNOUNCER: Thank you, Count Luckner. This concludes our Five Star

Theatre presentation for this evening, brought to you by the Standard Oil companies of New Jersey, Pennsylvania and Louisiana, and the Colonial Beacon Oil Company. These associated companies maintain a system of service stations and dealers from Maine to Texas. They are the makers and marketers of Essolube, the new lubricating oil Count Luckner told you about; of Esso, the giant power fuel; of Atlas Tires and other motor accessories. Go to an Esso station for *all* your motoring needs.

Don't forget about the Five Star Theatre presentation tomorrow night at ten p.m., Eastern Standard Time, of Josef Bonime's Symphony Orchestra with John Charles Thomas as guest soloist. This is the finest musical unit ever assembled on the air. It will be a great treat for music lovers. Look in your local newspaper for the station listings.

AFTERPIECE

CHICO: Ladies and gentlemens. Dis isa very important what I gonna say, so first I'll tell you what I'm gonna tell you. Den I'll *tell* you. And after dat I'll tell you what I tole you.

GROUCHO: Take it easy, Chico. You're working yourself into a temperature.

CHICO *(laughs):* Dat ain't from da speech, Groucho. It's from da suit I bought.

GROUCHO: The suit you bought?

CHICO: Yeah, it's a two-pants suit and two pairs of pants is too warm when you ain't outside.

GROUCHO: I see. Well, it's human to make mistakes, and *you're* only human. However, no one would know it to look at you.

CHICO: Aw, Groucho, you'ra too grouchy. Why don't you do tings to make people glad?

GROUCHO: I suppose I don't. Why, yesterday I went to visit Uncle Charlie and it made him *very* happy. And that wasn't all. An hour later I *left*, and that made him *twice* as happy.

CHICO: Yeah, I don't know what to do about Uncle Charlie. He's a case. He's such a crank.

GROUCHO: You mean a crankcase. Well, Essolube, that famous hydrofined motor oil, is the best thing in the world for a crankcase.

CHICO: Hey! You didn't say nuttin about Esso, which is more powerful than any gasoline.

GROUCHO: Well, we can mention Esso next week. So—

BOTH: Goodnight, ladies . . . goodnight, ladies . . .
(Signature music.)

FIVE STAR THEATER
PRESENTS

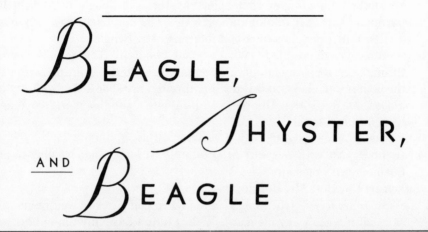

Beagle, Shyster, AND Beagle

EPISODE NO. 2   DECEMBER 5, 1932

CAST

Groucho Marx as Waldorf T. Beagle
Chico Marx as Emmanuel Ravelli
Miss Dimple
Mr. Scrooge
Man
Cop
Woman

(*Music; phone rings.*)

MISS DIMPLE: Law offices of Beagle, Shyster, and Beagle . . . Oh, hello, darling. I was just thinking about you . . . I can't talk now. My boss, Mr. Beagle, just came in. Good morning, Mr. Beagle.

GROUCHO: Good morning? What's good about it? The rain is coming through the roof, the landlord's coming through the door, my wife goes through my pockets, and I'm going through my shoes. And you say it's a good morning. Miss Dimple, you were late again this morning. Where were you last night?

MISS DIMPLE: Last night? Why, I was out with you.

GROUCHO: Out with me, eh? Miss Dimple, it isn't a good policy to mix business with pleasure.

MISS DIMPLE: But, Mr. Beagle, I—

GROUCHO (*quickly*): Oh, I know what you're going to say. you're going to say that it wasn't any pleasure. Well, I didn't have any fun either.

MISS DIMPLE: But you asked me to go out.

GROUCHO: Yes, but you didn't have to go out on the second drink, Miss Dimple!

MISS DIMPLE: Yes, Mr. Beagle.

GROUCHO: Today is Monday. What have we got on the books besides red ink? What's on the court calendar for this afternoon?

MISS DIMPLE: You know you have a suit on today.

GROUCHO: Certainly I have a suit on today. Do you expect me to come in in my nightshirt? I only wear that for night court. Where's that assistant I hired last week?

MISS DIMPLE: Oh, Mr. Ravelli. He just phoned.

GROUCHO: Oh, he phoned did he? Where did he get the nickel? He's been holding out on me. I thought I told him to go out and chase ambulances. How's he going to get clients unless he finds accidents? What did Ravelli have to say?

MISS DIMPLE: He said he's coming in to see you.

GROUCHO: Oh, so he's coming in to see me. I suppose he doesn't think I'm good enough to go out and see him! Maybe he's ashamed to let me see where he lives. Where *does* he live?

MISS DIMPLE: He's been living here in the office ever since you hired him.

GROUCHO: Oh, he has, has he? No wonder he's ashamed. Well, you tell him he'll have to sleep in the hall tonight. I'm having people up here for dinner. Have I any appointments today?

MISS DIMPLE: No, Mr. Beagle, you haven't got any appointments at all.

GROUCHO: Well, make some. Do you expect me to sit here alone all day? Don't you think I ever get lonesome? What do you take me for?

(Pause.) Well, go on—make me an offer. *(Knock on door.)* Miss Dimple, get off my lap and see who's at the door.

MISS DIMPLE *(whispers):*   It's probably Mr. Scrooge, the landlord, coming in to see you about the rent. He's looking for his money.

GROUCHO: Tell him to look next door. There's more light there . . . and more money, too.

MISS DIMPLE: The landlord's been in five times already when you were out.

(Door opens.)

GROUCHO: Is this him?

MISS DIMPLE *(whispers):*   Yes, it's Mr. Scrooge.

GROUCHO: Bring him in. I'll talk to him.

SCROOGE *(approaching):*   Are you Mr. Beagle?

GROUCHO: Am I Mr. Beagle? What right have you got to walk into a man's office and insult him? Did you ever get a load of Mr. Beagle?

SCROOGE: No. I've been looking for him long enough, but I've never been able to find him in.

GROUCHO: Well, then I can speak freely. As man to man I advise you to give it all up.

SCROOGE: What's *your* name?

GROUCHO: What's my name, eh? Hmm. There's ignorance for you. Why, I've got a ten-year-old boy who knows my name.

SCROOGE: That's about enough of this. When's Beagle coming in?

GROUCHO: Now I'll ask *you* one. When are you going out?

SCROOGE *(bewildered):*   Why . . . a . . .

GROUCHO: Stuck, eh? All right, I'll ask you another. What's a two-letter word meaning a piece of office furniture?

SCROOGE *(annoyed):*   Oh, I don't know what—

GROUCHO: Give up? The answer is desk.

SCROOGE: Desk! there are more than two letters in desk!

GROUCHO: There's only two letters in my desk. I tore the others up.

SCROOGE: Are you crazy?

GROUCHO: Don't you ever do anything but ask questions? Don't you know any other games? I'll tell you what. You go out in the hall and hide and I'll bet you ten to one we won't find you. I'll bet you twenty to one we won't even look for you.

SCROOGE: I'm going to stay here until Beagle gets back.

GROUCHO: Have you got a reservation? We're pretty full up now. I think I may be able to fix you up in March. No, now that I've looked you over, I think it'll take longer than that to fix you up. How's your liver today?

SCROOGE: My liver's all right.

GROUCHO: Fine, we'll take a pound. Miss Dimple, get some bacon to go with that liver and we'll have lunch. Perhaps Mr. Stooge would like to join us?

SCROOGE *(enraged):*   My name is not Stooge, it's Scrooge, and I want to see Mr. Beagle about the rent. I'm not going to sit around here waiting for Beagle. You tell him when he comes back that if he doesn't pay me the rent for the past six months, I'll sue him.

GROUCHO: Oh, you're gonna sue him? I'll take that case, Scrooge. We'll collect that rent if it takes the last cent you have.

SCROOGE: I'm not going to waste my time talking to an egg like you! Goodbye. *(Door slams.)*

GROUCHO: So, I'm an egg, am I? That reminds me, I haven't eaten today. Miss Dimple, is there any more of that telephone book left? As I recall it, yesterday I ate as far as Levy and that was only page ninety-three. By the way, Miss Dimple, can you stuff a turkey?

MISS DIMPLE: Of course I can stuff a turkey.

GROUCHO: Well, the next time you pass a butcher shop, stuff one in your pocket and bring it up here.

(Knock on door.)

GROUCHO: If that Scrooge is loose again, I'm out.

MISS DIMPLE: I'll see who it is.

(Door opens.)

MISS DIMPLE: It's your assistant, Mr. Ravelli. Can you see him?

GROUCHO: Certainly not! I can't see him. I can't see him for dust. Dust him off and bring him in.

CHICO *(enters singing):*   For dere'sa no place like home,
Dere'sa no place like home.
For dere'sa no place like home,
Dere'sa no place like home.
For dere'sa—

GROUCHO: Ravelli, what are you singing?

CHICO: "Home Sweet Home."

GROUCHO: It sounds terrible.

CHICO: Well, my home is terrible. *(Sings again.)*

GROUCHO: Ravelli, will you stop that confounded noise!

CHICO: That's not noise, that's singing.

GROUCHO: Well, if that's singing, make some noise. What are you singing for anyhow?

CHICO: Just to kill time.

GROUCHO: Well, you've certainly got a swell weapon. What have you been doing all week?

CHICO: Chasing ice wagons.

GROUCHO: You've been doing what?

CHICO: Chasing ice wagons. I just came in to get warm.

GROUCHO: I thought I sent you out to chase ambulances.

CHICO: You did, but ambulances go too fast.

GROUCHO: Well, this is a fine how-do-you-do. One of the finest how-do-you-dos I've ever seen.

CHICO: How do you like to give me some salary?

GROUCHO: Oh, you want salary and we haven't even got olives. Listen, Ravelli, unless you get me some clients, we're going to get thrown out of here.

CHICO: It's awright, I no like the place very much anyhow.

GROUCHO: No? Listen, Ravelli, I mean business. You're going to stand out in the street in front of this office and bring in a client if it kills you.

CHICO: Me stand out in the street and get clients? I no think that's very good. Suppose my wife sees me.

GROUCHO: Oh, you're married? Where is your wife?

CHICO: My wife? She's home.

GROUCHO: Yeah, how do you know she's home?

CHICO: I got her shoes on.

(Music in strong.)

(Traffic and street noises, fade down.)

CHICO *(yelling):*   Anybody want a lawyer? Anybody want a lawyer? You want a lawyer, lady? Nice fresh lawyer today? Awright, it don't hurt to ask, you know. Hey, mister, how about you? You want a lawyer?

MAN: No, I don't want a lawyer.

CHICO: Well, what do you want?

MAN: I want you to leave me alone.

CHICO: That's no good. What else you want? Nice lawyer, maybe? Nice fresh lawyer today.

MAN: I got no use for your lawyer.

CHICO: Well, I got no use for him either, but I gotta get a client.

MAN: Say, what are you trying to do? What sort of a game is this? Lay off me! Beat it or I'll call a cop.

CHICO: You want to *sue* me? I got a good lawyer for you.

MAN *(receding):*   Oh, you . . . Officer, will you keep this nuisance away from me?

COP *(Irish):*   Here you . . . move . . . move, you're obstructing traffic.

CHICO: Can't move, officer. We no pay the rent.

COP: Listen you . . . I know you don't mean any harm.

CHICO: How do you know that? Sure I do.

COP: Oh, so you're a wise guy!

CHICO: Oh no, my boss Mr. Beagle, he's the wise guy. You want a lawyer?

COP: What would I be wantin' a lawyer for?

CHICO: I don't know. Take him home, wash him up, show him to the kids.

COP: Listen, what are you trying to do?

CHICO: Mr. Beagle, my boss, sent me down here to get clients.

COP: Well, you're not going to get any clients for a lawyer standing around here.

CHICO: At'sa fine. How am I gonna get clients?

COP: You better hustle around and look for an accident. That's the way to get clients. Now move on out of here. *(Receding.)* If you're here when I get back, I'll run you in.

CHICO *(to himself):* He'll run me in! He'll run me in! *(Yells.)* Anybody want a lawyer? Anybody want a lawyer? Anybody got an accident? Anybody got a nice fresh accident? Hey, mister, you got an accident?

MAN: Accident? What are you talking about?

CHICO *(to himself):* Awright, awright. I maka my own accidents. *(Sound of horses' hooves.)* Ah, here comes a wagon. At'sa fine. The next man comes along, I push him under it.

(General confusion; taxi horns; screeching of brakes; horse whinnies; crowd murmuring; fades down a little.)

GROUCHO *(approaching):* Who pushed me? Who pushed me? Me, Waldorf T. Beagle, an innocent bystander! Well, fairly innocent. Oh, so it was *you*, Ravelli. What's the big idea of pushing *me*? Don't you know you might have killed that horse?

CHICO: Ha-ha! I didn't know that was you, Mr. Beagle. The joke's on me.

GROUCHO: Oh, the joke's on you. Well, the *horse* was on me! Did you ever have a horse on your stomach?

CHICO: No, but I once had a colt on my chest.

GROUCHO: Well, enough of this horseplay! Where are those clients?

CHICO: I walka up and down three hours. I ask everybody, but nobody wants to see you.

GROUCHO: You're telling me! Listen, Ravelli, what we've got to do is make America Beagle-conscious. Let America wait.

CHICO *(calling feebly):* Anybody want a lawyer? Anybody want a lawyer?

GROUCHO: Shh! Be careful, someone might hear you!

CHICO: I don't think so. Nobody's heard me yet.

GROUCHO: What you need, Ravelli, is technique. What *I* need is nobody's business. What I need even more is anybody's business.

CHICO: Well, you so smart. You go geta some clients.

GROUCHO: Oh, so you're trying to taunt me? All right, you'll eat those words, and if I don't get some food soon, *I'll* eat those words. Well, we can't stand here all day. The next client that comes along, let *me* do the talking!

CHICO: At'sa fine. Hey, here comes a lady.

GROUCHO: A lady. Pull up your socks, Ravelli.

WOMAN: Can one of you gentlemen direct me to Forty-Second Street and Times Square?

CHICO: At'sa fine. Now we got a case. How do you do, lady?

GROUCHO: Well, madam, it's about time you showed up. And even now you don't show up very well. Ravelli, get off that fireplug and let the lady sit down. Now, what can we do for you, madam? How about getting you a divorce? It'd be a nice Christmas present for your husband.

WOMAN: Divorce? I merely asked how to get to Forty-Second Street and Times Square.

GROUCHO: Don't beat about the bush. You need a divorce. And I need a divorce. I need your divorce if I'm gonna pay my rent. Now, madam, out with it! How did the whole thing start?

CHICO: She asked us how to get to Times Square.

WOMAN: Why, I don't know—

GROUCHO: I can see it all. You married this man, this innocent little man . . . Oh, no . . . that's another client.

CHICO: Hey boss, we got another client?

WOMAN: I tell you, I won't stand for this.

GROUCHO: Who's telling this story, you or me? You married him when you were only a girl. *He* was only a man. So far it hangs together pretty well.

CHICO: Yes, and if you no watch out, *we* hang together.

WOMAN: Will you please explain to me what you're talking about?

GROUCHO: You gave him everything . . . everything, and what did you get out of it? And all the time that beast was running around with beautiful, luscious, sensuous blondes. Hey, Ravelli, where are you going?

CHICO: Well, you just gave me an idea.

GROUCHO: You come back here.

WOMAN: I won't stand for this one moment longer.

GROUCHO: I don't blame you. But don't worry. Beagle is on the trail. Now, what grounds can we divorce you on? How about the Polo Grounds? By the way, I think you'd like the Polo Grounds, especially if you decide to play ball with us. Later on we might trade you for Babe

Ruth. We might even trade you in for a Buick. Say, you're getting to be pretty useful. I can't understand why your husband wants to divorce you. Maybe we can talk him out of it. By the way, where is he?

WOMAN: Where is who?

GROUCHO: Do I have to go through all that again?

CHICO: He just wants to know where your husband is.

WOMAN: I have no husband.

BOTH: What?

WOMAN: I'm not married, and I won't be married till August.

GROUCHO: All right then, we'll give you the divorce in September.

(Music in strong.)

CHICO *(exhausted):* Don't anybody want a lawyer? Don't anybody want a lawyer?

SCROOGE: Here . . . here! What do you want to stand out here for?

CHICO: I don't want to stand out here. Maybe you got a chair?

SCROOGE: Say, listen, you can't park in front of this building and sell things.

CHICO: Oh, you found that out, too? What is it *you* don't sell?

SCROOGE: I don't sell anything.

CHICO: Well, so do I. Shake. *(Doubtfully.)* You wouldn't want a lawyer, would you?

SCROOGE: How do you know I wouldn't?

CHICO: Well, you wouldn't want this one.

SCROOGE: As a matter of fact, I want a lawyer and I want one bad.

CHICO: I got just the man for you. He's terrible.

SCROOGE: That's his name?

CHICO: What'sa difference what's his name? You don't know him.

SCROOGE: Listen, I'm Mr. Scrooge and I got a tenant who hasn't paid his rent in six months. I want a lawyer to dispossess him. Come on, I'll take a look at your man.

CHICO: I think you better hire him first and look at him afterwards!

SCROOGE: You're not a very good salesman. Where's his office?

CHICO: Where's his office? Right here in this building. Come on, I show you.

SCROOGE: Oh, his office is in *this* building?

CHICO: Sure, and he lives here. I live here, too. Come on.

SCROOGE: Don't you know it's against the law to live in an office building?

CHICO: What we care? We cook here, too. Yesterday we have corn beef and cabbage. Oh boy, that wasa good. The tenants all complain, but the landlord, he don't say anything. He's scared of us.

SCROOGE: So . . . he's scared of you, is he?

CHICO: Sure, He's yellow. *(Pause.)* You'll like this lawyer. I hope he got time to see you. He's a very rich man. He doesn't take many cases.

SCROOGE: He'll see me, all right.

CHICO: Here we are. No, not here, the nexta door—Beagle, Shyster, and Beagle. You stay here, I see if Mr. Beagle can see you.

SCROOGE: Well, be quick about it.

CHICO: Don't move.

(Door opens and closes.)

CHICO: Hey, Miss Dimple, guess what I got outside?

MISS DIMPLE: Shh! Mr. Beagle is busy.

CHICO: Well, wake him up. I got a client.

GROUCHO: I heard you, Ravelli. You got a client! You can't lie to me. I wasn't born yersterday. If I was, what am I doing with these long pants on?

CHICO: Boss, I tell you I'm not lying. I got a client.

GROUCHO: A client? Quick Miss Dimple, my shoes. And get those mice off the typewriter. Show the client up, Ravelli. No, never mind. You show him in, *I'll* show him up.

(Door opens.)

CHICO: You can come in now.

SCROOGE: Thanks.

CHICO: This is my boss, Mr. Beagle. Boss, this is our new client, Mr. Scrooge.

SCROOGE: Are *you* Mr. Beagle?

GROUCHO: That's just what you said the *last* time you came in here. Am I sick of you.

SCROOGE: Oh, so you're Mr. Beagle. Now look here, Beagle, I'm not going to speak to you again about that rent . . .

GROUCHO: Well, that's a relief. I'm glad you came around to my way of thinking. This is probably the beginning of a beautiful friendship, Scrooge. I could feel a spark the moment you came in this office. I can feel another spark now. You'll have to put out that cigar. My pants are on fire.

CHICO: Let 'em burn. It will be the first time we've had heat in this building all winter.

SCROOGE: If you would pay the rent, you'd get enough heat in this office.

CHICO: If we could pay the rent, we'd get out of this office.

SCROOGE: Listen, Beagle. I've had just about enough of you. Your friend tells me you're a rich man and I want my rent.

GROUCHO: Oh, he told you I was rich, did he? Well, he's just a dreamer.

Aren't we all? Mind you, Scrooge, I'm not blaming you. You're only doing your duty. You're just a white-collar man. And unless you change that collar soon, you won't even be that. How am I doing, Ravelli?

CHICO: At'sa fine, boss. I think he likes it.

SCROOGE: For the last time, Beagle, will you or won't you pay the rent?

GROUCHO: Is there a choice?

CHICO: Sure, there's a choice. There'sa Peggy Joyce.

GROUCHO: You, too, Ravelli? *(Phone rings.)* Pardon me, Mr. Scrooge. That's the phone. Hello . . . can you hear me? . . . I can hear you, too. *(Aside.)* Marvelous inventions, these telephones. Oh, so it's *you*, Astorbilt. How many times have I told you not to disturb me during office hours? . . . Oh, you want me to represent your railroads. Well, you know my terms. Send over a five-thousand-dollar retainer at once. Oh, yes, and a half a pound of butter.

CHICO *(whispering):*   See that, Mr. Scrooge? Everybody is after him, and you want to bother him with a little thing like rent.

SCROOGE *(whispering):*   Well, maybe I *was* a little hasty.

GROUCHO: Listen, Astorbilt, I wouldn't consider your proposition for a minute if I wasn't in love with your wife. As it is, I'll think it over. I'll tell you what I'll do. I'll sleep on it. That is, if the desk doesn't get too uncomfortable. I'll phone you in the morning. Goodbye.

SCROOGE: Well, Mr. Beagle, I had no idea you were handling such big cases. Maybe I'd better come back some other time when you're not so busy.

CHICO: At'sa fine. Maybe you better not come back at all.

SCROOGE: You're sure everything is satisfactory around the office?

GROUCHO: Well, now that you speak of it, there are a few things I don't like about the place. In fact, I don't like you about the place. Of course, we could always have you painted. We could even shellac you. Boy, how we could shellac you!

SCROOGE: Well, I'll be seeing you again.

GROUCHO: Drop in any time, old man. You'll always find welcome on the mat. And you'll always find the mat at the pawnbroker's. And lock that door after you.

SCROOGE: Yes, Mr. Beagle.

(Door opens and shuts.)

GROUCHO: And now, Ravelli . . .

CHICO: Yes, boss?

GROUCHO: Statistics show that there are about eight million people in this city. Two million go by this office every day. And out of those two million you had to pick the landlord to bring in here! Well, what have you got to say for yourself?

CHICO: I think I should get a raise.

GROUCHO: That sounds reasonable. That sounds familiar, too. Where do you think I'm going to get the money?

CHICO: Well, you just told Astorbilt you wouldn't take a million-dollar case.

GROUCHO: Astorbilt my eye. That was the telephone company calling.

CHICO: They offer you million-dollar cases?

GROUCHO: No, you sap. They just called up to say they've cut off the phone service.

CHICO: They cut off the phone service? At'sa too bad. So how you going to call up Astorbilt in the morning?

GROUCHO: Ravelli, the next time you cross the street, make sure the traffic lights are against you.

(*Signature music.*)

FIVE STAR THEATER
PRESENTS

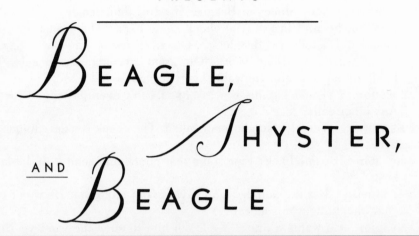

BEAGLE, SHYSTER, AND BEAGLE

EPISODE NO. 3   DECEMBER 12, 1932

CAST

Groucho Marx as Waldorf T. Beagle
Chico Marx as Emmanuel Ravelli
Miss Dimple
Client
Cop
Woman
Butler
Keeper

(*Sound of typing; phone rings.*)

MISS DIMPLE: Law offices of Beagle, Shyster, and Beagle . . . Mr. Beagle? No, he isn't in . . . The check came back? There must be some mistake. I'll tell Mr. Beagle . . . Okay. (*Click of phone . . . She resumes typing . . . Door opens.*) Oh, good morning, Mr. Beagle. The landlord called again. He wants his rent paid.

GROUCHO: *I* should pay his rent? Why, I can't even pay my own rent. Any other calls?

MISS DIMPLE: Yes, the laundry man called. The check you gave him came back.

GROUCHO: It came back? Fine, take that check and send it to the landlord.

MISS DIMPLE: But the laundry man says it isn't any good. He won't take your check, he wants a draft.

GROUCHO: He wants a draft? Well, tell him to open the window. Hereafter, Miss Dimple, send my laundry home to my wife. Her customers tell me she does *very* good work.

MISS DIMPLE: Yes, sir. By the way, Mr. Beagle, how did you make out in court?

GROUCHO: Splendid, splendid, Miss Dimple. I got my client off.

MISS DIMPLE: You got him off?

GROUCHO: Yes, I got him off the streets for six months. They put him in the workhouse.

(*Knock on door.*)

MISS DIMPLE: Come in.

(*Door opens.*)

CHICO: Hello, boss. I wasa looking for you in the poolroom.

GROUCHO: Oh, it's you, Ravelli. A fine assistant *you* are. What do you mean by coming in at *this* hour of the day?

CHICO: Well, boss, I wouldn'ta come in, but a cop he come and chased me out of the park.

GROUCHO: Listen, Ravelli, you're loafing on the job. Look at that table. That dust has been on there for *ten weeks!*

CHICO: Well, you can't blame me for that. I only been working here *tree* weeks. But listen, boss, I gotta some good news.

GROUCHO: You mean you're quitting?

CHICO: No, I no quit—I gotta some good *news* for you.

GROUCHO: Listen, Ravelli, the only good news you could bring me would be a noose around your neck.

CHICO: Ha, you no understand. I got a new client.

GROUCHO (*excited*):   A new client? Where is he? Why doesn't he come in?

CHICO: He can't. He can't come in. He's a little bit unconscious. You gotta come out and help me carry him in.

GROUCHO: *I* should carry *him*? Let him go to my creditors. They've been carrying me for ten years. Ravelli, he's got to be brought in. I don't care how—by hook or by crook. And we haven't got a hook, so it's up to you.

CHICO: At'sa fine. I go and push him in.

(*Door opens and closes.*)

GROUCHO: Miss Dimple, quick, make out a bill for five hundred dollars for legal services.

MISS DIMPLE: Who is the client?

GROUCHO: I don't know. Ravelli hasn't brought him in yet. And when you're through, run down to the corner and get me a couple of cigars.

MISS DIMPLE: The kind I got yesterday?

GROUCHO: No, get me stronger cigars.

MISS DIMPLE: Stronger cigars?

GROUCHO: Yes, much stronger. The ones you got yesterday broke in my pocket.

(*Door opens.*)

CHICO: Well, here's the old geezer, boss. Where shall I put him?

GROUCHO: Drop him in that chair. Say, he looks pretty good for an old geezer.

CHICO: I look pretty good for an old geezer, too. I look for this old geezer all day.

CLIENT (*squeakily*): Gentlemen, I don't like being called an old geezer.

CHICO: Awright, awright, den I call you Old Sourpuss, eh, old geezer?

CLIENT: My name is John Smith.

GROUCHO: Not *Captain* John Smith? Say, how's Pocahontas? Miss Dimple, send that bill to Captain John Smith, in care of Pocahontas. Captain, have you got a stamp on you?

CHICO: At'sa fine, boss—if he got a stamp on him I won't have to carry him no more. We can mail him home.

CLIENT: Please, Mr. Beagle. I'm here on business. I was on my way to my banker's next door when I met your assistant, Mr. Ravelli.

GROUCHO: Well, that's your hard luck.

CLIENT: He persuaded me that I ought to have my will looked over. So I went home and got it. I thought I'd kill two birds with one stone.

GROUCHO: Listen, Smith, first let's see the will; we can go hunting for birds later.

CLIENT: Very well, I will read you my will now: "I, John Smith, being of sound mind—"

GROUCHO: Sound mind, eh? Well, that's the first thing we'll have to eliminate.

CHICO: At'sa fine. I take some.

GROUCHO: You'll take some what?

CHICO: Eliminate. I take a nice cold glass e'liminate.

GROUCHO: That's very good, Ravelli, that's very good. Here, stuff this handkerchief down your throat and eliminate yourself.

CLIENT: If you don't mind, I'll go on with the reading . . .

GROUCHO: And stuff a handkerchief down *your* throat.

CLIENT *(continuing):* "One million dollars in cash, which I . . . "

GROUCHO: You have a million dollars in cash? Ravelli, Captain Smith is our guest. Take your hand out of his pocket.

CHICO: Ha! Just a little mistake, boss. His suit looka so much like my suit I thought I had my hand in my own pocket.

GROUCHO: Pay no attention to him, Captain. Go on with the will.

CLIENT: "One million dollars in cash, which I give and bequeath to my dear and beloved Aunt Sarah."

GROUCHO: *Aunt Sarah!* You mean you're going to give all that money to a woman you're not even married to? Captain, you know how people will talk. You know what they'll say, Captain. Think of her good name. Aunt Sarah is a very good name. Just ask yourself, are you being fair to that little, wire-haired old lady who has struggled all these years to get your money? No, Captain, no. A thousand times, no.

CLIENT: Mr. Beagle, this is very surprising.

GROUCHO: Splendid, Captain, splendid. I *knew* you'd see it our way. Now, as to that million dollars, I suggest charity. I've got just the charity for you. The Beagle Foundation for the Advancement of Beagle.

CHICO: Hey, boss, what about me? Didn't I carry him in?

GROUCHO: All right, Ravelli, we'll split the old geezer two ways. Half a million for the *Beagle* Foundation for the Advancement of Beagle, and half a million for the *Ravelli* Foundation for the Advancement of Beagle.

CHICO: At'sa fine, boss. From now on I think I'm gonna call you Square-Deal Beagle.

CLIENT: Don't I have anything to say about it?

GROUCHO: All right, Captain. Let's hear a word from you.

CLIENT: Mr. Beagle—

GROUCHO: There you are. That's two words. I let you have a word and you take two. And I thought I could trust you.

CLIENT *(indignant):* See here, Mr. Beagle, I'll have you know I'm just as honest as you are.

CHICO: Hey. Just one minoots. You're just as honest as Mr. Beagle, eh? Hey, boss, I think we better lock up the safe.

CLIENT: If you don't mind, I'll continue reading my will. Now . . . ah . . . my house on Long Island, my villa in Newport, my yacht, and three motor cars I leave to my loyal brother, Hector.

CHICO: Hector? What kind of a hector—a movie hector? . . . Hey, what's his name?

CLIENT: His name is Hector—Hector Smith. He's an inventor.

CHICO: Inventor, that's no good. It's too cold in ventor. In summer . . . ah, boss, at'sa fine in the summer.

CLIENT: Perhaps I'm not making myself *clear!*

GROUCHO *(sotto voce):* Yes you are, Captain. I can see right through you.

CLIENT: I want to leave the balance of my estate to my brother, Hector.

GROUCHO: Captain John Smith, I'm amazed. You mean to say that you're going to cut Pocahontas off without a nickel? After all she's done for you! Why, man, she saved your scalp, and what other hair tonic can do that? Furthermore—

CLIENT *(indignant):* Gentlemen, I want to say that I never—

GROUCHO *(cutting in):* It's nothing at all, Captain. It's settled. That rat—

CLIENT: What rat?

GROUCHO: I mean your brother Hector . . . is disinherited. The house—

CHICO: Awright, boss, awright. I take the house.

GROUCHO: *You'll* take the house? Do you think *I* like living in this office?

CHICO: Awright, boss. You take the house. I'll take the three automobiles.

CLIENT: See, here, Mr. Ravelli, I wish—

GROUCHO: Shut up, Smith. I can fight my own battles. Ravelli, let's talk this thing over. What'll you take for one of those cars?

CHICO: Oh, no, I no wanna sell, boss. These cars have been in the family for a long time.

GROUCHO: But I'm willing to pay, Ravelli, and handsomely. I'll give you the villa and I'll throw in my girl's telephone number.

CHICO: I don't want your girl's telephone number. Every time I call her up, *you* answer.

CLIENT: Gentlemen, it strikes me that you're not considering my wishes in the matter. I . . . ah . . .

GROUCHO: Captain, you're absolutely right. You can sign right here. If anything else turns up, you can see me at my office or at my home. I am home every evening but Thursday.

CHICO: Where do you go Thursday?

GROUCHO: Thursday is the maid's night out, and, eh, I always go out with *her*.
(*Music in strong.*)

(*Street noises; honking horns; sounds of automobile engine.*)
CHICO: Hey boss, not so fast. We're in Long Island. Maybe Captain Smith's house is in the next block. You better drive slower.
GROUCHO: Where's your sporting blood, Ravelli? A race is a race. Do you think I'm going to let that motorcycle cop beat us?
(*Sound of siren.*)
CHICO: Hey, hey boss, watch that lamppost.
GROUCHO: *You* watch the lamppost. I've got my hands full *driving* this car.
CHICO (*excited*): Hey, look out! I tell you, look out! The lamppost!
(*Car crashes. Motorcycle policeman's siren approaches.*)
GROUCHO: Ravelli, Ravelli, where are you?
CHICO: Here I am, boss. Here I am, up here on top of the lamppost.
GROUCHO: I told you to *watch* the lamppost. I didn't tell you to *sit* on it. Come on down.
(*Siren approaches and stops.*)
COP: Hey, you guys, where's the fire?
CHICO: I don't know, Mr. Policeman, we come from out of town.
COP: Yeah? Well this is gonna cost you plenty.
CHICO: Whata you mean, cost me plenty? We no bet *nuttin* on dis race.
COP: You were going seventy miles an hour.
CHICO: Ah, you make a mistake, officer. We haven't been out an hour. We only stole dis car fifteen minutes ago.
COP: Do you guys know that you're driving on the wrong side of the street, that you crashed through a fence, knocked down a lamppost, smashed a wagon and damaged the car in front of you?
GROUCHO: See here, officer. I paid three dollars for my driving license. Doesn't that entitle me to *any* privileges?
COP: Pipe down, pipe down, and take this ticket.
CHICO: Hey, officer, how about a ticket for me? Make it a Wednesday matinee. I got a date.
GROUCHO: You can give him my ticket, officer. I don't think I care to go. The last time I got a ticket it cost me fifteen bucks.
COP: You'll take this ticket, all right. There you are. I'm going.
(*Motorcycle starts and fades out.*)
CHICO: Say, boss, what about the car?
GROUCHO: Let it lay there. It probably isn't paid for anyway. Well, what

do you know about that! We broke down right in front of the house we're looking for. Captain Smith said it was a brown house with a porch in front.

CHICO: What kind of porch? A front porch or a back porch?

GROUCHO: He didn't say. He just said it was a house with a porch in front.

CHICO: All right, I'll go in back and see if there's a front porch. You look in the front and see if there's a back porch. Hey, I bet Captain Smith is gonna be surprised when *we* walk in.

GROUCHO: Good old Smith. It's nice of him to will us the house. You know, I'll be almost sorry to see him kick the bucket.

CHICO: At's awright boss. We get him a new bucket. Hey look, here's a window. We can get in through here.

GROUCHO: Ravelli, a gentleman never enters a house through a window. So *you* go through the window and answer the door when I ring the bell.

(Window is raised, sounds of entering.)

WOMAN: Jameson, who *is* this man?

BUTLER: I really down't knaow, modom. He must have flown in through the window.

WOMAN: Sir, who are you?

CHICO: Me? I'm Emmanuel Ravelli, and I know who you are, too. You can't fool me. You're Aunt Sarah.

WOMAN: You must be mad.

(Doorbell rings.)

CHICO: Oh, I'm not mad, Aunt Sarah. My boss—he's gonna be mad if I don't open the door pretty quick.

WOMAN: Jameson, what will my guests think? Take this man out at once.

CHICO: Oh no, I'm not going out with him, but I go out with *you* some night, hey baby? What do you say, okay?

(Doorbell rings.)

WOMAN: This is unbearable. Jameson, open the door and see who it is.

BUTLER: Yes, modom. *(Opens door.)*

GROUCHO *(indignant):* Where's that Ravelli? This is a pretty kettle of fish.

CHICO: Hey, fish ain't kettle. Horses and cows is kettle.

GROUCHO: Here I am being kept waiting at the threshold of what is practically my own home.

WOMAN: *Your* home! You must be crazy.

CHICO: You're right, Aunt Sarah, this ain't his home. It's half mine. *I* brought the old geezer into the office.

WOMAN: Old geezer! Just what are you talking about?

GROUCHO: Playing dumb, eh? Well, two can play that game as well as one, and Ravelli isn't even playing.

WOMAN: *Sir*, just *what* can I *do* for you?

GROUCHO: Madam, we'll discuss that later. Right now my mind is on business. If the old geezer wants me to take over this house when he kicks off, he'll have to fix it up to suit my taste. Look at those pictures on the wall. They're terrible!

WOMAN: Why, those pictures are masterpieces. They're two hundred years old!

GROUCHO: Two hundred years old? Yes, and they look it. Why, that's older than my overcoat, Ravelli. Take those pictures down off the wall and hang up my overcoat instead.

WOMAN: Keep your hands off those pictures. I tell you they are valuable old masters.

CHICO: That's an old master? It looks more like a lady to me.

GROUCHO: Shut up, Ravelli. Well, the pictures are not the only thing that needs improving. Tomorrow we give the house a coat of paint. We'll give it a good coat, then the next day we'll give it the pants and vest.

WOMAN: *What is the meaning of all this?*

GROUCHO: The will I have with me explains everything. If you will join me in the parlor, I will read it. Jameson, a whiskey and soda . . . a whiskey for me and a soda for Ravelli. Bicarbonate of soda.

WOMAN: All this . . . is simply intolerable.

GROUCHO: Madam, if you'll be good enough to dry up, I'll read the will. Ahem. Here we go. "I, Captain John Smith, known to my attorney as 'Old Geezer,' being sixty-eight years of age and *very* repulsive . . . " How do you like it so far, Mrs. Smith?

WOMAN: I'm not Mrs. Smith. You must have the wrong address.

CHICO: Aw no, we got the right address. You must be in the wrong house.

WOMAN: Ridiculous. I've lived here for years. And I tell you there are *no Smiths here*!

GROUCHO: No Smiths! Well, why didn't you say that before?

WOMAN: That's just what I tried to—

GROUCHO: I know. You thought you'd have a little fun at our expense. Madam, I'm a lawyer; my time is valuable, and you're going to pay for it. In the morning you'll get a bill for sixty cents.

CHICO: Hey, boss, what about me? I'm here, too.

GROUCHO: He's right, madam. He's here too. I'll reduce the bill to . . . er . . . er . . . forty cents.

(*Music in strong.*)

. . .

MISS DIMPLE *(wearily):* Hello, Mr. Smith? Are you the John Smith who came into the office of Beagle, Shyster, and Beagle about six weeks ago to have a will drawn up? . . . No? . . . Well, you don't have to get fresh about it . . . Goodbye. *(Hangs up receiver.)* It's no use, Mr. Beagle, I've tried every John Smith in the phone book and I haven't found him yet. I simply don't know where to look for him.

GROUCHO: Oh, I know where to look for him, all right! What I'd like to know is where to find him. The sneak! He promises to leave me his fortune and all he does is to leave *me.*

MISS DIMPLE: Will that be all?

GROUCHO: No, I want you to take my law book back to the library and get me *The Rover Boys in the Pants Business.* My friends are all talking about it.

(Door opens.)

CHICO: Hello, boss. How's things?

GROUCHO: Ravelli, what are you doing *here?* I thought I told you to go outside and look for Smith.

CHICO: I know, boss, but it's raining outside.

GROUCHO: Well, let it rain.

CHICO: That's just what I was going to do.

GROUCHO: That settles it—you're fired. Go, Ravelli. Go, and never darken my office towels again. Miss Dimple, take his name off the payroll.

CHICO *(sadly):* See, Miss Dimple, I looka and looka for a job for eighteen years. I look, and when I find one, the boss he fires me.

MISS DIMPLE: Mr. Ravelli, you looked for a job for eighteen years! How is it you didn't find one?

CHICO: I don't know, Miss Dimple. I think it was just good luck.

(Knock at door.)

MISS DIMPLE: I'll open it, Mr. Beagle . . . Why it's *Mr. Smith!*

GROUCHO: Smith? Ravelli, Ravelli, it's Smith!

CHICO: Hey, it'sa the Cap. Hey, look, he'sa lookin fine.

GROUCHO: That's too bad, but don't let that trouble you, Ravelli. From now on he'll be under *our* care.

SMITH: How do you do, gentlemen? I came—

CHICO: Here you are, Cap, take a seat.

GROUCHO: No, no, Ravelli, not there. Sit him by the window. There's a good draft there. There you are, Captain, sit right down. How's that?

SMITH *(sneezes):* It's kind of chilly. I'll catch cold.

GROUCHO: That's fine. Ravelli, open the other window.

SMITH: No, no, you'd better *shut* the window. It's raining outside.

CHICO: What do you care? If I shut the window it'll still be raining outside.

SMITH: Mr. Beagle, about that new will you drew up for me. I've been somewhat troubled by the middle clause.

CHICO: He's got a mistake. He don't mean the middle clause. He means the *centa* clause, but he no fool me. There ain't no centa clause.

SMITH: That's beside the point. I was just thinking, instead of leaving a million dollars to those foundations you mentioned, it might be a good idea to leave half a million to my children and half a million to an orphanage.

GROUCHO: Nonsense, Smith. That involves too much bookkeeping. Instead of leaving half of your money to your children and the other half to the orphanage, why not leave your children to the orphanage . . . and the million to me?

SMITH: Leave you a *cool million*?

"There ain't no Sanity Clause." The contract-tearing scene from *A Night at the Opera.*

CHICO: Don't worry, Cap, don't worry. We warm it up for you.

(Knock heard on door.)

GROUCHO: Miss Dimple, open the door. Ravelli, hide the captain, it might be his relatives.

MAN *(gruffly):* I'm looking for—oh, there you are Smith. You're coming with me.

CHICO: Aw no, we saw the captain first.

MAN: Come along, Smith.

SMITH *(crankily):* You leave me alone. I've got business to attend to. With my lawyer.

GROUCHO: See here, stranger, if you want to take Smith away, you've got to leave us a deposit. We got a million dollars tied up in Old Sourpuss.

MAN: I've got to take him away. He escaped from the asylum.

GROUCHO: *What?*

CHICO: Whata you say?

MAN: Yep. He may become violent at any moment.

SMITH: You let me alone. You let me *alone. (Starts yelling.)*

MAN: Hold him, hold him.

GROUCHO: Hold him? *You* hold him, we're through with him.

SMITH: I'll get you, Beagle.

GROUCHO: Out of my way, Ravelli. *(Terrible crash.)* Hey, Ravelli, what do you mean by jumping out of a window ahead of your boss?

(Signature music.)

FIVE STAR THEATER
PRESENTS

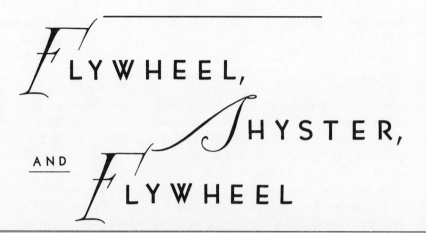

FLYWHEEL, SHYSTER, AND FLYWHEEL

EPISODE NO. 4   DECEMBER 19, 1932

CAST

Groucho Marx as Waldorf T. Flywheel
Chico Marx as Emmanuel Ravelli
Miss Dimple
Mrs. Brittenhouse, society woman
Bride
Butler
Man

(Phone rings.)

MISS DIMPLE: Law offices of Flywheel, Shyster, and Flywheel . . . Yes, I know that used to be the name of the firm, but the boss got a divorce and changed his name back to Flywheel . . . You want to speak to Mr. Ravelli? He's not in now, madam. Mr. Flywheel's here. Do you want to speak to him? . . . Oh, you don't want to speak to Mr. Flywheel?

GROUCHO: Who doesn't want to speak to Mr. Flywheel? Give me that phone, Miss Dimple. I'll show her a thing or two. Hello . . . hello . . . So, madam, you don't want to speak to me? . . . No, this isn't Ravelli; this is Flywheel . . . *F* like in Flywheel, *l* like in fly, *y* like in Flywheel, *wheel* like in wheel cutlet, and *fly* like in milk . . . Oh, you still want to speak to Ravelli? Listen, madam, I'll have none of your lip, but I'll take an ear of corn. Goodbye! *(Hangs up phone.)* I guess that put her in her place. Say, I wonder where her place is? I'd like to go up and see her. Miss Dimple, am I doing anything today?

MISS DIMPLE: No, Mr. Flywheel, not a thing.

GROUCHO: Ah me, the same old grind. Well, Miss Dimple, to work! What's at the movies this afternoon?

MISS DIMPLE: *Grand Hotel* with John Barrymore.

GROUCHO: I'd rather have a small boarding house with Greta Garbo.

MISS DIMPLE: Oh, I love Greta Garbo.

GROUCHO: I think she's pretty Swede myself. By the way, Miss Dimple, it's cold today. Look in the filing cabinet under *W* and get me my winter underwear.

MISS DIMPLE: Your underwear isn't there, Mr. Flywheel. Your assistant is wearing it today.

GROUCHO: Oh, so Ravelli is wearing my underwear! Quick, Miss Dimple, look under the letter *X* and see if he's taken my extra golf socks.

(Filing cabinet drawer slides.)

MISS DIMPLE: Your golf socks?

GROUCHO: You know, the socks with the eighteen holes.

MISS DIMPLE: They're here, Mr. Flywheel.

GROUCHO: Yes, the socks are here, but there are thirty-six holes now.

MISS DIMPLE: Isn't that a shame! The rats have probably been at them, Mr. Flywheel. This office is alive with them.

GROUCHO: Rats at my age? What are we going to do about it?

MISS DIMPLE: Don't you think I'd better get some rat biscuit?

GROUCHO: Rat biscuit? Nonsense! These rats'll eat what *we* eat or they'll go hungry. Why do you think this is—a rathskellar?

(Door opens.)

MRS. BRITTENHOUSE: Good morning. I *beg* your pardon . . .

GROUCHO: What?

MRS. BRITTENHOUSE: I *beg* your pardon.

GROUCHO: Sorry, madam, but they don't allow beggars in this building. You'll find the beggary shop next door. And furthermore, you'll have to leave your dog outside.

CHICO: Hey! At'sa no dog. At'sa me, boss.

GROUCHO: Oh, so it's you, Ravelli. Well, you'll have to leave your woman outside.

CHICO: Hey, Mr. Flywheel, this lady, she wants to see you.

MRS. BRITTENHOUSE: Is this a detective agency?

GROUCHO: A detective agency? Madam, if there's anything in it for me, this is Scotland Yard.

MRS. BRITTENHOUSE: This man told me he was taking me to a detective bureau.

CHICO: You're cuckoo, I did not. You stop me in the hall. You say you want a detective. I say, you go see Flywheel. You say awright. Well, here's Flywheel.

MRS. BRITTENHOUSE: Sir, are you or aren't you a detective? My time is money.

GROUCHO: Your time is money? I wonder if you could lend me ten minutes for lunch, or maybe a half an hour for the rent?

MRS. BRITTENHOUSE: For the last time, are you a detective?

GROUCHO: Madam, for the first time I *am* a detective.

MRS. BRITTENHOUSE: Well, you don't look much like a detective to me.

GROUCHO: That's the beauty of it. See? I had you fooled already.

MRS. BRITTENHOUSE: Is this man who brought me in a detective too?

CHICO: Sure, I'm a detective. I prove it. Lady, you lose anything today?

MRS. BRITTENHOUSE: Why, I don't think so. Heavens! My handbag has disappeared.

CHICO: Here it is.

MRS. BRITTENHOUSE: Where did you find it?

CHICO: Right here in my pocket.

GROUCHO: Isn't he marvelous, madam? He has the nose of a bloodhound, and his other features aren't so good either.

MRS. BRITTENHOUSE: Well, you're just the men I'm looking for.

CHICO: You're looking for us? Hey, are *you* a detective?

MRS. BRITTENHOUSE: No, no. You misunderstand me. You see, my daughter is getting married this afternoon.

GROUCHO: Oh, your daughter's getting married? I love those old-fashioned girls.

MRS. BRITTENHOUSE: We're having a big wedding reception, and I want you two men to come out this afternoon and keep an eye on the wedding presents. They're very valuable, and I want to be sure that nothing is stolen.

CHICO: How mucha you pay us? You know it'sa very hard work not to steal nothing.

MRS. BRITTENHOUSE: Would you take fifty dollars? I think that would be adequate.

CHICO: Adequate? I had to quit the last job for taking fifty dollars when the boss wasn't looking.

MRS. BRITTENHOUSE: Very well, fifty dollars, but you understand; of course, that you're not to mingle with the guests.

GROUCHO: Well, if we don't have to mingle with the guests we'll do it for forty dollars.

MRS. BRITTENHOUSE: Dear, dear, I must hurry. My daughter can't get married unless I get her trousseau.

CHICO: Trousseau? You mean Robinson Trousseau?

GROUCHO: Your daughter's marrying Robinson Crusoe today? Monday? Wouldn't she be better off if she'd marry the man Friday?

MRS. BRITTENHOUSE: In order that no one suspect anything, I want you to dress like my guests.

GROUCHO: I'm sorry, madam, but this is the frowziest suit I've got.

MRS. BRITTENHOUSE: No, no, you don't understand. I want you to wear a cutaway.

CHICO: It's no use, lady. I can'ta wear a cutaway. I only got the *pants*. Last week I gave the cutaway.

MRS. BRITTENHOUSE: Well, I'll be looking for you this afternoon.

GROUCHO: Well, why look for us this afternoon when we're here right now?

MRS. BRITTENHOUSE: I must hurry along now. Goodbye, gentlemen.
(*Door closes.*)

CHICO: Well, boss, I guess we gotta fine job.

GROUCHO: Ravelli, for once I think I've underrated you. From now on your salary is raised. Hereafter I'll owe you twenty dollars a week instead of fifteen.

CHICO: At'sa fine, boss, you raise me like that.

GROUCHO: Why shouldn't I raise you, Ravelli? I've raised pigs.

CHICO: Umm—I hope they gotta good food at this wedding.

GROUCHO: What do you care? You won't get anything to eat.

CHICO: Well, even when I don't get anything to eat, I lika the food good.

GROUCHO: Jumping Jupiter, Ravelli! We're ruined. We're sunk!

CHICO: What's the matter, boss?

GROUCHO: We forgot to get the address where the woman lives.

CHICO: Don't get excited. Don't get excited. I know where she lives.

GROUCHO: You know where she lives?

CHICO: Sure, I know. I got the address right in here.

GROUCHO: In where? Ravelli, what have you got there?

CHICO: Ha! *I got the lady's handbag.*
  (*Music in strong.*)

  (*Soft music in distance, fades down. Murmur of voices, fades.*)

MRS. BRITTENHOUSE: How do you do, Mr. Flywheel? How do you do, Mr. Ravelli? So, you got here at last.

CHICO: Yes, we had trouble with our car.

MRS. BRITTENHOUSE: Oh, that's too bad. Was it serious?

CHICO: Nota very much. The motorman, he just threw us off.

MRS. BRITTENHOUSE: Well, I'll take you right over to the table where the presents are being displayed.

GROUCHO: Madam, before we go into that, permit me to say that you've got the goofiest-looking collection of guests at this brawl that I ever hope to see.

MRS. BRITTENHOUSE: How dare you! Why, my guests are the social lights of the community.

GROUCHO: Ravelli, let's put out the lights and go to sleep.

MRS. BRITTENHOUSE: Here's my butler. Hives, these are the detectives I spoke to you about.

GROUCHO: Oh, so you've been discussing us with the servants behind our backs?

MRS. BRITTENHOUSE: Hives, take these gentlemen's hats and coats, and show them where they're to guard the presents.

HIVES: Very good, milady.

GROUCHO: Very good, my eye. Who's going to guard our hats and coats while we guard the presents?

CHICO: At'sa right. I no wanta lose this coat. It don't belong to me. It belong to a friend of mine.

GROUCHO: Oh, you've got a friend, have you? Where is he?

CHICO: He'sa looking for his coat.

MRS. BRITTENHOUSE: Well, Hives will take care of you. Oh, dear, I'm always so nervous at weddings. I'm really not myself today.

GROUCHO: You're not yourself, eh? Well, whoever you are, you're no bargain.

MRS. BRITTENHOUSE: Hives, you attend to these gentlemen and show them their duties. I really must fly now.

GROUCHO: Well, happy landing.
  (*Door closes.*)

HIVES: Come with me, gentlemen. The presents are over here.

CHICO: Never mind about the presents. We wanta see where is the kitchen.

GROUCHO: Such a question, Ravelli! What will Hives think of you? Where were you brought up?

CHICO: Hey, don't you remember? I was brought up in the elevator with you.

GROUCHO: Don't mind him, Hives. He hasn't been the same since his hat fell out of a fourth-story window.

HIVES: His hat fell out of the window, sir? But I don't understand.

GROUCHO: Well, unfortunately, he was wearing the hat at the time. Now, Hives, let's get down to business. Have you seen any suspicious-looking characters around here today . . . that is, besides yourself?

HIVES: Oh, no, sir. All the guests are close friends of the bride and groom's.

GROUCHO: Hmm. By the way, who is that dummy in the corner?

HIVES: That man in the corner? Why, that's the groom, sir.

GROUCHO: He just gave me a dirty look. They ought to take him upstairs and give him a bath. Then the bride would have a groom and bath. If I were the bride, I wouldn't stand for him.

CHICO: If you were the bride, he wouldn't stand for you.

HIVES: Now, on these two tables here, gentlemen, are the presents. Please watch them very carefully. *(Receding.)* I'll have to leave you now.

GROUCHO: Ravelli . . . take your hands off that butter dish.

CHICO: This butter dish?

(Crash.)

GROUCHO: Well, that's fine. There's one present they won't steal, unless they bring a broom. Now get to work. Er . . . you sit in this chair and watch the presents . . . and I'll lie down over here and watch you.

CHICO: At'sa fine. But who'sa gonna watch you?

GROUCHO: Who's going to watch me? I never thought of that. Ravelli, this job is getting to be too big for two men. Maybe we ought to get an assistant.

(Tap at the window.)

CHICO: Hey, what'sa that noise?

GROUCHO: I think there's somebody at the window. You'd better let him in.

CHICO: Hey, boss. He's a great biga guy and he looks very tough.

(Tap again.)

GROUCHO: Ravelli, open the window, there's nothing to be afraid of. Er . . . if you need me, I'll be hiding under the table.

CHICO: Awright, boss. I open the window and ask him what he wants. *(Opens window.)* Hey, biga boy, what you want?

MAN *(approaching):* What's de big idea of keepin' me out in de cold? . . . Well, I said what's de big idea?

GROUCHO: Oh, it's not such a big idea. It's just a little thing I thought up.

MAN: Oh, yeah?

CHICO: Hey, who are you?

MAN: Never mind who I am. Who are you guys?

CHICO: We're a coupla detectives.

MAN: Oh, you're a coupla detectives. Ha, ha, ha! That's a hot one!

GROUCHO: Well, I've heard better ones than that, but it's fairly good.

CHICO: Honest, we're detectives. If you don't believe us, we'll call da lady in and prove it.

MAN: Wait a minute, you mugs. You call the lady and I'll croak yuh. I'm giving the old girl a surprise party. But the biggest surprise will come when I blow out of this joint. Hey, what are youse guys supposed to do here?

CHICO: I watcha da presents. Flywheel, he watcha me, but we gotta no one to watcha Flywheel.

MAN: Flywheel? What are you talking about? Who ever heard of Flywheel?

GROUCHO: What, you've never heard of me? Flywheel, the old gray fox? The pride of Scotland Yard?

MAN: Well, you punks can clear out of here. I'll do the whole ting for you. You won't even have to watch de presents. That's gonna be my job. And to show you what a good guy *I* am, I won't charge youse a cent.

GROUCHO: Stranger, I bet you'd give a fellow the shirt off your back. That's white of you . . . and that's more than I can say for the shirt.

MAN: Go on, scram. Scram! I'll take good care of the presents. Don't worry. I'll handle those presents like they was my own.

GROUCHO: Ravelli, that fellow certainly is a prince. Let's hurry out of here before he changes his mind. *(Opens door.)* Come on.

CHICO: I'm coming. *(Closes door.)* Hey, look out. Here comes de old lady of da house.

MRS. BRITTENHOUSE: Well, gentlemen. Why aren't you watching the presents?

CHICO: We don't have to watch dem any more. We know what dey look like.

MRS. BRITTENHOUSE: Why . . . er . . .

GROUCHO: You'll pardon us, madam, we're very busy. There's something that must be investigated immediately. I must question the servants at once.

MRS. BRITTENHOUSE: Question the servants? What for?

GROUCHO: I want to find out when we eat.

(Music in strong.)

CHICO: Hey, boss, dere's data pretty girl again.

BRIDE: See here. Who are you two? I'm getting awfully tired of you following me around.

CHICO: I no follow you. I follow my boss, Mr. Flywheel. He follow you.

BRIDE: Well, I don't like it.

GROUCHO: I'm with you there, babe. I don't like it either. This is the *worst* wedding I ever went to except my own. Say, how about you and me ducking out of this dump and going someplace else?

BRIDE: Sir, do you know who I am? I am the bride.

GROUCHO: You're the bride? Look here, if you're the bride, why aren't you wearing a train?

CHICO: I guess she missed her train. At'sa why she's running so fast. Ha, ha, at'sa good.

BRIDE: You go away, or I'll call my father!

CHICO: I don't want your father. You call anodder girl and we all go away.

BRIDE: I certainly don't know any girls who'd go out with *you*.

CHICO: Neither do we. Dat's why we ask you.

GROUCHO: I still think it's a dull wedding. Maybe we can liven it up. Do you like riddles?

BRIDE: No!

GROUCHO: Fine. Then I'll ask you one. What has eight legs and sings?

BRIDE: I don't know.

GROUCHO: Give up? A centipede.

BRIDE: But a centipede has a hundred legs.

GROUCHO: Yes, but it can't sing.

BRIDE: Listen to me. If you people have been hired for this wedding, then you belong outside. The servants have quarters of their own.

CHICO: Oh no, lady. We joosta been shooting crap wit dem and dey got no more quarters left.

BRIDE: I've had enough of you two. Kindly get out of my way.

GROUCHO: Ravelli, you heard what the bride said. Get off the bridal path. See you later, Googoo.

CHICO: She's a nice kid. Hey, boss, here comes old battle-axe again. Hey, she looks pretty mad. I think I better go back and watcha the presents.

GROUCHO: Oh, so you're going to walk out on me, Ravelli? All you think about is saving your own face. And I think you're making a big mistake to save it. All right, go on and watch the presents.

MRS. BRITTENHOUSE *(away):* Mr. Flywheel!

CHICO: Awright, boss, I'll see you later.

MRS. BRITTENHOUSE: Why, Mr. Flywheel, I thought you were supposed to stay in that room with the presents!

GROUCHO: Madam, I couldn't stand being alone in that room. I just *had* to have another look at *you*. And now that I've had that look, I can hardly wait to get back to the presents.

MRS. BRITTENHOUSE: Why, Mr. Flywheel!

GROUCHO: Don't call me Mr. Flywheel, just call me Sugar and I'll call you Cocaine.

MRS. BRITTENHOUSE: Why, my name isn't Cocaine. Cocaine's a dope.

GROUCHO: Well, so are you.

MRS. BRITTENHOUSE: Oh, Mr. Flywheel, I simply love the things you say.

GROUCHO: Oh, Mrs. Brittenhouse—I know you'll think me a sentimental old softie, but would you give me a lock of your hair?

MRS. BRITTENHOUSE *(coyly):* Why, Mr. Flywheel!

GROUCHO: I'm letting you off easy—I was going to ask you for the whole wig.

MRS. BRITTENHOUSE: Well, we'll discuss that later. It's too bad you can't join us now for refreshments, but maybe some evening you'd like to have me for dinner.

GROUCHO: Have you for *dinner?* Well, if there's nothing better to eat, I wouldn't mind, but personally, I'd prefer a can of salmon.

HIVES: Mrs. Brittenhouse! Mrs. Brittenhouse!

GROUCHO: Is there no privacy here?

MRS. BRITTENHOUSE: Why Hives, what's the matter?

HIVES: The presents! The presents!

MRS. BRITTENHOUSE: What about the presents?

HIVES: They're gone. We've been robbed!

GROUCHO: Robbed? Where's Ravelli? Quick, find Ravelli!

CHICO: Here I am, boss. How you makin out?

GROUCHO: Listen, Ravelli. I thought I told you to watch the presents.

CHICO: Dat's just what I was doing.

GROUCHO: There you are, Mrs. Brittenhouse. You have nothing to worry about.

HIVES: But, madam, the presents are gone.

MRS. BRITTENHOUSE: Gone!

GROUCHO: Hmm. We'll have to question some of your guests. Ravelli, we'll have to grill all these people.

MRS. BRITTENHOUSE: Grill my guests!

CHICO: Sure, we're a couple of gorillers.

MRS. BRITTENHOUSE: But, Mr. Flywheel, if your man was watching the presents, how does it happen that they disappeared?

GROUCHO: Say . . . that's a *very* interesting point you just brought up, Mrs. Brittenhouse, a *very* interesting point. Ravelli, maybe you can elucidate.

CHICO: Sure I can elucidate. And if we don't hurry up out of here, I'm gonna lucidate with my girl.

MRS. BRITTENHOUSE: But I hired you men to watch the presents and now they've disappeared under your very eyes. You couldn't have been watching them. How could it have happened? Answer me. *Answer me!*

GROUCHO: Ravelli, answer the nice lady and I'll give you a nickel to get yourself a great big box of rat poison. *Did you watch the presents?*

CHICO: Boss, I watch dem joosta like a bloodhound. You remember dat big fellow? He come in da room . . . well, I watch him . . .

ALL: Yes . . .

CHICO: He walk over and pick up da presents and I watch him . . .

ALL: Yes . . .

CHICO: He take dem out da window! He put dem on a truck and I watch him . . .

ALL: Yes . . .

CHICO: But when da truck drives away . . . den I cannot watch no more.

GROUCHO: You're a genius. And now, Mrs. Brittenhouse, how about our fifty dollars?

(*Signature music.*)

FIVE STAR THEATER
PRESENTS

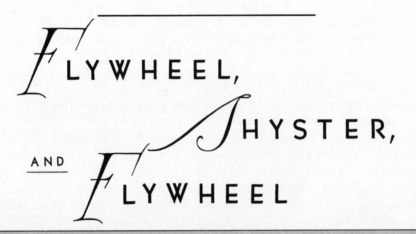

*F*LYWHEEL, *S*HYSTER, AND *F*LYWHEEL

EPISODE NO. 5   DECEMBER 26, 1932

CAST

Groucho Marx as Waldorf T. Flywheel
Chico Marx as Emmanuel Ravelli
Cop
Horace, seven-year-old child
Check girl in restaurant
Headwaiter in restaurant
Man
Pierre
Lady
Manager

(*Heavy pounding on the door.*)

GROUCHO: This is an outrage, Ravelli—locking us out of our own office on Christmas Day. *Me*, an American citizen—and *you* not even an American. A fine Christmas this is. When I woke up this morning I looked in my stocking and what do I find? *Your foot.*

CHICO: Ah, what'sa matter? You *gave* me that stocking.

GROUCHO: *I* gave you that stocking?

CHICO: Sure, lasta night, I ask you what you give me for Christmas, and you say you give me a sock.

GROUCHO: Just for that, Ravelli, you get no present from me.

CHICO: You got a present for me, boss? At'sa fine. What is it?

GROUCHO: I can't tell you, Ravelli. It's a secret.

CHICO: Ah, I no smoka segrets. I smoka cigars.

GROUCHO: One more crack like that and you'll get cigars. Scars all over your body.

CHICO: I kicka some more. I busta da door in.

(*Heavy pounding.*)

GROUCHO: Harder, Ravelli, harder. We got to get into this building.

CHICO: Hey, why don't *you* kicka da door awhile?

GROUCHO: I'd like to, Ravelli, but my foot's asleep.

CHICO: Your foot's asleep? Well, wake it up.

GROUCHO: Ravelli, I always believe in letting sleeping dogs lie.

CHICO: Awright den, *I* kick.

(*More pounding.*)

GROUCHO: That won't do any good. Not if you kick till the *cows* come home.

CHICO: I didn't know da cows went out. Hey, look out, boss. Here comes a cop.

COP (*approaching*): Hey, what are you guys doing out here?

GROUCHO: You bulls make me sick. What are you hanging around for?

CHICO: Is dat a bull? I guess he'sa waitin for dose cows to come home.

COP: What are you trying to break into this building for?

CHICO: We live in dis building, Mr. Policeman.

COP: Oh, you live here! Do you expect me to believe that? You can't take me in that way.

GROUCHO: We can't take you in any way. That's the trouble. If we could, we'd all go in together. Say, officer, you got nice big feet. How about you kicking the door for a while?

COP: Oh, fresh guys! Well, listen, you mugs, if it wasn't Christmas Day, I'd throw you both in jail. (*Receding.*) Now clear out of here and be quick about it.

GROUCHO: Well, Ravelli, this day is starting out in great shape. I must

Groucho as Ulysses H. Drivel (Ulysees H. Drivvle in the show's press release), "eagle-eyed news hound," and Chico as his "doughty" assistant Penelli, from their short-lived CBS comedy show broadcast in the spring of 1934 on Sunday nights.

have gotten up on the wrong side of the desk this morning. Santa Claus has certainly forgotten us.

CHICO: Maybe Santa Claus no come down our chimney because he's afraid of da crickets.

GROUCHO: Crickets in the chimney?

CHICO: Sure. You heard of chimney crickets.

GROUCHO: Listen, Ravelli, don't make matters any worse. This whole thing's your fault anyway. If you hadn't walked in your sleep and I hadn't been sleeping with you, we never would have walked out of that office.

CHICO: I no can help it. I dream dat a beautiful lady ask me to go to a big Christmas dinner and I start to walk home with her. Then I wake up . . . and no lady, no dinner, no home. Just Flywheel.

GROUCHO: Say, you don't happen to remember her address, do you?

CHICO: Sure, she hadda on a reda dress.

HORACE *(away):* Wahhh!

CHICO: What's dat?

HORACE *(nearer):* Wahhh!

GROUCHO: Unless my memory fails me, it's a child. Why look, Ravelli, he can't be more than seven years old. What's the matter, little man? Are you locked out of *your* office, too? What's your name?

HORACE: My name's Horace and I'm lost. Wahhh!

GROUCHO: Turn your face away, Ravelli. Can't you see you're frightening the child? What's wrong, Horace? Are you sick?

HORACE: No, I'm hungry. Daddy was taking me to Christmas dinner and he heard some little boys singing Christmas carols . . . and he went to give them some money and I lost him.

CHICO: Dey gotta money for singing? At'sa fine. I sing very good.

GROUCHO: Maybe there is something to this Christmas-carol gag. Only I don't know any carols. The only one I ever knew got married and moved out of town.

CHICO: Say, I know two carols.

GROUCHO: You know two carols. Well, let's hear you sing one.

CHICO *(singing tenor):* "Carolfornia, here I come . . . "

HORACE: Wahhh!

GROUCHO: That's awful, Ravelli. You'd better sing the other one.

CHICO: Awright. I sing de odder one. *(Singing bass:)* "Carolfornia, here I come . . . "

GROUCHO: Why, that's the same song.

CHICO: Yes, but dis is *lower* Carolfornia. *(Starts singing again.)*

HORACE: Wahhh!

GROUCHO: You're in a bad state. Look, Ravelli, Horace is only crying, and he sounds better than you.

CHICO: You know, boss, I sing by ear.

GROUCHO: You sing by ear? Well, try using your mouth sometime. It might be an improvement.

HORACE: Wahhh! I want to eat.

GROUCHO: Say, you're getting to be a problem child. You want to eat? Well, how much money have you got on you?

HORACE: I haven't got any money.

GROUCHO: No money? Ravelli, see if he has any gold teeth.

CHICO: Awright . . . Ouch! He bit my finger! Boss, I tink he must be hungry.

GROUCHO: He's hungry? All right, we'll go to the best restaurant in town and we'll all have Christmas dinner.

CHICO: Hey, boss, you crazy? We got no money.

GROUCHO: You heard me, Ravelli. The best restaurant in town. The better the restaurant, the older the waiters. And the older the waiters, the softer we fall when we get thrown out.

(Music in strong.)

GIRL: Check your coat, sir? Check your coat?

GROUCHO: Check my coat? I don't want any checks. What's the matter with these stripes?

GIRL: If you're going to eat in the restaurant, sir, you'll have to leave your coat here with me.

GROUCHO: Listen, girlie, I got a better idea. I'll send my coat in and stay here with you myself.

CHICO: Come on, boss, I'm hungry.

HORACE: Wahhh . . . I want to eat.

GROUCHO: All right, young lady, here's the coat. And be sure to toss it to me as I get thrown out.

GIRL: Thank you, sir. And *your* coat please, sir.

CHICO: Whata you give me for it?

GIRL: I'll give you a check, sir.

CHICO: Oh, you wanna buy it? Den I don't want a check. You got to give me cash.

GROUCHO: Come on, Horace. Come on, Ravelli. Say, this is a pretty swell restaurant. It'll be an honor to be thrown out of here.

HEADWAITER: Table for three, sir?

GROUCHO: Yes, captain, and make it near the door. You couldn't put a table on the street, could you? We like to eat out.

HEADWAITER: Eat out, sir?

CHICO: Sure, we eat out. We eat out of anything.

HEADWAITER: Here's a very nice table right here, sir.

CHICO: What'sa very nice about it?

HEADWAITER: Well, it's right by a window, sir. You can see the street.

GROUCHO: Don't worry. We'll see the street soon enough.

CHICO: Awright, we taka da table, Cap, but you gotta take away da tablecloth.

HEADWAITER: The tablecloth, sir?

CHICO: Sure, we no wanna pay cover charge.

HORACE: Hooray, hooray, hooray! Food, food, food! It's about time we're going to eat.

HEADWAITER: What will you have, sir?

GROUCHO: Er . . . I don't want anything. I had a late breakfast. I had it late in August. On second thought, I think I'll have the two-dollar dinner. How much is it?

CHICO: I think it's a dollar fifty.

GROUCHO: Very well, waiter. I'll take the two-dollar dinner and you can owe me fifty cents.

HORACE: Hey, I thought you didn't have any money!

GROUCHO: Ha, ha, ha. Isn't he a witty little fellow? He's quick as a trap. And I wish he'd keep his trap shut.

HEADWAITER: And what do *you* want, sir?

CHICO: First, I wanna some minestrone, den some ravioli, den some spaghetti with cheese, den some spaghetti without cheese, den some cheese without spaghetti, and *den* I tink I have some pastafazole.

HEADWAITER: Would you like some dessert?

CHICO: Dessert? Awright. For dessert I think I taka the two-dollar dinner.

HORACE: Ha, ha, ha! You ain't got no money. Ha, ha, ha! You ain't got no money.

GROUCHO: Ha, ha, ha. Isn't he a card? He always keeps saying we haven't any money.

HEADWAITER: I like him. I wish I had a boy like that.

GROUCHO: Well, knock a half dollar off the bill, and he's yours.

HEADWAITER: What?

GROUCHO: All right, make it a quarter, but you'll have to take Ravelli too.

CHICO: Hey, boss, keep quiet. Come on, Mr. Waiter, bring in the food. I'm ready to eat.

HEADWAITER: Right away, sir. *(Exits.)*

GROUCHO: Ravelli, what are you unbuttoning your shirt for?

CHICO: I joosta remember dat da doctor he tell me when I eat I should watch my stomach. Hey, boss, looka quick. Who's dat fat man coming over here?

MAN: Excuse me, gentlemen, am I intruding?

GROUCHO: Sure, you're intruding, but if you button your coat, nobody will ever notice it.

MAN: You'll pardon me, but I'm sure we've met before.

GROUCHO: Say, you aren't by any chance Flywheel, the lawyer, are you?

MAN: No, I'm afraid I'm not.

GROUCHO: Well, it's nothing to be afraid of. You just don't know how lucky you are.

MAN: Gentlemen, I want to introduce myself. I am a millionaire who—

CHICO: We don't care whata you are. What we want to know is, have you got any money?

MAN: Why, I have plenty of money. More than I can use. But then, what is money without a home . . . and loved ones?

GROUCHO: What is money without a home? Say, that's a pretty good riddle. But I'll bet I can guess the answer.

CHICO: Hey, I know a better riddle. What is it you brush your teeth with and sit on?

MAN *(puzzled):*   Brush your teeth with and sit on?

CHICO: Give up? A toothbrush and a chair!

GROUCHO: Ravelli, your mind is wandering. And the longer it stays away, the better off you are.

HORACE: Wahhh! I'm hungry.

MAN: Gentlemen, I wonder if you'd do me a great favor? I'm a lonely old man and I love children. I was wondering if you two gentlemen and your boy would consent to have Christmas dinner as my guests?

GROUCHO: Nonsense! We wouldn't hear of it. You must be *our* guest. But you can pay for the dinner.

MAN: Splendid, splendid. That's just what I wanted to do. And now, little man, what would you like?

HORACE: I'd like you to go away.

GROUCHO: Horace! Is that a way to treat a kind man?

CHICO: Treat *him?* I tought he was going to treat us.

HORACE: Wahhh!

GROUCHO: Shut up, Horace!

MAN: Oh, don't scold the child. I'm sure he didn't mean it.

HORACE: I did so mean it. I don't like you. I *hate* you.

MAN: What?

GROUCHO: Ha, ha, ha. He always talks that way to people he likes, don't you, Horace?

HORACE: No, I don't. He's just a big, fat lobster.

MAN: Why . . . why . . . I've never been so—

CHICO: Horace, you shutta your mouth. Ha, ha. I guess dat's telling him, eh, big fat lobster?

MAN: That settles it. You can pay for your own meals.

GROUCHO: We can pay for our own meals? What makes you think we can?

MAN: I'm through. Goodbye!

GROUCHO: Horace, take off your glasses.

(Crash in the distance.)

CHICO: Hey, what'sa dat?

GROUCHO: Waiter, waiter. What's that noise?

HEADWAITER: Oh, it's nothing, sir. They just threw out a man who couldn't pay his check.

CHICO: I don't tink I feel so hungry no more.

HEADWAITER: Oh, don't worry, sir. It's really all right. They only broke his leg.

GROUCHO: Waiter, on second thought, I don't believe we'll dine here. Cancel those three dinners.

HEADWAITER: I can't cancel them now, sir. The order's in.

GROUCHO: You can't cancel them?

HEADWAITER: No, sir.

GROUCHO: All right then, but I'd like to add something to our order. With the dessert, bring us three cushions and a bottle of liniment.

(Music in strong.)

HEADWAITER: Wise guys, eh? Thought you could get a meal for nothing! Well, you're gonna stay in this kitchen and wash dishes for that meal. Come on, come on.

CHICO: Hey, who you tink you're pushin?

HEADWAITER: I'm pushing you.

GROUCHO: Ravelli, the man is right. I saw him pushing you with my own eyes. Now we'll push *him* and see if *he* can guess who it is.

HEADWAITER: Stop it . . . Stop pushing me! *(Crash of dishes.)* Look what you've done—you've broken those dishes!

GROUCHO: Good! In that case we won't have to wash them.

HEADWAITER: You numbskulls! Do you realize you've broken over a hundred dishes?

CHICO: Yeah, boss, it's worse dan I tought. Da dishes is broken on both sides.

HEADWAITER: Pierre! Pierre! Come over here.

PIERRE: Bien zut alors! Don't you know I am busy wiz ze cooking? Remembair, I am ze chef . . . ze cook . . . ze chef!

GROUCHO: Well, make up your mind. Are you the cook or the chef?

CHICO: Hey, I need a chef.

HEADWAITER: You need a chef?

CHICO: Sure, I'll take a chef and a haircut.

HEADWAITER: Pierre, these men didn't pay for their dinner, and they insulted *me*, the headwaiter. Keep this man in the kitchen and put him to work.

CHICO: Hey, at'sa no fair. Flywheel tell me if we no pay we get arrested, maybe we get thrown out on our heads. But he no say nothing about work.

HEADWAITER: You'll work, or I'll kick those shabby pants of yours until you do.

GROUCHO: See here, pardner, beneath those shabby pants of his there may be a heart of gold.

HEADWAITER: And as for *you*, you're going to come out and wait on the tables.

GROUCHO: You want me to wait on one of those little tables? Nothing doing. If I'd wait on a little table like that, I'd fall off.

HEADWAITER: You heard what I said. Here, take this plate of roast beef out to table twenty-eight.

GROUCHO: Why table twenty-eight? I can eat it right here in the kitchen.

HEADWAITER: That dish is for a customer! Come with me. *I'll* show you where to take it.

GROUCHO: I see, you can dish it, but you can't take it, eh? Come on.

CHICO: Hey, boss, wait a minoot, where's little Horace?

GROUCHO: They've got him working, too. He's weighing groceries.

CHICO: Weighing groceries? Say, dat's a pretty big job for a little shrimp.

GROUCHO: Well, he's only doing it on a small scale.

HEADWAITER: You come along and stop talking to him. He's gotta wash dishes.

GROUCHO: Why can't we all go to the movies and leave the dishes in the sink till we get home?

CHICO: At'sa fine, boss. I wanna see the funny picture they got next door. I was there yesterday and, oh boy, I laughed and laughed and laughed. But I didn't like it.

GROUCHO: You laughed and laughed and didn't like it?

CHICO: Sure I didn't like it, at'sa why I laft . . . I laft da theatre as soon as da picture started.

GROUCHO: Ravelli, you're just wasting your breath. Why don't you stop breathing?

HEADWAITER: Come on, Flywheel.

(They exit; CHICO *hums "Daffodils.")*

PIERRE: Mon Dieu! Shut up and get to ze dishes. Wash them, you dog, wash them.

CHICO: Hey, whata you tink? I'm a wash dog?

PIERRE: Oh, you ze smart fellow. You zink you eat for nozzing, yes?

CHICO: I no unnerstan whata you talk. I no tink you spikka so good Engleesh.

PIERRE: Oh, you no unnerstan? Maybe zis *club* help you unnerstan. You know what I'm gonna do wiz zis club?

CHICO: Sure I know. You're going to make a club sandwich. Hey, cook, you ever make tomato yum-yum?

PIERRE: Tomato yum-yum? I have nevair heard of such a ting.

CHICO: Well, it'sa very good. I tell you how to make it. First you take a little bit of spinach, den you mix it up wid a whole bunch of spinach. Den you put in . . . let me see . . . I tink a half a pound of fresh spinach. Den you let it cook for a couple of hours. And, oh boy, at'sa tasta good. At'sa fine, I like it.

PIERRE: You said *tomato* yum-yum. Why, zat is plain spinach!

CHICO: I know. I call it tomato yum-yum because I don't *like* spinach.

(Door opens.)

GROUCHO *(approaching):*   Oh, chef!

PIERRE: Yes.

GROUCHO: You know that delicious cut of roast beef you just gave me? With the crispy baked potatoes and the tender truffles and green peas on the side?

PIERRE: Ah yes, yes. Zat is my specialty, my masterpiece.

GROUCHO: Your masterpiece. Well, I just dropped it.

PIERRE: Oh, zis is *terrible.* Zat beautiful dish on ze floor!

GROUCHO: Don't get alarmed, Frenchy. It didn't fall on the floor. I dropped it in the customer's lap.

PIERRE: Oh you . . . you drive me crazy!

GROUCHO: That's no drive, it's just a short putt. I'd show you if I had a caddy.

CHICO: Hey, cook, I know dat song.

PIERRE: What song?

CHICO: Caddy . . . "Caddy Me Back to Old Virginia."

(Door opens.)

HEADWAITER: Hey, Flywheel. What are you doing here? Come on back to your duties. You're loafing half the time.

CHICO: At'sa fine. You know, half a loaf is better dan none.

HEADWAITER: See here—the last guy who loafed around here lost his job and—

GROUCHO: Well, it's better to have loafed and lost than never to have loafed at all.

HEADWAITER: Listen, Flywheel. See that lady at table twelve? She's one of our best customers, and I want you to take pains with her.

GROUCHO: That sounds easy, captain. I take pains just looking at her.

HEADWAITER: Get over to that table.

(*Door opens.*)

LADY (*away*): Waiter. Waiter.

GROUCHO: What is it, babe?

LADY: Look at this steak! It's burnt.

GROUCHO: Burnt? It's a mere trifle. Just rub it with vaseline.

LADY: Ridiculous! I want to order something else.

GROUCHO: Very well, how about some lamb chops? They're very nice today. I chopped them down myself.

LADY: I don't want any lamb chops. I think I'll have a chicken dinner.

GROUCHO: Chicken dinner? Okay. I'll get you some stale bread.

LADY: Stale bread?

GROUCHO: Certainly. That's a chicken dinner . . . our chickens *love* it. How about the two-dollar dinner?

LADY: Two dollars for a chicken dinner? They have the same thing next door for seventy-five cents.

GROUCHO: Well, why don't you go next door?

LADY: I did, but they didn't have any more chicken.

GROUCHO: Well, if we didn't have any chicken we could sell it for sixty cents. Besides, you can't compare *our* restaurant with that dump next door. Look at this beautiful place. Look at those fine paintings. Don't you think you have to pay for that?

LADY: I don't care about your paintings.

GROUCHO: All right, then I'll give you the dinner for seventy-five cents, but you'll have to eat it with your eyes closed.

LADY: Please hurry. I've had *just about enough.*

GROUCHO: You've had enough? Very well, then I'll bring you your check.

LADY: Headwaiter, headwaiter!

HEADWAITER: Yes, madam.

LADY: I've been grossly insulted by this waiter. I'll never eat in this restaurant again.

GROUCHO: I'm with you there, madam. The bread is *stale*, the customers are *fresh*, and the only *tips* I get are asparagus.

LADY: *Good day!*

HEADWAITER: But, madam—
(Crash of dishes.)
HEADWAITER: Heavens! What's happening in the kitchen?
CHICO *(running into scene):*   Hey Flywheel! Hey boss!
GROUCHO: What's the matter?
CHICO: I saw a mouse in da kitchen.
GROUCHO: Well, what did you expect to find in the kitchen—an elephant?
CHICO: I don't know . . . I didn't look for an elephant.
HEADWAITER: This has gone far enough! Here comes the proprietor. He'll see that both of you are thrown in jail. Oh, Mr. Cordwell.
MANAGER: What's the matter?
HEADWAITER: These two men ate a big dinner and couldn't pay for it. They've wrecked the kitchen and insulted our best customers, Mr. Cordwell.
MANAGER *(sadly):*   Don't bother me. I'm upset. I'm terribly upset. My child has disappeared. My little boy.
CHICO: A little boy? You've lost a little boy? Was he a big redheaded kid about six foot four whose name is Angelo?
MANAGER: No.
CHICO: No? Den it must be Horace.
MANAGER: Horace! That's my boy's name. Have you seen him? Where is he?
HORACE *(approaching):*   Daddy, daddy. Where have you been?
MANAGER: Horace, my boy, my boy . . . *(Embrace.)*
GROUCHO: And now, Mr. Cordwell—about the reward.
MANAGER: Who said anything about a reward?
CHICO: My boss, Mr. Flywheel. Joosta now, don't you remember?
MANAGER: Gentlemen, I'm afraid I can never repay you.
CHICO: You can't pay us? Den we gonna take Horace back.
GROUCHO: Say, that's an idea. That's the worst idea I've ever heard.
CHICO: Why, we take Horace back, den I can go horse-back riding.
MANAGER: Gentlemen, you understand . . . I want you to know how grateful I am. Is there anything in the world I can do for you?
GROUCHO: Yes.
MANAGER: Tell me what it is.
GROUCHO: Mr. Cordwell, you own this restaurant.
MANAGER: Yes.
GROUCHO: Well, you can give us a dollar so that we can go next door and get a decent meal.
(Music interlude.)

CLOSING ANNOUNCEMENT

ANNOUNCER: You have just heard another of the adventures of *Flywheel, Shyster, and Flywheel, Attorneys at Law,* which are presented for your pleasure each Monday night at this hour. Groucho and Chico Marx, world-famous comedians, star in this program. They have just come out from behind the screens and are bowing. The audience is giving them a big hand.

(Applause.)

ANNOUNCER: You will now hear a short speech from Groucho Marx and also a few words from Chico Marx.

GROUCHO: And the fewer the better. Get away from that microphone, Chico.

CHICO: Ladies and gentlemen—

GROUCHO: That'll be enough, Chico. I can get along without you.

CHICO: What'sa matta with me, Groucho?

GROUCHO: You're much too cheeky.

CHICO: Ladies and gentlemen—

GROUCHO: We're not going to talk about the product.

CHICO: No. We're not going to talk about Essolube.

GROUCHO: Shut up, Chico. Our job is to sell the Christmas spirit and not Essolube.

CHICO: Yeah, but if we don't sell the Essolube, we no got the job.

GROUCHO: Listen, Chico, we're not going to mention the product.

CHICO: Awright. We not talk about Essolube.

GROUCHO: In a minute I'm going to knock you for Essoloop. Remember, the only thing we're selling is Christmas.

CHICO: At'sa fine. Ladies and gentlemen, we no got anything to sell except Christmas. So go to your nearest filling station and have your crankcase drained and filled with Christmas. And me and my boss, we wish you a very Merry Essolube.

(Signature music.)

FIVE STAR THEATER
PRESENTS

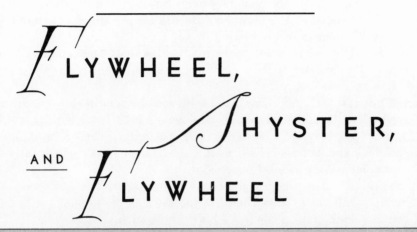

Flywheel, Shyster, and Flywheel

EPISODE NO. 6   JANUARY 2, 1933

CAST

Groucho Marx as Waldorf T. Flywheel
Chico Marx as Emmanuel Ravelli
Miss Dimple
Mailman
Cop
Mrs. Van Regal
Jailer
Warden
Attendant
Clerk of the Court
Judge
District Attorney
Foreman of the Jury

(Sound of typing; phone rings.)

MISS DIMPLE: Law offices of Flywheel, Shyster, and Flywheel . . . You want to speak to Mr. Flywheel? He's in his private office. Here's Mr. Ravelli, you can talk to him.

CHICO: Hello, you want to speak to Mr. Flywheel? You can't talk to him now. He's in conference . . . Who's with him? Nobody. He's just practicing . . . Goodbye.

MISS DIMPLE: Oh, Mr. Ravelli, Mr. Flywheel wants to see you. He . . . why Mr. Ravelli! What happened to your hand? Those bandages!

CHICO: Aw, it'sa Mr. Flywheel's fault. Yesterday I come to work at tree o'clock and da boss he gets mad. He tells me I gotta come in early and punch da clock. Well, I punched it.

MISS DIMPLE: You punched the clock with your *fist?*

CHICO: Only once, Miss Dimp. Da boss wants me to punch it again at five o'clock, but I no do it. I'll hit it with a stick.

*(*MAILMAN*'s whistle heard.)*

MISS DIMPLE: Excuse me, Mr. Ravelli. There's the mailman.

(Door opens.)

MAILMAN: Good morning. Let's see . . . Just one letter this morning. It's for Mr. Flywheel.

MISS DIMPLE: Thank you.

CHICO: Hey, mailman, I tink you got a coupla letters for me.

MAILMAN: Letters for you? What's your name?

CHICO: My name? It's on the letters.

MAILMAN: *What* letters?

CHICO: Any letters. Letters and tomato . . . letters and gentlemen . . . or maybe you got some step letters.

MAILMAN: You don't know what you're talking about.

CHICO: Is dat so? Well, you don't know what I'm talking about either.

MAILMAN: *Good day!*

(Door slams, GROUCHO*'s door opens.)*

GROUCHO: Miss Dimple, did I just hear the postman?

MISS DIMPLE: Yes, Mr. Flywheel.

GROUCHO: Well, that's fine. Bring him in and we'll play post office. Oh, there you are, Ravelli! I thought I sent you over to Western Union to find out the correct time.

CHICO: Oh, I find out da time dis morning. Here, I put it down on dis piece of paper. Da big hand was on nine o'clock, da little hand was on seven. I tink it was half past twelve . . . but da clock wasn't running.

GROUCHO: It wasn't running? Why didn't you tell me? I had money bet on that clock. Pretty slow thinking, Ravelli. Isn't there *anything* you're quick at?

CHICO: Sure. I get tired quick. Boss, I don't sleep so good at night.

GROUCHO: That's strange. You sleep well enough during the day.

CHICO: Last night I walk in my sleep, all night long. And I'm tired.

GROUCHO: You *walked* in your sleep? Well, there's a remedy for that. Next time you go to bed, take carfare with you.

CHICO: But I gotta no carfare. I gotta no notting. You never pay me. Boss, I want my money.

GROUCHO: You want *your* money? You mean you want *my* money.

CHICO: Mr. Flywheel, you owe me tree hunnerd bucks, and I gotta have it.

GROUCHO: Well, let's see what I got. Fifty, sixty, eighty, eighty-five, ninety, a dollar . . . No, I've only got a dollar.

CHICO: At'sa fine. I'll take it.

GROUCHO: I'm sorry, Ravelli, but this happens to be Miss Dimple's purse. But I'll tell you what I'll do. I haven't got the three hundred dollars, so I'll give you the business instead. And *I'll* work for *you*.

CHICO: You'll work for me? How I gonna pay your salary?

GROUCHO: Well, as soon as you owe me three hundred dollars you can give me back the business, and then you can work for me again.

CHICO: At'sa fine. Den we gotta put my name on da door.

GROUCHO: You're a fine businessman, Ravelli! It costs two bucks to change the name on the door and we can change your name for nothing. Let's see . . . Flywheel, Shyster, and Flywheel. I'm both Flywheels, and Shyster doesn't belong to the firm.

CHICO: Den what's his name on dere for?

GROUCHO: Well, Shyster ran away with my wife. And I put his name on the door as a token of my gratitude. Say, why can't you use Shyster's name?

CHICO: Awright, I change my name. From now on, I'm Shyster Ravelli.

(*Knock on door.*)

GROUCHO: Come in.

(*Door opens.*)

MISS DIMPLE: Heavens! It's a policeman!

GROUCHO: You're in the wrong place, officer. The speakeasy is on the floor above.

COP: I don't care about any speakeasy. What I want to know—does a man named Ravelli work here?

CHICO: I'ma Ravelli.

COP: Well, I've got a summons for you.

GROUCHO: Ah, summons coming to our house.

COP: I tell you, I'm here to serve a summons.

CHICO: I don't want any.

COP: See here—I came to get Ravelli.

CHICO: Get *me*? What do you want me for? I no done nuttin.

GROUCHO: I'll vouch for that, officer. He hasn't done anything since the day I hired him. Please don't take him away. He's all I have. And that gives you a pretty fair idea of how hard up I am.

COP: Enough of this! I arrest you in the name of the law!

CHICO: In the name of the law? You got the wrong fellow. My name's Ravelli.

COP: Yes, and it's you I'm taking to jail.

GROUCHO: What are the charges, officer? And don't make them too high. I left my wallet in my other trousers and I got my other trousers on.

COP: Oh, you want to know what the charges are? Well, I'll tell you . . . Here. Read them for yourself, and hurry up because the wagon's waiting downstairs.

GROUCHO: Listen to this, Ravelli. This is good. One—insulting women on Pine Street. Two—fighting in the street. Three—insulting women on Seventh Street. Four—obstructing traffic. Five—insulting women on Central Avenue and hurling a brick through a glass window. Six—resisting an officer. Seven—insulting women on Broadway and Main Street. Ravelli, have you got anything to say for yourself?

CHICO: You betcha I have, boss. He got the streets all wrong.

(*Music in strong.*)

MRS. VAN REGAL: Jailer, I'd like to speak to the warden.

JAILER: Come right in, Mrs. Van Regal. He's expecting you.

MRS. VAN REGAL: How do you do, warden?

WARDEN: Hello, Mrs. Van Regal. We haven't seen you here in quite a while.

MRS. VAN REGAL: Well, this isn't the only social service work I do, you know. The Christmas charities took all my time. Are there any new prisoners I might be able to help?

WARDEN: Well, we got a man here named Ravelli. He's been with us a week and he comes up for trial Monday. We don't seem to be able to manage him.

MRS. VAN REGAL: Why not let me talk to him.

WARDEN: He might be a little bit dangerous, but if you wanna talk to him, it's okay with me. He's right down this corridor.

(Approaching sound of RAVELLI's *voice singing "Happy Days Are Here Again.")*

VOICES *(away):*   Pipe down . . . Hey, will you cut out that singing . . . Shut up . . . Boo . . .

WARDEN: Here we are, Mrs. Van Regal. Ravelli, Ravelli! This is Mrs. Van Regal.

CHICO: Well, put her in da cell next door. I no got enough room in here myself.

WARDEN: See here, Ravelli, this kind lady is here to help you.

MRS. VAN REGAL: Yes, to help you lead a new life.

CHICO: I don't want a new life. I'm not through with de old one yet.

MRS. VAN REGAL: You poor misguided soul! Perhaps I can show you the light.

CHICO: Never mind da light, lady. I tink you look much better in da dark. *(Sings:)* Happy days are here again . . .

WARDEN: Be quiet, Ravelli. See what we're up against, Mrs. Van Regal? Still, if you feel you can do anything for him, go right ahead. If you want me, I'll be in my office.

CHICO: At'sa fine. And if you want me, warden, I'll be right here.

MRS. VAN REGAL: You unfortunate man. Why are you in jail? What did you do?

CHICO: I no do nuttin, lady. Two men were fightin. I don't even know dem.

MRS. VAN REGAL: They put you in jail because two strange men were fighting?

CHICO: Yeah. Dey was fightin with me.

MRS. VAN REGAL: Did they start the fight?

CHICO: Sure, dey start da fight . . . dey start it right after I trow da brick. *(Sings:)* Happy days are here again . . .

MRS. VAN REGAL: Please, Mr. Ravelli, your case interests me. Do you think you've inherited your criminal tendencies from your father?

CHICO: No, lady, my father still got his.

MRS. VAN REGAL: I don't quite understand. Perhaps I ought to get in touch with your parents. What are their names?

CHICO: Their names? Momma and poppa . . . *(Sings:)* Happy days are here again . . .

MRS. VAN REGAL: You sound as though you *like* being in jail.

CHICO: Like it? Lady, I love it. I eat, I sleep . . . I sleep, I eat. I don't see my boss, Flywheel. Nobody bothers me . . . till you come here. Hey, why you gotta come here for?

MRS. VAN REGAL: Why, I came to *help* you.

CHICO: You wanna *help* me? Awright, you sing tenor. *(Sings:)* Happy days are here again . . . *(Sings softly during next couple of lines.)*

ATTENDANT *(away):* You can't come in here. Ravelli's got one visitor already.

GROUCHO: See here, flunky, Flywheel is not in the habit of being kept *out* of jail. Out of my way, or I'll break you. Ravelli, Ravelli . . . where are you?

CHICO: If dat'sa Flywheel, tell him I'm out.

GROUCHO: I heard you, Ravelli. You're out to me, eh? Me, who went to the trouble and expense of getting you a beautiful chocolate cake and carrying it through crowded streets and street cars. Ravelli, there's only one thing I can say to you.

CHICO: What's that, boss?

GROUCHO: I'm glad I ate the cake myself.

CHICO: At'sa fine. I don't like da chocolate cake you get from a lawyer.

MRS. VAN REGAL: What kind of cake are you talking about?

CHICO: A chocolate lawyer cake.

GROUCHO: Ravelli, I ought to let you stay here. But having you in jail is a disgrace to the firm of Flywheel, Shyster, and Flywheel. Having you out of jail is disgrace enough.

MRS. VAN REGAL: Mr. Ravelli, can't you see we both want to help you? Don't we, Mr. ah . . .

GROUCHO: Ravelli, who's this cluck?

MRS. VAN REGAL: Cluck? Why, I've never been so insulted before in my life.

GROUCHO: Madam, that covers a lot of ground. And I don't mind saying you cover quite a bit of ground yourself. Say, you better beat it before they tear you down and put up an office building in your place.

MRS. VAN REGAL: I wash my hands of the whole case.

CHICO: At'sa fine. You can wash your neck, too.

MRS. VAN REGAL: The warden will hear about this. *(Exits.)*

GROUCHO *(calling after her):* If you see the warden, tell him I've got a jigsaw puzzle with me. It's for the man who cut up his wife. Now, Ravelli, about getting you out—

CHICO: Go away, boss. I like it here. *(Sings:)* Happy days are here again . . .

GROUCHO: You like it here, after the way they treat you? You *live* here, and look at the size of your room. The warden has a room ten times as big, and he only works here. Ravelli, the style you're living in hardly becomes a man worth five thousand dollars.

CHICO: I'm worth five tousand bucks?

GROUCHO: Well, that's what the Albany police are offering.

CHICO *(indignant):*   De Albany police is offering five tousand bucks for *me?* Dey gotta some noive. Da Boston police—

GROUCHO: What do you mean, the Boston bulls?

CHICO: At'sa da same ting. Dey are offering seven tousand bucks dead or alive. But dey no fool me because I know if dey're dead, dey can't pay.

GROUCHO: They're offering seven thousand dollars? Say, that isn't bad. I think I'll take it. On second thought, maybe we ought to shop around a little. Were you ever in Chicago?

CHICO: Sure, I opened a little business dere.

GROUCHO: *You* opened a business?

CHICO: Yeah, I opened a little bank . . . when da watchman wasn't looking.

GROUCHO: That's splendid. I'll give you up to the Chicago police, but I won't take a cent less than nine thousand.

CHICO: You gonna give me up? Say, if dey wanna pay nine tousand, I give *myself* up.

GROUCHO: There you go, thinking only of yourself when there's money and glory enough for both of us. Here's what we'll do. First, I'll get you out of this jail, where you're only wasting your time. Then I'll turn you over to the Chicago police, which will be a pleasure, and we'll split the reward three ways—three thousand for me, three thousand for you and three thousand for the fellow who gives you up, who by a strange coincidence turns out to be me.

CHICO: Ha, ha, ha!

GROUCHO: What are you laughing at?

CHICO: Da last time a friend gave me up, I only got twenty bucks.

GROUCHO: Ravelli, a real good friend would give you up for nothing.

(Music in strong.)

(Murmur of voices.)

CLERK: Hear ye, hear ye, the municipal court is now in session and stands until adjournment.

(More murmurs.)

CLERK: Silence in court. His honor, the judge.

ATTENDANT: Good morning, judge.

JUDGE: Good morning, bailiff.

CLERK: Good morning, judge.

(These good mornings allow JUDGE *time to get to bench.)*

JUDGE *(raps gavel):*   Court is now convened for the third day of trial of Emmanuel Ravelli. Mr. District Attorney, will you proceed with the case?

Groucho as attorney J. Cheever Loophole mistries his case in MGM's *At the Circus* [1939].

DISTRICT ATTORNEY: Your honor, ladies and gentlemen of the jury, and my estimable opponent, Counselor Flywheel, the state rests.

GROUCHO: Oh, the state rests, does it? I suppose you expect *me* to do the work while you're resting. Your honor, this whole trial has been a sham, a mockery . . . a hollow mockery.

CHICO: I know that song, mockery.

GROUCHO: What song?

CHICO: You know, mockery. *(Sings:)* Mother Moc-ree.

(JUDGE *pounds gavel*.)

GROUCHO: There you are, judge. I change my plea to insanity.

CHICO: At'sa fine, boss. You look a little bit crazy.

JUDGE: Counselor Flywheel, the court cannot accept a change of plea at this time. The state has produced three witnesses who saw Ravelli fighting and insulting women.

GROUCHO: That's nothing, judge. I can get three *thousand* witnesses who *didn't* see him fighting and insulting women.

JUDGE *(indignant):* Counselor Flywheel, are your witnesses ready?

GROUCHO: No, your honor, and that's my complaint. There are only three of my witnesses here and I paid for eight.

JUDGE: So, you were tampering with witnesses? Did you give them anything?

CHICO: Sure. He gave dem tamper.

JUDGE: He gave them *what?*

CHICO: Tamper. Tam per cent of what dey asked.

DISTRICT ATTORNEY: Your honor, I move you strike that from the record.

JUDGE: Stenographer, strike that from the record.

CHICO: Hey, boss, dat's two strikes. One more strike and I'm out.

JUDGE *(pounds gavel):* Gentlemen, the court warns you that it will tolerate no more of your insolence. Ravelli, will you take the stand?

CHICO: Where should I take it, judge?

JUDGE *(furious):* Mr. Flywheel, will you put your client on the stand?

GROUCHO: Okay, judge, but remember, you brought it on yourself. Ravelli, get up in that chair.

CHICO: Tanks, boss, but I can see awright from where I am.

GROUCHO: Ravelli, step up to the stand!

CHICO *(irritated):* Awright, awright, I go. *(He walks to stand.)*

CLERK: Emmanuel Ravelli, you are about to be sworn in. Raise your right hand.

CHICO: Why should I raise my hand? I don't have to leave da room.

CLERK: *Put that hand up!* Now, do you promise to tell the truth, the whole truth, and nothing but the truth?

CHICO: I gotta speak to my lawyer first.

CLERK: Answer yes or no!

CHICO: Awright. No!

JUDGE: Order! Order! *(Pounds gavel.)*

CHICO: Hey, judge, what'sa idea making so much noise? At'sa fine business—an old man like you playing with a little hammer.

JUDGE: Counselor Flywheel, please proceed with the examination.

GROUCHO: Ravelli, who did, where were you on the night of December fifth?

CHICO: What do you mean, "Who did, where were you?"

GROUCHO: I'm in a hurry. I'm asking two questions at one time.

CHICO: Boss, can I ask you a question?

GROUCHO: Shoot.

CHICO: Shoot? At'sa fine.

(He fires gun. Buzz of voices in the court, gavel pounds.)

GROUCHO: Ravelli, you'll have to stop shooting at the judge. You haven't got a license to carry a gun.

JUDGE: Counselor Flywheel, for a member of the bar your conduct is most unbecoming.

GROUCHO: Unbecoming? Do you think it would be more becoming if I wore a shirt?

JUDGE *(pounds gavel):*   Counselor! Will you *please* proceed with the examination?

GROUCHO: Very well, judge. I'll go on with the examination, but you know you don't have to be so cross about it. After all, this isn't the *cross* examination. Ravelli, name three presidents of the United States.

CHICO: Ha, ha! You no fool me, boss. Dere's only one president of da United States.

DISTRICT ATTORNEY: Your honor, the state objects to these irrelevant questions. Why doesn't Counselor Flywheel ask the defendant whether he insulted those women?

GROUCHO: Don't be silly. That question is too easy. Crafty old Flywheel has his own way of working. Watch him trap his witness. Ravelli, take a number from one to ten.

CHICO: Eleven.

GROUCHO: Right. Now, Ravelli, tell the court—did you insult that woman?

CHICO: What woman?

GROUCHO: The one you called a sloppy old scarecrow.

CHICO: I no insult her, boss, I only told her if she was a little better looking, she look just like a cow.

GROUCHO: Ravelli, I resent that. My wife happens to look like a cow.

DISTRICT ATTORNEY: Your honor, the state objects. The defendant is changing his testimony. That's the second story he's told.

CHICO: Whata you mean, *second* story? I fight, I insult women, but I ain't no second-story man.

JUDGE *(pounds gavel):*   Mr. Ravelli, don't address your remarks to the district attorney. Talk to the jury.

CHICO: Awright, I talk to da jury. Hello, jury, how you feel? It's pooty nice da judge don't charge you nuttin for sleepin here.

JUDGE *(pounds gavel):*   Just a moment . . . just a moment. Counselor Flywheel. Go on with your questioning.

GROUCHO: I'm sick of asking him questions. Why doesn't the district attorney ask him a few?

DISTRICT ATTORNEY: Ahem. Your honor, the state has no questions to ask. The defendant's own testimony is, we feel, sufficiently incriminating to convict him on every allegation.

GROUCHO: Oh, you with your big words. Just trying to show off in front of the judge. Well, he doesn't understand them either, do you, judge?

Ladies and gentlemen of the jury, I ask you to pay attention to my closing speech. You can pay a little now and the balance when the speech is delivered. Gentlemen, all that Ravelli wants is vindication.

CHICO: Hey, boss, I no wanna vindication. I just wanna vindi *case.*

GROUCHO: See that, gentlemen? It's been my lifelong ambition to win a case, and look what I'm stuck with. Give me a break, fellas, will yuh? Convict him the next time he comes here, when he's got another lawyer. Gentlemen, let me tell you Ravelli's life story. From the time of his first crime at the age of nine, he has been arrested thirty-four times, but the convictions number only thirty-three. Proving conclusively, gentlemen, that he is a good boy, but that he has bad friends. Now don't misunderstand. His criminal record is not altogether bad. In the San Quentin prison he won first place in the stone-crushing event. When he graduated from there he went to Sing Sing. He left during the great jailbreak. I mean it was a great break for the jail when he left. And *why* did he go to Sing Sing, gentlemen? He went to Sing Sing only because he likes music.

CHICO: At'sa right, boss. *(Sings:)* Happy days are here again . . .

JUDGE *(pounds gavel):* Order!

GROUCHO: Ravelli, will you do me a favor and stick your head under the judge's gavel? The state told you that Ravelli went to the penitentiary for three years. That's a malicious lie. He escaped after the second week. He wouldn't have stayed that long, but he was crazy about the meals. The district attorney has told you that Ravelli spent six months in the state prison. Gentlemen, that's true. But does the state tell you *why* he spent six months in the state prison? No, gentlemen, no. *I'll* tell you why. Ravelli spent six months in the state prison because he was locked in and besides that he didn't want to be separated from his father.

JUDGE: Ladies and gentlemen of the jury, as presiding judge I instruct you to retire and bring back a verdict of guilty or not guilty.

FOREMAN: Your honor, we the jurors have already reached a verdict. We pronounce the defendant, Emmanuel Ravelli, not guilty.

(Cheers.)

GROUCHO: Congratulate me, Ravelli. I guess I'm pretty good, eh?

JUDGE: Gentlemen of the jury, I find your verdict most unsatisfactory. I discharge you without thanks.

GROUCHO: Just a minute, judge. You can't discharge these jurors. I hired them.

(Signature music.)

FIVE STAR THEATER
PRESENTS

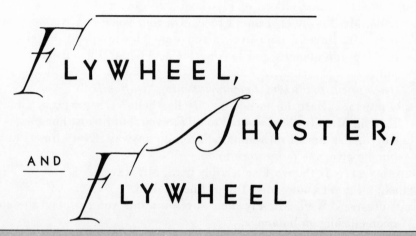

Flywheel, Shyster, and Flywheel

EPISODE NO. 7   JANUARY 9, 1933

CAST

Groucho Marx as Waldorf T. Flywheel
Chico Marx as Emmanuel Ravelli
Miss Dimple
Mrs. Carroway
Mailman
Taxi Driver
Jamison, butler
Doctor Perrin

(*Phone rings.*)

MISS DIMPLE: Law offices of Flywheel, Shyster, and Flywheel . . . Oh, hello, Mr. Flywheel, I didn't recognize your voice . . . No, your assistant, Mr. Ravelli, isn't in . . . You want him to spend the afternoon chasing ambulances and looking for accidents? I'll tell him . . . Uh-huh.

(*Door opens and* RAVELLI *enters humming "Daffodils."*)

MISS DIMPLE: Here he is now . . . Hello, hello? (*To* RAVELLI:) Oh, Mr. Ravelli, Mr. Flywheel wanted to talk to you, but he just hung up.

CHICO: At'sa fine. I no wanna talk to him anyway. Every time I talk to him he gives me more work to do.

MISS DIMPLE: Is the work so terribly hard, Mr. Ravelli?

CHICO: I don't know, Miss Dimp, I never do it.

MISS DIMPLE: Well, Mr. Flywheel says he wants you to spend the afternoon chasing ambulances.

CHICO: At'sa no good. I chased one ambulance all morning.

MISS DIMPLE: Well?

CHICO: Well, it went into a hospital. So I went home.

MISS DIMPLE: You went home? Why didn't you go into the hospital?

CHICO: Go in? I no was feelin sick.

MISS DIMPLE: But Mr. Flywheel wanted you to follow the *ambulance*.

CHICO: Yeah, but I tell you de ambulance went into da hospital. I no tink da boss wants a sick ambulance.

MISS DIMPLE: Mr. Ravelli, I don't think you understand your job. Mr. Flywheel isn't interested in ambulances. He's interested in people who are *in* ambulances. People who have been in accidents and might need a lawyer.

CHICO: Oh, he wants sick people. (*Sighs.*) You know, Miss Dimp, my brudder got trown in jail because he had sinus trouble.

MISS DIMPLE: Thrown in jail for *sinus trouble?*

CHICO: Yeah. He sinus name to a bad check.

MISS DIMPLE: Don't you think you ought to get going? You know Mr. Flywheel is going to be here any minute, and he'll be furious if he finds you hanging around the office.

CHICO: You're right, Miss Dimp. It's very bad to hang around de office. I tink I go back to da pool room. *Arrivederci.*

(*He exits, phone rings.*)

MISS DIMPLE: Flywheel, Shyster, and Flywheel. Mr. Flywheel isn't in yet. Oh, just a minute. That may be him at the door. (*Door opens.*) Oh, Mr. Flywheel. There's a phone call for you.

GROUCHO: If it's the doctor, tell him I'm too sick to see him.

MISS DIMPLE: It's that politician you've been trying to get in touch with all morning.

GROUCHO: I'll talk to him. Hello . . . Yes, this is Flywheel . . . Run for judge, eh? I see . . . I don't think so, but I'd like to consider it. Call me in the morning. Goodbye. (*To* MISS DIMPLE): See that, Miss Dimple? (*Gloating.*) They want me to run for judge.

MISS DIMPLE: Run for *judge?*

GROUCHO: Yes, for Judge Bulingham. They want me to run his errands. But I'm not interested in politics. I've got too many other things on my mind.

MISS DIMPLE: You seem troubled, Mr. Flywheel. What's happened?

GROUCHO: Nothing much. Just a little trouble with my bankers.

MISS DIMPLE: Your bankers?

GROUCHO: Yes. A fine lot of businessmen they are. I went down this morning to open an account, and they turned me down.

MISS DIMPLE: They wouldn't let you open an account? How much did you want to deposit in the bank?

GROUCHO: I didn't want to deposit anything. I wanted to open a charge account. (*Sneers.*) Hmm. They call themselves the Citizens Trust Company and then they won't trust me. Don't they think I'm a citizen? (*Heavy hammering on door.*)

MISS DIMPLE: Heavens! Someone's hammering on the door!

GROUCHO: Is there? (*Heavy pounding again.*) So there is. I couldn't hear him at first, he made so much noise.

MISS DIMPLE (*opening door):* Why, it's Mr. Ravelli.

CHICO: Hello, boss.

GROUCHO: Ravelli, what's the idea of pounding on the door? Are you crazy?

CHICO: Ha, ha, ha! Sure I'm crazy—crazy like a fox.

GROUCHO: Well, listen, crazy fox. I thought you were supposed to be out chasing ambulances.

CHICO: Aw no, boss. I'ma too smart. I no gotta look in ambulances for sick people no more. Sick people is gonna look for us.

GROUCHO: Ravelli, that sounds very interesting. Now tell me what you're talking about.

MISS DIMPLE: Why look, Mr. Flywheel! He's been hammering Dr. Jones's sign on our door. Why, that's the doctor downstairs.

CHICO: Aw, don't worry. He ain't a doctor no more. I put Mr. Flywheel's sign on his door.

GROUCHO (*approvingly):* Ravelli, I always knew I could make something of you. I think I'll make a punching bag.

CHICO: At'sa fine, boss. I knew you'd like it. *(Door opens.)* Hey, look! *(Whispering.)* Here comes a nice big lady.

MRS. CARROWAY: Oh, I'm so glad I found you in, Doctor. I'm just about half dead.

GROUCHO: That's fine. If you're half dead, we can collect half your insurance. Say, there's good money in medicine. Where you going, Ravelli?

CHICO: I'm going to the drugstore.

GROUCHO: To the drugstore?

CHICO: Sure. You say there's good money in medicine, so I tink I go and get a coupla bottles.

GROUCHO: Good. On your way, mail this letter for me.

CHICO: Hey, boss, dis letter no gotta stamp.

GROUCHO: Well, drop it in the box when no one's looking.

CHICO: I don't tink I go. We can write for some medicine.

GROUCHO: Write for *medicine*? Where?

CHICO: Medicine, Wisconsin.

MRS. CARROWAY *(impatient):* Doctor, please. My friend, Mrs. Gillingham, recommended you very highly. She told me you made a great fight for her life.

GROUCHO: Great fight? I made a terrific fight for her life. And I'd have gotten it, too, only she wouldn't take my advice. As for you, madam, I prescribe a sea trip.

MRS. CARROWAY: But doctor, I haven't told you about my ailment.

GROUCHO: No, you haven't told me, and I want to thank you. A sea trip will be just the thing. We leave for Bermuda on Monday.

MRS. CARROWAY: That's impossible, doctor. I can't go to Bermuda.

GROUCHO: Very well, then. I'll go myself. Ravelli, put my clothes in the trunk.

CHICO *(surprised):* You mean you gonna go naked?

MRS. CARROWAY *(impatient):* *Doctor!* Aren't you going to examine me?

CHICO: Awright, take off your coat.

MRS. CARROWAY *(removing coat):* Why, yes . . . there you are.

CHICO: Here lady, I tink you can put your coat on again. It don't look good on me.

MRS. CARROWAY: Doctor, your methods seem very curious. But I suppose you know your business. Goodness knows you charge enough. Mrs. Gillingham said you charged her eight hundred dollars for her operation.

GROUCHO: But madam, I had to take six stitches.

MRS. CARROWAY: But isn't that rather high—eight hundred dollars for six stitches?

GROUCHO: Not at all. I gave her fancy embroidery.

MRS. CARROWAY: Doctor, that's all beside the point. I've been having dizzy spells. I think—

GROUCHO: Never mind what you think, madam. I'll examine your eyes. Look at that calendar on that wall and see if you can tell me what day it is.

MRS. CARROWAY: Very well. *(Reading.)* It's December twenty-eighth.

GROUCHO: Just as I thought. Madam, you need glasses. It's January ninth.

MRS. CARROWAY: Why, I'm *sure* that calendar says December twenty-eighth.

GROUCHO: I know, but that's last year's calendar.

CHICO: Boss, I'm gonna try her dis time. Lady, close one eye and read dat sign on da wall.

MRS. CARROWAY: That sign? It says "No smoking."

CHICO *(astonished):* Oh, is *dat* what is says? You know, dat big word "Smoking" always had me fooled.

MRS. CARROWAY: Doctor, I think you'd better forget about my eyes. The trouble is with my general condition. I'm not feeling very strong.

GROUCHO: Well, you look strong enough. However, I'll examine you. Push that desk across the room.

MRS. CARROWAY *(astonished):* Why doctor, I—

GROUCHO: Come on, madam. Stop horsing around and push that desk.

MRS. CARROWAY: It seems very strange, but very well.

(Sound of desk being moved and woman grunting.)

GROUCHO: Ravelli, maybe you better give her a lift.

CHICO: Give her a lift? Hey, boss, you need a coupla piano movers to pick her up.

MRS. CARROWAY *(sighing wearily):* Well, there you are, doctor, I got the desk moved. *(Breathes heavily.) Now* what do you think?

GROUCHO: What do I think? I think the desk looked better where it was before. Madam, you'd better push it back.

(Music in strong.)

(Knock at door.)

MISS DIMPLE: Come in. *(Door opens.)* Oh, it's *you*, mailman. Good afternoon.

MAILMAN: Afternoon, miss. Is Mr. Flywheel in? I got a special delivery for him. Another one of those books.

MISS DIMPLE: Oh yes, he's been waiting for it. It's from a correspondence school. Mr. Flywheel has taken an interest in medicine.

MAILMAN: Let's see. I may have a letter here . . . No, I guess that's all, just that little book. Can you sign for it?

MISS DIMPLE: Of course . . . There you are. (GROUCHO *enters*.) Oh, hello, Mr. Flywheel.

GROUCHO: Hello, Miss Dimple. Good afternoon, professor.

MAILMAN: Professor?

GROUCHO: Yes, didn't you bring my lessons?

MISS DIMPLE: Here it is, Mr. Flywheel. Another book from that correspondence school.

GROUCHO: Professor, what's the idea of bringing the mail in so late? Do you think this is night school? The dean will hear about this.

MAILMAN: What dean?

GROUCHO: Gunga dean.

MAILMAN: I don't quite know what you mean, Mr. Flywheel, but I admit I don't get around as fast as I used to with the mail. You see, I'm troubled with flat feet.

GROUCHO: You only *think* your feet are flat. Columbus thought the world was flat. But it wasn't . . . it wasn't flat until 1929. Say, I think I'll take out your appendix.

MAILMAN: But there's nothing wrong with my appendix.

GROUCHO: Well, if there's nothing wrong with them, I'll put 'em back. It won't hurt to take a look.

MAILMAN: My appendix is *all right*. If anything is wrong with me, it's my tonsils.

GROUCHO: You're probably right, professor. But I'd much rather take out the appendix. There's more money in a job like that.

MAILMAN: Say, you're not a doctor.

GROUCHO: Well, I make allowances for that. I'll knock ten percent off the bill.

MAILMAN: I've got my *mail* to deliver. I'm *going*.

GROUCHO: Wait a minute, professor. Don't go. I've got a better offer. I'll take out one tonsil, too, and I won't charge you a cent extra.

MAILMAN: I haven't time to—

GROUCHO: I'll make that *two* tonsils.

MAILMAN: *I'm going.*

GROUCHO: See here, professor. I don't want you to go out dissatisfied. You're a man after my own heart—and I'm a man after your appendix.

MAILMAN: *Please*, Mr. Flywheel.

GROUCHO: All right. Forget the appendix. I'll take out two tonsils and five teeth. I'll go even farther than that. You give me that appendix job and I'll take out three tonsils and five teeth free of charge. And if we strike gold in those teeth we split, fifty-fifty.

MAILMAN: Why, er. . . .

GROUCHO: It's a bargain. I'll operate as soon as my assistant, Mr. Ravelli, comes in with the instruments I sent him after. He's on his way over from the junk shop now.

MAILMAN: Mr. Flywheel, I'm afraid you—

GROUCHO: Nonsense, there's nothing to be afraid of. You won't feel a thing. Because I'm going to give you an anaesthetic. A local anaesthetic. And if you don't care for a local anaesthetic, I'll get you one from out of town. Personally, I think we ought to patronize the neighborhood stores.

MAILMAN: Good day!

GROUCHO: Don't go, professor. Here comes my assistant with the instruments.

(CHICO *heard humming "Daffodils."*)

CHICO: Hullo boss, hullo mailman.

GROUCHO: Ravelli, I'm going to operate. Have you got the instruments I sent you for?

CHICO *(sneers):*   Dose instruments! I got better ones. Listen to dis. *(He plays a few harsh notes on saxophone.)*

MAILMAN: I've had enough of this, Mr. Flywheel. *Good day!*

GROUCHO: Wait a second, professor.

(Door slams.)

GROUCHO: A fine assistant you are, Ravelli. I send you out to select medical instruments and you pick a saxophone.

CHICO: Ha! You make a mistake, boss. You no pick a saxophone, you pick a mandolin.

GROUCHO: I see. Ravelli, something tells me this little incident is going to end in violence.

CHICO: Violence? I brought dat too, see? *(Plays a few notes on violin.)*

GROUCHO: Ravelli, I'm going to raise your salary.

CHICO: At'sa fine, boss.

GROUCHO: It's nothing at all. I'm only raising your pay so you'll feel worse when I fire you.

CHICO *(sadly):*   Aw, boss, you no gonna fire me—after I bring you such a good lunch today. I bringa you two sandwiches, rawsta biff and nicea pimento cheese.

GROUCHO: Ravelli, I was willing to forget, but now that you mention it, I want to tell you that I *ate* one of those sandwiches.

CHICO: Which one, boss?

GROUCHO: I don't know. It tasted like glue.

CHICO *(very seriously):*   Oh, dat was da *cheese.* Da rawsta biff tastes like an old shoe.

(Phone rings.)

GROUCHO: Don't stand there—answer that phone.

CHICO: I'ma too busy, boss.

GROUCHO: Busy? Doing what?

CHICO: Can't you see, boss? I'm growing a beard.

GROUCHO: Well, grow your beard outside office hours and answer that phone.

(*Phone rings again.*)

CHICO: Howado you do? . . . Dis is da law office of Flywheel, Shyster, and Flywheel . . . Oh, you wanna Doctor Jones? Awright, den it's Doctor Jones's office too . . . Me? I'm Emmanuel Ravelli . . . You no wanna talk to me? . . . Awright, you shut up an' I talk to you. I give you a riddle. What is it crawls on trees and sings? Ha! I knew you no guess. It's a caterpillar. (*Surprised.*) What? A caterpillar can't sing? Say, no wonder I never seen any caterpillars in grand opera.

GROUCHO: Give me that phone, Ravelli. Hello . . . Oh, it's *you*, Mrs. Carroway . . . You're feeling worse? Well, that's easily understood. I happened to give you the wrong medicine . . . What? . . . Well, I wouldn't really say it was the *wrong* medicine. It happens to be very good for the rheumatism . . . Is it *my* fault that you haven't got rheumatism? . . . Well, we'll be over. Get the guest room ready. We'll be there as soon as we finish packing. Goodbye. Ravelli, I think I've got just the medicine for Mrs. Carroway.

CHICO: She still sick, boss? Whatta you tink she's got?

GROUCHO: My guess is that she's got a hundred thousand dollars. That's why I want to give her the best medicine there is. I've got it right in my desk—something I worked out myself.

CHICO: Oh, at'sa fine. We gonna be rich.

GROUCHO: Not so fast, Ravelli. The correspondence school says I should first try out my medicine on a guinea pig.

CHICO: Awright, I get my little brudder.

GROUCHO: Your little brother? What's the matter with you? Here, drink this, Ravelli.

CHICO: Tanks, boss, but I ain't tirsty.

GROUCHO: Drink it, Ravelli. It if kills you, you'll be a martyr.

CHICO: Me be a motter? You crazy, boss. I tink you mean a fotter.

GROUCHO: *Come on*, Ravelli. Drink the medicine.

CHICO: Naw, boss. I'ma too young to die.

GROUCHO: Ravelli, even if it kills you, we'll have something to be thankful for.

CHICO: Tankful for what?

GROUCHO: Thankful that we didn't waste money on a guinea pig.

(*Music in strong.*)

. . .

(Sound of cab in traffic.)

GROUCHO: There's Mrs. Carroway's house, Ravelli. Tell the cab driver to stop.

CHICO: He's stopping, boss.

DRIVER: Here you are, fellows. Here's the house.

GROUCHO: Okay, driver, here's a dollar. Keep the change.

DRIVER: But the bill is a dollar ten.

GROUCHO: All right. Then *I'll* keep the change.

DRIVER: I tell you the meter on this cab reads a dollar ten.

CHICO: A dollar ten to ride in your cab? Hey, dat'sa too much for cabbage. I can get spinach for a nickel.

DRIVER: Do you fellows want me to wait here?

GROUCHO: Yes, wait here until I can get a policeman to arrest you for parking.

DRIVER: Aw rats!

GROUCHO *(frightened):*   Rats? Where, where? Oh, wise guy! Just trying to scare us.

DRIVER *(disgusted):*   Aw, I haven't got time to argue with you mugs. *Goodbye. (Drives away.)*

GROUCHO: Well, Ravelli, here we are. Did you bring the medicine with you.

CHICO: Yeah, boss, but I tell you it's no good. It needs a little more ketchup.

GROUCHO: I don't know. I rather like that vanilla flavor. Ring the bell, Ravelli.

(Doorbell rings.)

BUTLER *(opening door):*   Whom do you wish to see?

CHICO: Are you Mr. Carroway?

BUTLER: Mr. Carroway? Indeed not. I'm Jamison, the butler.

CHICO: Awright, I'll take one.

BUTLER: You'll take what?

CHICO: A butler. A butler beer.

BUTLER: Quiet, gentlemen. Mrs. Carroway isn't feeling well.

GROUCHO: See here, doorman. I'm the doctor.

BUTLER: I'm glad you're here. Mrs. Carroway has been quite ill.

GROUCHO: That's too bad. Maybe we ought to come back when she's feeling better.

BUTLER: Oh! She's coming downstairs.

MRS. CARROWAY *(approaching):*   Why doctor! I've been waiting for you. I've been dreadfully upset.

GROUCHO: Well, what seems to be the trouble?

CHICO: Don't tell him, lady. If he's gonna be a doctor, make him find out himself.

MRS. CARROWAY: Doctor, I think it's purely a case of frayed nerves.

GROUCHO: Your nerves are frayed? What are they afraid of? Madam, you need rest, plenty of rest.

MRS. CARROWAY: But doctor, I—

GROUCHO: Stick your tongue out. Just as I thought. Your tongue needs rest too.

MRS. CARROWAY: I don't quite understand. Oh, doctor, I hope you won't mind, but I've called in another doctor for a consultation. *(Door bell rings.)* I believe that's the doctor now.

BUTLER: Doctor Perrin.

DOCTOR PERRIN: How do you do, Mrs. Carroway?

MRS. CARROWAY: Oh, doctor, these are the physicians I told you about. Gentlemen, this is Doctor Perrin. Doctor Perrin, this is—

GROUCHO: This is an outrage, Perrin, muscling in on our territory.

CHICO: Some doctor. He ain't even got a beard.

MRS. CARROWAY: Gentlemen, perhaps I ought to retire to my room, so you three can talk over my case.

GROUCHO: You can take this quack with you. I'll talk to Ravelli.

DOCTOR PERRIN: Doctor, your attitude is very unethical.

GROUCHO: Oh, a wise quack! Well, run along, Mrs. Carroway, we'll handle him.

CHICO: Leave it to me, lady, I'll have him eatin outta my hands.

GROUCHO: In that case, Ravelli, you'd better wash your hands.

MRS. CARROWAY: Call me when you're ready.

(Door opens and closes.)

DOCTOR PERRIN: Gentlemen, I have a special interest in this case, because I have a great affection for Mrs. Carroway.

GROUCHO: Yes, the dear old soul. It's too bad she cheats at cards.

DOCTOR PERRIN *(haughtily):* Let's not indulge in personalities. I'm a nerve specialist myself, but I suspect that Mrs. Carroway is suffering from rheumatism. Ah . . . do you know anything about rheumatism?

CHICO: I know sometin about rheumatism. I know a funny joke about it. Ha, ha, ha! I wish I could remember it.

DOCTOR PERRIN: Gentlemen, as medical men you amaze me. I've been practicing for twenty-two years—

CHICO: Oh, you're just practicin, too? I tought you was a *real* doctor.

DOCTOR PERRIN: Please, gentlemen. Let's discuss the case.

GROUCHO: Okay, doc. Now *I* think she's suffering from a case of locomotor ataxia, which we can easily cure at fifteen cents a mile. Ravelli, get out the book. Say, look at this picture. I think it's a map of New Jersey.

DOCTOR PERRIN: Ridiculous! Why, that's a diagram of the digestive tract.

GROUCHO: I've never been at that tract, but I lost a lot of money at Latonia. Where are you going, Ravelli?

CHICO: I'm going to Latonia to look for your money.

DOCTOR PERRIN: Doctor! All this is beside the point. Our first problem is, what's to be done about Mrs. Carroway's rheumatism?

GROUCHO: That's our second problem, doctor. Our first problem is: How are we going to split the fees? You know, doctor, with me it's *strictly* one price. That price is anything I can get.

DOCTOR PERRIN: Doctor, we'll come to that later. Now, the drugs I would prescribe—

CHICO: Aw no, doc. Drugs is no good. Last time I go to a doc he gimme so much drugs I was sick long after I got well.

DOCTOR PERRIN: Gentlemen, after all, this is a consultation. I would like to see Mrs. Carroway drink a glass of hot water an hour before breakfast every morning.

CHICO: Drink hot water an hour before breakfast? Nobody can do it, doc. I tried it once. I dranka hot water for ten minutes, den I couldn't hold anudder glass.

DOCTOR PERRIN: That's my wish in the matter, doctor. What would you like to do?

GROUCHO: Frankly, doctor, I'd like to sell you an insurance policy.

DOCTOR PERRIN: I *don't want* any life insurance.

GROUCHO: This isn't life insurance. It's fire insurance. It would be just the thing for you—if you had a wooden leg.

CHICO: Hey, wait a minoot. I sell you a better policy—my father's. He won't need it no more. Dey only give him tree days to live.

DOCTOR PERRIN: Is he that sick?

CHICO: No, he feels fine.

DOCTOR PERRIN: Then what makes you think he'll die in three days?

CHICO: Well, dat's what da judge said.

(*Door opens.* MRS. CARROWAY's *excited voice heard approaching.*)

MRS. CARROWAY: I know it all now! I was talking to Mrs. Gillingham, and she says she's with Doctor Jones right now. These two men are imposters!

DOCTOR PERRIN: I thought they were imposters. They certainly didn't talk like doctors.

GROUCHO: What do you mean, I didn't talk like a doctor. Didn't I ask for my money? Madam, how about kicking in with about a hundred bucks for my advice.

MRS. CARROWAY: Why should I pay you? What advice have you given me?

GROUCHO: If you want advice, I can give you some. Never play cards on trains. Especially with people like yourself.

MRS. CARROWAY: I mean *medical* advice.

GROUCHO: Oh, that's easy. If you've rheumatism, I prescribe a mustard plaster. If you don't like mustard, horseradish.

MRS. CARROWAY: Jamison, throw these men out.

BUTLER: Very well, Madam!

(Scramble heard: "Ouch!" "Hey!" Groans; door slams; street noises to show they are outside.)

CHICO: Hey, my arm, my arm. Hey boss, I tink maybe it's broke.

GROUCHO: In that case, we'd better go back into the house. There's a doctor inside.

(Signature music.)

FIVE STAR THEATER
PRESENTS

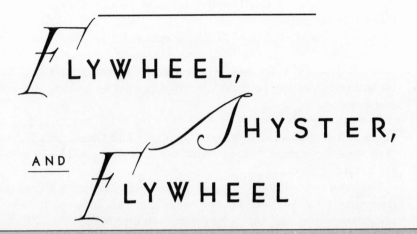

FLYWHEEL, SHYSTER,
AND FLYWHEEL

EPISODE NO. 8   JANUARY 16, 1933

CAST

Groucho Marx as Waldorf T. Flywheel
Chico Marx as Emmanuel Ravelli
Miss Dimple
Mrs. Jackson
Taxi Driver
Cop

(Fanfare. Trumpet)

ANNOUNCER: The Five Star Theatre presents Groucho and Chico Marx.

(Signature music.)

ANNOUNCER: The Five Star Theatre is sponsored by the Standard Oil Companies of New Jersey, Pennsylvania, and Louisiana, and the Colonial Beacon Oil Company, which markets Colonial Gasoline. All of these companies market Essolube, that famous hydrofined motor oil, and Esso.

Monday night is comedy night in the Five Star Theatre and we are about to hear those Mad Marxes, Groucho and Chico, in another of their three-act comedies concerning the adventures of Flywheel, Shyster, and Flywheel.

But before we get into our program we would like to ask all our radio friends to do something for us, something that involves no cost or obligation to you, and will be of great assistance to us.

For many years we have enjoyed the patronage of a host of loyal customers. We appreciate your support keenly and in return we wish to give you only the very best of radio entertainment.

We have diversified the programs of the Five Star Theatre to fit every mood and taste. Each week it includes smart comedy, beautiful symphony music and singing by opera stars, popular music and mystery drama. We and the artists want to know how you like our offerings, and we've arranged an easy way for you to vote for your favorite Five Star Program. Stop in at an Esso station, ask the salesman for a ballot, cast your vote for the program *you* like best, and leave it with the salesman. Your votes will enable us to give you the kind of entertainment you like best.

Now for the Mad Marxes. This program is coming to you tonight from Hollywood, California. There is Groucho. He looks just the way you see him on the stage and screen with those black, black brows and the famous mustache. Chico is here, too, in the little green hat and the corduroy suit. The audience is applauding. *(Applause.)* Our orchestra leader, Harry Jackson, has prepared some delightful numbers for you tonight. He's raising his stick, the overture is in, and the show is about to begin.

(Orchestra—medley from "Sweet Adeline.")

(Phone rings.)

MISS DIMPLE: Hello? Law offices of Flywheel, Shyster, and Flywheel. Hello . . . Who? Who did you want to speak to? . . . I can't understand you . . . Mr. Flywheel, I can't make out what this man is saying. You'd better talk to him.

GROUCHO: Give me that phone. Hello . . . Hello! What's that? You want to speak to Mr. Tilson? Mr. Tilson senior or Mr. Tilson junior? . . . Oh, you don't know! Well, is he a tall man or a short man? He's short? Oh, you mean Mr. Tilson *junior*. Well, there's nobody here by that name. You must have the wrong number. Goodbye.

MISS DIMPLE: Why, Mr. Flywheel, what have you got that string tied around your finger for?

GROUCHO: String? Oh, yes. I put that on last night to remind me to ask you to do something for me this morning.

MISS DIMPLE: Well, what did you want me to do?

GROUCHO: I can't imagine, unless it was to get you to untie the string. Oh, now I remember. I was going to deposit that ten cents we found yesterday in the bank. By the way, where *is* that ten cents?

MISS DIMPLE: It's in that drawer, Mr. Flywheel, where you put it last night.

(Drawer slides open.)

GROUCHO: *This* drawer? Miss Dimple, look! Look! It's gone! The money's gone!

(CHICO's *humming of "Daffodils" heard faintly.*)

MISS DIMPLE: Your assistant, Mr. Ravelli, is coming in. Maybe he knows something about it.

(Door opens.)

CHICO: Hello, boss. Hello, Miss Dimp.

GROUCHO: Never mind that, Ravelli. What happened to the ten cents that was in that drawer?

CHICO *(innocently):* Search me.

GROUCHO: Search you—a very good suggestion, Ravelli. Hold him, Miss Dimple. *(Pause.)* Ahhh! I knew it! Here it is right in his pocket. Now, Ravelli, I guess you'll sing a different tune.

CHICO: All right. I'll sing da ten-cent tune.

GROUCHO: The ten-cent tune?

CHICO: Sure. " Dime on My Hands"—

GROUCHO: You hand that money over! Look, Miss Dimple, a dime and two cents. Where did the two cents come from? Say, this money is beginning to yield interest. Maybe we ought to keep it in Ravelli's pocket instead of in the bank. Well, what have you got to say for yourself?

CHICO: Boss, I took da ten cents, but it was joost a mistake. You see, I tought it was a quarter.

GROUCHO: Ravelli, I'm amazed—You'd rob your friend and employer for ten cents . . . a measly bit of change.

CHICO: Well, boss, da doctor said da change would do me good.

THEY'RE FUNNY That WAY

So long as you laugh at them and they get paid, the Four Marx Brothers are happy

By

SIDNEY SKOLSKY

The cast of the Marx men in the order of their appearance on this earth is Chico, Harpo, Groucho and Zeppo (left). Harpo, the red-wigged and silent one (above), was named Adolph, at thirteen changed it to Arthur, and now has graced himself with a middle name, Duer.

This profile of the Four Marx Brothers noted, "The four of them play the stock market. That's why they're still in show business." (From *The New Movie Magazine*, Jan. 1932.)

GROUCHO: I see. All right, Miss Dimple, let go of him. Ravelli, *you* let go of Miss Dimple.

CHICO: Scusa please, boss, I forgot what I was doing.

GROUCHO: You'd forget your head if it wasn't on Miss Dimple's shoulder. Where have you been all morning?

CHICO: I was standing on da corner looking at an accident.

GROUCHO: An accident? Was it a good one? Will it make a law case? What happened?

CHICO: Well you see, a man he walk right in front of a baker's wagon. It was da baker's fault. He shoulda turned to da left.

GROUCHO: Nonsense. The baker had no choice in the matter. You know bakers can't be choosers.

CHICO: Well, it was da baker's fault. He was sitting and driving at da same time he was eating a piece of cake.

GROUCHO: Driving and eating cake? Didn't he give his horn a honk?

CHICO: No, he ate it all himself. He didn't give anybody a hunk. Not even da horse.

GROUCHO: What! He didn't give that poor horse any cake? Why not?

CHICO: I don't know, boss. Maybe it was because he didn't have a horse. He was driving an automobile.

(*Door opens.*)

MISS DIMPLE (*whispers*): Here comes a lady. She looks like a client.

MRS. JACKSON: Aw . . . pardon me. Are you Mr. Flywheel?

GROUCHO: Am I Mr. Flywheel? Before I answer that, there's one thing I want to know. Are you *Mrs.* Flywheel?

MRS. JACKSON: Certainly not.

GROUCHO: All right, then I'm Mr. Flywheel. And I bet I can guess who you are.

MRS. JACKSON: Well then, who am I?

GROUCHO: I give up. Who are you?

CHICO: I give up, too. And I wasn't even playing.

MRS. JACKSON: My name is Mrs. Jackson, and, er, I've come in to get you to help me with my income tax.

GROUCHO: Help you with your income tax? A big woman like you? You'll pay your own taxes.

CHICO: Taxes? Hey, I got a brudder living in Taxes.

GROUCHO: Quiet, we're talking about taxes—money, dollars.

CHICO: Well, dat's where my brudder lives, Dollas, Taxes.

GROUCHO: Ravelli, if you were only deaf, you'd be deaf and dumb.

MRS. JACKSON: Gentlemen, I don't know what you're talking about.

GROUCHO: Well, madam, what you don't know, won't hurt you—and that ought to make you practically safe from anything.

MRS. JACKSON: I didn't come here to be insulted!

CHICO: Den you must be in da wrong office.

GROUCHO: Keep quiet, Ravelli. I can defend myself! Now, madam, about that income tax?

MRS. JACKSON: I've got a blank right here with me—

GROUCHO: So have I. His name is Ravelli.

MRS. JACKSON: I mean I've got a tax blank with me, and there are a few things I don't understand.

GROUCHO: Madam, let me see that blank. Hmm. This income tax isn't very entertaining reading. You haven't got an amusement tax with you, instead?

MRS. JACKSON: I'm afraid it's rather complicated.

GROUCHO: Complicated? Why, a child of four could explain this. Ravelli, run out and see if you can find a child of four. I can't make head or tail out of it.

CHICO: Hey, dis is no good at all. It gotta no pictures.

GROUCHO: Now, let's see. We'll start at the beginning. It says here, "Are you a resident of the United States?"

CHICO: Ha, ha. At'sa crazy. Dat paper wants to know if da lady is a resident of da United States. Everybody know Mr. Hoover, he's da resident of da United States.

GROUCHO: Say, here's a good one. It says, "A fiduciary filing the return for an estate in process of administration may claim"—now get this, this will kill you—"in lieu of this deduction provided in Section 162(a) of the Act of 1928(b)." How do you like it so far, Ravelli?

CHICO: Ha! At one's too easy, but I know a mucha better riddle. Hey, lady, tirteen men was under an umbrella and only one of dem got wet. Why was dat?

MRS. JACKSON (*impatiently*): I'm sure I *don't know!*

CHICO: It wasn't raining!

MRS. JACKSON: Well, how did the one man get wet?

CHICO: Oh, him. He went home and took a bath.

MRS. JACKSON: *Please*, gentlemen. What about my income tax?

GROUCHO: Your income tax? Haven't you anything else to occupy your mind? What do you do for a living?

MRS. JACKSON: I have a millinery shop.

CHICO: Hey, my little brudder he goes to a millinery school. He's gonna be a soldier.

MRS. JACKSON: Well, that's all very nice, but I wish you'd attend to my income tax.

GROUCHO: Madam, if wishes were horses, I'd drive you home. However, leave your tax with me and I'll drop over to your shop this afternoon and let you know how much you lose.

MRS. JACKSON: I'll be expecting you, then, this afternoon.

GROUCHO: Fine. And now let's have a paper chase.

MRS. JACKSON: A paper chase?

GROUCHO: Sure. I'll read the paper and Ravelli'll chase you out of here. (*Music in strong.*)

(*Street noises.*)

GROUCHO: Taxi! Taxi!

CHICO: Hey, boss, what you want a taxi for?

GROUCHO: Do you expect me, Flywheel, to walk to Mrs. Jackson's shop? What kind of impression do you think we'd make? Where's your pride, Ravelli?

CHICO: Hey, I ain't got no pride. I ain't even engaged.

GROUCHO: Taxi! Taxi!

(*Cab drives up.*)

DRIVER: Okay, mister. Here you are.

GROUCHO: Driver, we want to go to Mrs. Jackson's Millinery Shop—555 Boulevard Avenue.

DRIVER: All right, buddy. Hop in.

(*Door slams, car starts up.*)

CHICO: Hey, boss. Hey, boss. How we gonna pay for dis cab?

GROUCHO: Ravelli, don't cross a bridge until you come to it. (*Squealing of brakes.*) And that goes for you too, driver.

CHICO: Hey, driver, why don't you look where you're going wit dis old tin can?

GROUCHO: Listen, Ravelli. You'll have to stop berating this car. What do you think you are, a carburetor?

DRIVER: Hey, youse guys, if you don't like this cab, you can get out and walk.

GROUCHO: Oh, a wise guy.

DRIVER: Yeah, I'm a wise guy. What do you tink of dat?

GROUCHO: Well, if you're so wise, answer me this. If I mail this letter today, will it be delivered in Philadelphia in the morning?

DRIVER: Sure, it will. It'll get dere foist thing in de morning.

GROUCHO: That's where you're wrong. It won't get to Philadelphia in the morning. This letter is addressed to Boston.

CHICO: Hey, boss. Hey, boss. Look at da cop running disa way. What'sa matter?

(*Sound of shooting.*)

GROUCHO: He's jumping on the running board. Hey, officer, what's the big idea? We didn't invite you to come with us.

COP: Shut up, you. Listen, driver, follow that touring car ahead of you. It's full of gunmen and they just held up a bank. Come on. Drive like the devil and look out for the bullets.

DRIVER: Okay, chief, we'll catch those rats.

CHICO: Rats? Hey, we better stop at dat corner and get some cheese.

COP: Cheese? What for?

CHICO: For my lunch.

COP: You guys had better get down on the floor if you don't want to get hit.

(*Burst of machine-gun fire and breaking glass.*)

GROUCHO: Move over, Ravelli. Quick. Let Flywheel have the floor.

CHICO: Ouch. Ouch.

COP: Did they hit you, buddy?

CHICO: Dey no hit my buddy, but dey almost got me in da neck.

(*Bang, bang, bang.*)

GROUCHO: Turn to the right at the next crossing, driver. I want to pass my girl's house. She'll enjoy seeing Ravelli shot at.

COP: Shut up! Keep chasing that car, driver. I tell you those fellows just stole *ten thousand dollars!*

GROUCHO: See here, officer, you can chase that car if you like, but I'm not in the habit of running after people just because they have money. Officer, you may be poor, but I'm sure you're just as nice as those rich fellows you're running after.

COP: I tell you, *those guys are thieves—bandits.*

GROUCHO: Well, I *still* insist you are just as nice as they are. The trouble with you is you're suffering from an inferiority complex.

COP: Duck. Duck, they're going to shoot.

CHICO: Oh, are dey duck-shooting?

(*More shots.*)

GROUCHO: If you were a man, officer, you'd arrest those fellows. This isn't the duck-hunting season.

(*Machine-gun fire, breaking glass.*)

CHICO: Say, I wish my fadder was here. He's a dead shot.

COP: A dead shot?

CHICO: Yeah. He's been dead for tree years.

COP: Look out, you two, here comes a hand grenade.

CHICO: Hey, boss, look at what I catch—it looksa joosta like a pineapple.

COP (*excitedly*): Hey, throw that out of the window—it's a hand grenade!

(*Sound of explosion.*)

GROUCHO: Well, Ravelli, a big help you are! Too bad they didn't throw pneumonia. I'd like to see you catch that.

COP: Faster, driver. They're only a block ahead.

CHICO: Blockahead. Flywheel, he's a blockahead too, but we no talk about it.

(More shooting.)

COP: We're gaining! We're gaining!

GROUCHO: Say, you *are* gaining, officer. If I were you, I'd stop eating potatoes.

CHICO: Yeah, dat reminds me, you know what I weighed yesterday, boss?

GROUCHO: No—what did you weigh?

CHICO: A pound of sugar. Ha, ha, some joke! Hey, boss, look what dat meter says.

GROUCHO: Jumping Jupiter, it's six dollars and a quarter. Officer! Officer!

COP: Well, what is it?

GROUCHO: Where are we going?

(Bang, bang.)

COP: They're headed out for the open country, and we're following them.

GROUCHO: Well, I wonder if you'd ask those gunmen to do us a big favor?

(Bang, bang.)

COP: What do you want?

GROUCHO: If it's all the same to them, I wonder if they'd mind being chased to Mrs. Jackson's Millinery Shop. We have a business appointment at three o'clock and we're late now.

(Music in strong.)

(Sound of cab driving.)

CHICO: Hey, boss, it'sa lucky dose bandits got away over da state line. I was afraid for a while we catch up to dem.

DRIVER: Well, here we are. Dis is de dive youse guys wanted. 555 Boulevard Avenue.

GROUCHO: Yes, this is it. Mrs. Jackson's Millinery Shop. *(Door opens.)* Thanks for a delightful outing, driver. You must come over and go shooting with *us* some time. Come on, Ravelli.

DRIVER: Hey, wait a minute. Wait a minute. How about the fare?

GROUCHO: What fare?

DRIVER: Da fare is fifty-six dollars and thirty cents.

GROUCHO: Fifty-six thirty! Impossible!

DRIVER: See here, buddy, after that long ride around this country, you ain't gonna stand there and argue about fifty-six thirty, are you?

GROUCHO: Argue about it! Why, certainly not. I'm not going to argue about it. I'm just not going to pay it.

DRIVER: You'll pay it, all right!

CHICO: Hey, don't get excited. You joosta wait here till we come out. We gotta see dat lady on business.

DRIVER *(menacing):*   All right. I'll wait!

GROUCHO: If we're not out in ten minutes, don't bother to wait any longer.

DRIVER: I'll be here, don't worry!

GROUCHO: And I'll be in there, but I can't promise you I won't worry. Come on, Ravelli.

CHICO: Hey, it'sa pretty nicea shop.
   (Door opens.)

MRS. JACKSON: Well, Mr. Flywheel, this is a fine time to be coming.
   (Door closes.)

GROUCHO: Never mind about that. The important thing is, has this place got a back door?

MRS. JACKSON: What about my income tax?

GROUCHO: Answer *my* question first. Has this place got a back door?

MRS. JACKSON: No, it hasn't.

GROUCHO: Well, in that case, you owe the government fifty-six dollars and thirty cents.

CHICO: Hey, at'sa funny ting. At'sa joosta what we owe da taxicab— fifty-six dollars and tirty cents.

MRS. JACKSON: Why, that's far too much! I won't pay it.

GROUCHO: Well, that makes three of us who won't pay it. By the way Mrs. Jackson, do you know the best way to avoid falling hair?

MRS. JACKSON: Why I—

GROUCHO: Well, it's very simple. The next time you see it falling, just step quickly out of the way. And now about that fifty-six dollars and thirty cents. Unless you can build a back door, we'll take it in cash.

MRS. JACKSON: Nonsense! If I really owe that much I'll send it to the government myself.

CHICO: What'sa matter, lady? Don't you trust me?

MRS. JACKSON: Oh, you misunderstand me. It isn't that I don't trust you. But I always pay my tax in installments—every three months.

CHICO: At'sa no good. We can't keep da cab waiting dat long.

MRS. JACKSON: And now, gentlemen, aside from what I owe the government, what do I owe you for the work you've done?

GROUCHO: Just a moment, I'll figure it out. *(Mumbling to himself.)* Let's see. Three hours labor, time and a half for overtime, one hour for lunch, horse, one dollar. That's four times four is twenty-eight and twelve to carry makes thirty-two, minus Ravelli . . . which adds up to . . . *(Brightly.)* Mrs. Jackson, you owe us exactly fifty-six dollars and thirty cents.

MRS. JACKSON: Why that's just what you told me I owe the government! Mr. Flywheel, do you mind telling me how you arrived at that figure?

GROUCHO: You want to know how we arrived at that figure? Well, I'll tell you. We left town by Hemingway Avenue, came back through Tenth Street, cut across to Billy Boulevard, and before you could say Jack Robinson we arrived at fifty-six dollars and thirty cents.

MRS. JACKSON: I'm very confused. I wish you'd come upstairs to my office and show it to me on paper.

GROUCHO: Okay, babe. You lead the way and I'll go ahead of you. You stay here, Ravelli, and watch the store.

MRS. JACKSON: Yes—and Mr. Ravelli, if any customers come in, please call me.

CHICO: Awright, lady.

MRS. JACKSON: Come, Mr. Flywheel.

(Door opens and closes; CHICO *starts singing "All Alone"; door opens.)*

DRIVER: Hey, you! How long do I have to wait?

CHICO: Hello, Mr. Taxi Driver. You wanna buy something?

DRIVER: I want my fifty-six dollars, and I want it quick.

CHICO: You want fifty-six dollars? What happen to da tirty cents? Anyhow, you gotta da wrong man. I never saw you before. Hey, maybe you wanna buy something. Nicea lady's hat?

DRIVER: What would I do with a lady's hat?

CHICO: Here, trya one on. At'sa very nicea hat.

DRIVER: Well, dat isn't a bad hat. Maybe dat wouldn't look so bad on de wife. How much is it?

CHICO: It's just fifty-six dollars and tirty cents. You want I should wrap it up, or will you wear it?

DRIVER: Say, you got your noive with you. Fifty-six thirty for that little hat?

CHICO: Awright, awright. Here's a *bigger* hat, and it won't cost a cent more than fifty-six tirty.

DRIVER: Say, what are you trying to do, kid me? I know you! You're one of the two guys I'm waiting to collect from. Where's the guy with the mustache?

CHICO: He's inside shaving off his mustache!

DRIVER: What's he doing that for?

CHICO: He's shaving it off so you won't know him.

DRIVER: Oh, he thinks he can fool me, does he?

CHICO: Sure. I coulda fool you too, only it take me longer. I'd have to stay here until I *grow* a mustache.

(*Door opens.*)

MRS. JACKSON: Mr. Flywheel, this is an outrage! You haven't put a single figure down on this income-tax blank. Why, I don't believe you've even *looked* at it.

GROUCHO: That's all right, I've got the whole thing in my head. If you had an X-ray machine I could show it to you.

DRIVER: Oh, so there's the other guy. Listen, punk, I'm tired of waiting for you.

GROUCHO: Driver, I thought I told you to wait outside with my car.

CHICO: Did we buy da car, now?

MRS. JACKSON: I'm sick of all this horseplay. I won't pay you a cent. I'm going right down to the tax collector's office now and get them to figure it out for me.

GROUCHO: You're going to the collector's office now? Ravelli, call a taxi-cab for Mrs. Jackson. On second thought, driver, you take Mrs. Jackson wherever she wants to go.

DRIVER: Yeah, well, what about that money?

GROUCHO: Driver, the lady is in a hurry. Mrs. Jackson, you'll pay the taxi driver whatever the meter says when you get there, won't you?

MRS. JACKSON: Why certainly. I always pay my taxi fares!

GROUCHO: There you are, driver, Mrs. Jackson will take your cab.

MRS. JACKSON: Very well.

DRIVER: Okay, boss. I guess it's all right. Come on, lady.

(*Door opens and closes.*)

GROUCHO: Here, Mrs. Jackson. Allow me to help you in.

CHICO: Goodabye, lady.

MRS. JACKSON: *Goodbye!*

CHICO: Well, boss, we got out of dat pretty good.

GROUCHO: Out of it! How we going to get back to the office?

CHICO: Why? How far is it?

GROUCHO: Well, it's forty miles as the crow flies, it's sixty as the house flies.

CHICO: Don't worry, boss, I call Miss Dimp and tell her to come out here right away.

GROUCHO: What good will that do us? She hasn't got any money either.

CHICO: At'sa fine—den da tree of us can walk home together.

(*Music in strong.*)

ANNOUNCER: You have just heard another of the adventures of Flywheel,

Shyster, and Flywheel, Attorneys at Law, which is the Monday-night feature in the Five Star Theatre. Groucho and Chico Marx are the stars of this show. They have just come out to take a bow, and the crowd in the studio is applauding wildly.

(*Applause.*)

ANNOUNCER: Now here are Groucho and Chico again.

CHICO: Lay-deez and, and . . . ah . . . gentlemens! Ha, I knew I'd guess it. Ladies an' gentlemens, I—

GROUCHO: That was very good, Chico. *Very* good.

CHICO: Hey, I kin do even *better* dan dat.

GROUCHO: That's easy to believe. But fortunately our time is short and—

CHICO: Why, what time is it?

GROUCHO: I don't know. But it can't be seven o'clock, because I'm supposed to be at a friend's house for dinner at seven o'clock and I'm not there yet.

CHICO: Why don'tcha look at your watch?

GROUCHO: My watch isn't going.

CHICO: Why? Wasn't your watch invited?

GROUCHO: I see. You're getting sleepy. Now say good night to the nice people and I'll put you to bed.

CHICO: Izesso?

GROUCHO: Yes, Esso, which is better than any gasoline, and Essolube, too, that hydrofined motor oil. *Say,* we worked that in pretty neatly. I guess we better say good night before we spoil everything. Good night, good night.

(*Applause.*)

ANNOUNCER: Don't forget to go to the nearest Esso service station this week and cast your ballot in the Five Star Theatre popularity vote. It won't cost you a cent, entails no obligation. Just go in and ask the salesman for a ballot, record your vote, and he will send it to us. We are very anxious to know which of the various Five Star programs— comedy, fine music, famous short stories, or mystery drama—you prefer. You can help us to give you the entertainment you like best by casting your vote. Thank you.

(*Signature music.*)

FIVE STAR THEATER
PRESENTS

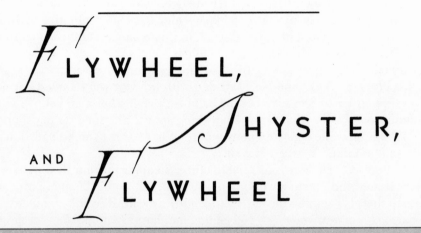

FLYWHEEL, SHYSTER, AND FLYWHEEL

EPISODE NO. 9   *JANUARY 23, 1933*

CAST

Groucho Marx as Waldorf T. Flywheel
Chico Marx as Emmanuel Ravelli
Miss Dimple
Mrs. Dalloway
Boy
Streetcar Conductor
Cranky Tailor

(Phone rings.)

MISS DIMPLE: Law offices of Flywheel, Shyster, and Flywheel . . . No, Mr. Flywheel is in court. I expect him back any minute . . . Hmm, Hmm . . . I'll tell him. Goodbye. *(Hangs up phone.)* Oh, good morning, Mr. Flywheel. Mrs. Carrington called.

GROUCHO: Complaining again, I suppose.

MISS DIMPLE: Yes. She isn't satisfied with the way you handled her non-support case. She says her husband isn't giving her a nickel.

GROUCHO: Well, what is she squawking about? She *sued* for nonsupport. Well, now she's *getting* nonsupport. Where's that thick-headed assistant of mine? Where's Ravelli?

MISS DIMPLE: He's in your private office, sleeping on your desk.

GROUCHO: So he sleeps on my desk, does he? Well, I'll soon put a stop to that. I'll sell the desk. *(Calling out.)* Ravelli, Ravelli!

CHICO *(From next room):* You calling me, boss? *(Approaches yawning.)*

GROUCHO: Oh, there you are. I didn't recognize you with a clean shirt on. Listen, Ravelli, you'll have to snap out of it. Here it is Monday. Tomorrow's Tuesday, and the day after that's Wednesday. A half a week's gone by and you're still sleeping on the desk.

CHICO: I'ma feel sorry, boss. But I joosta can't sleep at home.

GROUCHO: Why not?

CHICO: I ain't gotta no desk.

GROUCHO: Well, I'm not sure that you've got a job either. I waited in court all morning for you to bring me those Carrington divorce papers. Why didn't you show up?

CHICO: Well, I no tink doze papers wasa very important.

GROUCHO: *My* legal papers and *you* didn't think they were important? Well, they were *very* important . . . I had my *lunch* wrapped in those papers!

CHICO: Awright, I bring you another lunch. I bring you nicea tomayto sandwich.

GROUCHO: *Tomayto?* Ravelli, in my social circle we call it tomahto.

CHICO: Oh, you want it *tomahto.* I thought you wanted it *today.* Awright, I bring you a tomato sandwich tomahto.

GROUCHO: Ravelli, I think I've been overestimating your intelligence. Why, I've been telling everybody you're a halfwit.

CHICO: Halfwit? Dat's da kinda sandwich I gonna bring you. Half wit butter and half witout.

GROUCHO: I see. You know, you're in a position to do me a great favor.

CHICO: Okay, boss, whata you want I should do?

GROUCHO: I want you to get out of this office before I throw you out. Miss Dimple, put a sign on the door saying, "Boy Wanted."

CHICO: Never mind, Miss Dimp. I already put up dat kinda sign. I'm gonna quit.

GROUCHO *(excitedly):*   You're quitting? Shake hands, Ravelli. I want you to be the first to congratulate me. *(To* MISS DIMPLE:*)* Oh, Miss Dimple, I'll be in my office. Call me as soon as Ravelli scrams.

MISS DIMPLE: Okay, Mr. Flywheel. *(Door opens and closes.)* Really, Mr. Ravelli, I'm terribly sorry to hear you're going.

CHICO: Hey, *you* didn't hear me going. I didn't go yet. Say, Miss Dimp, didja see my hat around here anyplace?

MISS DIMPLE: Your hat? Why, it's on your head!

CHICO: Awright, den don't bodder. I'll look for it when I come back. *(Knock on door.)*

MISS DIMPLE: Come in.

Groucho as Rufus T. Firefly, President of Freedonia, in *Duck Soup,* the film made immediately after *Flywheel*'s first and only season.

BOY *(fresh, tough kid):*   Say, lady, you lookin' for a boy?

MISS DIMPLE: Yes, Mr. Flywheel was—

CHICO: Hey, waita minoot. Dat'sa my sign on da door, I need a boy to work for me. Hey kid, you wanna job?

BOY: Sure. Whata yuh tink I come in for?

CHICO: Awright, you're hired. Come on, get to work.

BOY: Take it easy. What am I supposed to do?

CHICO: Well, first ting you gotta do is call me boss. Den you gotta go out and find me a job.

BOY: Find *you* a job? Say, you gotta lotta crust. Why don'tcha go lookin' for a job yourself?

CHICO: Hey, shut up. Ain'tcha gotta no respeck for da boss? You know, I was a much smarter boy dan you when I was your age. And when I was your age, I wasn't even as old as you.

BOY: Yeah?

CHICO *(angry):*   You hearda what I say. An' when I was your size, I wasa much smaller dan you too. Hey, didn't you never go to school?

BOY: Soitanly, I went to school.

CHICO: Yeah? Den maybe you know my brudder Tony. He went to school too.

BOY: Is that so? What class was he in?

CHICO: He's in every class—he's da janitor.

BOY: Say, listen, mister—

CHICO *(admonishing):*   Hey, please! Calla me boss. Now we gotta talk money. How about dis? You find a job an' I give you halfa da pay.

BOY: Half the pay? Say, that sounds pretty good!

CHICO: You like da way it sounds? Awright, I say it again, but dis time I give you only a quarter of da pay.

BOY: Let me get this straight. If I find this job I get a quarter of da salary?

CHICO: At'sa fine!

BOY: Okay, what kinda work do you wanna do?

CHICO: Anyting you like.

BOY: Anyting I like? Why, *you're* gonna do the work, ain'tcha?

CHICO: *Me* do da work? Whatta you tink I'm givin' you quarter da pay for?

BOY: Say, you got some noive!

CHICO: Hey, what'sa matta wit you? Ain'tcha gotta no ambish'? Don'tcha wanna grow up an' be a boss like me?

BOY: Soitanly not!

CHICO: Awright, den I tink I fire you. G'wan, beat it!

BOY: I'll beat it, you fathead! *Goodbye! (Slams door.)*

CHICO *(calling out):*   Hey, Mr. Flywheel.

GROUCHO: What? Are you still here? I thought—

CHICO: Well, boss, I no find a new job yet.

GROUCHO: Why don't you go to the bank next door? I hear they're looking for a new cashier.

CHICO: Dey're looking for a new cashier? But dey joosta hired one yesterday.

GROUCHO: That's the one they're looking for . . . You know, being a bank cashier isn't such a bad job, Ravelli.

CHICO: Yeah? I might take it. What about da salary, boss? You tink twenty-five a week is too much?

GROUCHO: Twenty-five a week to be *cashier?* If I were you, I'd offer to pay them *fifty* dollars a week . . . Say, while you're at the bank, see if you can get me change for a nine-dollar bill.

CHICO: You crazy, boss. Dere'sa no nine-dollar bill.

GROUCHO: There aren't, eh? What about the nine-dollar bill the gas company has been trying to collect?

CHICO: Don't bodder me, boss. I tink I better look for my own job. Gimme dat newspaper. *(Newspaper ruffling is heard.)* Now lemme see. Hey, what it says here, boss?

GROUCHO: Ravelli, you'll never find a job there. You're looking in the lost and found column.

CHICO: That's awright, maybe somebody else lost a job and I can find it.

GROUCHO: Give me that paper. Hmm. Look at this: "Bulldog wanted." Say, that might be a job for you. With a little coaching, you ought to be able to do anything a dog can do.

CHICO: Awright, I take it.

GROUCHO: Just a minute! *(Excited.)* Here's something about a dog worth a thousand dollars!

CHICO: A tousand dollars? Hey boss, at'sa crazy, how could a little dog save up so much money?

GROUCHO: Shut up while I read this. "Lost—a tiny brown Pekingese . . ."

CHICO: Say, a man had my brudder arrested for dat.

GROUCHO *(impatient):*   Arrested for *what?*

CHICO: For Pekingese. You know, peekin' hees pockets. Ha, some joke, eh boss?

(Phone rings.)

MISS DIMPLE: Flywheel, Shyster, and Flywheel . . . Yes, here he is. Mr. Flywheel there's a man on the phone wants to talk to you.

GROUCHO: Miss Dimple, can't you see I'm reading the paper? Tell him to wait. Hmm, now let's see . . . "Lost—tiny brown Pekingese answering name of Foo-Foo." Get that name, will you? Foo-Foo! "Return to Mrs. J.Q. Dalloway, Seven-Eighty Sixth Street. Reward, five hundred dollars."

MISS DIMPLE: Mr. Flywheel, what about the man on the phone?

GROUCHO: Tell him to wait, tell him to wait. Hear that, Ravelli? *Five hundred dollars' reward!*

MISS DIMPLE: Mr. Flywheel. This man on the phone is getting impatient. He says he wants a lawyer.

GROUCHO: He wants a lawyer? Well, hang up on him. From now on I'm a dogcatcher.

(*Music in strong.*)

(*Barking dogs heard from next office. Phone rings.*)

MISS DIMPLE: Law offices of Flywheel, Shyster, and Flywheel . . . Yes, of course, I know—you're the tailor in the next office . . . Well, I'm sorry the noise is disturbing you, but there's nothing I can do about it. If Mr. Flywheel wants to keep dogs in his office, I think he has a perfect right to . . . Well, if you want to talk to him, I'll call him. (*Calls.*) Oh, Mr. Flywheel, Mr. Flywheel . . .

(*Door opens; loud barking heard.*)

GROUCHO: Yes? (*Closes door and barking is subdued.*)

MISS DIMPLE: The tailor in the next office wants to talk to you.

GROUCHO: Well, tell him he'll have to wait. The dogs were here first.

MISS DIMPLE: I'll tell him you're busy. Hello, hello? I think he hung up.

(*Knock on door.*)

MISS DIMPLE: Come in.

(*Door opens.*)

TAILOR (*cranky old man*): Excuse me. I'm the tailor in the next office, and—

GROUCHO: Well, what do you mean by walking into my office without knocking?

TAILOR: I did knock. I knocked three times.

GROUCHO: Well, I only heard *two* knocks. You'd better go out and knock once more.

TAILOR: Mr. Flywheel, I'm tired of hearing those dogs bark.

GROUCHO: I'm tired of it too, but I don't come complaining to *you.*

TAILOR: You! You have nothing to complain about.

GROUCHO: I haven't, eh? Well, what about the job you did on my suit? You didn't even know enough to take the crease out of my pants.

TAILOR: Take the crease *out* of your pants?

GROUCHO: Sure, the axle crease. But I'll forget that.

TAILOR: See here, Mr. Flywheel.

GROUCHO: Now don't get yourself excited. Let's talk this thing over. Sit down. Here—have a cigar. I'm sorry it isn't a whole one.

TAILOR: Thanks . . . ah . . . if you don't mind, I'll smoke it after dinner.

GROUCHO: Smoke it now and you won't *want* any dinner.

(*Scratching at door.*)

MISS DIMPLE: Mr. Flywheel, someone's scratching at the door.

GROUCHO: That's a fine place to scratch. Have 'em come in and scratch my back.

(*Door opens; barking heard.*)

CHICO (*entering*): Hullo, boss. I tink we gonna get five hunnerd bucks.

GROUCHO: Ravelli, you're hired again. Where's the money?

CHICO: Hey, I no gotta da money yet, but I find littla Foo-Foo. An we get da five hunnerd bucks reward when we get to Mrs. Dalloway's house. Here Foo-Foo! Here Foo-Foo! (*HEAVY barking.*) See, he answers when I call him Foo-Foo!

TAILOR: That dog looks *mad* to me.

GROUCHO: You'd be mad too if they called you Foo-Foo!

TAILOR: This is an outrage, bringing another dog into the building. Why that makes thirteen you've got now.

GROUCHO: Thirteen dogs in the office? That's an unlucky number. Ravelli, you'd better get out.

CHICO: Whata you talkin', boss? (*Indignant.*) Din't I find littla Foo-Foo? Ain't we gonna get da reward?

GROUCHO: But the lady said in her ad that her dog is brown.

CHICO: Aw, she'sa crazy. Anybody can see dat dis dog is black.

(*Dog barks*).

TAILOR: Get that dog away from me. He's biting me, he's biting me!

(*Dog barks.*)

GROUCHO: Some mutt you brought in, Ravelli. Doesn't that hound know that a barking dog never bites?

TAILOR: I tell you, that dog is vicious!

CHICO: Aw, no, mister, you make a mistake. He'sa no vicious. He joosta hungry.

TAILOR: Take that pooch away from me.

CHICO: Shut up! How you like it if I call you a pooch? Pooch yourself in da dog's place.

TAILOR: I don't think you know what a pooch is!

CHICO (*insulted*): Aw, you crazy. Dey got a pooch in da housa next door. Dey gotta two pooches—a front pooch and a back pooch.

(*Barking dogs.*)

TAILOR: Keep that dog away from me. I think he has fleas.

GROUCHO: Oh, you can pet him. A few more fleas won't hurt him.
(*Barking again from all the dogs.*)

TAILOR: There's that noise again! *(Threatening.)* I'll get those dogs out of here if—

GROUCHO: Say! You can take this one out of here for five hundred dollars. That'll save us the carfare to Mrs. Dalloway's house.

CHICO: Sure. You'll lika littla Foo-Foo. Watch, I teach him tricks.

GROUCHO: Nonsense, Ravelli. You can't teach a dog anything unless you know more than the dog.

TAILOR: See here, Mr. Flywheel, I—

GROUCHO *(quickly):* I know. You're afraid this dog hasn't got a pedigree. Well, I happen to know that he comes from a long line of thoroughbreds. In fact, I can assure you that he comes from a much better family than I do.

CHICO: You bet. Dis dog's fadder took first prize at da cat show.

TAILOR: First prize at the *cat* show?

CHICO: Yeah, he took da cat.

TAILOR: It seems to me, Mr. Flywheel, you forget why I'm here!

GROUCHO: Not at all, tailor! You want this dog for five hundred dollars? He's yours. And now, if you don't mind, I'd like to borrow Foo-Foo for a couple of hours so I can take him to his owner's house and get the reward, too.

TAILOR: I *can't* waste any more time here. If you won't get those dogs *out* of the building, *I'll report it to the landlord. Good day!* (*Slams door.*)

GROUCHO: The piker!

CHICO: It's too bad, boss. It looks like all we gonna get outa dis is Mrs. Dalloway's five hunnerd bucks reward. Hey, Miss Dimp. Where does da lady live? You know, da one who lost da dog.

MISS DIMPLE: There's no point to your taking that dog to Mrs. Dalloway. The ad distinctly said that her dog had white spots.

GROUCHO: Ravelli, Miss Dimple is right. If we're too lazy to paint a few white spots on that dog, we don't deserve the reward. Go out and get some paint.
(*Music in strong.*)

(*Traffic sounds; streetcar approaching; dog barking.*)

CHICO: Hey, boss, I no feel like walkin to Mrs. Dalloway's house. My shoes hurt.

GROUCHO: Well, *my* shoes feel fine, but my feet ache a little. Pick up the dog and we'll get on this streetcar.

CHICO: Aw, no, boss—let's take da car across da street.

GROUCHO: *That* car? Why, that's going in the direction we came from.

CHICO: I know, but we can get *seats* on *dat* car.

(Bell clangs as car comes to stop.)

CONDUCTOR: All aboard. Watch your step there! Hey, you guys, you can't get that dog on this car!

CHICO: We can't? Hey, it's easy—watch! Oop, Foo-Foo . . . At'saboy! See, Mr. Conduck, he's onna car and we didn't even help him.

CONDUCTOR: "No Dogs Allowed." There it is—right on the sign.

CHICO: I know, Mr. Conduck, but dis littla dog can't read.

CONDUCTOR: But what about you? *You* can read.

GROUCHO: Listen, conductor, that flattery won't get you anywhere with us. Furthermore, *if you lay a hand on that dog*—

CONDUCTOR: Yeah?

GROUCHO *(blithely):* Well, we'd have to wash him again.

(Dog barks, runs into car.)

CONDUCTOR: Hey, stop that dog! Don't let him go inside the car!

CHICO: Awright. I go in an' get him.

CONDUCTOR: *No you don't.* You don't leave this platform until you drop your fare in the box. I don't trust you.

GROUCHO: Sir, I resent that. My assistant doesn't steal. Why, he worked in a bathhouse for over five years and never even took a bath.

CONDUCTOR: Why, er . . .

GROUCHO: Never mind. Here's your money. *(Drops coin in box.)*

CONDUCTOR: What about the other guy? Ain'tcha gonna pay for him?

GROUCHO: *Pay* for him? I wouldn't take him for nothing.

CHICO: Hey, boss, come on! Let's go in quick, before dat lady gets dat seat!

CONDUCTOR: Come on with that other fare!

CHICO: Whata you mean? Da boss, he joosta paid for me.

CONDUCTOR: Don't gimme that. There are twelve people on the car an' only eleven fares are registered.

GROUCHO: In that case, conductor, we'll have to put you off the car.

CONDUCTOR: *Come on with that fare!*

CHICO: Awright, awright. Don't get excited—here'sa quarter. Keep da change. Come on in, boss. *(They walk in.)*

GROUCHO *(whispers):* A quarter? Ravelli, what's the idea of throwing away money?

CHICO: Dat's awright, boss. I gave him a lead quarter.

GROUCHO: That's *still* extravagance. You should have given him a lead nickel.

(Dog barks.)

CHICO: Here, Foo-Foo. Here, five hunnerd bucks!

GROUCHO: Say, what street do we get off at, do you remember?

CHICO *(thinking):*   Yeah, I . . . I tink it's I-Don't-Feel-So-Good Street.

GROUCHO: I-Don't-Feel-So-Good Street?

CONDUCTOR *(calling out):*   Sixth street. Sixth street!

CHICO: Sick street! At's it, boss. Let's get off. Come on, Foo-Foo.
   (Bell rings; dog barks.)

CONDUCTOR *(yelling):*   Well, get off if you're goin' to. An' take that mutt
   with you.

GROUCHO: Goodbye, conductor. We'll be back in half an hour. You wait
   right here.

CONDUCTOR: Go on, beat it!
   (Car bell rings; car leaves.)

GROUCHO: Here's the house, right on the corner. Seven-eighty Sixth
   Street. *(Dog barks.)* Ring the bell.
   (Doorbell rings; dog barks; door opens.)

MRS. DALLOWAY: What is it, gentlemen?

GROUCHO: Are you Mrs. Dalloway?

MRS. DALLOWAY: Yes.

GROUCHO: Well, trot out that five hundred bucks.

MRS. DALLOWAY: What for?

GROUCHO: For your little dog. You're going to get your Foo-Foo back.

MRS. DALLOWAY: I don't know what you're talking about. That dog isn't
   my Foo-Foo. *My* Foo-Foo was returned to me this morning. *(Thin little
   barking.)* Here he is. Come here, darling.

GROUCHO: Madam, you're being made the victim of a fraud. That mutt
   is an imposter. He's a wolf in sheep's clothing.

MRS. DALLOWAY: Why! Why your dog's back is all painted!

CHICO: Well, your face is all painted. And you don't look half as good as
   da dog. Well, yes, you do—joost about half.

MRS. DALLOWAY: Why, I was never so humiliated—

GROUCHO: Madam, if you want the advice of a lawyer, which you can
   have for only fifty dollars extra, you'll quit stalling and fork over that
   five hundred bucks.
   (Dog barks.)

MRS. DALLOWAY: Get that dog away from me! Oh! I think he bit me!

GROUCHO: Let me see . . . Oh, it's nothing at all. *(Coyly.)* At least, it's
   nothing that a kiss won't cure.

MRS. DALLOWAY: A *kiss? (Growing coy.)* Why, I hardly know you.

GROUCHO: Well, what's the difference? Come on, come on . . . Foo-Foo,
   kiss the lady.

MRS. DALLOWAY *(furious):*   Oh you! *I've stood about as much of this as I'm going to. (Little dog barks lightly.)* There . . . itsy-bitsy Foo-Foo . . . come to mama.

GROUCHO *(imitating):* Aw, now, bigsy-stingy mama, you ain't gonna cheat the drate big mans outa an itsy-bitsy five hundred buckos, are you?

MRS. DALLOWAY: Please leave here at once. I won't pay you *anything*.

GROUCHO: Not even the five hundred dollars? Well, will you give us the money we spent on the paint?

MRS. DALLOWAY: I tell you, he *isn't my dog*! Good day! *(Slams door.)*

GROUCHO: Ravelli, that's a fine Foo-Foo you found. If that dog were a skunk, I wouldn't be able to tell you two apart.

CHICO: Not even wit my *hat* on? Well, don't worry, boss. Ravelli, he's no dumbbell. Da people in da house next door is offerin a reward for a lost dog. I tinka dis is da dog.

GROUCHO: What makes you think *this* is the dog that belongs next door?

CHICO: Well, dat's where I stole him from.

(Music in strong.)

AFTERPIECE

CHICO: Lay-dees and gentlemens . . .

GROUCHO *(whispering):* Hey, Chico . . .

CHICO: What'sa matter?

GROUCHO: The people in the studio are looking at you. You've got your shoes on the wrong feet.

CHICO: Hey, dese are my feet.

GROUCHO: I know, but they aren't your shoes.

CHICO: Go way, please. I gonna make a speech.

GROUCHO: Well, that can wait. I want to tell my wife a few things.

CHICO: Hey, you can tell her when you get home.

GROUCHO: I know, but if I tell her on the radio, she can't talk back. You know, for an opportunity like that, any husband ought to be thankful.

CHICO: Tankful? I got one of doze. I got a pretty tankful of Esso, which is better dan any gasoline. And I got some Essolube, dat hydrofined motor oil, too.

GROUCHO: Very well done, Chico. But you forgot what we came out here for.

CHICO: What's dat?

GROUCHO: To say good night.

CHICO: Dat's right.

BOTH *(singing):* Good night, ladies.

(Signature music.)

FIVE STAR THEATER
PRESENTS

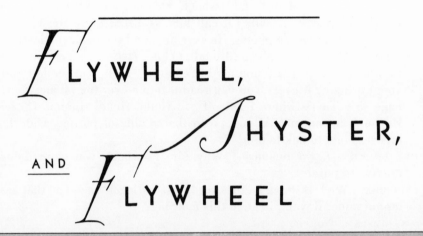

FLYWHEEL, SHYSTER, AND FLYWHEEL

EPISODE NO. 10   JANUARY 30, 1933

CAST

Groucho Marx as Waldorf T. Flywheel
Chico Marx as Emmanuel Ravelli
Miss Dimple
Mrs. Willoughby
Gombatz, fighter
Jackson, promoter
Boy
Attendant
Announcer
Referee

(*Phone rings.*)

MISS DIMPLE: Law offices of Flywheel, Shyster, and Flywheel . . . Mr. Flywheel? Just a second; I'll call him. *(Calling out.)* Mr. Flywheel! There's a man on the phone. He says he found the book you lost.

GROUCHO: Give me the phone, I'll talk to him. *Hello* . . . Yes, this is Mr. Flywheel . . . So you found my book, eh? . . . Oh, you needn't bother about bringing it over. You can read it to me over the phone. Start at page 150. That's where I left off . . . Hello! Hello! Hmmm. *(Sneers.)* He hung up on me. After I go to the trouble of putting aside legal business just to talk to him!

MISS DIMPLE: *Legal* business? Why Mr. Flywheel, you were doing a crossword puzzle.

GROUCHO: Well, is doing a crossword puzzle *il*legal? Say, has that assistant of mine, Ravelli, been in this morning?

MISS DIMPLE: No, sir.

GROUCHO: He hasn't, eh? Well, when he gets here tell him to go down to the post office and have our inkwells filled. And while he's there, he can mail this letter.

MISS DIMPLE: But this letter has no stamp on it.

GROUCHO: Well, tell him to drop it in the box when nobody's looking.

MISS DIMPLE: But, Mr. Flywheel, a stamp only costs *three cents.*

GROUCHO: For *three cents* I'd deliver it *myself.*

MISS DIMPLE: Anyway, this letter is too heavy for one stamp. I think we'd better put two stamps on it.

GROUCHO: Nonsense. If we put two stamps on the letter, it'll be still heavier. On second thought, never mind the letter. It's just a little note to my friend, Sam Jones, asking for a loan of two dollars. But poor old Sam probably has his own troubles. I hardly think he can spare it. And even if he *had* it, I think he'd be a little reluctant to lend me the dough. He's kind of tight that way. Why, I don't think he'd let me have it if he thought I was going hungry. In fact, that guy wouldn't give me a nickel if I were *starving. And he calls himself a friend* . . . the cheap, four-flushing swine. I'll show *him* where to get off at. Take a letter to that snake and tell him I wouldn't *touch* his two dollars. And if he ever comes near this office again I'll break every bone in his body.

(CHICO *heard whistling "Daffodils."*)

MISS DIMPLE: Oh, here comes Mr. Ravelli.

(*Door opens.*)

CHICO: Hello, boss. Hello, Miss Dimp.

GROUCHO: Don't try to change the subject . . . Where have you been?

CHICO: I was in da barbershop, getting my hair cut.

GROUCHO: I see. Getting your hair cut during *office* hours.

CHICO: Well, my hair *grows* during office hours, don't it?

GROUCHO: When you're in the office, I want you to concentrate on your work. You can grow your hair at home.

(Phone rings.)

MISS DIMPLE: Flywheel, Shyster, and Flywheel . . . Yes, Mr. Ravelli is here . . . Who's calling? *Who?* . . . Mr. Ravelli, there's a man on the phone who wants to talk to you. He says his name is One-Round Gombatz.

CHICO: Oh, dat's my new prizefighter. *I* talk to him. Hello, One-Round . . . How you feel? At'sa fine . . . Yeah? . . . At'sa fine . . . Hmm . . . At'sa fine . . . Goodbye. *(To* GROUCHO.*)* Boss, I just gotta some bad news.

GROUCHO: Bad news? Well, at'sa fine!

CHICO *(sadly):*   My new prizefighter, he don't feel so good today.

GROUCHO: You've got a *fighter?* Where'd you get him?

CHICO: It was easy. I was at da prizefights watchin him fight, and da other guy knock him right into my lap.

GROUCHO: Oh, so *that's* how you picked him up.

CHICO: I no pick him up. Tree ushers, dey picked him up.

MISS DIMPLE: Oh, that's too bad. Did they have to carry him home?

CHICO: Not One-Round Gombatz. Dey don't have to carry *him* home. Dey carry him to da *hospital.*

GROUCHO: Ravelli, I'd be better off if they carried *you* there instead.

CHICO: No, boss. We're gonna make plenty of money wit One-Round Gombatz. He's gonna sign a contract wit me as soon as he learns to write his name.

GROUCHO: That's a good one. Who's going to sign *your* name?

CHICO: Gombatz. He's learning dat, too. Yeah, pretty soon, boss, we gonna own a fighter.

GROUCHO: We're going to *own* him? That's fine. Run down to the pawn-shop and see what we can get for him.

CHICO: I don't know what we can get for him, but he could *use* a set of false teeth.

(Knock at the door.)

MISS DIMPLE: Come in.

MRS. WILLOUGHBY: Excuse me . . . I am Mrs. Willoughby—

GROUCHO: You come busting in here just to tell us *that?*

MRS. WILLOUGHBY: You misunderstand. I came to your office to transact some business.

GROUCHO: You want to use *my* office for *your* business?

MRS. WILLOUGHBY: No, no, no, gentlemen. I'm here for legal advice . . . I've just been left a very large estate, with considerable money. I feel

"How much have you got to invest?" Groucho as private detective Wolf J. Flywheel tries not to drool as Margaret Dumont counts out some greenbacks in this scene from MGM's *The Big Store*.

that before making some of the investments I have in mind, I ought to consult a lawyer.

CHICO: Lady, you come joosta to da right place. How'd you like to buy a prizefighter?

MRS. WILLOUGHBY: A prizefighter?

GROUCHO: Yes, madam. He punches like a mule, and if you don't believe it, I can have him punch you around a little—

MRS. WILLOUGHBY: No, no. I want to make some conservative investments. Some people have been trying to interest me in a wholesale grocery which I can buy for ten thousand dollars.

GROUCHO: What would you want with ten thousand dollars' worth of groceries? Why, you can get a regular dinner for sixty-five cents.

MRS. WILLOUGHBY: I'm talking about *investments!*

GROUCHO: Well, why didn't you say so? How much have you got to invest?

MRS. WILLOUGHBY: Oh, roughly about . . . two hundred thousand dollars.

GROUCHO: Two hundred thousand dollars? Ravelli, lock the door and tie her to that chair. Now, madam, I've got just the thing for you—a prizefighter.

MRS. WILLOUGHBY: I don't want a prizefighter!

CHICO: But lady, he's a fine, clean fighter. Why, yesterday I bring him a big piece of spoiled meat and before he eats it, he wipe it off good wit his sleeve.

GROUCHO: You brought *our* fighter *spoiled* meat? Why didn't you bring him *good* meat?

CHICO: Well, when I bring him *good* meat, he never leaves any for me.

MRS. WILLOUGHBY: I'm *not interested* in your prizefighter.

GROUCHO: Madam, if it's the price that stands in the way, you don't have to worry. You can buy our fighter on the installment plan. Ten dollars down, and ten dollars when he gets up.

MRS. WILLOUGHBY: I tell you, I *don't want your fighter.*

CHICO: Maybe she's right, boss. It'sa no use buying Gombatz unless she buys da referee, too.

MRS. WILLOUGHBY: Gentlemen, I'm afraid you're giving me bad advice.

GROUCHO: *Giving* you bad advice? Madam, you're gonna *pay* for it.

MRS. WILLOUGHBY: For the last time, gentlemen, *I don't want a prize-fighter!*

GROUCHO: All right, then, how about a pugilist?

MRS. WILLOUGHBY: Perhaps I'm not making myself clear. I distinctly said I don't want anything of that kind.

GROUCHO: Very well, let's forget about it. Mrs. Willoughby, how would you like to invest some money in a heavyweight boxer?

MRS. WILLOUGHBY: *No, no, no,* Mr. Flywheel! What I want is some high-grade, gilt-edge securities. Now, is *that* clear?

GROUCHO: Yes, *perfectly* clear. I'll get you some gilt-edge securities, but I warn you—it's going to be a prizefighter.

(*Music in strong.*)

MISS DIMPLE (*on phone*): Hello, is this Morningville 3355? . . . Mrs. Willoughby's residence? . . . Well, hold the wire. Oh, Mr. Ravelli! I got that number for you.

CHICO: At'sa fine. I talk to 'em . . . Howadoyoudo. Is Mrs. Willoughby home? . . . She is? Well, as soon as she goes out, tell her I called. Goodbye . . . What? . . . She wantsa talk to me? . . . Awright . . . Hello, Mrs. Willoughby. How you feel? . . . Oh at'sa too bad . . . You're a little pale? Aw, you crazy, you ain't a little pale. You look more like a big tub. Ha, ha, ha! Some joke, huh? . . . What? . . . Oh, your fighter? Well, don't worry about One-Round Gombatz. We got him a great fight for tomorrow night. He's gonna fight Cyclone Wilson . . . Oh, sure, Gombatz, he's in great shape. They let him out of the hospital today . . . Huh? Oh, don't worry. After the fight we send him back to the hospital . . . You bet. Goodbye.

MISS DIMPLE: Oh, Mr. Ravelli, I meant to tell you. One-Round Gombatz is on his way over. Mr. Flywheel wants you to give him his instructions for tomorrow night's fight.

(*Knock on door.*)

MISS DIMPLE: Oh! Here comes Mr. Gombatz now.

GOMBATZ (*punch-drunk goof*): Hello dere, Mr. Ravelli.

CHICO: Hello, palooka.

GOMBATZ (*slow-witted anger*): Say, what'sa idea of sayin "Hello, *palooka*"?

CHICO: Whatta you tink? Just because you're a palooka I don't say *hello?*

GOMBATZ: Aw, cut de wisecrackin an' gimme my tings. Mr. Flywheel said you'd gimme a new fightin outfit—shoes, an' trunks, an' all dat stuff.

CHICO: Awright, dope, awright. Here's you tings.

GOMBATZ: Wait a minute. Dere's only *one shoe.*

CHICO: Well, dat'sa Flywheel's idea. He told me to have your shoes half-soled, so I sold one shoe to da janitor.

GOMBATZ: An' look at dem red socks. Dey're too loud.

CHICO: Well, if da socks is loud, your feet won't fall asleep. Ha, ha, ha! Some joke . . . Come on, now. Get to work.

GOMBATZ: Whatta you want me to do?

CHICO: I tink some road work she fix you up fine. You better run down to da beach.

GOMBATZ: Hey! Dat's too far. Dat's ten miles.

CHICO: What are you talking? Ten miles! Ain't I going dere with you?

GOMBATZ: Well?

CHICO: Well, den it's only five miles apiece.

GOMBATZ: Say-y-y! I never tought of dat!

(*Door opens.*)

CHICO: Shut up, palooka, here comes da big boss, Mr. Flywheel.

GOMBATZ: Hullo, Mr. Flywheel. I wanna tell you—

GROUCHO: Just a minute, Gombatz. I had a very tough day in court.

CHICO: What happened, boss?

GROUCHO: Oh, some pawnbroker accused my client of stealing an eight-day clock and—

CHICO: Did you win the case?

GROUCHO: Well, we compromised. The pawnbroker got the clock and my client got the eight days.

GOMBATZ: Listen, Mr. Flywheel, I'm worried about dat fight. I don't tink I'm in good shape.

GROUCHO: *You'll* be in good shape. We'll let you fight in a corset. However, I'll soon find out if you're in good condition. Ravelli, get me a pair of boxing gloves. I want to take a sock at Gombatz.

CHICO: I ain't got no gloves, boss. But here's a chair you can hit him wit.

GOMBATZ: Hey, wait a minute. What'm I gonna get for dis fight?

GROUCHO: Gombatz, I was figuring it out this morning. It seems to me that . . . for my share as manager, ah . . . five thousand dollars would be reasonable. Then of course, there are also other items. Training expenses, forty cents; movie tickets for me and my girl, a dollar and a half—but *she* paid for the tickets, so we'll make that just a dollar. Now let's see. That leaves you exactly two dollars and eighty cents.

CHICO: Hey, boss, what about me?

GROUCHO: He's right, Gombatz. I think Ravelli ought to get that two-eighty.

GOMBATZ: Say, I thought there was gonna be a *tousand*-dollar purse!

CHICO: Hey, palooka, for the money *you're* going to get, you won't *need* any purse.

GOMBATZ: You mean I ain't gonna get nuttin' outa dis fight?

GROUCHO: Now don't get excited. We *bought* something for you.

GOMBATZ: Yeah? What didja buy?

GROUCHO: We bought the referee.

(*Knock on door.*)

MISS DIMPLE (*whispering*): I think it's Mrs. Willoughby.

CHICO: I'm sick of talking to her. Miss Dimp, I'll go in de odder office. You tell her I ain't in.

MISS DIMPLE: But Mr. Ravelli, she won't believe me if I tell her you're not in.

CHICO: Awright. Den I stay here and tell her myself.

(*Door opens.*)

MRS. WILLOUGHBY: Oh, gentlemen, I've been—

GROUCHO *(with exaggerated cordiality):* Well, if it isn't dear, *dear* Mrs. Willoughby! You know, Willoughby, you're getting better looking every day.

MRS. WILLOUGHBY *(kittenish):* Oh, Mr. Flywheel. You exaggerate.

GROUCHO: Well, maybe I do. But you'll have to admit that your looks couldn't get any *worse.*

MRS. WILLOUGHBY: Please, let's not indulge in personalities . . . Mr. Flywheel, I've been thinking about this curious investment you persuaded me to make. I mean that prizefighter.

GOMBATZ: You mean me?

CHICO: Shut up your face, Gombatz. She don't know what she's talking about.

MRS. WILLOUGHBY: It seems that all I do is lay out money for this pugilist. There's that hospital bill, money for trainers . . . and what about that five hundred dollars I gave you last week? I thought you were going to build a gymnasium.

GROUCHO: I thought I was going to build a gymnasium, too. But I didn't have a thing to wear to the fight, so I bought myself a couple of new suits instead.

MRS. WILLOUGHBY: That settles it. I'm through with the whole mess. I'm through with you. I'm through with this fighter . . . I'm—

GROUCHO: Don't desert him, madam! One-Round Gombatz needs a woman's care. He's just a kid at heart. You ought to see him cutting out paper dolls.

MRS. WILLOUGHBY: Mr. Flywheel, I . . . *(suddenly amazed by what she sees.)* Oh! Mr. Ravelli! Did I see you put your *hand* in my overcoat pocket?

CHICO: I tink you did. But I bet you won't see me *next* time.

GROUCHO: Ravelli, didn't I tell you that if you stopped stealing I'd give you a dollar?

CHICO: I know, boss. But I wanted to save you da dollar.

MRS. WILLOUGHBY: Mr. Flywheel. I'm willing to forget what I spent on this fighter. *That* money I consider lost. But what about the other money—the five thousand you were going to invest more conservatively?

GROUCHO: Oh *that?* You have nothing to worry about, Mrs. Willoughby. I was lucky enough to get you in on a *very sound* investment with that five thousand dollars.

MRS. WILLOUGHBY: Well, I'm glad you've done at least *one* sensible thing. Now tell me, Mr. Flywheel, just what did you do with the money?

GROUCHO: Madam, I took that five thousand dollars and bet it on One-Round Gombatz.
(Music in strong.)

(Open in fight auditorium, crowd yelling: "Knock him out!" "Oh, boy, what a sock!" etc.)
JACKSON *(promoter):*   Hey, Slim, it looks like this fight won't last long. Run down to the dressing rooms and tell the boys on the next bout—Gombatz and Wilson—to get ready.
BOY: Okay, Mr. Jackson.
(Yelling from fight fans continues for about five seconds, fading; boy knocks on door.)
GROUCHO *(from within):*   Come in.
BOY *(door opens):*   Gombatz-Wilson fight is next, Mr. Flywheel. You better get your man ready.
GROUCHO: Just a minute, son. You run down the hall and tell Cyclone Wilson to come in for a short rehearsal.
BOY: I don't know what you're talking about. But you'd better hurry up.
(Door opens; distant cheering heard. Door shuts; cheering ends.)
GROUCHO *(like a coach):*   Just listen to that crowd cheering. They love you, Gombatz. They want you to win . . . But win or lose, they hope you get killed.
GOMBATZ: Huh?
GROUCHO: Gombatz, in a little while you'll be out in front of that crowd, fighting . . . Your little mother will be at home at the radio—
GOMBATZ: I ain't got no mother.
GROUCHO: Well, you've got a *radio*, haven't you? Just remember, Gombatz, we've done everything we could for you. We've paid the referee to give you the decision. We've paid the other fighter to let you win. Now, Gombatz, the rest is up to you. And don't forget, my boy—I've got great plans for you. If you win this fight, I'm going to let you fight my landlord.
GOMBATZ: What do I want to fight your landlord for?
GROUCHO: You can fight him for the rent. *(Knock on door.)* Come in.
CHICO *(opens door):*   Hullo, boss. Hullo, Gombatz.
GROUCHO: Oh, here you are, Ravelli. Late again. Didn't I tell you to get here early?
CHICO: Well, you see, boss, I left my house too late to come early.
GROUCHO: Well, why didn't you leave your house early?
CHICO: I couldn't. It was too late to leave early. Anyway, on da corner a

fellow lost a nickel, and a whole bunch of kids was standing around looking for it.

GROUCHO (*contemptuous*):   And I suppose *you* were standing there *watching* them!

CHICO: No, I was standing on da nickel.

ATTENDANT *(opens door):*   Gombatz-Wilson fight next. Three minutes to go!

GROUCHO: Three minutes? Ravelli, get busy. Run over to Cyclone Wilson's dressing room and ask him to wear red fighting trunks so Gombatz will know him when they meet in the ring.

CHICO: Wilson? Hey, he ain't here yet. He's home sleepin.

GROUCHO: What? We've only got three minutes to go and Wilson isn't even up!

CHICO: Sure he's up. Tree o'clock in da morning I saw da janitor carry him up.

GROUCHO *(excited):*   Jumping Jupiter! Do you think he was *drugged?*

CHICO: Sure, he was drugged. Da janitor drugged him up tree flights of stairs.

GROUCHO: Quick! Gombatz, run out and find Jackson, the fellow who's promoting this fight.

(Door opens.)

GOMBATZ: Here comes Jackson.

JACKSON: Mr. Flywheel! I've got terrible news. Wilson has run out on us . . . We can't find him anyplace.

CHICO: Don't worry, Mr. Jackson. Gombatz is much better when he fights alone.

JACKSON: I tell you, we got to get someone to fight Gombatz.

GROUCHO: I'd go in there and fight him myself, but I've got my glasses on. Ravelli, it's up to you.

CHICO: Hey, boss, you got anodder pair of glasses? I don't wanna fight him either.

GROUCHO: Come on! You're going in to fight for Wilson.

CHICO: Awright, I'll go in and fight for Wilson if somebody else go in and fight for me.

GROUCHO *(commanding): Put on these gloves!*

CHICO: I don't need da gloves, boss. My hands ain't cold.

(Door opens.)

ATTENDANT: Mr. Jackson, the crowd's hollering for the fight.

GROUCHO: Okay, we're ready. Gombatz, don't forget—you go down for a count of four in the third round. Ravelli, you go down for the count of three in the fourth round. *(Confused).* No, you go down for the count of four . . . no, the count of three . . . Well, never mind. The referee has all the instructions. Open the door . . . Let's go.

(As they start for ring, cheering is heard.)

CHICO: Hey, boss, let's walk down de odder aisle . . . Here comes Mrs. Willoughby.

MRS. WILLOUGHBY: Oh, Mr. Flywheel . . . I've been looking for you. The seat you got me is right behind a post.

GROUCHO: Well, come back tomorrow and we'll have the post torn down.

MRS. WILLOUGHBY: Now, what about that money wagered on Gombatz . . . my five-thousand-dollar bet?

GROUCHO: Your bet? Madam, you've made your bet, now lie in it.

MRS. WILLOUGHBY: But, Mr. Flywheel—

GROUCHO: Aw, stop crabbin' . . . run along. I've got to look after these two bums. Now, Ravelli, you're going into that ring and you may never come out again. Before you step through those ropes, is there anything you want to say?

CHICO *(solemnly):*   Yes, boss, I'd like to ask a question. What building has tree hunnerd stories and no elevator?

GROUCHO: I give up, Ravelli. *What* building has three hundred stories and no elevator?

CHICO: A public library. Ha, ha, ha! Some joke.

GROUCHO: Come on! Get in that ring. And don't forget, you're supposed to take a beating. But while you're taking it, just remember . . . I'll be out there cheering.

(A couple of gongs.)

ANNOUNCER: Main bout . . . Ten rounds to a dee-cision . . . In this corner, One-Round Gombatz, the terror of the East Side. *(Cheers.)* And in *this* corner, Emmanuel Ravelli, the pride of the gas-house district. *(Cheers.)*

GROUCHO: Wait a minute! . . . Ravelli—is that a horseshoe I feel in your glove?

CHICO *(laughs):*   Sure, I put it dere for good luck.

(Gong sounds.)

GROUCHO: All right, boys, go to it. If you need me, I'll be at the microphone.

(Cheers, and cries of "Geev it to heem," "Put out the lights, they want to be alone!")

GROUCHO *(jumping to microphone):*   Well, folks, here's Flywheel, bringing you a round-by-round account of the big fight. Zowie! There they go! . . . Gombatz is leading, but Ravelli is close behind . . . chasing him around the ring. Ravelli's in a corner . . . He's fighting back savagely . . . thus proving the old adage that if you get a rat in a corner, he'll fight back. Boy, oh boy, oh boy, what a battle! . . . Folks, I'm going to put the mike in the ring so you can hear the grunting

of the gladiators, the pounding of leather against leather . . . *Listen to this.*
(Silence.)

CHICO *(whispering):*   Hey, Gombatz, what'sa matter wit you? . . . You hit me dat time.

GOMBATZ *(whispers):*   Well, what about you? You got me all covered with blood.

CHICO *(whispers):*   I know, but it's *my* blood. *(Calling out.)* Hey, Mr. Flywheel, I'm tired . . . stop the round.

GROUCHO *(calling back):*   We can't, Ravelli. The timekeeper can't find his watch.

CHICO: Tell him to look in my back pocket.

GROUCHO *(taking mike back):*   Hear that, folks? What a battle . . . *What a battle* . . . Gombatz looks great . . . Gombatz is down . . . He looks even *better* when he's down . . . listen to the count.

REFEREE: One . . . two . . . *(Count continues.)*

GROUCHO *(yelling):*   Get *up*, Gombatz . . . Get up!

CHICO *(calling back):*   Leave him lay dere, boss. He's got till ten to get up . . . and it's only half past nine now.

REFEREE: . . . six . . . seven . . .

GROUCHO: Get up, Gombatz! How am I going to explain to Mrs. Willoughby?

REFEREE: Nine . . . ten . . . OUT! The winner is Emmanuel Ravelli!
(Audience cheers.)

GROUCHO *(angrily):*   Ravelli, Ravelli, come here!

CHICO: Well, I guess I did pretty good, huh, boss?

GROUCHO: I thought you were supposd to *throw* the fight.

CHICO: I *did* trow it . . . *(Suddenly realizing.)* Oh yeah, boss, I made a mistake. I trew it da wrong way. Say, here comes Mrs. Willoughby. I tink I better go back into da ring.

MRS. WILLOUGHBY: Mr. Flywheel, this is terrible! You've tossed away my five thousand dollars with your preposterous bet.

GROUCHO: Now, just calm youself, Mrs. Willoughby. I've got a very pleasant surprise for you. I didn't bet your five thousand dollars after all.

MRS. WILLOUGHBY *(delighted):*   You didn't?

GROUCHO: No, I used the money to buy myself a little house in the country.

MRS. WILLOUGHBY: You bought a house with *my money?*

GROUCHO: Yes—you must come out and visit me some time. But if I catch you stepping on the grass, I'll have you arrested.
(Music in strong.)

AFTERPIECE

CHICO: Mr. Chairiman, Mrs. Chairiman, all da little chairimen, and *ladeez and chairimen!*

GROUCHO: Chico, are you talking English or Chairmen?

CHICO: Oh, boy, dat was some speech I joosta made, huh?

GROUCHO: You'll be all right, Chico. I think it's just a case of overwork. What you ought to do is take up golf for six months to get your mind off work, and then after six months you can take up work to get your mind off golf.

CHICO: I don't like golf. I can't drive a golf ball so good, but I can drive my boss *witout* an automobile.

GROUCHO: You drive your boss without an automobile?

CHICO: Sure. I drive him crazy. Ha, ha, ha! Some joke!

GROUCHO: No, no, Chico! You were supposed to say something about driving *with* an automobile. Then *I* could get in a few words about the product. *Now* do you remember?

CHICO: Don't tell me. I wanna guess.

GROUCHO: Not *guess. Guessoline.* And of course, Esso is better than any gasoline. And you know that Essolube is that famous hydrofined motor oil.

CHICO: *Now* can we say it?

GROUCHO: Say what?

CHICO: Good night to the peoples?

GROUCHO *(fatherly):* I think so.

BOTH *(singing):* Good night, ladies.

(Signature music.)

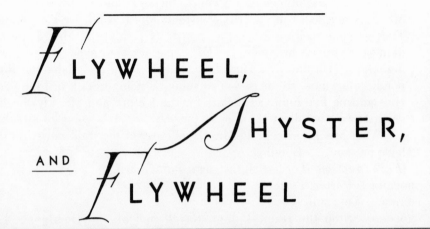

FLYWHEEL, SHYSTER, AND FLYWHEEL

EPISODE NO. 11   FEBRUARY 6, 1933

CAST

Groucho Marx as Waldorf T. Flywheel
Chico Marx as Emmanuel Ravelli
Miss Dimple
Porter
Train conductor
Lady
Pullman conductor
Voice
Clubwoman
Mahatma Rahpondi
Khayam

(Phone rings.)

MISS DIMPLE: Law offices of Flywheel, Shyster, and Flywheel . . . No, Mr. Flywheel isn't in . . . His assistant, Mr. Ravelli, isn't in, either. They've gone to Pine City on a case . . . Oh, it's *you*, Mr. Melford. I didn't recognize your voice . . . Of *course*, it's your case they're working on . . . Uh-huh . . . That fake Indian lecturer, Mahatma Rahpondi, you know, the man you're suing, is going to talk in Pine City. He's getting five hundred dollars for the lecture and Mr. Flywheel is going to try to collect the money for you . . . He's going to attach it . . . Yes, Mr. Flywheel and Mr. Ravelli are on the train now with the legal papers . . . Goodbye.

(Fade in to sound of locomotive, which dies down.)

GROUCHO: Porter! Porter!

PORTER: Yes, suh.

GROUCHO: Stop the train. I think Ravelli fell off . . . He's gone. I'm afraid I've lost Ravelli.

PORTER: You mean that gemmeman dat got on de train with you? You don't need to be afraid. He's on the train someplace. He didn't fall off.

GROUCHO: Well, that's what I was *afraid* of.

PORTER: There's the gemmeman you talkin' about.

GROUCHO: Ravelli, where have you been? Where did you get that black eye?

CHICO: At'sa no black eye, at's a birthmark. I got into da wrong berth . . . Hey look, boss, here comes da conductor for da tickets.

GROUCHO: Ravelli, I've got only a half-fare ticket for you. Quick! Roll up your pants, look like a child of eight . . . No, better make it *seven*. You've got to look dumb . . . just be yourself. *(Very pleasantly.)* How do you do, conductor?

CONDUCTOR: Get your tickets out. I want to punch your tickets.

GROUCHO: I'll tell you what, *I'll* keep the tickets and *you* can punch Ravelli.

CONDUCTOR: Come on, *give me those tickets*.

CHICO: Hey, boss, I tink he wants da tickets.

GROUCHO: Hush, little Emmanuel, or father will knock you unconscious. Here are your tickets.

CONDUCTOR: What's the half-fare ticket for?

GROUCHO: That's my little boy, Emmanuel. Kiss the nice conductor, Emmanuel, but first take that chewing tobacco out of your mouth.

CONDUCTOR *(skeptically):* Say, how *old* is he?

GROUCHO: Emmanuel's just eight.

CHICO: At'sa right, conductor, I joosta ate and I no like da food on dis train.

CONDUCTOR: Do you mean to say that this great big lummox is only eight years old?

GROUCHO: He *is* a repulsive-looking child. I'm taking him out now to try to lose him in the country.

CONDUCTOR: Say, if that kid's eight years old, I'm Christopher Columbus.

CHICO: Hey, you no foola me, you ain't Columbus. Columbus is in Ohio. *(Laughs.)* Some joke.

CONDUCTOR *(menacingly):* Say you—

GROUCHO: Pay no attention to the nasty mans, Emmanuel. Anyway, I think it's time for your bottle.

CHICO: Dere's nothing left in dat bottle; we killed it dis morning. Now, pop, can I kill da *conductor?*

CONDUCTOR: What you ought to give that boy is a few lessons in good behavior.

GROUCHO: Good behavior? Why, do you realize that it was *because* of his good behavior that they let him out of prison?

CONDUCTOR: *Prison?* I thought you said he was eight years old.

CHICO: Well, I *was* eight years old, but dat was *before* I went to prison.

CONDUCTOR: I *thought* so. You're going to pay the full fare for this guy.

GROUCHO: You mean to say you expect a full fare for a halfwit?

CONDUCTOR: Absolutely. It's a good thing you've got a round-trip ticket; I'll just keep the whole thing. *(Receding.)* And you're lucky I don't throw you both off. *(Conductor exits.)*

CHICO: Hey, boss, you put me in a fine fix. You take me to Pine City and den I won't be able to get back.

GROUCHO: Ravelli, you don't know what a break that is for me. I think you're going to love Pine City. It's out in the farmlands. Why, you could become a gentleman farmer—if only you were a gentleman.

CHICO: I no wanna stay dere. I no like da country.

GROUCHO: Well, if you don't like the country, why don't you go back where you came from? Porter! Porter!

PORTER: Yes, suh.

GROUCHO: What time do we get to Pine City?

PORTER: We get there at six-fifteen tomorrow morning, suh.

GROUCHO: Well, tell the engineer to slow down. I never get up that early.

CHICO: I got a better idea, boss—you tell de engineer to stop da train. I can't sleep when dere's bumping.

GROUCHO: Say, the train's beginning to run smoother. We must be off the tracks. Porter, I'm sleepy. How about making up our berth?

PORTER: It's all ready for you, suh. I'll get the ladder, so you can get in the upper berth.

CHICO: Do we gotta sleep on dat shelf? Why can't we sleep downstairs?

PORTER: Well, suh, the lower berth costs more than the upper.

GROUCHO: Just a minute, porter, are you trying to tell us that the lower is higher than the upper?

CHICO: No, boss. I explain it to you. He means da higher is lower dan da lower—but if we want to hire a lower for tonight, we'll have to go a little higher.

PORTER: Yas, er . . . but if you excuse me, suh, I think you better climb up in your berth 'cos I gotta take the ladder down to the end of the car . . . some passengers *there* wants to use it.

GROUCHO: Why take the ladder to them? Let them come here and use it. Come on, Ravelli, hop up there.

(Pause while climbing up.)

CHICO: Hey, boss, I can't sleep in dis little hammock.

GROUCHO: That's no hammock, that's for your clothes. Here, help me up.

CHICO: Ooop, atta boy. Boss, I wonder who lives downstairs . . . Hey, it's an old lady. I tink I play a joke on her. I hit her with a shoe . . . Watch!

(LADY screams.)

CHICO *(laughs)*:   Hello dere, lady. My name's Ravelli. Me and Mr. Flywheel, we just moved in da second floor . . . Maybe a little later we'll drop in on you.

LADY: Sir! How dare you? Porter! Porter!

PORTER: Yes, ma'am. You call me?

LADY: Yes, there's an idiot in the upper berth bothering me.

GROUCHO: Madam, I resent that. There are two of us up here.

PORTER: You gemmemums better stop making noise, 'cos this lady can't sleep.

GROUCHO: Well, we can't sleep either if she's going to yell every time she gets hit with a shoe. Ask her to be quiet. And wake us up in time to get off at Pine City.

PORTER *(receding)*:   Yes, suh. Goodnight, suh.

CHICO *(groans))*:   Oooh, boss.

GROUCHO: What's the matter, Ravelli? (CHICO *groans again.*) Are you sick? Are you sick? Speak to me. Speak to me!

CHICO *(in strangled tones)*:   Water . . . water.

GROUCHO: Ravelli, have you been poisoned? What's the matter? Speak man, speak!

CHICO: Water . . . water!

GROUCHO: I'll get you water. I'll jump down.

(Crash; loud squawk from LADY.)

LADY: Oh! He stepped on my face.

GROUCHO: Madam. How was I to know it was your face? There's a man dying up there. Where's that water cooler?
(Various voices: "What's the matter?" "What's happened?" "What's wrong?" "Who's sick?")

GROUCHO: Keep your heads, everybody. Stay where you are. I have the situation under control. *(Sound of water pouring.)* I'm coming, Ravelli. Be brave. Flywheel is coming with water. Out of my way, madam, I'm on an errand of mercy.

CHICO *(dying):* Water . . . water . . . water.

GROUCHO *(approaching):* Here I am, Ravelli. Here I am, pard. Can you hold the cup? Here, *I'll* hold it for you. Drink, Ravelli, drink. *(Sound of drinking.)* There you are. How do you feel, Ravelli? Are you all right?

CHICO: At'sa fine, boss. I feel great now.

GROUCHO: You feel great? *What* a relief! Now tell me, what was the matter?

CHICO: Oh, boy, was I tirsty!
(Music in strong)

(Sound of train whistle; interior train sounds, die down; sound of snoring.)

PORTER: Wake up, suh. Wake up. Time to get up. *(Loud snores again.)* It am five minutes to six.

CHICO *(drowsily):* What you say?

PORTER: Ah said it was just five to six.

CHICO: Five to six? Say, dat's a pretty close score. You come back when da game's over and tell us how it came out.

PORTER: But, mister, you said you all wanted to get off at Pine City. We gets there in ten minutes.

CHICO: Ten minutes? Hey, boss, boss! Wake up! Wake up! *(Sound of snoring.)*

CHICO: Wake up!

GROUCHO *(awakening with a start):* Huh . . . what? . . . What's all the noise? Ravelli, why didn't you wake me up? You know I can't sleep when there's noise.

PORTER: Say, you gemmemums better hurry up and get dressed, or you miss the station.

GROUCHO: How far does this train go, porter?

PORTER: Well, it goes all the way to California, but we won't be there for three days.

GROUCHO: That's fine. Wake me up when we get there.

PORTER: Yes, er, but ain't you all supposed to get off at Pine City? Here comes the Pullman conductor to pick up the tickets for your berth.

CHICO: Da conductor? Hey, porter, run to da dining car and get me an apple.

PORTER: An apple?

CHICO: Sure. An apple a day keeps da conductor away. *(Laughs.)* Catch on?

CONDUCTOR: Show your pullman tickets, please. *(Raising his voice.)* How many are there in that upper berth?

GROUCHO *(calling down):*   There's only one up here, conductor. Here's our ticket.

CONDUCTOR: Only *one* up there, eh?

CHICO: He's right, conductor. There's only one of us up here . . . me and Flywheel.

CONDUCTOR *(angry):*   Yeah? Well, I heard about you guys from the other conductor. Come on with the other ticket.

GROUCHO: All right, all right. Here's *three* tickets. They're for Mahatma Rahpondi's lecture in Pine City.

CONDUCTOR: *I don't want these tickets.* You're getting off at Pine City if I have to *put you off in your pajamas.*

CHICO: You can't put us off in our pajamas. We're wearing *nightshirts* . . . I guess *dat'sa* telling 'im where to get off, heh?

GROUCHO: You've got it all wrong, Ravelli. He's telling *us* where to get off.

CONDUCTOR: *Come on!* Get on your clothes!

GROUCHO: By the way, where *are* my clothes? Ravelli, where did you put my pants?

CHICO: I put all our clothes away so nobody can steal 'em. I put dem up here in dis little closet.

GROUCHO: Well, don't sit there. Get them out. We're almost at the station.

CHICO *(excited):*   Hey, boss, dey gone! Dere's nothing in dis closet.

GROUCHO: Closet? Closet? That's the ventilator! Ravelli, you threw our clothes out the window!

CHICO: Oh, I *tought* dere was a lot of room in dat closet.

(Train whistles and slows down.)

VOICE *(away):*   All off for Pine City!

CONDUCTOR: Come on, you two. You get off here.

GROUCHO: But, conductor, what about our clothes?

CONDUCTOR: Clothes or no clothes, you get off. Come on, out you go.

(Crash and sound of scuffling; train stops, air brakes whistle; confusion away.)

CHICO: Hey, who you pushin? Who you pushin?

CONDUCTOR: I'm pushing *you!* Do you want to make something out of it?

GROUCHO: *I'd* like to make something out of it. I'd like to make a pair of pants out of it!

CHICO: Your pants didn't *last* so long, eh, boss? You know, *I* know how to make a pair of pants last.

GROUCHO *(tolerantly):* All right, Ravelli, just *how* do you make a pair of pants last?

CHICO: Make the coat first. *(Laughs.)* Boss, I tink I die laughing.

CONDUCTOR: *Get off those steps.*

(Bang, crash.)

VOICE *(away):* All aboard!

(Train starts, gathers speed and start to fade; one long whistle.)

CHICO: Hey, Flywheel, listen to dat whistling. I tink the engineer musta lost his dog! Say, dat conductor, he put us off pretty fast, eh, boss?

GROUCHO: He certainly did. He must be a lightning conductor. Ravelli, we got to get some clothes. We can't find an Indian Mahatma in our nightshirts.

CHICO: You're right, boss. I joosta look in my nightshirt and dere's no Indian dere. Hey . . . look. Here comes a lady!

GROUCHO: A lady? Hide, Ravelli, hide. Not behind *me*, you dope.

LADY *(approaching):* Gentlemen, gentlemen. This is indeed a pleasure.

GROUCHO: I guess she doesn't have much fun at home.

LADY: Oh, Mahatma Rahpondi! I'm the chairman of the reception committee. I think your costume is too lovely for words.

GROUCHO: Yeah? Well, I'll trade it with you for a pair of pants.

LADY: You know, Mahatma, you don't look at all like I thought you would.

GROUCHO: Well, to tell you the truth, madam, I didn't expect to look like this either.

LADY: You know, Mahatma, your lecture isn't scheduled until ten o'clock. How would you and your secretary like to walk over to the clubhouse with me for something to eat?

CHICO: Aw, no, lady, we no gonna walk over to eat. We gonna *run*.

GROUCHO: Ravelli, you can't eat that way. Look at yourself. Your *face* is clean, but how did your *hands* get so dirty?

CHICO: My hands? From washin my face.

(Music in strong.)

. . .

LADY: Come right in, gentlemen. This is the anteroom to the lecture hall. If you look through this drapery, you can see the crowd. *(Murmur of crowd voices.)*

GROUCHO: If you look through *this* drapery, you can see me.

LADY: Gentlemen, if you're thirsty, there's something to drink on that table.

CHICO: Lady, I can't drink dis punch. It's full of lumps.

GROUCHO: Ravelli, you're at the wrong table. You're drinking out of the goldfish bowl.

LADY: Oh, I almost forgot. I'd better give you the money now. Here it is —five hundred dollars.

GROUCHO: Sorry, madam, I can't take your money.

LADY: You can't take it?

GROUCHO: No, I have no place to put it. On second thought, give me the money. I'll keep it in Ravelli's mouth.

LADY: Oh, by the way. Since I have to introduce you, what city in India did you say you came from?

GROUCHO: Hmm. What cities *are* there in Indian?

CHICO: I know one, boss—Indianapolis.

GROUCHO: Indianapolis isn't in India. You're thinking of Minneapolis.

CHICO: Dat's what I always say. Minneapolis a day keeps da doctor away.

GROUCHO: That isn't what you said *last* time. You said conductors.

LADY *(puzzled):* Mahatma, evidently your secretary isn't from India.

CHICO: Sure I'm an Indian. Listen. *(Does Indian war whoops.)*

LADY *(annoyed):* *Please*, gentlemen! Now, if you'll wait here, Mahatma, I'll go out and introduce you. As soon as you hear me say "Ladies, now I present the great Mahatma Rahpondi," you come out and deliver your lecture.

GROUCHO: Lecture? Why can't I tell 'em a story? Why, only last week I got a hundred dollars for a story I wrote.

CHICO: A hunnerd dollars? Who from, boss?

GROUCHO: From the post office. They lost the story and I collected the insurance.

(Murmur of voices heard from lecture hall.)

LADY: The audience is getting restless, Mahatma. I'd better go out and announce your lecture. And remember, you're to come out as soon as I say, "Ladies, now I present the great Mahatma Rahpondi." *(Receding.)* Get ready, I'm going to announce you.

(Sound of applause outside; dies down.)

GROUCHO: This is a fine mess. I never expected to have to talk to five hundred woman without clothes.

CHICO: Five hunnerd women without clothes? Let *me* talk to 'em.

GROUCHO: Control yourself, Ravelli. Mahatma Flywheel has never shirked his duty.

LADY *(away):* Ladies, now I present the great Mahatma Rahpondi.

GROUCHO: I'll bet she tells that to everybody. She said the same thing to us only a minute ago.

LADY *(away):* Ladies, now I present the great Mahatma Rahpondi.

CHICO: Hey, she's saying it over again.

GROUCHO: That's right. She's probably stuck. Maybe if she keeps on saying it, everybody will go home and I won't have to make my speech.

LADY *(very loud): Ladies, now I present the great Mahatma Rahpondi.*

GROUCHO: Say, this is getting pretty dull. I could do better than that myself.

LADY *(approaching excitedly):* Mahatma! Mahatma! The ladies are waiting to hear you. Please come out on the stage.

CHICO: What are you gonna do, boss?

GROUCHO: I'm going to be honest with these ladies. They gave me the five hundred, I'm going to give them the lecture. Ravelli, you stay here and see that the back door stays open. Madam, lead the way.

(Sound of applause; GROUCHO *is heard in distance saying, "Ladies of Pine City . . . "; fade into knock on door.)*

CHICO: Awright, come in.

KHAYAM: This way, sire.

CHICO: Hey, you guys! You can come in, but you gotta keep quiet. My boss is making a speech.

KHAYAM: Out of our way, fool! This is the great Mahatma Rahpondi, who sees the past, present, and future.

CHICO: At'sa fine, joosta so he don't see Flywheel.

MAHATMA: Silence, dog. Khayam, you have our ceremonial robes with you?

KHAYAM: Yes, sire.

MAHATMA: Then we'll change our clothes right here.

CHICO: You're gonna take off your clothes? Hey, at'sa fine. Dey won't fit me, but maybe dey'll fit Flywheel.

KHAYAM: Step aside, fool! Do you not know that the great Mahatma is sacred?

CHICO *(hoarse whisper):* Awright, I no tell nobody. I can keep a sacred.

MAHATMA: Come, Khayam. I am in my ceremonial robes. Let us leave our traveling clothes here.

KHAYAM: Yes, sire. We will go and greet our public.

CHICO: Hey, wait a minoot. I got an idea. I take your clothes and I go out and tell da ladies you're ready.

KHAYAM: He is right, sire. We cannot walk out on the platform unannounced. Very well, fellow, go announce us. And be careful of our clothes.

CHICO *(receding):*   Sure, boss. I'll treat your clothes like dey was my own.

GROUCHO *(voice fades in):*   As I was saying, girlies, the traveling salesman—

CHICO *(interrupting):*   Hey, Mr. Flywheel.

GROUCHO *(calling back):*   Shut up, Ravelli, let me finish this lecture. *(In lecture voice.)* And as I was saying, girlies, the traveling salesman then asked the farmer where he could sleep. And the farmer sent him to a hotel. *(Laughs.)* Of course, a story like that isn't any good if you have to clean it up. Now are there any questions?

CHICO: I got a question, boss. It's a riddle. What's da best way to keep a fish alive out of water?

GROUCHO: You got me there, Ravelli. What *is* the best way to keep a fish alive out of water?

CHICO: Boss, I don't know either. That's why my fish died.

GROUCHO: Hey, shut up. I'm going into a trance. *(In voice of medium.)* I hear voices of the past . . . from another world. What do they bring before my eyes?

CHICO: Two pair of pants, boss.

GROUCHO: Right. I will now saw a woman in half. If you will return at this time next Monday I will try to put her together again. *(Heckling from women.)* Meanwhile, can one of you ladies lend me a silk hat? No? Well, maybe you can lend me a pair of pants.

CHICO *(whispers):*   Hey, Mister Flywheel. Mister Flywheel!

GROUCHO *(in voice of medium):*   Ah, I hear the voice of little Periwinkle talking to me from another world.

CHICO: Boss, we gotta get outta here.

GROUCHO: You're telling *me*, Periwinkle.

CHICO *(excitedly):*   Hey, da real Mahatma is here. We gotta beat it.

GROUCHO: Hold everything, Ravelli. And now, ladies, we come to the most sensational part of my lecture. The famous Mahatma Rahpondi disappearing act. Throw me those pants and let's go, Ravelli.

CHICO: Dis way, boss.

(From here to the finish angry murmurs grow louder, building to a climax.)

CHICO: Hey, look out! Here comes da real Mahatma.

GROUCHO: The Mahatma? Quick—Mahat, ma coat, ma pants, we're leaving.

VOICES: Arrest that Mahatma! Throw out that faker!

GROUCHO: Hey, Mahatma, your public is calling for you.

MAHATMA: I am ready. But first we must receive the five hundred dollars.

CHICO: Don't worry, Mahat. You gotta dat five hundred bucks right in your pants pocket. But Flywheel's wearing your pants. *Goodbye!* (*Music in strong.*)

AFTERPIECE

CHICO: Ladies and gentlemens, I—(*suddenly*)—hey, where you going, Groucho?

GROUCHO: I'll be right back. I just want to call my wife and tell her I won't be home for dinner. Some friends are dropping over and if I show up, there will be fourteen at the table, and fourteen is an unlucky number.

CHICO: Hey, you crazy! *Tirteen* at da table—*dat's* an unlucky number.

GROUCHO: Well, fourteen is even unluckier when your wife has prepared only enough dinner for *three*.

CHICO (*expansively*):   Oh yeah, *I* know. Today's your birthday. Well, I no forget. I'm gonna buy you a nice blue fountain pen wit a little gold band and your name on it.

GROUCHO: That's mighty nice of you, Chico, but strangely enough, I already have a fountain pen exactly like that.

CHICO: Well, you ain't got it any more. I just dropped it out da window.

GROUCHO: Hmm. (*Sneer.*) You dropped it out the window. Why, if there weren't so many people here, I'd knock you for a loop.

CHICO: Loop? You mean Essolube.

GROUCHO: *No*, Essolube is that famous hydrofined motor oil, and of course you know about Esso, which is better than any gasoline.

CHICO (*in manner of singer vocalizing*):   Mi, mi, mi, mi.

GROUCHO: What are you *doing*, Chico?

CHICO: I'm tuning up to sing good night.

GROUCHO: Well, let's do it.

BOTH (*singing*):   Good night, ladies. Good night, ladies. (*Signature Music.*)

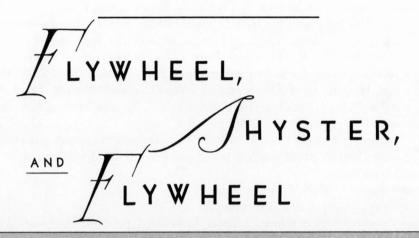

FIVE STAR THEATER
PRESENTS

FLYWHEEL, SHYSTER, AND FLYWHEEL

EPISODE NO. 12   FEBRUARY 13, 1933

CAST

Groucho Marx as Waldorf T. Flywheel
Chico Marx as Emmanuel Ravelli
Miss Dimple
Salesman
Bardwell
Dealer
Crookley
Slim
Buck
Bailiff
Judge
Clerk
District Attorney

(Sound of typewriter; phone rings.)

MISS DIMPLE: Law offices of Flywheel, Shyster, and Flywheel . . . No,
Mr. Flywheel isn't in. He's in court, trying your husband's case . . .
Uh-huh . . . *(Door opens.)* Just a second . . . *here* he is . . . *(To*
GROUCHO:*)* Oh, Mr. Flywheel. Here's Mrs. Watson on the phone.

GROUCHO: *Good.* I was just going to call her. *(Jovial.)* Hello, Mrs. Watson. How are you? That's fine . . . Your husband? Oh yes, I meant to
tell you . . . He got five years in prison . . . But *don't worry*, Mrs. Watson. I've got a very pleasant surprise for you. I'm going to knock ten
percent off my bill . . . Goodbye. Miss Dimple *(hangs up phone)* . . .
Miss Dimple, put down that telephone book. This office is no place for
a bookworm.

MISS DIMPLE: Yes, Mr. Flywheel.

GROUCHO: Any mail this morning?

MISS DIMPLE: Yes, there's a letter from the typewriter company. They
say you haven't paid for the typewriter yet.

GROUCHO: Why should *I* pay for the typewriter? You're the one who uses
it.

MISS DIMPLE: But Mr. Flywheel, I—

GROUCHO: Never mind. Take a letter to those cheap chiselers. Ah . . .
Gentlemen . . . I never *ordered* that typewriter. *(Pause.)* If I did, you
didn't send it . . . If you sent it, I never got it . . . If I got it, I paid for
it . . . And if I *didn't*, I won't. Best regards . . .

MISS DIMPLE: Anything else, Mr. Flywheel?

GROUCHO: Yes . . . Love and kisses. But don't send them. They're for
you . . . And now . . . take a letter to the Peerless Building Supply
Company. *(Pompously.)* Gentlemen, I refuse to accept a penny less
than fifty dollars for the electrical fixtures in my office. In case I do not
hear from you, I shall conclude you do not wish to pay more than *twelve*
dollars . . . So, in order to lose no time, I shall *accept* the twelve dollars.

MISS DIMPLE: But Mr. Flywheel! You can't sell those fixtures. They belong to the landlord.

GROUCHO: Well, he ought to be glad. I'm only *selling* his fixtures so I can
pay him his rent . . . Say, tell that assistant of mine to wrap up the
chandelier.

MISS DIMPLE: Mr. Ravelli? He isn't in yet.

GROUCHO: Well, when he comes in you better tell him to take out more
fire insurance. I'm gonna fire him on Saturday.

(Door opens.)

MISS DIMPLE: Why, *here* he comes. Hello, Mr. Ravelli.

CHICO: Hello, Miss Dimp. Hello, boss.

GROUCHO: Ravelli, do you realize you're a half hour late?

CHICO: I couldn't help it, Mister Flywheel. I fell down a whole flight of stairs.

GROUCHO: Well, does it take you a half hour to fall down one flight of stairs? Anyway, I don't believe that story.

CHICO: Awright, if you don't believe *dat* story, I tell you anodder one . . . I came late because we had a little money trouble at our house.

MISS DIMPLE: Money trouble, Mr. Ravelli?

CHICO: Yeah, my little brudder he swallowed a nickel.

MISS DIMPLE: Really? What did you do?

CHICO: Well, next week's his birthday anyway, so I let him *keep* da nickel.

GROUCHO: Hey, *stop jabbering* and clean out my desk.

CHICO: I cleaned out da desk yesterday . . . Dat's where I got da nickel. (*Knock on door.*)

MISS DIMPLE: Come in.

GROUCHO: Ravelli, I'm going into my private office. When I come back, I don't want to catch you loafing.

CHICO: Awright, If you don't want to catch me loafing you better *whistle* before you come in. (*Knock on door.*)

MISS DIMPLE: I said *come in*. (*Someone enters; to* CHICO:) Mr. Ravelli, I think he's selling something.

SALESMAN (*very breezy*):   Well, well, well. Just what I like to see . . . a busy little office, with nice bright smiling faces.

CHICO: Aw, *shut up.*

SALESMAN: Ah . . . er . . . er . . . Excuse me, you see, I represent the Excelsior House-to-House Merchandise Company . . .

CHICO: Well, dere's nobody here by dat name. Dis is Flywheel's office.

SALESMAN: You don't understand. If you'll just give me a moment of your time, I'd like to show you a few choice values in neckties, safety razors, hair tonic . . . Say, let me *tell* you something about this tonic. It's the *real* thing.

CHICO: Awright, gimme a taste.

SALESMAN (*trying to be patient*):   No, no. Now before I began using this tonic, my hair was getting *pret-tee* thin.

CHICO: Well, it don't look so fat now.

SALESMAN: You just *try* it once. We guarantee every bottle.

CHICO: Oh, the *bottle* looks all right, but I tink the stuff inside is no good . . . Hey, how much is that necktie?

SALESMAN: *Now* you're talking. I'm going to sell you that tie for a dollar.

CHICO (*incredulous*):   A *dollar?*

Chico, Zeppo, Groucho, and Harpo surround a helpless microphone in this photograph, circa 1933.

SALESMAN: Yes, brother, and it's a steal at that price.

CHICO: Hey, if I'm gonna *steal* it, I can get it for nothing.

SALESMAN: A dollar and the tie is yours. Why, I paid ninety-five cents for it myself.

CHICO: Well, if *you* paid only ninety-five cents, why should *I* pay a dollar?

SALESMAN: Well, the nickel's my profit. You know, I got a *wife* to support.

CHICO: You tink I'm gonna help support *your* wife? Nobody supports *my* wife—not even me . . . *I* tell you what—you leave da necktie, and I'll send you ninety-five cents in care of da Woodlawn Cemetery.

SALESMAN *(indignant):*   Woodlawn Cemetery? That's not my address.

CHICO: Well, it will be by da time I send you da ninety-five cents. *(Laughs.)* Some joke, eh?

SALESMAN *(furious):*   Aw, I can see I'm wasting my time here.

CHICO: Well, it took you a long time to find it out.

SALESMAN: Goodbye!

(Door slams.)

GROUCHO *(coming from other door):*   Did I hear someone come in?

CHICO: Yeah, a wise guy. He wanted a nickel for his wife.

GROUCHO: A nickel for his wife? Well, that's cheap enough . . . Was she good-looking?

(Knock on door.)

CHICO: Awright, come in.

(Door opens.)

BARDWELL: Mr. Flywheel. Permit me to introduce myself. I'm Bertram T. Bardwell. I suppose you've been hearing about my charity work and my fight against crime?

GROUCHO: Oh yes, I've been hearing about it for a number of years, and I'm getting *pretty sick* of it too.

BARDWELL: Why, er, er . . . I happened to be in court this morning when your thrilling address to the jury sent that man to prison for five years, where he belongs.

GROUCHO: *My* speech sent him to prison? *(Laughs.)* That's a good one on the jury. I was *defending* that guy.

BARDWELL: Just a moment, Mr. Flywheel. Let me ask you a question.

CHICO: Hey, I got a question too, boss. What animal likes dirt, always plays in the mud, and eats anyting?

GROUCHO: I know, Ravelli, it's *you.*

CHICO *(disappointed):*   Awww . . . somebody told you.

BARDWELL *(annoyed):*   Mr. Flywheel, my organization is waging an intensive fight against crime in this city, and I feel that you're a man who can help us drive the crooks out of town.

CHICO: *Hey!* Why should we *drive* 'em out? Let 'em *walk.*

GROUCHO: Nice work, Ravelli.

BARDWELL: You see, gentlemen, my committee is determined to rid the city of Public Enemy No. 1, Big Joe Crookley. Although Crookley himself is in hiding, he has crime organized like a big business. In fact, some of his gangsters have an office only two doors from here.

GROUCHO *(dramatically):* Bardwell, you came to the right man. There isn't room enough in this town for gangsters and me, Waldorf T. Flywheel. However, we're putting up a *big hotel* in the spring.

CHICO: Boss, you leave it to me. Ravelli'sa plenty smart. I go next door and tell dem gangsters to move.

GROUCHO: An excellent idea, Ravelli. But wait a minute. You've got your hat on wrong.

CHICO *(from door):* Well, I don't know which way I'm going yet. And say, if you see my brudder, you tell him to wait.

GROUCHO: *I* don't know your brother.

CHICO: I never tought of dat. Awright, den tell him *not* to wait. Goodbye. *(Door closes.)*

BARDWELL: Mr. Flywheel, I can see that you're a man of action. Some time later I'd like to interest you in our *charity* work *too.*

GROUCHO: Charity work . . . hmm . . . Bardwell, I'm not the kind of fellow who likes to talk about his good deeds, but it may interest you to know that I've been sending *pretty large*-sized checks to various charities, and not even the *charities* know that the money came from me.

BARDWELL *(mildly questioning):* But Mr. Flywheel, I don't understand. Couldn't they tell by the name on the checks?

GROUCHO: No, no, that's how *modest* I am. I didn't even *sign* the checks.

MISS DIMPLE: Why, Mr. Flywheel, What's this? Someone just put a note under the door.

GROUCHO: Well, pick up the door and get it.

MISS DIMPLE: It says . . . why, *good heavens.* It's from Crookley's gangsters. They've kidnapped Mr. Ravelli for meddling in their affairs.

BARDWELL: *Kidnapped* him?

MISS DIMPLE: Listen to this: "Unless you send us ten thousand dollars, we will kill Emmanuel Ravelli."

BARDWELL: They'll *kill* him? Mr. Flywheel, what are you going to do?

GROUCHO: Keep cool, Bardwell. Miss Dimple, take a letter to Big Joe Crookley. Dear Joe: Received yours of the fifth inst., in which you state that unless I send ten thousand, you will kill Ravelli . . . I haven't got

the money, but the proposition sounds very attractive. Send further details.
(*Music in strong.*)

(*Knock on door; second knock is louder.*)

SLIM (*hoarse whisper*):   Who's dere?

CROOKLEY: Open dat door. It's me, Crookley.

SLIM: Okay, chief, I was scairt it was de cops.

CROOKLEY: You don't have ta be scairt. De cops won't ever find dis place. Where's dat fella Ravelli?

SLIM: Inside eatin'. Dat's all he's been doing since we grabbed him off a week ago. Hey, chief, is dat lawyer Flywheel comin' trough wid de ten grand?

CROOKLEY: I tink so. He's on his way over here now.

SLIM: Say, what if he brings de cops?

CROOKLEY: Don't worry. He won't go shootin' off his mouth. I told Flywheel what's good for him. And now I tink I'll have a little *talk* wid Ravelli.

SLIM: Right in here, chief. (*Opens door.*)

CROOKLEY: Hey, Ravelli. (*Sound of moving dishes.*) *Ravelli, put dat dish down.* I'm talkin' to you.

CHICO (*cheery*):   Oh, hello, Mister Crookley. Sit down, have a piece of pie. I just had tree pieces and I'm afraid to *eat* any more.

CROOKLEY: *What?*

CHICO: Sure, if I eata too much pie maybe I get pie-areah.

CROOKLEY: Look here, mug. We been treatin' you pretty nice. You know why? Because if Flywheel don't show up with that ten thousand bucks today, you ain't gonna live very long.

CHICO: Hey, you *crazy*? I feela fine. I tink I eat some more pie.

(*Knock at door.*)

CROOKLEY: Who is it?

SLIM: Say, chief. There's a guy comin' in. I tink it's dat Flywheel.

CHICO: Flywheel? Don't let him in till I hide da pie.

CROOKLEY: Bring him up here.

SLIM (*from distance*):   Okay chief . . . This way mister.

CROOKLEY: Well, Flywheel, I—

GROUCHO: Cut out the formalities. When are you gonna kill Ravelli?

CHICO (*alarmed*):   Hey, boss. Is *dat* what dey wanna do?

GROUCHO: Don't be alarmed, Ravelli. I've fixed everything. I've written a farewell note to your wife, and I've sent flowers to your sweetheart. I've also arranged for a nice, quiet little funeral. There'll be eight carriages for your family and a motorcycle for your friends.

CROOKLEY: Quit your stalling, Flywheel. Did you raise that money?

GROUCHO: Oh, I *raised* the money all right, but unfortunately I had to spend it on Ravelli's funeral.
(*Knock on door.*)

CROOKLEY: Come on in.

SLIM: Hey, chief, I gotta talk to you.

CROOKLEY: Awright, I'll be right wid you. Listen, Flywheel, you an' Ravelli stay right here . . . Come over here, Slim. What is it?

SLIM (*hoarse whisper*): Chief, Butch just called and said we better lay low on deze guys. The cops is all steamed up about de kidnapping . . . and dey kinda suspeck *you.*

CROOKLEY (*whisper*): Okay I'll try to grab off the dough, an' t'row 'em both out.

SLIM (*whisper*): Yeah . . . (*Receding.*) Maybe you'd better, chief.
(*Door opens and closes.*)

CROOKLEY: Look here, Flywheel, forget the ten grand. You give me five thousand dollars and Ravelli can leave here.

CHICO: Sure, *I* like to leave here. It's a very nice house to leeve in.

CROOKLEY: Well, what about that five thousand?

GROUCHO: Five thousand? Crookley, can you make it *three* thousand?

CROOKLEY: All right, I'll make it three thousand.

GROUCHO: That's talking, Crookley. Now if you'll make it *two* thousand, I'll make it *one* thousand . . . I haven't got the thousand in cash, but I'll give you my note for thirty days, and if it isn't paid by then you can keep the note.

CROOKLEY: Listen, you guys. I'm gonna give you exactly five minutes to make up your minds. When I come back, you're either gonna fork over the dough, or it'll be curtains for both of you. Get me? *Curtains for both of you. (Receding.)* Now think fast.
(*Door closes.*)

CHICO: Boss, we're in a tight fix. Whata we gonna do?

GROUCHO: First, Ravelli, I think I'll have a piece of this pie. Take some yourself.

CHICO: Tanks, boss, I'm full.

GROUCHO: Well, put some in your pockets.

CHICO: Dey're full too.
(*Knock on door.*)

CHICO (*whispering*): It's Crookley!

GROUCHO: Crookley? He's probably bringing us the curtains.

CROOKLEY (*outside door*): Better hurry up, you guys. You got just two more minutes.

GROUCHO: Ravelli, I've got to give this a lot of thought.

CHICO: Hey, boss, I gotta idea—

GROUCHO: Be quiet! I can't hear myself talk.

CHICO: Dat's all right. You ain't missin anyting. *(Suddenly.)* Say, it's *cold* in dis room.

GROUCHO: It *is* kind of chilly. See what that thermometer says.

CHICO: Aw, you can't believe dat thermometer. One day it'sa sixty; next day it'sa sixty-five—it'sa no good.

GROUCHO: Well, the thermometer ought to be kept at seventy.

CHICO: I can fix dat easy. I just light a match under it. Watch. *(Scratching of match heard.)*

GROUCHO: Ravelli! Be careful of those draperies!

CHICO: Hey, boss! Dey're burning. Oh boy! Look at dat fire.

GROUCHO *(calling out):* Oh, Crookley!

CROOKLEY *(from outside):* Whata you want?

GROUCHO: Can I use your telephone?

CROOKLEY: You tink I'm *crazy?*

GROUCHO: Answer my question first. Can I use your phone?

CROOKLEY *(sneering):* *An' let you call the cops,* I suppose.

GROUCHO: Not at all, I just wanted to call the fire department . . . and ask them where the nearest alarm box is . . . Crookley, I don't want to seem like an old gossip, but your house is on fire.

CROOKLEY *(outside):* What! What's dat? *(Door opens,* CROOKLEY's *voice approaches mike.)* Whata you guys been up to? . . . Slim! Buck!

SLIM and BUCK *(from outside; excitedly):* What's up?! What's wrong?!

CROOKLEY: Quick! Bring some water.

GROUCHO: You can make mine *ginger ale.*

CHICO: And I'll take some *pie.* Hey, I know a song about pie. *(Begins singing.)* Good Pie Forever . . .

GROUCHO: Say, Crookley, why don't you call the fire department? I know all the boys at Hook and Ladder 78. And tell 'em to bring along a deck of pinochle cards.

CROOKLEY: Nothin' doin'! I don't want no cops or firemen snoopin' around here.

CHICO: He's right, boss. Dere's no usea callin' da fire department now. Da place is on fire *already.*

GROUCHO: Ravelli, open the windows! Open the windows! This smoke is beginning to get me.

CHICO: Yeah, dere's too much smoke. You better put out your cigar.

SLIM: Boys! The fire's spreading fast. Better start running.

CHICO: Hey, Flywheel! I know a good place to run to.

GROUCHO *(excited):* *Where,* Ravelli, *where?*

CHICO: To run to. Toronto, Canada. *(Laughs.)* Hot stuff, eh, boss?

(Fire engines and police siren approach.)

CROOKLEY: Slim! Buck! It's the fire department—the cops too! Watch your step.

(Smashing of door; breaking of glass.)

VOICES: This way! . . . I think there's somebody in there!

SLIM: Gee, Crookley! You better duck.

CROOKLEY: Don't worry, Slim. De cops around here won't recognize me. Listen, Flywheel. No cracks about me being Joe Crookley, if you know what's good for you.

GROUCHO: Count on me, Crookley, old boy. I'll see that your name isn't mentioned . . . Oh, Policeman! Policeman!

OFFICER: What is it?

GROUCHO: I want you to meet Emmanuel Ravelli, the fellow who started the fire—

OFFICER: What?

GROUCHO: And before I forget it—when you report this fire, don't mention Joe Crookley's name, because there's a warrant out for his arrest.

(Excitement.)

(Music in strong.)

(Buzz of conversation; gavel knocking.)

BAILIFF: Silence in the court . . . His honor, the judge . . . Everybody rise.

CLERK *(drones):*   Hear ye, hear ye, hear ye, the municipal court is now in session and stands until adjournment.

(Buzzing of conversation.)

JUDGE *(raps gavel):*   What's the next case, clerk?

CLERK: It's the preliminary hearing, your honor, in the case of Joseph "Big Joe" Crookley, charged with the kidnapping of Emmanuel Ravelli.

JUDGE: Proceed with the hearing.

BARDWELL: Your honor, please . . . one moment.

JUDGE: What is it, Mr. Bardwell?

BARDWELL: Your honor, I'd like to say a few words in behalf of the Citizens Committee Against Crime.

JUDGE: Of course, Mr. Bardwell.

BARDWELL: My organization regards this case as tremendously significant, and wants to commend Mr. Flywheel here in open court for his noble, fearless, public-spirited activities in bringing that archenemy of the people, Joe Crookley, to justice.

(Applause.)

GROUCHO: Thanks, folks. Thanks . . . I've waited and struggled a long time for this honor. Why, I began life as a barefoot boy—

CHICO: At'sa nuttin, boss. When *I* was born, I was *naked.*

(*Gavel pounding.*)

JUDGE: Gentlemen, the court *wants this case to proceed.*

GROUCHO: Very well, your honor, if you and Ravelli will keep your traps shut, I'll proceed . . . As I was about to say, before the judge horned in, when I was a wee bit of a tot, I was left an orphan—

CHICO: You was left an orphan? What did you do wit it?

(*Gavel pounding.*)

JUDGE: Mr. Flywheel! The court must ask you to sit down. Now, Mr. District Attorney, proceed with the hearing.

DISTRICT ATTORNEY: If your honor please, the state's attorney's office has been requested by the Citizens Committee to let Mr. Flywheel conduct the prosecution, because of his splendid work in tracking down Joe Crookley.

JUDGE: Very good. Joseph Crookley, where's your attorney?

CROOKLEY: Judge, I offered to pay plenty, but I couldn't get a lawyer in dis town with nerve enough to take my case. I even offered to pay as high as five thousand bucks.

GROUCHO (*jumping up, touched*): Just a minute, your honor. I'm talking now—*not* as Flywheel, the lawyer, but as Flywheel the man—the defender of human rights. In a court of justice, your honor, every man has certain inalienable rights. Every man has a right to the advice and counsel of a lawyer—*especially* if he has five thousand dollars. Crookley, *I'll* take your case. Trot out the five thousand clams.

(*Murmur in court.*)

JUDGE: Mr. Flywheel, the court was under the impression that you were going to *prosecute* Crookley.

GROUCHO: Well, I was under that impression too . . . until I heard about the five thousand. Let's start the case. The first witness for the defense is Emmanuel Ravelli.

JUDGE: Mr. Flywheel, you can't call Ravelli for the defense. He's the man who says he was kidnapped.

GROUCHO: Oh, so *that's* the story he's been spreading! Well, he's a *liar.*

CHICO: Hey, whata you mean, callin me a liar?

GROUCHO: You're a *liar.* I didn't call you a liar . . . See, your honor? He wouldn't tell the truth under oath. Ravelli, get up there and take the oath.

CHICO: Okay, boss.

(*Gavel.*)

CLERK: Order! Order! Emmanuel Ravelli, do you promise to tell the truth, the whole truth and nothing but the truth?

CHICO (*disturbed*): Hey, you want me to lose my job?

GROUCHO: Emmanuel Ravelli, where were you born?

CHICO: I wasn't born, I had a stepmotter.

JUDGE: Come, come, Ravelli. Tell the court your birthday.

CHICO: What *you* wanna know for, Judge? You ain't gonna buy me nuttin.

GROUCHO: He's right, your honor. You haven't bought a thing since you bought your place on the bench.

JUDGE: See here, Mr. Flywheel, the court considers that remark most unnecessary and vicious.

CHICO: Hey, judge, dat's what I got for my birthday.

JUDGE: You got *what?*

CHICO: Vicious—I got a telegram *with very best vicious. (Laughs.)* Some joke!

(Gavel pounding.)

JUDGE: Please, please! Let's get on with this hearing! *Mr. Ravelli, will you kindly state your age!*

CHICO: Sure, judge, I'm joosta twenty-eight.

JUDGE: Twenty-eight? Why, you said you were twenty-eight when you appeared here in court *two years ago!*

CHICO: Well, when Ravelli says sometin in court, he sticks to it.

GROUCHO: There you are, your honor. I guess that'll hold you for a while. I make a motion that you dismiss the charges against my client.

CHICO: Atta boy, boss. I second da motion.

(Gavel pounding.)

JUDGE: *Motion denied!* Mr. Flywheel, have you any other witnesses? I don't think this one is intelligent enough to understand court proceedings.

GROUCHO *(laughs):* Did *you* hear that, Ravelli? Your honor, just to show you what a *fool* you're making of yourself, I'm going to give my witness an intelligence test. Ravelli, what's the first letter of the alphabet?

CHICO: Give me a hint.

GROUCHO: Ravelli, is that question so hard for you?

CHICO: No, the question's easy. But the answer's hard.

GROUCHO: All right, I'll try you on another one. Where was the Declaration of Independence signed?

CHICO: At the bottom.

GROUCHO: Right!

(Gavel pounding.)

JUDGE: *The court cannot help but regard all this as irrelevant and immaterial!* Mr. Flywheel, you now claim that Crookley did *not* kidnap Ravelli? How is it that Crookley was found at the scene of the crime, where he was holding Ravelli as prisoner?

GROUCHO: Frankly, judge, that's got me kind of puzzled too . . . Say, maybe it was *Ravelli* who kidnapped *Crookley.*

(*Murmur of excitement in court.*)

JUDGE (*pounding gavel*): Silence in court.

GROUCHO (*becoming eloquent*): Your honor, in a case as important as this, we cannot be swayed by our emotions. Nothing matters but *hard, cold facts!* (*Becoming tearfully emotional.*) Remember, I too have a baby . . . I met her in a dance hall . . . and your honor, I couldn't go home and face my baby if I felt that I was defending a guilty man.

JUDGE: Just a moment, Mr. Flywheel. The prosecution hasn't been heard from yet. Do you expect to talk much longer?

GROUCHO: Certainly. The longer I talk, the longer my client stays out of jail. Your honor, Joe Crookley is really a fine boy at heart. He's very good to his family . . . he never goes home. Why, for a *whole year* he didn't talk to his wife. And *why* didn't he talk to his wife? Because he didn't want to *interrupt* her. Your honor, I demand a habeas corpus.

JUDGE (*astonished*): A habeas corpus?

GROUCHO: You needn't be embarrassed, judge, I don't know what it means either.

JUDGE: Mr. Flywheel, you've wasted enough of the court's time. Mr. District Attorney, call your witnesses.

DISTRICT ATTORNEY: Your honor, the state has been surprised in this case. We had counted on Emmanuel Ravelli as *our* witness. And since he's shifted to the defense, I'm afraid we have no case.

JUDGE: In that event, I am forced—much against my will—to dismiss the charges and release the defendant, Joseph Crookley. Crookley, you may go.

CROOKLEY: Tanks, judge. (*Receding.*) So long dere, Flywheel.

GROUCHO: Judge, he's leaving the courtroom! Bring him back!

JUDGE: Bring Crookley back? What for?

GROUCHO: He owes me five thousand dollars.

CHICO: Aw, you crazy, boss. We owe *him* five tousand dollars.

GROUCHO: We owe *him* five thousand dollars?

CHICO: Sure. He had ten tousand dollars in his pocketbook . . .

GROUCHO: Well?

CHICO: Well, I got his pocketbook.

(*Music in strong.*)

AFTERPIECE

ANNOUNCER: Keep your seats, people! The show isn't over. The mad Mr. Flywheel and his insane assistant, Emmanuel Ravelli, have gone for the night, it's true. But Groucho and Chico Marx are still very much with us, and are going to give us something brand new. They've concocted a little act entitled "The Marx Brothers Motoring." Scene: an Esso service station, anywhere from Maine to Texas. Characters: Groucho, Chico, and an Esso dealer. Here it is!

(*Sound of car approaching; sounds of horn, grinding brakes.*)

CHICO: Whew! *Boy*, dat was fast driving! Groucho, you know you was goin seventy miles an hour?

GROUCHO: Well, I was in a hurry. The brakes on this car don't work, and I wanted to get here before we had an accident.

CHICO: Well, whata we gonna do here?

GROUCHO: Get our oil changed, of course.

CHICO: Why you wanna change it? Don't you like it anymore?

GROUCHO: Sure I like it. But we've gone a lot of miles with it, and it's dirty.

CHICO: Dirty? Den what makes you think dey'll change it for you? Dis fellow here won't want your dirty oil.

GROUCHO: Maybe you're right. I think I'll take some free air instead. Oh, dealer!

DEALER: Yes, Sir. Shall I change your oil? It pays to change to Essolube.

GROUCHO: That's fine. How much does it pay?

DEALER: It pays in value, sir. Essolube is the first five-quality oil ever made. Until it was developed, folks had to choose between two types of oil—

CHICO: I know—olive oil and castor oil.

DEALER: No, I mean two types of *motor* oil. One had three of the five qualities a modern oil needs. The other had two of them. But there was no oil with all *five*. Then, after many years of work on a great invention so important that it won the Nobel prize, my company perfected *hydrofining*. And produced *Essolube*, the first five star oil.

GROUCHO: It sounds too expensive. Better fill up the car with castor oil instead.

DEALER: But it *isn't* expensive. That's another amazing thing about Essolube. It's *regular-priced*. Cost you less to buy than the oil you've got in here *now*, probably.

CHICO: At'sa fine.

DEALER: Will you take a couple of quarts for your car?

GROUCHO: A couple of quarts for this car? Sold! Give us the oil and the car is yours.

(*Signature music.*)

FIVE STAR THEATER
PRESENTS

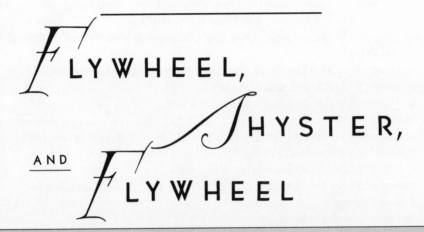

FLYWHEEL, SHYSTER, AND FLYWHEEL

EPISODE NO. 13   FEBRUARY 20, 1933

CAST

Groucho Marx as Waldorf T. Flywheel
Chico Marx as Emmanuel Ravelli
Miss Dimple
Abner Flywheel
Farmer
Squire Higbee, banker

(*Phone rings.*)

MISS DIMPLE: Law offices of Flywheel, Shyster, and Flywheel . . . Yes, Mr. Flywheel's in now, but I can't disturb him.

GROUCHO: What do you mean you can't disturb me? You're disturbing me already.

MISS DIMPLE: Mr. Flywheel, there's a man wants to talk to you.

GROUCHO: Tell him I can't pay him.

MISS DIMPLE: But you don't know who it is.

GROUCHO: No matter who it is, I can't pay him.

MISS DIMPLE: I'll tell him to call later. Hello . . . You'd better phone Mr. Flywheel tomorrow. All right, goodbye.

(CHICO *approaches humming "Daffodils."*)

MISS DIMPLE: I think that's your assistant, Mr. Ravelli, coming in.

(*Door opens.*)

CHICO: Goodbye, boss.

GROUCHO: Goodbye? What do you mean goodbye? You just *got* here.

CHICO: Sure. But I gotta leave again. I gotta go back to my brudder's wedding.

GROUCHO: Your brother's wedding? Why, I let you off at noon *yesterday* to go to that wedding. Is he getting married *again?*

CHICO: Oh, no, boss. Da wedding was lasta night, but da party's still going on.

MISS DIMPLE: Why, Mr. Ravelli. That must be some wedding party, to last two days.

CHICO: Whatta party! *Everybody's* dere—and, oh boy, are dey having fun! Everybody kissing da pretty bride. And oh boy, she's *some* grapefruit!

MISS DIMPLE: A grapefruit? Don't you mean a peach?

CHICO: Naw, she's a grapefruit. I squeezed her and she hit me in de eye. (*Laughs.*) Some joke, eh?

MISS DIMPLE: Did you wear full dress?

CHICO: Huh?

MISS DIMPLE: You know. Did you have on a soup and fish?

CHICO: Sure, all over my vest.

MISS DIMPLE: Oh, I don't mean that. How was you *brother* dressed?

CHICO: I don't know. I didn't see him.

MISS DIMPLE: Your *brother's wedding*, and you didn't see him?

CHICO: No. Dat crazy brudder of mine, he never showed up.

(*Knock on door.*)

MISS DIMPLE: Come in.

ABNER (*opens door.*): Good morning, folks, good morning.

MISS DIMPLE (*whispering*): He looks like a farmer.

ABNER: I just come in to the city and—

GROUCHO *(cordially):* Well, sit down. Take off your coat. Take off your whiskers and stay awhile.

ABNER: Sir, my name is Flywheel.

GROUCHO: Flywheel? *Your* name is Flywheel? Ravelli, lock the door. This man is an imposter.

ABNER: But I tell you gentlemen . . . that . . .

GROUCHO: Quick, Ravelli! Unmask him.

CHICO: Okay, boss.

ABNER *(squawks):* Hey, hey . . .

CHICO: Say, boss, da joke is on us. Dose are real whiskers. Dey won't come off.

GROUCHO: Those are real? . . . Come out from behind those bushes, farmer, or I'll shoot.

ABNER *(strained voice):* You skairt me when you pulled my whiskers. You skairt me so I can hardly talk.

CHICO: At'sa right, boss. He can hardly talk above a whisker.

ABNER: See here, I'm Abner Flywheel from Hickory Corners. I come to the city to look up my long-lost nephew, who's a lawyer.

GROUCHO: You mean you're Abner Flywheel . . . one of the Joplin, Missouri, Flywheels?

ABNER: I never heard of that branch of the family.

GROUCHO: Did you run away to Australia at the age of three and die over there?

ABNER: No, I never ran away from anyplace.

GROUCHO: Well, were you the Flywheel who was thrown into jail for smuggling Chinamen into China in 1891?

ABNER: No, I certainly was not. I never was in jail.

CHICO: You never was in jail? Hey, boss, he can't be a real Flywheel.

GROUCHO: You're wrong, Ravelli. He's passed the test. It's my long-lost Uncle Abner. Get Uncle Abner a chair. Let him rest his feet. Give him some farm relief.

ABNER: Well, this is more like it. So you're little Waldorf. Well, well, well, you certainly haven't changed much.

GROUCHO: Oh, come now, Uncle Abner. I don't look as young as all that.

ABNER: No, I wouldn't say that, but we always did say 'round home that you were the stupidest child in the family.

CHICO: At'sa your uncle, awright. He knows you.

GROUCHO: Listen, Ravelli, he's an uncle on my father's side. And if he's on my *father's* side, I'll fight on my *mother's* side.

ABNER: Just the same, you was a cute little brat, Waldorf. I can remember how you was able to walk around before you was a year old.

CHICO: At'sa nothing. I know a little dog dat can walk, and he's only six months old.

GROUCHO: Yes, but a dog has *twice* as many *legs*.

ABNER: Say, Waldorf, who's this little fellow? I don't like his face.

CHICO: Hey, mister, if I could see *your* face, I wouldn't like it, either.

ABNER: Waldorf, I'm getting old and I want someone to carry on my work at the farm after I'm gone.

CHICO: At'sa fine. Where are you going?

ABNER: Wal, to make a long story short, I'm looking for an heir.

CHICO: You're looking for an heir? Why don't you get some hair tonic?

ABNER: No, I mean an heir to leave my farm to. I figured on leaving the farm to you, Waldorf—providing you know how to take care of it.

GROUCHO: Don't worry about me, Uncle Abner. You just lie down and die and we'll do the rest.

ABNER: You see, I was going to leave my farm to your cousin Nicholas, but he's no good. I'm going to cut him off without a penny.

GROUCHO: What? You're going to leave Nicholas penniless?

ABNER: Yes, Nicholas worked on the farm for forty-three years and then he up and ran out on me.

GROUCHO: That's just like us Flywheels—*always* on the go.

ABNER: Remember, Waldorf, before I leave my farm to you, you gotta come out and show me you can really run it. But I know you city folks. *(Chuckles.)* I bet you don't even know a Jersey cow when you see one.

GROUCHO: I don't know a Jersey cow? Why, that's a cinch.

ABNER: Well then, how can you tell it's a Jersey cow?

GROUCHO: That's easy—All you have to do is look at the *license* plates! *(Music in strong.)*

(Train heard leaving.)

GROUCHO: Well, Ravelli . . . this is the Hickory Corners station all right, but I don't see any town.

CHICO: Yeah, boss. I wonder why dey built da railroad station so far from da town.

GROUCHO: I don't *know,* unless it was because they wanted the station near the railroad. Say, I wonder where Uncle Abner lives. I'm getting tired watching you carry those two heavy bags.

CHICO: At'sa fine, boss. How about *you* carrying dem?

GROUCHO: Oh, I'm not *that* tired.

CHICO: I tought your Uncle Abner was going to meet us at da station.

GROUCHO: He *said* he'd meet us . . . he said he'd meet the five-fifteen train on Saturday . . . and we came on the *five-fifteen.*

CHICO: But today ain'ta Saturday. It'sa Monday.

GROUCHO: I know. But it wouldn't have hurt him to *wait*.

(*Sound of horse and wagon approaching.*)

CHICO: Hey, look. Here comes a guy on a wagon. Maybe *he* knows where your Uncle Abner lives.

(*Horse and wagon come up.*)

GROUCHO: Hey, mister. Mister.

FARMER: Whooooooa there, Molly.

GROUCHO: I say, my good man, can you tell us where Abner Flywheel lives?

FARMER: Sure, I know where that old skinflint lives.

GROUCHO: Stranger, when you call my Uncle Abner a skinflint, *smile*.

FARMER: Your uncle? (*He laughs.*)

GROUCHO: I said smile, not laugh.

FARMER: Well, that uncle of yours is an ornery cuss. His house is over yonder.

GROUCHO: How much will you charge us to take us there?

FARMER: Oh, I reckon twenty cents.

GROUCHO: How much to take the bags?

FARMER: The bags? Oh, they can go free.

CHICO: At'sa fine. You take da bags and we'll walk.

FARMER: Oh, smart alecks. Well, you can *walk* with your old bags. Giddap, Molly.

(*Sound of horse's hooves receding.*)

GROUCHO: Ravelli! Ravelli! There's a garter snake!

CHICO: I don't need it, boss. My sock's ain't comin down . . . Come on. We go over dis fence.

GROUCHO: But don't you see that sign? It says "Keep out. This means you."

CHICO: It means me? How did dey know *I* was comin?

(*Distant bellowing.*)

GROUCHO: Run, Ravelli, run. It's a bull. He's going to charge you!

CHICO: He no can charge me. I didn't buy nuttin.

(*One enormous bellow.*)

CHICO: Hey, boss! He's comin after me!

GROUCHO: Quick! Let's jump over this fence!

CHICO: I'm comin.

(*Heavy splash, grunting of pigs.*)

GROUCHO: Ah, we're saved! (*Sputtering.*) Oh, Ravelli, Ravelli! . . . We jumped into a pigsty! . . . Where are you, Ravelli? . . . Oh, here you are. I'll help you up. (*Pig goes "oink oink oink."*) Pardon me, pig, I thought you were Ravelli.

CHICO: Here I am, boss.

GROUCHO: How do I know it's you? I made one mistake already.

CHICO: Sure it's me. Ask me someting, I *prove* it.

GROUCHO: That sounds fair enough. Well, how much is three and eight?

CHICO *(laughs):* At'sa easy. Tirty-eight.

GROUCHO: That proves it. You're Ravelli, all right. *No* pig could be that dumb. Come on, we've got to get out of this pigsty.

ABNER *(approaching):* Hey! Hey! What are you men doing in my pigsty. Stop or I'll shoot.

CHICO: Boss. Boss! It's your Uncle Abner, and he's got a gun.

GROUCHO: Uncle Abner! . . . Uncle Abner! Don't shoot. Don't shoot! It's Waldorf, your nephew. You can't shoot your nephew. Blood is thicker than water, and Ravelli's thicker than both.

ABNER: Wal, I'll be switched.

GROUCHO: That suits me, Uncle Abner. Ravelli, find me a switch.

CHICO *(sotto voce):* Hey boss, he'sa pretty mad. I better be nice to him. *(Aloud.)* Hey, Flywheel's uncle, dose are fine pigs you got in dat sty.

ABNER: I'll say they're fine pigs. Those pigs cost ten dollars apiece.

CHICO: Ten dollars a piece? How much for a whole pig?

ABNER: The whole pig costs ten dollars.

CHICO: Yeah? How much you gonna sell him for?

ABNER: Wal, the price has gone down. I expect to sell him in the spring for ten dollars.

CHICO: You buy the pig for ten dollars. And den you'll sell him for ten dollars. Hey, how can you maka money dat way?

GROUCHO: He doesn't make money, Ravelli. But he has the pleasure of the pig's company all winter.

ABNER: Here we are, Waldorf. There's the farmhouse you're going to inherit if you show me that you know something about farming.

GROUCHO: Just leave it to me, Uncle Abner. You won't know this place in a couple of days.

ABNER: Make any improvements you like, Waldorf. But take your time. Remember, Rome wasn't built in a day.

GROUCHO: Well, I wasn't in charge of that job. You'd better look out, Ravelli. I think that cow's following you.

ABNER: Shucks, that cow's going to the barn to get milked. You better go to the barn too.

CHICO: We go to da barn? Hey, we don't wanna get milked.

ABNER: There's the pail, Mr. Ravelli. Let me see what you know about milking a cow.

CHICO: Awright. Here, cow . . . here's da stool. Go ahead and sit down. *(Cow moos.)* Awright, stand up. See if I care . . . Come on, nice cow, here's your bucket . . . fill 'im up wit milk.

ABNER: Try using *two* hands on that cow. It saves time.

GROUCHO: Ridiculous, Uncle Abner—that cow's got plenty of time.

ABNER: You boys can look the place over while I go in and fix up a snack for supper. *(Receding.)* Make yourself to home.

CHICO: Awright, I finish up wit da cow. *Hey*, Bossy. *Hey*, Bossy!

GROUCHO: What do you want, Ravelli? And cut out the baby talk.

(Cow moos, kicks over bucket, and runs out.)

CHICO: Look boss, da cow kicked da bucket.

GROUCHO: That's too bad. I didn't even know she was sick.

CHICO: She'sa no sick. She's running away. Quick, Flywheel, let's jump on dis hay wagon and chase her.

GROUCHO: Okay, Ravelli, step aside. Let *me* in that driver's seat.

CHICO: Awright, *I* get up here on da hay.

GROUCHO: Be *careful* up there, you might knock over all that hay.

CHICO: Say, it's fallin down. Watch out! Watch out!

(Sound of hay coming down.)

ABNER *(approaching):* What's goin' on out here? What's the idea of knockin' all that hay over? It took me two hours to load that wagon.

CHICO: Don't worry, I put it back again.

ABNER: Well, never mind. Better come and eat your supper first.

CHICO: Awright, I go and eat supper, but my boss, Flywheel, he won't like it.

ABNER: Oh, come on and eat.

CHICO: I'll come, but I tell you my boss won't like it.

ABNER: Well, why not?

CHICO: Cause he's under the hay.

(Music in strong.)

(Knock on door.)

ABNER: Come in, there!

BANKER: Hello there, Abner.

ABNER: Howdy, Squire Higbee. Ain't seen you 'round these parts in quite a spell.

BANKER: Well, been so busy at the bank. But I was comin' by this way an' thought I'd see how you're feelin', and kinda talk over a liddle business.

ABNER: Certainly, Squire. I been figurin' to drop over to see you. You know my mortgage payment's due next week and—

BANKER: Well, I ain't worried about that. You always was good pay.

ABNER: Thanks, Squire, but this time I'd like to ask a little extension. 'Tain't that I ain't got the money, but my nephew, Waldorf Flywheel,

Trade advertisement for *Horse Feathers*, September 1932.

    is sorta runnin' the farm now, an' he's hankerin' after makin' some improvements.

BANKER: Well, I'd kinda like to have a talk with this nephew of yours. Just to sorta know how the money's gonna be spent.

    (CHICO *heard humming "Daffodils" outside. Door opens, he enters.*)

BANKER: Is this your nephew coming in?

ABNER: No, that's his business associate, Emmanuel Ravelli.

CHICO: Hullo, Flywheel's uncle.

ABNER: Ravelli, *this* is Squire Higbee.

CHICO: Well, who said it wasn't?

BANKER: Mr. Ravelli, as long as you're taking a financial interest in this farm, an' seein' as how I'm the banker, I reckon it'd be good business for us to have a little talk. Er, where do you live?

CHICO: I live wit my brudder.

BANKER: Well, where does you *brother* live?

CHICO: He lives wit me.

BANKER: Er, well, where do you *both* live?

CHICO: We bot live together.

BANKER: Oh, never mind that. Would you mind telling me what you do?

CHICO: When?

BANKER: When you *work*, of course.

CHICO: Hey, when I work, I *work*. I'ma Flywheel's assist'.

BANKER: Assist? . . . Do you know anything about farming?

CHICO: Sure, I'm a pharm*acist*. *(Laughs.)* Some joke, eh?
(Rumpus; sound of running.)

GROUCHO *(approaching):* Uncle Abner! Uncle Abner! There's a mouse in my room.

ABNER: My nephew afraid of a little mouse?

GROUCHO: Well, *I* would have fought back, but he came after me with a gat.

ABNER: A mouse came after you with a revolver?

GROUCHO: No, a gat. A pussy-gat.

ABNER: Oh, Waldorf! . . . Er, this is Squire Higbee—

GROUCHO: Good. Have him run down to the drugstore for some rat biscuits. If they haven't any rat biscuits, tell him to get some animal crackers.

ABNER: Er, never mind, Waldorf. I can phone to town. You want me to have the drugstore send over some rat poison?

GROUCHO: No, they needn't bother, Uncle. I'll send the rats over after it. *(Bang heard in grandfather's clock.)* Ravelli, what are you doing in that grandfather's clock?

CHICO: Grandfadder's clock! *(Laughs.)* At'sa my mistake. You said call the drugstore, and I thought dis was a telephone booth.

ABNER: Please, boys! Squire Higbee is here on business. You know he has a mortgage on this farm and—

GROUCHO *(dramatic):* A mortgage? Why did you *keep* it from me, Uncle Abner? There I was out in the city, frittering away my time, as only youth can, while your poor bald head was turning gray, and this wolf at the door was sitting in your parlor, drinking your poisonous corn liquor and eating your heart out. But don't worry, uncle, don't worry. He won't foreclose, not if *I* have anything to say.

BANKER: Sir, you have nothing to say.

GROUCHO *(breezily):* In that case, uncle, I guess he'll foreclose.

CHICO: Hey, a mortgage foreclose? Dat's no good. A suitcase for clothes —dat'sa much better.

GROUCHO: Nice work, Ravelli. Now go upstairs and wash your face. I can tell what you ate for breakfast this morning.

CHICO: Well, you're so smart, what did I eat?

GROUCHO: Eggs. You've still got some on your chin.

CHICO: You crazy. I ate dose eggs yesterday.

BANKER: See here, young Flywheel, I've decided to extend the mortgage. But being a businessman, I'd like to know what improvements you plan to make.

GROUCHO: Well, in the first place, Higbee, I'm getting pretty sick of waking up early in the morning to get milk from those cows. It would be a lot simpler if we had the milk delivered to our door in bottles, like the city folks have.

ABNER: Ridiculous, Waldorf. You're talking about milkmen and—

GROUCHO: That's just it. Why can't we sell the cows and buy a milkman instead?

CHICO: Hey, maybe we can get some *elephant*'s milk. I know a baby tree months old dat drinks elephant's milk and he weighs ninety-five pounds.

BANKER: A baby three months old weighs ninety-five pounds?

CHICO: Sure, it's a baby *elephant. (Laughs.)* Oh boy, I foola you dat time!

BANKER: Now see here, gentlemen. I'm a busy man. Just what improvements do you plan to make on this farm?

GROUCHO: Improvements? Well, first I think we'll get rid of Uncle Abner.

BANKER: What?

GROUCHO: Of course, we won't throw out the old idiot unless we can do it without hurting his feelings.

ABNER: So that's what's in your mind, Waldorf? You'd like to get rid of me? Well, you'll have to get up pretty early in the morning to fool your Uncle Abner.

GROUCHO: Is nine o'clock early enough?

BANKER: See here, you fellows. Just what *is* your game?

CHICO: My game's pinochle, but I gotta use my own cards.

BANKER: Abner, if this is your idea of improvements, we can't do any business together! Unless the payment is made by Wednesday, I'm going to foreclose.

ABNER: Don't worry, Squire. I can see I was wrong about letting my nephew handle the money. The mortgage payment will be made. Waldorf, where's that two thousand dollars I gave you?

GROUCHO: *That* two thousand? Well, you told me you wanted a new chicken coop.

ABNER: Two thousand for a chicken coop? You said you could buy a *first-class* coop for three hundred.

GROUCHO: Well, the one I bought *isn't* first-class. Anyway, the dealer didn't have a coupe, so I got a sedan instead.

BANKER: Abner, if he's thrown away your money, that's your business, not mine. You've made your bed; now—

CHICO: Hey, Uncle Abner, if you made *your* bed, why didn't you make mine too?

BANKER: Abner, I'm *leaving!* And unless the mortgage payment is made, *I'll foreclose!*

GROUCHO: Just a moment there! Squire Higbee, if you have any of the milk of human kindness, I'll take a quart. Poor Uncle Ab is sorry for what he did. *(Dramatic.)* Look at him, sitting there conscience-stricken.

CHICO: At'sa what *I* always say, boss. Don't conscious-strickens before dey're hatched.

BANKER: Abner, I'm through with this nonsense. You know very well that I've often put myself out for you—

GROUCHO: Well, why don't you put yourself out now? On second thought, don't bother. We can *throw* you out.

CHICO: Sure, boss. I kick him outa da house.

GROUCHO: Why wait till he's out of the house? You can start kicking him now.

BANKER: That's the finish! *(Receding.)* I'm going! Good day!

ABNER: Squire! Squire! *(Door slams.)* You scoundrels, you've driven him away.

GROUCHO *(genially):* Good. Now we can have a little chat about these farm improvements.

ABNER: Get out of my house! Both of you!

GROUCHO: What? You think we're the type of fellows that would run out on you when you need us most?

ABNER: Very well. Then maybe this shotgun will get you out.

CHICO: Hey, look out! Put down dat gun!

GROUCHO: Ravelli, step back! Don't fight with Uncle Abner while he's got a gun in his hand.
(Sound of quick scuffle.)

ABNER: Stop it! . . . Get your hand off my gun or . . . *(Gun fires, glass breaks.) Put down my gun. You've broken a window!*

CHICO: Come on, boss, I tink he's mad at us.

BOTH: Goodbye, uncle.
(Door slams.)

GROUCHO: Ravelli, you shouldn't have grabbed that gun. Do you realize you almost shot my uncle?

CHICO: Awright. When we get back home, you can take a shot at *my* uncle!
(Music in strong.)

AFTERPIECE

GROUCHO: Well, m'lads . . . and molasses too . . . if you enjoyed listening to this program as much as we enjoyed making it, they you enjoyed listening to this program as much as we enjoyed making it. Furthermore—

CHICO: Hey, Groucho!

GROUCHO: What is it, Chico?

CHICO: Can you give me a nickel for a poor old man who's crying outside?

GROUCHO: What's he crying about?

CHICO: Hey's crying "Peanuts, popcorn, ice cream!"

GROUCHO: Chico, didn't I ask you not to interrupt me when I started talking?

CHICO: Awright, don't get excited. It's only da foist time.

GROUCHO: Don't say foist.

CHICO: Awright, den it's da second time. *(Muttering resentfully.)* Every time I say sometin—

GROUCHO: Ladies and gentlemen—

CHICO *(still muttering):* Every time I say sometin you holler and—

GROUCHO: Chico, will you stop muttering!

CHICO: I *won't* stop muttering. Muttering isa very nice when I use Essolube, dat famous hydrofined mutter oil.

GROUCHO: Chico, your dentist must have a pretty tough time when he gives you gas. How can he tell when you're unconscious?

CHICO: I don't go to a dentist for gas. I go to a filling station for Esso, which is better than any gasoline.

GROUCHO: Well, I guess that covers everything.

BOTH *(singing):* Good night, ladies. Good night, ladies.

(Signature music.)

FIVE STAR THEATER

PRESENTS

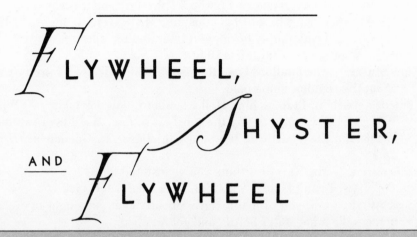

Flywheel, Shyster, and Flywheel

EPISODE NO. 14   FEBRUARY 27, 1933

CAST

Groucho Marx as Waldorf T. Flywheel
Chico Marx as Emmanuel Ravelli
Miss Dimple
Priscilla
Landlord
Thorndyke
Doorman
Customers
Sheriff

(Clicking of typewriter heard; phone rings twice.)

MISS DIMPLE: Law offices of Flywheel, Shyster, and Flywheel . . . No, Mr. Flywheel isn't in, but his assistant, Mr. Ravelli, is here . . . Hold the wire, I'll call him. *(Calling out.)* Oh, Mr. Ravelli.

CHICO: Whatta you want, Miss Dimp?

MISS DIMPLE: The landlord is on the phone again. He seems pretty angry about the rent not being paid.

CHICO: Awright, I talk to him. Hello, landlord, how you feel? . . . What? You give us *two days* to pay the rent? At'sa fine. We'll taka two days. We'll taka the Fourth of July and Christmas . . . Goodbye! *(Hangs up.)*

MISS DIMPLE: Mr. Ravelli, I think you've insulted him.

CHICO: Aw, I can't bodder with him. I'ma tired. I feel sick.

MISS DIMPLE: Oh, you probably have a cold. What you ought to do is go home, take a hot water bottle, and get into bed.

CHICO: Hot water bottle? Aw, dat'sa no good. Last night I put some water in a hot water bottle, and I wait and wait . . . but the water didn't even get *warm*.

MISS DIMPLE: Mr. Ravelli, maybe you ought to see a doctor.

CHICO: I *did* see a doctor. He give me some medicine to take wit my meals, but I *can't* take it.

MISS DIMPLE: Why not?

CHICO: Because I ain't gettin no meals.

MISS DIMPLE: Well, if you're hungry, I can give you this quarter. It's all I have with me, so get something to eat and don't spend the money for da movies.

CHICO: Don't worry, Miss Dimp. I won't spend your money for da movies. I *got* some money for da movies.

(Footsteps heard.)

MISS DIMPLE: Someone's coming in. I think it's Mr. Flywheel.

CHICO: Well, I don't wanna see him. I feel sick enough now. I go out da back door. *(Receding.)* Goodabye, Miss Dimp.

(Door closes; typing is heard; door opens.)

MISS DIMPLE: Good morning, Mr. Flywheel.

GROUCHO: Quiet! Quiet! I'm in no mood for small talk. Where's Ravelli?

MISS DIMPLE: He just went out the back door.

GROUCHO: Well, call him back, quick! We're gonna have a showdown around here.

MISS DIMPLE *(calling out as she opens door):*   Oh, Mr. Ravelli! Mr. Ravelli!

CHICO *(away):*   What?

MISS DIMPLE: Mr. Flywheel wants to see you.

CHICO *(approaching):*   Awright, awright, I'm comin. What you want, boss?

GROUCHO: Look here. I've been practicing law in this town for a good many years. And my reputation means more to me than anything else in the world. Ravelli, what was the idea of telling Sam Jones that you can beat me at pool?

CHICO: I did *not* tell Sam Jones I could beat you. I tole Louie Milano.

GROUCHO *(sneers):*   Hmm . . . And you told him that I steal pennies from the newsstands, didn't you?

CHICO: Yes, boss. But—

GROUCHO: And you also told him that I cheat at cards, eh?

CHICO: No, boss, I didn't tink of dat.

GROUCHO: Ravelli, hand me that water pitcher. I want to smash it over your head.

MISS DIMPLE: Please, Mr. Flywheel. The landlord may come in any minute. What will he think if he sees you and Mr. Ravelli in a rumpus?

GROUCHO: Why? Do the pants I'm wearing look like rompus?
(Knock on door.)

MISS DIMPLE *(whispers):*   I think that's the landlord now.

GROUCHO: I'm going into my private office. If it *isn't* the landlord, call me.
(Door opens and closes; knock on other door.)

MISS DIMPLE: Come in.

LANDLORD: I'm Mr. Scrooge, the landlord.

CHICO: Oh yes, Mr. Flywheel, he was expectin you.

LANDLORD: He was?

CHICO: Yeah, dat's why he ain't here.

LANDLORD: But Mr. Flywheel said he would see me.

CHICO: He did see you. He saw you comin' in da front door. Dat's why he went out da back door. *(Pause.)* But I gotta some news for you.

LANDLORD: Yes?

CHICO: Do you know I can beat Flywheel playing pool?

GROUCHO *(opening door and approaching):*   Ravelli, I *heard* what you said.

LANDLORD: See here, Mr. Flywheel.

GROUCHO: Pipe down, landlord. We've having enough trouble in this office without you butting in. Ravelli, that was the last straw.

LANDLORD: Mr. Flywheel! I came here Tuesday to ask for the rent. I came Thursday. And I came again Saturday. We've got to come to some definite arrangements.

GROUCHO: All right. Hereafter, you can come every Thursday.

LANDLORD: Why I . . . have never—

GROUCHO: Oh, it won't bother me. I'm never in on Thursdays.

LANDLORD: Mr. Flywheel, you have no excuse for not paying the rent.

GROUCHO: Well, it isn't my fault. I tried to think of an excuse. Anyway, all you talk about is money. I'm different. I don't care how much money a man has—just so he's rich.

LANDLORD: Please! Don't confuse the issues.

CHICO: Issues? You mean the ones I'm wearing? You're crazy. Flywheel just tinks dey're issues—but dey're *my* shoes.

GROUCHO: Nice work, Ravelli. Look here, landlord. You're a man who's gotten some place by hard work and—

LANDLORD: Well, I don't mind saying I'm a self-made man.

CHICO: You're a self-made man? Den why didn't you put more hair on your head?

GROUCHO: Don't listen to him, landlord. He's got *plenty* of hair, and he looks just as repulsive as you do—

LANDLORD *(exasperated):* I've put up with all that I'm going to. *(Receding.) You'll hear from me!*

GROUCHO: Drop in any time. This is Liberty Hall.

LANDLORD: Good day! *(Slams door.)*

CHICO: Hey, boss—

MISS DIMPLE: Shh . . . I think he's coming back . . . Oh, no, it looks like a client.

(Knock at the door.)

MISS DIMPLE: Come in.

THORNDYKE: My name is Reginald Thorndyke. I am here for business.

GROUCHO: Thorndyke, if you're here for business, I can tell you you're wasting your time. We can't find any business here ourselves.

THORNDYKE: You don't understahnd. I'm an actor.

CHICO: At'sa too bad, 'cause my boss, he don't like actors.

THORNDYKE: Well, I'm a playwright too.

CHICO: My boss don't like playwrights either.

THORNDYKE *(impatient):* Well, what *does* he like?

CHICO: I tink he likes spinach. *(Laughs.)* Some joke, eh?

THORNDYKE: Gentlemen, I'm with the Shakespearean Repertory Company.

GROUCHO: Is that so? Have a chair.

THORNDYKE: I'm the leading man.

GROUCHO: Good. Have another chair.

THORNDYKE: I want to sue our manager for back salary.

GROUCHO: Never mind that. How about a couple of passes for Saturday night's show?

THORNDYKE: We'll discuss that later. Mr. Flywheel, if you can get the money the manager owes me, I'd be willing to pay you—well, let's say a tenth of what you collect.

CHICO: A tenth ain't enough, boss. Make him give at least a twentieth.

THORNDYKE: Why . . . ah . . . we can discuss the terms later. Mr. Flywheel, our manager is a very slippery fellow. He is . . . rather reluctant to part with money—especially a sum as large as three hundred dollars, which he owes me.

GROUCHO: Don't worry, Thorndyke. I'll get your three hundred dollars from that guy!

THORNDYKE: Really? Well, just how will you approach him?

GROUCHO: I think I'll approach him with a blackjack.
   (*Music in strong.*)

DOORMAN: Good morning, Mr. Thorndyke.

THORNDYKE: Good morning, doorman. Have the rehearsals started yet?

DOORMAN: No, sir. I'm afraid there ain't gonna be any rehearsals. The manager's run outta town.

THORNDYKE: What! And left the show stranded?

DOORMAN: Yes, sir, and he took all the troupe's money with him.

THORNDYKE: The scoundrel! After I, Reginald Thorndyke, consent to star in his fly-by-night company! Tell me, has my leading lady come in?

DOORMAN: Miss Priscilla Kent? . . . Here she comes.

PRISCILLA: Oh, Reginald, have you heard the terrible news? What can we do?

THORNDYKE: Don't fret, my sweet. My lawyer, Mr. Flywheel, is coming right over. I'm sure *he'll* be able to do something.
   (*Scuffle heard at door.*)

DOORMAN *(away):*   You guys can't come in here.

GROUCHO *(away):*   Out of Flywheel's way, or I'll flog you within an *inch* of your life!

CHICO: And when my boss gets through, *I'll* flog you de *other* inch.

THORNDYKE: Doorman! Doorman! Let them in! They're my attorneys.

DOORMAN: Excuse me, Mr. Thorndyke.

THORNDYKE: Oh, Mr. Flywheel. I'm glad you came. We're facing a very serious problem.

GROUCHO: Well, that can wait. Who's the good-looking gal?

THORNDYKE: Pardon me. This is our leading lady, Miss Priscilla Kent. Miss Kent, this is Mr. Flywheel . . . and his assistant, Mr. Ravelli.

PRISCILLA: Mr. Flywheel, Mr. Thorndyke has been telling me all about you.

GROUCHO: Well, he's a liar.

THORNDYKE: Why, I said you were a splendid lawyer and a fine gentleman.

CHICO: Boss, you were right. He *is* a liar.

THORNDYKE: Mr. Flywheel, we don't know what to do. The manager of our company has run out on us with all the money!

GROUCHO: It's very simple. Just charge it to running expenses.

THORNDYKE: But what are we going to do? The show is scheduled to open in three days and—

GROUCHO *(pompously):* Thorndyke, you may not know it, but I'm a theater lover.

THORNDYKE: Really?

GROUCHO *(excess modesty):* Well, maybe I shouldn't go as far as to say I'm a theater *lover,* but you ought to see me in a dark movie theater with my girl.

THORNDYKE: Mr. Flywheel, I cahn't disappoint my public. I'm counting on *you* to get us out of this mess.

GROUCHO *(pompously):* Thorndyke, I've thought it all over. *The show must go on.*

THORNDYKE *(eagerly):* What do you plan to do?

GROUCHO *(breezily):* I don't plan to do anything. I just said that the show must go on.

THORNDYKE: Do you gentlemen know what the name Reginald Thorndyke means in the American theatah?

CHICO: I give up. Now I ask *you* a riddle. What do you look through if you wanna see through a brick wall?

THORNDYKE *(bewildered):* Look through to see through a brick wall?

CHICO: A window. *(Laughs.)* Oh boy, dat's some nifty.

GROUCHO: Shut up, Ravelli! I'm not paying you to interrupt my business conferences.

CHICO: I know, boss, but I like it so much I do it for nothing.

THORNDYKE: Mr. Flywheel, if you could only find the right man to take over the show and manage it.

GROUCHO: Does Miss Kent go with the show?

THORNDYKE: Why yes, of course.

GROUCHO: Then I'm just the man I'm looking for. Ravelli, we're in the show business. Run over to the box office and see if there's any money there.

CHICO: Money? Hey boss, dat reminds me. Did you lose a big roll of bills?

GROUCHO: Why yes, I believe I did.

CHICO: Did it have a rubber band around it?

GROUCHO: Come to think of it, it did.

CHICO: Well, I found da rubber band.

THORNDYKE: Mr. Flywheel, as long as you're going to take over the show, I think we ought to get busy. We haven't much time left. You know we are going to present *Romeo and Juliet*.

CHICO: *Romeo* AND *Juliet*. Hey, one show ought to be enough.

THORNDYKE *(snooty)*:   *Romeo and Juliet* is the title of the play.

GROUCHO: Well, I don't care much for that title. Why not call it *Grand Hotel?* They're using that name on another play and it's cleaning up.

THORNDYKE: That's ridiculous!

CHICO: Awright, den how about *Mickey Mouse?* At'sa *very* good name.

THORNDYKE: *Mickey Mouse?* Why, we're presenting a classic. It's important . . . it's *big* . . . ah—

CHICO: Well, if it's big we'll call it *Mickey Rat*.

THORNDYKE *(impatiently)*:   The title is *Romeo and Juliet*. Here's a copy of the play.

GROUCHO: Hmm . . . let's see . . . What's *this?* It says "balcony scene."

THORNDYKE: Why, that's Romeo and Juliet's famous balcony scene!

GROUCHO: Fine business! See here, Thorndyke, while *I'm* running this company you'll do your acting on the stage. Leave the balcony for the customers.

PRISCILLA: But Mr. Flywheel, Mr. Thorndyke and I have played that scene—

GROUCHO: All right, babe. You can play it in the balcony, but Thorndyke will have to stay on the stage.

PRISCILLA: Why, I—

GROUCHO *(whispering)*:   Keep it under your hat, but I'll be up there in the balcony with you. *(Louder.)* Ravelli, I want to reserve two seats in the balcony for tonight. Ring for the box-office man.

CHICO: Aw, let him ring for himself. I wanna read dis play an' see what it's all about. *(Clears throat.)* Roma . . . Room . . . Roomyeow and Jollio . . . ah . . . Joliet . . . It's a crazy show, eh boss?

GROUCHO: Well, with some fixing up here and there, I may be able to make something out of it. Let me read a couple of lines. Listen to this: "And yet I wish for but the thing I have. My bounty is as boundless as the sea—"

CHICO: I know de answer to dat one, boss. It's a window.

GROUCHO: Quiet, Ravelli. I'm reading. "My bounty is as boundless as the sea. My love as deep. The more I give thee, the more I have, for both are infinite." I think I'll cut that out. There's no sense to it. Thorndyke, run out and get some scissors.

CHICO: Hey, boss, dat's a better show.

GROUCHO: What's a better show?

CHICO: Scissors. Julius Scissors.

THORNDYKE: Gentlemen, your suggestions are impossible. The play will go on as Shakespeare wrote it.

GROUCHO: Are you *crazy?* Look at this love scene! Even *you* ought to realize that it needs something to liven it up.

THORNDYKE: Why, I—

GROUCHO: But leave it to Flywheel. As soon as the scene begins to sag, I'll come out and announce the election returns. That's sure-fire stuff. It always gets applause.

THORNDYKE *(temperamentally):*   Oh, all these strange proceedings have upset me. I'm going to my room. I must rest.

GROUCHO: That's fine. You go with him, Ravelli. I'm going to stay here and rehearse Miss Kent in the love scene, eh, Miss Kent?

CHICO: Okay, boss, I go. But remember, tomorrow it's my turn to rehearse, eh, Miss Kent? *(Receding.)* Come on, Shakespeare.

THORNDYKE: Very well, lead the way.

(Door closes.)

PRISCILLA: Mr. Flywheel, in all my career, I have never—

GROUCHO: Aw, cut out the shop talk. How about you and I running over to your house for a nice little dinner?

PRISCILLA: My house?

GROUCHO: Well, if it's good enough for you, it's good enough for me.

PRISCILLA: Mr. Flywheel, please—I might as well tell you right now . . . I'm in love . . . I'm in love with the handsomest, sweetest, most talented man in the world.

GROUCHO *(coyly):*   And I like you too . . . Miss Kent, I've got something for you. It's a ring. I got it from the nose of a savage, so it ought to look well on you.

PRISCILLA: Mr. Flywheel, I can't accept your ring.

GROUCHO *(dramatic):*   You mean . . . there's another man?

PRISCILLA: Why, yes.

GROUCHO: Tell me . . . I must know . . . Who is he?

PRISCILLA: Why do you want to know? Do you want to *harm* him?

GROUCHO: Not at all. I want to sell him the ring.

PRISCILLA: Mr. Flywheel, our relations must be strictly businesslike.

GROUCHO *(indignant):*   Listen. You keep my relations out of this. You needn't be so uppish with me. You know, I can marry anybody I please. The only trouble is I don't *please* anybody. *(Very romantic.)* Oh come, Priscilla, let's end all this shallow pretense. The air is filled with

"How about playing post office?" Groucho romances "college widow" Thelma Todd in this scene from *Horse Feathers*.

love, and my very soul cries out to be held in your arms. How about playing post office?

PRISCILLA: Stop! Mr. Flywheel, you're making a *show* of yourself.

GROUCHO *(dramatically):*   I know Priscilla, but the . . . show . . . must . . . go . . . on.

(Music in strong.)

(Street noises heard away; phone rings twice.)

CHICO: Hullo. *Dis* is da box office . . . Huh? Sure. Da show, she opens tonight . . . The curtain goes up in ten minoots . . . You want two seats in de orchestra? What instrument do you play? . . . Oh! You wanna bring your gal! Awright, I put her in da gallery. I can't talk to you. Dere's customers at da window. Goodbye. *(Hangs up.)*

FIRST CUSTOMER: Oh, box-office man! That seat you gave me isn't any good.

CHICO: Well, what are *you* hollering about. You only got one seat at'sa no good. We got tree hunnerd at'sa no good.

FIRST CUSTOMER: Oh, I'm not going to argue. *(Receding.)* I—

CHICO: Hey, wait a minoots! What about a ticket for dat kid wit you?

FIRST CUSTOMER: This little boy? I don't need a ticket for him. He's only six years old.

CHICO: Awright, I let him in. But if I catch him lookin at da show, I'll trow him out. Next.

SECOND CUSTOMER: Say, mister. You gave me the wrong tickets. These tickets are for *next* Monday night.

CHICO: What's da difference? It's for da same show.

SECOND CUSTOMER: But see here!

(Door opens)

CHICO: Here comes da boss, Mr. Flywheel. You can talk to him.

GROUCHO: What's the trouble here?

SECOND CUSTOMER: Mr. Flywheel, I asked for tickets for tonight, and this . . . *person* gave me tickets for next week!

GROUCHO: You're lucky. The show won't be here next week. Now run along.

SECOND CUSTOMER *(receding):*   Why, I never heard of . . .

DOORMAN *(approaching excitedly):*   Mr. Flywheel! Mr. Flywheel!

GROUCHO: What is it, doorman?

DOORMAN: A man just fell out of the balcony! Right into the orchestra seats.

GROUCHO: Tell him he can stay there, but it'll cost him a dollar-and-a-half extra.

CHICO: Hey, boss. Mr. Thorndyke's very mad da way you changed his part in da play. He was in here lookin for you. He wanted to beat you up.

GROUCHO: Well, what did you tell him?

CHICO: I said I was sorry you wasn't in. I tink he's drinkin again.

GROUCHO: What? On the opening night? Ravelli, I told you to keep an eye on him and see that he doesn't do any drinking.

CHICO: I did. He only had one little glass.

GROUCHO: One glass?

CHICO: Yeah, but he kept filling it up.

GROUCHO: Doesn't he know that that stuff is slow poison?

CHICO: Well, he wasn't in a hurry. *(Knock on the door.)* Come in. *(Door opens.)*

GROUCHO: Hello, Priscilla.

PRISCILLA *(excitedly):* Mr. Flywheel! That dressing room you gave me is impossible! I *cahn't* dress in there.

GROUCHO: What's the matter with that room? It's got everything. Hot and cold water—

PRISCILLA: In *that* dressing room . . . hot and cold water?

GROUCHO: Certainly. Hot in summer and cold in winter.

PRISCILLA: And besides, there's no lock on the door. That numbskull assistant of yours—

CHICO *(blandly):* She means *me*, boss.

PRISCILLA: He's walked in on me several times without knocking . . . Why, I might not have been *fully dressed!*

CHICO: You don't got to worry, lady. I always look through da keyhole first. If you ain't dressed, I don't come in.

PRISCILLA: And another thing, Mr. Flywheel. Look at this costume you bought for me. I'm playing Juliet, and you got me a cowboy suit.

GROUCHO: Well, the cowboy suits were cheaper. Anyway, that cowboy stuff is great for the kids.

PRISCILLA: And Mr. Thorndyke is furious! He's to play Romeo, and they sent him a policeman's uniform.

GROUCHO: They sent him a policeman's uniform? Those blundering idiots! I ordered a baseball suit.

(Knock at door.)

DOORMAN: Mr. Flywheel!

GROUCHO: Yes, doorman.

DOORMAN: The curtain goes up in five minutes. The overture's on . . . and with that soprano singing.

GROUCHO: Doorman, you come in here and watch the box office.

DOORMAN: Okay.

GROUCHO: Everybody else come on backstage. We can go through the theater . . . right through this door.

(Door opens; buzz of audience; orchestra heard with soprano's voice; GROUCHO, PRISCILLA, RAVELLI *walk toward it.)*

CHICO: Hey, boss, what's dat orchestra leader shaking a stick at da lady for?

GROUCHO: He's not shaking a stick at her. That's the baton.

CHICO: He's not shaking a stick at her? Den what's she screaming for?

GROUCHO: Say, there's been some complaint about that. I'll talk to her. Madam! *(Singing and music continue.)* Madam! . . . Hey! Stop that music.

(Buzz of astonishment from orchestra and audience; singing stops.)

WOMAN: What is the idea of interrupting my solo?

GROUCHO: Well, you'll have to cut out singing so loud. We got a complaint from the factory next door.

WOMAN *(astonished):* The factory next door?

GROUCHO: Yes, the men mistook your voice for a whistle. And they quit working.

WOMAN: Why, I—

GROUCHO: Never mind that. Go next door and whistle so the men can start work again . . . Come on, crawl under this curtain, Miss Kent. Watch out for that scenery, Ravelli.

(Door opens; bell jingles softly as curtain warning.)

PRISCILLA: It's eight-thirty, Mr. Ravelli. You'd better run up the curtain.

CHICO: Hey, whatta you tink I am, a squirrel?

DOORMAN *(approaching):* Oh, Mr. Flywheel, Mr. Flywheel!

GROUCHO *(impatient):* *Now* what is it, doorman?

DOORMAN: Mr. Thorndyke has walked out on the show!

ALL: *What?*

DOORMAN: He said he wouldn't think of playing Romeo in a policeman's uniform.

PRISCILLA: Oh! I suppose we'll have to call off the show.

GROUCHO: No, *no.* The show must go *on,* even if it has to go on the rocks. *I'll* play Romeo. Ravelli, you stand here in the wings and if I forget any of the lines, you prompt me.

CHICO: Okay, boss.

VOICE *(away):* The curtain's going up.

(Curtain rises; buzz of anticipation heard from audience; applause.)

GROUCHO: Thanks for the big hand, folks. I'm going to give you a Romeo tonight that'll knock you right into the aisles . . . so you'd better hold onto your seats. *(Becoming Shakespearean.)* Ah, my Juliet! See, how she leans her cheek upon her hand! Oh, that I were a glove upon that hand . . . that I might touch that cheek.

PRISCILLA *(whispering):*   Mr. Flywheel, that's the wrong scene.

GROUCHO *(whispering):*   Well, it's the only scene I know. *(Shakespearean again.)* She speaks: Oh, speak again bright angel! For thou art as glorious . . . for thou art as glorious . . . glorious . . . *(Whispering.)* Ravelli, what comes next?

CHICO *(away, whispering excitedly):*   Hey, boss. The landlord's joosta come over from de office wit da sheriff!

GROUCHO: For thou art as glorious as the landlord . . . landlord's just come over from the office with the sheriff.

PRISCILLA *(whispering):*   Those aren't the lines, Mr. Flywheel.

GROUCHO *(whispering):*   Pipe down, Juliet. Ravelli ought to know—he's got the script right in his hands.

(Buzz of astonishment from audience.)

GROUCHO: My ears have not yet drunk a hundred words of that tongue's utterance, yet I know the sound: Art thou not Romeo, and a Montague?

PRISCILLA *(whispering):*   Mr. Flywheel, you're taking my lines!

GROUCHO *(whispering):*   All right, tomorrow you can take some of *my* lines. I wish you'd stop interrupting! *(Acting.)* Lady, by yonder blessed moon I swear.

CHICO: Boss, boss! Da sheriff's coming on da stage!

GROUCHO *(whispering):*   Sheriff? I don't seem to remember any sheriff in this play. Why wasn't he at the rehearsals?

SHERIFF *(approaching):*   Mr. Flywheel, I'm the sheriff. And I'm going to attach all the scenery to pay the rent at your office.

(Buzz of excitement from audience.)

GROUCHO: Ah, noble sheriff, a fine time thou has picked to squawk about the rent. Go, wait in yonder alley whilst I whisper sweet words of love into the fair Juliet's ear . . . Juliet, if my heart's dear love—

SHERIFF: I arrest you in the name of the law.

GROUCHO: Ah, what's in a name? That which we call a rose . . . by any other name would smell as sweet . . . Noblest of noble sheriffs, I beg of thee to *scram*.

(Hissing from audience.)

PRISCILLA *(whispering):*   Oh, this is so humiliating.

SHERIFF: I'm sorry, lady, but I'm going to attach all the properties and scenery belonging to this show. *(Commanding.)* Ring down the curtain!

CHICO *(approaching):*   Boss, boss!

GROUCHO: What is it, Ravelli?

CHICO: We're saved! We're saved!

GROUCHO: What's happened?

CHICO: Leave everyting to me, boss. I'll talk to da sheriff. Looka here, sheriff, you can't ring down dis curtain.

SHERIFF: I can't, eh? Well, why not?

CHICO: Because I tried it, and it's stuck.

(Music in strong.)

AFTERPIECE

CHICO: Laydeez and gentlemens! Please excuse me. I gotta talk to me brudder. Hey, Groucho, what's da matter? You looka so sad.

GROUCHO: I got some bad news, Chico. See this letter with the black border? Well, my old pal Bill Cooper is dead.

CHICO: How do you know it's Bill Cooper? You didn't open de envelope yet.

GROUCHO: I don't have to. I can recognize Bill's handwriting.

CHICO: At'sa too bad, because I feela very happy. I find out today dat my kid didn't pass in school.

GROUCHO: Your child failed in school and you're happy?

CHICO: Sure. When he stays in de same class, I don't have to buy him any new books.

GROUCHO: I see. A chip off the old blockhead. You know, a dumber father than you would be hard to find.

CHICO: Hard to find? Don't you mean hydrofined?

GROUCHO: No. You're thinking of Essolube, that famous hydrofined motor oil. Or am I thinking of Esso, which is more powerful than any gasoline?

CHICO: Hey, Groucho! I joosta got a *great* idea!

GROUCHO: Well, let's hear it.

CHICO: I tink we oughta say good night.

BOTH *(singing):* Good night ladies. Good night ladies.

(Signature music.)

FIVE STAR THEATER
PRESENTS

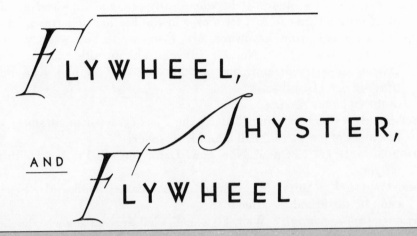

FLYWHEEL, SHYSTER, AND FLYWHEEL

EPISODE NO. 15   MARCH 6, 1933

CAST

Groucho Marx as Waldorf T. Flywheel
Chico Marx as Emmanuel Ravelli
Miss Dimple
Fischer, department-store manager
Woman Employee
Old Joe
Clancy, store detective
Collector
Customer
Officer
Kleptomaniac
Woman Customer
Secretary

(Typing heard; phone rings.)

MISS DIMPLE: Law offices of Flywheel, Shyster, and Flywheel . . . No, Mr. Flywheel isn't in . . . He's over at the Fischer department store, in conference with the owner, Mr. Fischer . . . You want Mr. Flywheel's assistant? . . . No, Mr. Ravelli isn't in either. He's at the Fischer department store too. I think you can get him over there. *(Fading out.)* Goodbye.

(Fade in phone ringing.)

SECRETARY: Good morning. This is the Fischer department store, Mr. Fischer's office . . . I'll call him. Mr. Fischer!

FISCHER *(away):* Not now. Now now. Can't you see I'm busy with my lawyers?

SECRETARY: I'm sorry, Mr. Fischer. *(Into phone:)* Hello. Mr. Fischer can't be disturbed . . . Goodbye.

FISCHER *(approaching):* Well, Flywheel, what are you going to do about it?

GROUCHO: Fischer, there's a lot of money involved, and I don't want to do anything that I might regret later.

CHICO: Come on, boss, make up your mind.

GROUCHO: Ravelli, I couldn't have gotten where I am today by making hasty decisions.

FISCHER: Oh, come, come, Flywheel, what do you say?

GROUCHO: Don't hurry me. Don't hurry me.

FISCHER: It's about time you made up your mind.

GROUCHO *(deliberating):* W-e-l-l, all right then, I'll take three cards.

CHICO: Here you are, boss. *(Slap of cards.)* One . . . two . . . tree.

GROUCHO: Well, Fischer, what have you got?

FISCHER: I've got four kings.

GROUCHO *(chuckles):* Too bad, Fischer, old boy. I happen to have five aces.

CHICO *(chuckles):* You lose, boys. Cause I got *six* aces.

FISCHER *(indignant):* Mr. Flywheel, what kind of game do you call this. Your assistant deals himself six aces!

GROUCHO: Well, it was his deal, wasn't it? The trouble with you, Fischer, is that you don't trust anybody. You're a bad loser. However, I'd rather play with a bad loser than a good winner.

FISCHER: Well, gentlemen. The game's over. I'm washed up.

GROUCHO: You'd never know it to look at you.

FISCHER: Come, gentlemen, let's forget the game. I want to talk over with you the serious financial difficulties that my store is in.

CHICO: Sure, dat'sa right, Mr. Fischer, but first let me ask you a riddle. What'sa difference between you and a skunk?

FISCHER: I'm sure I don't know.

CHICO: I don't know, either. Maybe dere ain't no difference. *(Laughs.)* Oh, boy, dat's some joke!

FISCHER *(annoyed)*: Please, gentlemen. I brought you here to give me legal advice. Mr. Flywheel, my store has not been doing very well lately. Unless I can pay off my creditors by the fifteenth of the month, I will lose the store.

CHICO: Hey! Dis is a big store. And if you do lose it, you could find it again easy.

FISCHER: No, no, gentlemen. If I do not have the money my creditors will take the store away from me. As my lawyer, what would you advise?

GROUCHO: Fischer, I advise you to take a vacation. Remember, all work and no play makes Jack a dull boy. And a duller boy than you, Fischer, I've never seen.

CHICO: You're right, boss. It was da same ting with my wife. She needed a rest, so I got her a job.

FISCHER: She needed a rest and you got her a job?

CHICO: Sure, when she no got a job, she no gets a vacation, so I got her a job washing clothes. And next summer she gets a week's vacation.

GROUCHO: Ravelli, you ought to be ashamed of yourself—an able-bodied man like you letting your wife wash clothes for a living.

CHICO: Well, I don't want her to wash clothes, but dat's de only ting she knows how to do. Dey wanna give her a fine job in de Eagle laundry, but I no let her take it.

FISCHER: No? Why not?

CHICO: Ah! My wife, she don't know nuttin about washin eagles.

FISCHER: Gentlemen, you don't seem to understand the seriousness of the problem. Our business was very good until they opened that big chain store on the next corner.

CHICO: Well, if da chain store isa doing so good, why don't you sell chains, too?

(Angry voices heard outside door.)

FISCHER: What's that racket? *(Knock on door.)* Come in.

(Door opens.)

CLANCY *(approaching)*: Come on in here, you!

KLEPTOMANIAC: Let go of me! Let go of me!

FISCHER: What's the trouble, Detective Clancy?

CLANCY: Sorry to disturb you, Mr. Fischer, but we just caught a woman.

CHICO: At'sa fine. What you use for bait?

GROUCHO: Say, she looks pretty small. Maybe you better throw her back in the water again.

CLANCY: No, no, I caught this woman shoplifting.

KLEPTOMANIAC: Let me go. I didn't mean to do it, I tell you. I can't help it when I take things. I'm a kleptomaniac.

GROUCHO: Not one of the Boston Kleptomaniacs? Say, do you happen to know the Ginzbergs of old Virginny?

FISCHER: Mr. Flywheel, let me handle this. If it's the last thing I do, I'm going to *stop* stealing in my store.

CHICO: You oughta stop stealing in your store. If you're gonna steal, steal in somebody else's store.

CLANCY: Mr. Fischer, this woman's been trying to get away with silk underwear and—

KLEPTOMANIAC: Oh, please, please, give me another chance!

GROUCHO: Go ahead, Fischer, give her one more chance at the silk underwear, but if she doesn't get away with it next time, let her wear cotton.

FISCHER: Maybe I'll let her go this time, Flywheel. Jail is a pretty bad place.

GROUCHO: Nonsense, Fischer. If jail was good enough for your father, it's good enough for her.

FISCHER: We won't discuss that now, Flywheel. Young woman, I'm going to give you another chance. But don't let it happen again. All right, Clancy, let her go.

KLEPTOMANIAC: Oh, thank you, thank you—

CLANCY *(receding):*   Come on, lady.

(Door opens and closes.)

FISCHER: See what I'm up against, Flywheel? It isn't enough that the store is losing money; I also have to contend with stealing. Maybe that's where my profits are going. I'll admit I'm at my wit's end.

CHICO: *Wits* end do you mean? *(Laughs.)* Catch on?

GROUCHO: Ravelli, if you'd only wait to speak until you're spoken to, you'd never have to open your mouth.

FISCHER: Gentlemen, I've got to raise five thousand dollars to pay off my creditors, and I don't know what to do. I've exhausted all my resources.

CHICO: Resources? At'sa too bad. Racehorses don't runa very fast whena dey are exhausted.

FISCHER *(annoyed):*   I'm talking about financial resources.

GROUCHO: Look here, Fischer, I'm not going to spare your feelings. You've made a botch of things. But as my father used to say—or was it my uncle Charlie?—no, it couldn't be my uncle Charlie because I haven't *got* an uncle Charlie. *However,* it doesn't matter who said it because I've forgotten what he said anyway.

FISCHER: Flywheel, I don't quite see what you're getting at.

GROUCHO: It's all very simple, Fischer. What this store needs is something to stimulate business. I suggest a dollar sale.

FISCHER: A dollar sale?

CHICO: Sure, Mr. Fisch. I explain it for you what a dollar sale is. If you sell a dollar for ninety-eight cents, you'd sell 'em like hotcakes.

GROUCHO: Couldn't we save time by just selling the hotcakes?

FISCHER *(confused):*   Well . . . in the present condition of my nerves, I'm afraid I can't handle the situation. Perhaps I *do* need a vacation. Flywheel, what I'd like you to do is to take the place over for a couple of weeks . . . and maybe Ravelli could be a floorwalker.

CHICO: Sure, I can be a floorwalker. Whata you tink—I walk on da *ceiling?*

GROUCHO: Don't worry, Fischer. He'll make a good floorwalker. All you've got to do is supply the baby. As for my running the store, don't worry, I'll put an end to shoplifting. I'll have your business looking up before you come back.

FISCHER: You really mean you'll have my business looking up?

GROUCHO: Certainly. It'll have to look up. It'll be flat on its back.

(Music in strong.)

(Buzzing of voices.)

WOMAN EMPLOYEE: Fellow employees of the Fischer department store, you've all been assembled here to hear a few words from our new manager, that celebrated lawyer and efficiency expert, Waldorf Tecumseh Flywheel.

(Applause.)

GROUCHO: Quiet! Quiet! . . . That's enough applause—We're cutting down on everything. Employees of the Fischer Bon Ton Merchandise Company, I called this meeting today because I want to publicly reward old Joe Feffer for his forty-five years of loyalty to this firm. Step up, Joe.

OLD JOE *(approaches):*   Yes, Mr. Flywheel.

GROUCHO: Shut up, Joe . . . Joe, I want to tell the folks that you're a faithful, loyal, model employee. Folks, Joe is a faithful, loyal, model employee. *(Applause.)* In all his forty-five years of service, Joe has never been known to watch the clock. One reason is that he can't tell time. It's now my privilege to do something for Joe. For his forty-five years of loyal service I'm going to present him with this package of canary seeds. I could have bought him a canary, but I'm sure that Joe would rather plant these seeds and raise his own canaries.

OLD JOE: Thankee, Mr. Flywheel.

From MGM's *The Big Store*, based on Nat Perrin's *Flywheel* Episode 15. The film's working title, incidentally, was *The Bargain Basement*.

GROUCHO: But that isn't all, Joe. Someday next week I'm going to give you a half-day's holiday.

OLD JOE: Thanks again, Mr. Flywheel.

GROUCHO: Not at all, Joe. My only regret is that I'll have to dock you for the half day. *(Buzz of astonishment from audience.)* And now, Joe, get back to work. And remember, old boy, if I catch you loafing, I'll fire you. In fact, I think I'll fire you anyway. Give me back those canary seeds and beat it. And that goes for the rest of you, too! What do you all mean by loafing here when you should be working? Come on, get going. Scram.

(Buzz of voices receding.)

CHICO *(approaching):* Hey, boss! Boss!

GROUCHO: What is it, Ravelli?

CHICO *(excitedly):* Oh, boy, what a close shave!

GROUCHO: A close shave? What happened?

CHICO: Nuttin. I just used a very sharp razor.

GROUCHO: Well, why weren't you at the employee's meeting? I could have fired you too.

CHICO: I went out to get my lunch.

GROUCHO: Lunch? Why, it isn't nine o'clock yet.

CHICO: I know, boss. But if I get my lunch right after breakfast, I ain't so hungry. And I save money on da lunch. You know, I'm pretty broke, boss. Maybe you could give me a dollar?

GROUCHO: Well, here's a dollar, and remember, spend it carefully, because I worked hard for this money.

CHICO: Hey, you borrowed it from me.

GROUCHO: Well, that was hard work. Ravelli, while I'm in charge of the store, everybody's got to keep busy. I've picked out a job for you. I'm going to put you to work in men's clothing.

CHICO: Hey, boss, you're crazy. I'm in men's clothing now, except dat I'm wearing my wife's shoes.

GROUCHO: Come on, Ravelli. Get over to that clothing counter. And remember our slogan, "The customer is always right."

CHICO: You mean I gotta be wrong *all* da time?

GROUCHO: Don't worry. That'll take care of itself. Just bear in mind: The customer is always right.

CHICO: Okay, boss, here comes somebody. Maybe I can sell him someting.

GROUCHO *(receding):* All right, but before I go, I want to remind you that in this store, it's strictly one price. And that price is anything we can get. *(Away.)* See you later.

CUSTOMER: Say, clerk, I want to buy a suit.

CHICO: Hey! Don't kid me. You're wearing a suit.

CUSTOMER: That's a nice way to talk to a customer.

CHICO: You a customer? At'sa fine. Anyting you say is all right wit me, even if you're crazy. Whatta you want?

CUSTOMER: I thought of getting a tweed suit, but I think I'd rather look at a herringbone.

CHICO: Okay, customer, you sit here. I go out and find a herring.

CUSTOMER *(loudly):* I said herringbone! It's a kind of cloth. Herringbone!

CHICO: Hey, whatta you hollering for? You tink I'm hard of herring?

CUSTOMER: On second thought, I don't think I'd look so well in a herringbone suit.

CHICO: You're right, customer. You'd look terrible.

CUSTOMER: Say, you're not a very good salesman, are you?

CHICO: Dat'sa right. I'ma rotten!

CUSTOMER: How much is this brown suit?

CHICO: Dat suit? Well, da regular price is fifty dollars. It costs us sixty. It's worth a hunnerd. But we'll give it to you for tirty, and we only make twenty bucks profit.

CUSTOMER: Thirty dollars for that suit? Why, that's highway robbery.

CHICO: At'sa right, customer. We oughta be arrested.

CUSTOMER: Well, the suit seems all right . . . but what's this stain on the coat? It looks like rust.

CHICO: Rust? At'sa fine. Dat means it wears like iron.

CUSTOMER: Do you expect me to believe that? You must think I'm crazy.

CHICO: At'sa right, customer. I tink you're nuts.

CUSTOMER: Why, you insolent fool!

CHICO: You said it, customer.

CUSTOMER (thinking aloud): However, the suit isn't bad. It's a size thirty-eight, isn't it?

CHICO: Right, customer, it's a size tirty-eight. It's even more dan tirty-eight. It's a size forty-two.

CUSTOMER: I don't seem to be getting anywhere with you. Where's the manager? Call the manager.

CHICO: Sure, customer. Hey, boss! Hey, Mr. Flywheel!

GROUCHO (approaching): Ravelli, I can only be in one place at a time— and I'm pretty sick of that place. What's the trouble here?

CUSTOMER: I'm having a little difficulty with your clerk. I'd like to get a suit.

GROUCHO: Well, step right in front of this mirror. No, maybe you'd better not. You might scare yourself. Here, try on this coat and vest.

CUSTOMER: All right. (Puts coat on.) Why, this coat doesn't fit me at all. It looks like a sack.

GROUCHO: Well, it's a sack coat. Besides, is it my fault if you're too thin?

CUSTOMER: Well, do you think you could cut it down to fit me?

GROUCHO: Why should we bother? Why don't you go home and fatten up?

CUSTOMER: But I tell you, it's too big. Why, *two* men could get into this suit.

CHICO: At'sa right, customer. Maybe you can get a friend to wear it wit you.

CUSTOMER: Hmm. The vest is a little loose, but that I don't mind. I like a little room in the vest.

CHICO: A little room in da vest. We'll give you a little gray home in da vest with nine rooms.

CUSTOMER: Now, what about the trousers?

GROUCHO: Stranger, with a coat that long you don't need any trousers.

CUSTOMER: That's preposterous. I want trousers.

GROUCHO: Very well. How long do you want the trousers?

CUSTOMER: I want them as long as the ones I'm wearing.

CHICO: You want 'em dat long? Boss, I tink he wants 'em about twenty years.

CUSTOMER: Do you think you can fix the suit in time for me to wear it out this afternoon?

GROUCHO: Certainly not. It'll take you at least a week to wear out this suit.

CUSTOMER: Why! You're even more stupid than your clerk!

(CHICO *laughs loudly.*)

GROUCHO: What are you laughing at, Ravelli?

CHICO: Dis time da customer *is* right.

CUSTOMER *(indignant):* I'll never buy here again! *(Receding.)* Goodbye!

GROUCHO: You did a nice job, Ravelli. At this rate, we won't have any customers in the store.

CHICO: At'sa fine. If we gotta no customers, we gotta no shoplifters. Hey, boss, dat reminds me. I just saw a very crooked-looking guy in the sheet-music department.

GROUCHO: Is that so? Maybe he wanted to steal a march on us.

CHICO: He was a big, tough guy. I don't like da way he looks. I tink he was a shoplifter.

GROUCHO: That doesn't follow, Ravelli. I don't like the way you look, and you're no shoplifter.

CHICO: Hey! Here comes that big guy I was telling you about.

GROUCHO: That guy? Why, you sap, that's Clancy, the store detective.

CLANCY *(approaching):* Mr. Flywheel, I was told that Mr. Ravelli would help me watch the store. He's supposed to be an undercover man in the basement.

GROUCHO: Are you crazy?

CLANCY: Why, what do you mean?

GROUCHO: You ought to know that we can't put Ravelli in the basement.

CLANCY: Well, why not?

GROUCHO: Because he's no bargain.

(*Music in strong.*)

(*Phone rings.*)

SECRETARY: This is the Fischer department store . . . No, Mr. Fischer isn't back yet. We expect him back today. Mr. Flywheel is still in charge of the store . . . Goodbye.

(*Knock on door.*)

SECRETARY: Come in.

COLLECTOR *(opens door):* Good morning. I'm Harvey Jones, of the Whole-sale Mercantile Company. Mr. Flywheel sent for me.

SECRETARY: He's in his private office. I'll call him. Mr. Flywheel! Mr. Flywheel!

GROUCHO *(opens door; harshly):* See here, Miss Brown!

SECRETARY: Yes, Mr. Flywheel?

GROUCHO *(softening):* Didn't I ask you to call me Snookums?

SECRETARY: Ah . . . This is Mr. Jones, of the Wholesale Mercantile Company.

COLLECTOR: Yes, Mr. Flywheel. I suppose you know that this store bought five hundred bolts of cloth from us *two years* ago, and hasn't paid for them yet?

GROUCHO: Yes, that's why I sent for you.

COLLECTOR: You want to pay for the cloth?

GROUCHO: *No,* I want to order five hundred more bolts on the same terms. We need the cloth to make more pants for our new three-pants suits.

COLLECTOR: I've got to get paid first.

GROUCHO: Suppose I give you a note?

COLLECTOR: Well—I don't know. Is the note good?

GROUCHO: Jones, if our notes were any good, we'd make notes, not pants. Now run along, I've got a lot of work to do.

COLLECTOR: I'll never do business with this firm again. *Good day! (Slams door.)*

SECRETARY: Mr. Flywheel . . .

GROUCHO: Yes, Miss Brown.

SECRETARY: A customer wants to know if the store will take back a dress she bought here.

GROUCHO: Certainly we'll take it back.

SECRETARY: Now about refunding the money—

GROUCHO: Who said anything about refunding the money? I just said we'd take back the dress.

SECRETARY: Why . . . yes . . . Oh, I meant to tell you. Someone has taken out all the fire extinguishers.

GROUCHO: What? Send for Ravelli! Send for Ravelli!

CHICO *(opens door):* Here I am, boss. Say, boss, I wanna ask you some-tin. Can I get in trouble for sometin I didn't do?

GROUCHO: Well, as a lawyer, I would say no. Why do you ask?

CHICO: Well, a lady gave me a ten-dollar bill, and I didn't give her no change. Boy, was I worried!

GROUCHO: Never mind that. I wanted to see you about something else.

A fine floorwalker you are! Someone has stolen all the fire extinguishers and you didn't even know about it.

CHICO: Da joke's on you boss. Nobody stole 'em. I took 'em out and sold 'em.

GROUCHO: You sold them?

CHICO: Sure. We wasn't using them. Dis store ain't had a fire since we been here.

GROUCHO: See, here, Ravelli, Fischer's coming back today, so you'd better get busy. Make as many sales as you can, and at the same time watch out for shoplifters.

CHICO: Okay, boss. You leave it to Ravelli.

(*Door opens and store noises are heard.*)

CHICO: Hello, lady, you lookin for somebody?

WOMAN CUSTOMER: I'd like to see a chaise lounge.

CHICO: Oh, you wanna eat? The lounge room is downstairs.

WOMAN CUSTOMER: I said a chaise lounge!

CHICO: Sure, I had dat kind of lounge yesterday—chaise and crackers.

WOMAN CUSTOMER: Well, never mind that. I also want to see some pictures.

CHICO: At'sa fine. If you got some money, we go to the picture show next door.

WOMAN CUSTOMER: I don't mean moving pictures. I mean paintings, photographs—

CHICO: Oh, dose kinda pictures. I gotta joosta what you want. I sell you a nicea picture of me when I was a littla baby.

WOMAN CUSTOMER: *Such* stupidity! The manager will hear about this! Where's the manager?

GROUCHO (*away*): Ravelli, what's happening over here?

CHICO: Aw, she don't know what she wants. First, she asks for lounge, then she asks for pictures—

GROUCHO: Pictures? Madam, I've got a very nice picture that you might be interested in. It's a picture of Washington crossing the Delaware.

WOMAN CUSTOMER: Splendid! I'd like to see it.

GROUCHO: Well, I'll have to take off my shirt first. I've got the picture tattoed on my chest.

CHICO: Aw, I don't wanna see dat picture again. I'm gonna beat it. (*Receding.*) Goodbye, lady. I'll see you in da chaise lounge room.

WOMAN CUSTOMER: See, here, manager, I came here to buy things.

GROUCHO: Very well, if you'll step over to this counter. I'll try and sell you a few choice articles that we haven't been able to *give* away. Now, here's a genuine, imported Chinese rug. It was made by a couple of Russians in Tennessee.

WOMAN CUSTOMER: I don't want a rug!

GROUCHO: All right, then how about this nice blue ribbon? It's the kind they give to thoroughbred dogs. Of course, I realize that you're not a thoroughbred, but it wouldn't look bad in your hair.

WOMAN CUSTOMER: A ribbon in my hair? That's much too youthful.

GROUCHO: Tush, tush, madam. You could have your face lifted. Two or three truckdrivers could lift it easily.

WOMAN CUSTOMER: This is outrageous! I'll never come into this store again. *(Receding.)* Idiot!

CHICO *(approaching):*   Oh, boss. Boss!

GROUCHO: What is it, Ravelli?

CHICO: Dere's Clancy standing by da jewelry counter. He'sa puttin tings in his pockets when nobody's looking.

GROUCHO: What do you mean, nobody's looking? We're looking, aren't we?

CHICO: Boss, be careful. You know dat Clancy's a great bigga guy and plenty tough.

GROUCHO: Ravelli, you may be right. Notify me when you see a small guy shoplifting. Look, Ravelli, he just stuffed a necklace and some diamond bracelets in his pockets.

CHICO: Hey, boss, he's coming over here!

CLANCY *(approaching):*   Say there, Ravelli, what are you doing snooping around here? You look like a suspicious character to me.

CHICO: At'sa right, Clancy.

CLANCY: So you admit you're a suspicious character.

CHICO: Sure, I'm suspicious of you. *(Laughs.)* And dat's no joke.

CLANCY *(nervously):*   What are you talking about? What do you mean you are suspicious of me? Well . . . aw . . . I gotta go. *(Receding.)* So long.

GROUCHO: Oh, no, you don't. Come back here, Clancy.

CHICO: Boss, dere's a cop! Hey, cop! Stop Clancy! He's a crook.

OFFICER *(away):*   This fellow? . . . I got him.

(Sound of scuffle.)

CLANCY: Let go of me! I'm the store detective.

GROUCHO: Well, look in his pockets, officer. He's stolen some jewelry.

OFFICER: Yeah? I'll take a look.

(Scuffle; CLANCY *ad libs protests.)*

OFFICER: Say! Here's the jewelry all right. I'll put the bracelets on him and take him away. *(Receding.)* Come along.

CHICO *(laughs):*   Mr. Flywheel, he can't put da bracelets on Clancy.

GROUCHO: He can't?

CHICO: No. He can put da necklace on him, but I took da bracelets outa Clancy's pocket. Say, here comes Mr. Fischer.

FISCHER: Gentlemen, I just heard how you trapped Clancy. Clancy, of all people! And I'm very happy. I guess you put an end to shoplifting in this store, all right.

WOMAN EMPLOYEE *(approaching very excitedly):* Oh, Mr. Fischer, Mr. Fischer!

FISCHER: Just a moment, floorlady.

WOMAN EMPLOYEE: But the basement is a regular riot! We've got to have more merchandise in the bargain basement. We're selling everything we got.

FISCHER: Oh, that is wonderful! Mr. Flywheel, how did you do it?

GROUCHO *(modestly):* Oh, it was nothing, Fischer, I just gave them good values, that's all.

WOMAN EMPLOYEE: And, Mr. Fischer, as long as you're back in charge, will you okay this order for twenty thousand more pianos?

FISCHER: Twenty thousand pianos! Flywheel, we can't get rid of twenty thousand pianos! Why, we're overstocked now.

Groucho, here as private detective Wolf J. Flywheel, takes a nap on company time in *The Big Store* [1941].

GROUCHO: That's where you're wrong, Fischer. I got rid of the five hundred pianos we had in less than an hour.

FISCHER: You did?

GROUCHO: Of course. That's how I increased business.

FISCHER: Oh, that's marvelous. That is superb! But, Flywheel, you think you can sell twenty thousand more pianos?

GROUCHO: Sell them? Who said anything about selling them? I'm giving away a piano free with every purchase over a dollar.

(*Music in strong.*)

AFTERPIECE

GROUCHO: Ladies and gentlemen—

CHICO: Wait a minute, Groucho! I gotta some bad news. They joosta told me I got a raise.

GROUCHO: You got a raise, Chico, and you call that bad news?

CHICO: Sure I gotta raise two hundred dollars or dey'll trow me outta my house.

GROUCHO (*dramatically*): Chico, you have nothing to worry about. I wouldn't see a brother of mine thrown out on the street. No, not while I have a roof over my head. I have a little room over at my place, Chico, and it's yours for seven dollars a day. But I'll have to remind you that unless you bring baggage, you'll have to pay in advance.

CHICO: Hey! Is dat a way to treat a brudder? Last time I come to your house I bring you a present—a big phonograph record.

GROUCHO: A phonograph record? I meant to talk to you about that, Chico. That was a manhole cover.

CHICO: Dat'sa funny. I found it in front of a phonograph store. And didn't I bring you a fine oil painting?

GROUCHO: Oil painting? That was a pencil drawing of a bottle.

CHICO: I know, but it was a bottle of Essolube—dat famous hydrofined motor oil.

GROUCHO: Now a word about Esso, which is more powerful than any gasoline and—

CHICO: No, we got no time to talk about Esso. We better say good night.

BOTH (*singing*): Good night, ladies. good night, ladies.

(*Signature music.*)

FIVE STAR THEATER
PRESENTS

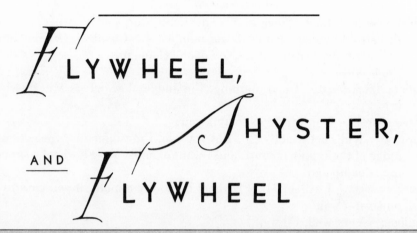

FLYWHEEL, SHYSTER, AND FLYWHEEL

EPISODE NO. 16   *MARCH 13, 1933*

CAST

Groucho Marx as Waldorf T. Flywheel
Chico Marx as Emmanuel Ravelli
Miss Dimple
Plunkett
Spike, a photographer
Reporter
District Attorney
Judge
Doorman
Bailiff

(Typewriter clicks; phone rings twice; lifting of receiver cuts off second ring.)

MISS DIMPLE: Law offices of Flywheel, Shyster, and Flywheel . . . No, I'm afraid you've got the wrong number . . . Goodbye. *(Hangs up receiver, resumes typing; knock on door.)* Come in.

(Door opens.)

JUDGE *(pompous):* Good morning. I'm Judge Maxwell. Is Mr. Flywheel in?

MISS DIMPLE: No, was he expecting you?

JUDGE: Well, not exactly . . . But you see, I'm running for reelection as judge of the criminal court, and I want to enlist Mr. Flywheel's support in my campaign.

MISS DIMPLE: I expect Mr. Flywheel back any minute, if you care to sit down and wait.

JUDGE: Very well, I'll wait.

(Typing resumes; someone humming "Daffodils" heard distantly.)

MISS DIMPLE: That sounds like Mr. Ravelli. He's Mr. Flywheel's assistant. Maybe *he* can help you.

(Door opens.)

CHICO: Hello, Miss Dimp.

MISS DIMPLE: Mr. Ravelli, this is Judge Maxwell.

CHICO: Jawdge Maxwell? Hey, mister, are you any relation to Gawge Washington?

JUDGE: No, no, I'm a *judge.* Do you know when Mr. Flywheel will be in?

CHICO: Who cares about Flywheel? I got *enough* to worry about.

MISS DIMPLE: Why, what's the trouble, Mr. Ravelli?

CHICO: Well, I buy a nice bigga dog and my little baby is afraid of him.

MISS DIMPLE: What are you going to do?

CHICO: I don't know—I tink I sell da baby.

JUDGE: See here, young man, *you can't sell a baby.*

CHICO: No? Well, maybe I can *raffle* him off.

MISS DIMPLE: Mr. Ravelli, I'm sure you can't mean that. You wouldn't want to give up your little boy.

CHICO: Aw, I tink you're right, Miss Dimp. Dat kid and me have *some* fun together. You know, last Christmas I buy him a sled and we both take turns using it. I take it going *down* da hill and he takes it back *up* da hill.

(Footsteps heard.)

MISS DIMPLE: Oh, judge, I hear Mr. Flywheel.

(Door opens.)

MISS DIMPLE: Good morning, Mr. Flywheel.

GROUCHO: Can't you think of anything *else* to say? You say that to me *every* morning.

JUDGE: Oh, Mr. Flywheel, you remember me, Judge Maxwell. I've been planning for a long time to drop in and talk to you about the coming election.

GROUCHO *(impatiently):*   I know. I know.

JUDGE: Really? How did you *know?*

GROUCHO: Why, you just told me.

JUDGE: Mr. Flywheel, while I have been judge of the criminal court, I have fought for social reform, tax reform, prison reform, and—

CHICO: Hey, what about *chloro*form?

GROUCHO: Nice work, Ravelli. I think I'll get you some.

JUDGE: Mr. Flywheel, my reelection is being bitterly fought by a faction of grafting politicians. Their leader is Big Boss Plunkett, who, as you know, is going to be tried for bribery shortly after the election. He doesn't want me on the bench because he knows I can't be tampered with.

GROUCHO *(indignant):*   See here, Judge Maxwell. *Did you come here to buy my vote?*

JUDGE: Why, no, of course not.

GROUCHO: Then you're wasting my time . . . and *my* time is valuable. Do you realize that while you're here talking nonsense, I could be at my desk, sleeping?

JUDGE: You don't understand, Mr. Flywheel. *I am here to enlist your support in my election campaign.*

CHICO: At'sa fine. I take two bottles.

JUDGE: Two bottles of what?

CHICO: Two bottles of campaign. *(Big laugh.)* At'sa some joke!

JUDGE: I said campaign, not *champagne!*

CHICO: Oh yeah! I know whata champagne is, too. Jack Sharkey—he's the heavyweight champagne. Hey, you wanna box?

JUDGE: Gentlemen! From your attitude I can only conclude that you are in sympathy with Boss Plunkett and his crooked politics. *I'm going.*

CHICO: Just a minoots, judge. I wanna ask you a question.

JUDGE: Well?

CHICO: If it takes two pints to fill a quart, how much does it take to Philadelphia?

JUDGE: I've heard enough of this. *Good day.*
   (Door slams.)

GROUCHO: Ravelli, I'm ashamed of you. I saw you taking your hand out of Judge Maxwell's pocket.

CHICO: Well, I had to take it out sometime.

(*Knock on door.*)

MISS DIMPLE: There's someone at the door. (*Louder knock.*) Come in.

(*Door opens.*)

MISS DIMPLE (*whispering*):   Why, it's Boss Plunkett, the politician!

PLUNKETT: Hello, Flywheel. How do you find yourself?

GROUCHO: Very easily. I just get up in the morning and there I am. Ravelli, take Plunkett's hat.

CHICO: *You* take it, boss. It won't fit me.

PLUNKETT: Flywheel, my pal. Joe Crookley tells me that if it hadn't been for the way you defended him in court, he'd have gone to prison for twenty years. He says you're a pretty smart lawyer.

GROUCHO (*coyly*):   Oh, I don't take his flattery seriously. That Joe Crookley is just a silly old cutthroat.

PLUNKETT: Listen, Flywheel, I want to talk turkey to you.

GROUCHO (*whispering*):   I think you'd better talk English. I don't want Ravelli to understand.

PLUNKETT: Look here, I'm against Judge Maxwell's being reelected. I'm in a position to get you nominated to run against him if you're willing to take orders.

CHICO: Hey! Maybe you can use my brudder. *He* takes orders—for spaghetti.

GROUCHO: Yes, Plunkett, the last order his brother got was from the Board of Health. They ordered him to stop selling that spaghetti.

PLUNKETT: Well, Flywheel, what do you say? If you join our party, I'll see to it that you get the nomination for judge.

GROUCHO: Plunkett, I'm willing to accept the nomination, but I'm afraid I can't join your party.

PLUNKETT: Why not?

GROUCHO: Frankly, I haven't a thing to wear.

(*Music in strong.*)

(*Horns blowing, excited crowd, street noises.*)

DOORMAN: You guys can't come in this door. If you wanna hear the Flywheel-Maxwell political debate, you've got to go around to the main entrance.

PHOTOGRAPHER: But we're from the press.

REPORTER: We want to interview one of the candidates, Mr. Flywheel, about tomorrow's election.

PHOTOGRAPHER: And I wanna get some pictures.

DOORMAN: Okay, come on in. (*Opens door; street noises fade.*) Waldorf Flywheel's in that room down the hall. (*Receding.*) First door to the right.

PHOTOGRAPHER: Thanks.

REPORTER: Funny how this man Flywheel has jumped into prominence so *suddenly*.

PHOTOGRAPHER: Well, when Big Boss Plunkett gets behind a candidate, he's as good as elected. . . . Here's the room . . . I think I ought to knock. *(Knocks on door.)*

GROUCHO *(inside):* Come in.

(Door opens and closes.)

PHOTOGRAPHER: Good evening, Mr. Flywheel.

REPORTER: Mr. Flywheel, we're from the press.

GROUCHO: Good, you can press my pants.

REPORTER: No, we are from the newspapers. We're here for an interview.

GROUCHO: Reporters, eh? Well, you can quote me as saying that *(Shifting to broad French accent.)* I am seemply cray-zee about your bee-oo-ty-ful coun-*tree*. I zink your bee-oo-ty-ful American women are—how is it you say in your bee-oo-ty-ful language—bee-ooo-ty-ful! And your handsome men, zay are so *strong*, but all zay zink of is money, money, money. But in zee *old countree* . . . ah . . . zay always zink of money, money, money.

REPORTER: No, no, Mr. Flywheel. What we want is your views on tomorrow's election.

(Door opens and closes.)

CHICO *(running in, excited):* Hey, boss!

GROUCHO: What's the matter, Ravelli?

CHICO: Dere's *some* big crowd outside. When I tried to come in here, a policeman wanted to hit me.

GROUCHO: How do you *know* he wanted to hit you?

CHICO: Because he *hit* me. Whata you gonna do about it, boss?

GROUCHO: I'm busy now, but I'll thank him later.

REPORTER: Mr. Flywheel, our paper would like to get a record of all that you've done in this town.

CHICO: Come on, don't bodder my boss. You can get his record at da police station.

GROUCHO: Shut up, Ravelli. Reporter, I'd like to say that everything I am I owe to my great-grandfather, old Cyrus Tecumseh Flywheel. If he were alive today, the whole world would be talking about him.

REPORTER: Just why, Mr. Flywheel?

GROUCHO: Well, if he were alive today, he'd be a hundred and forty years old.

REPORTER: But, Mr. Flywheel—

CHICO *(interrupting):* Excuse me, please, Mrs. Reporter. I gotta sometin very important to ask my boss. Hey, Flywheel, was dat *hair tonic* you had in dat bottle on your desk?

GROUCHO: No, it was glue.

CHICO: *Glue? (Big laugh.)* No *wonder* I can't get my *hat* off!
(Door opens.)

CHICO: Hey, here comes Big Boss Plunkett. He looksa mad.

PLUNKETT: Flywheel, Flywheel!

GROUCHO: Just a minute, old boy, I want you to meet the reporters. Reporters, this is my friend and manager, Big Boss Plunkett. There are two things I want to say about Plunkett. *First,* he's never been in prison. And *second,* I don't know why.

PLUNKETT: See here, Flywheel. What kind of campaign do you call this? You've got the town plastered with posters saying "Flywheel Is *For* and *Against* Beer."

GROUCHO: Certainly. I want to get the votes from both sides.

PLUNKETT: And who put your picture all around town with the slogan "Vote for Roosevelt" under it?

CHICO *(pleased):* I did dat, Mister Plunkett.

PLUNKETT: *You* did?

CHICO: Sure, dat's a great slogan. It's da same one our *president* used, and *he* got elected.

REPORTER: Sorry to interrupt, Mr. Plunkett, but we've got to get back to the paper. And we'd like to get a photograph of Mr. Flywheel.

GROUCHO: A picture of me? Certainly. Wait till I get my hat.

REPORTER: But Mr. Flywheel, you're *wearing* a hat.

GROUCHO: I know, but a candidate needs *two* hats. One to *wear* and one to *talk* through.

PHOTOGRAPHER: Hold that smile, Mr. Flywheel. Here goes! *(Flashbulb explosion.)* Thank you! And goodbye!
(Door opens and closes.)

PLUNKETT: See here, you guys, I didn't want to say this in front of the reporters, but—

GROUCHO: *Now* what are you going to squawk about, Plunkett?

PLUNKETT *(coldly accusing):* There's a thousand dollars missing from the campaign fund.

CHICO: Awright, Plunkett. *You* putta back five hunnerd, *I'll* putta back five hunnerd and we both forget about it.
(Knocking on door.)

PLUNKETT: Come in.

DOORMAN: Time for the debate.

PLUNKETT: Come on, boys . . . right through this door. *(Door opens.)*

This is a shortcut to the platform. *(Sounds of them walking.)* Remember, Ravelli, I had a tough time getting you the job as chairman of this debate. Do you *know* anything about a debate?

CHICO: Aw, sure! I explain it to you. When you wanna catch fish, you usea debate.

GROUCHO: There you are, Plunkett. You'd have to go pretty far to find a better chairman than Ravelli. And I wish you'd start now.

PLUNKETT *(annoyed):*   Come on! Let's get going—right through this door. *(Door opens, sounds of audience cheering, horns blowing and ad libbed cries of "we want Flywheel," "Flywheel for judge," "hooray for Maxwell," "we want Maxwell.")*

MAN'S VOICE: Ladies and gentlemen. The debate on judicial reform between Judge Herbert Maxwell and Waldorf Tecumseh Flywheel is about to begin. I now present the chairman of the meeting, Mr. Emmanuel Ravelli.

(Applause.)

CHICO *(oratorical):*   Awright, everybody please shut up your mouths. De foist guy I wanna interduce is a man who everybody isa crazy about. A man who'sa very smart, good to littla kids, and to big kids too . . . and he ain't afraid of nuttin. Ladies and gentlemens, dat man is *me! (Loud applause.)* Now I gonna call on Georgie Maxwell.

(Applause.)

JUDGE: Mr. Chairman, ladies and gentlemen. I was born in this city forty-eight years ago. I studied law here. I married here. And I do not hesitate to say that in all my forty-eight years, man and boy, judge and layman,—

GROUCHO: Just a minute, chairman.

CHICO: Whata you want, boss?

GROUCHO: If this guy's gonna talk only about himself, I'm going home.

JUDGE: *Please*, Mr. Flywheel, you'll get your chance later . . . Ladies and gentlemen, my candidacy is being fought by a group of men who are dishonest, grafting and meretricious!

CHICO: Tank you, judge, and I wish you da same.

JUDGE: You wish me *what?*

CHICO: A meretricious. A meretricious and a happy new year!

JUDGE: Kindly let me proceed. *(To audience.)* Ladies and gentlemen, my opponent now straddles the wet and dry question. But isn't it a fact, Mr. Flywheel, that you voted *in favor* of prohibition?

GROUCHO: Well, I was drunk at the time. However, don't let *that* mislead you folks. I don't drink anything stronger than pop—but my pop drinks *anything*.

JUDGE: *Mr. Flywheel, will you let me go on with my address?* Friends, my political views are an open book. I'm not afraid to submit to any question from anyone in this great auditorium.

CHICO: All right. *I* ask you a question. What has tree wheels and flies? Give up? A broken garbage wagon. *(Laughs.)* Oh, boy, at's some nifty!

JUDGE *(enraged):* Mr. Chairman, will you or will you not let me go on with my speech? Fellow citizens, I feel that—

CHICO *(pounds gavel):* At's all, Georgie. Your time is up.

JUDGE *(astonished):* My time is up? Why, how long have I talked?

CHICO: I don't know. I ain't got a watch. You sit down. *(To audience:)* And now, peoples, you gonna hear from my boss, Mister Flywheel, the *winner* of this debate. Okay, Flywheel.

(Buzz of astonishment.)

GROUCHO: Well, folks, I'm sorry my speech had to be delayed, but Maxwell insisted on talking. *(Eloquent.)* Fellow citizens, I'm here to tell you that if you elect Judge Maxwell tomorrow, this government of the people, by the people, and for the people . . . will fall into the hands of the people . . . And Big Boss Plunkett will never stand for that. A vote for Flywheel means a vote for free speech, free press, free wheeling and free cheers for the red, white and blue. *(Applause.)* My esteemed opponent . . . is all steamed up. And why? Because I broke a few promises. Well, I can make new ones just as good. And to you women in the audience, I can only say that I am *for* you. There's one thing I'll *never forget* as long as I can remember it . . . and that is, that the mothers of some of our *greatest* men were women. *(Applause.)* Judge Maxwell has been talking about restoring the franchise. Folks, I'm enough of a patriot to say that franch eyes are no prettier than American eyes. *(Applause.)* In the words of the immortal poet, whose name eludes me at the moment, I want to say:

(Dramatic:) Twinkle, twinkle, little star
        How I wonder where you are
        Up above the sky so high—

CHICO *(cutting in excitedly):* Hey boss! Whata you talkin about?

GROUCHO: Quiet, Ravelli! I'm trying to get the *children's* vote.

JUDGE: Mr. Flywheel, as long as you've seen fit to challenge my integrity, I'd like to ask you a question. Isn't it true that your organization has bought twenty thousand votes to swing tomorrow's election?

GROUCHO: *Say*, Maxwell, I'm glad you brought that up. We *did* buy twenty thousand votes.

JUDGE: What?

GROUCHO: But don't get excited. I've got some good news for you.

JUDGE: Good news?

GROUCHO: Yes, we bought five thousand more votes than we need, and we'll sell 'em to you at cost price.
(*Music in strong.*)

SPIKE: Well, Plunkett, Judge Flywheel owes a lot to you.

PLUNKETT: Yeah, we ran away with the election.

SPIKE: It's a lucky thing for you that your trial's coming up in *his* court.

PLUNKETT: Lucky? What do you think I got him put in office for? Judge Maxwell woulda given me twenty years on this bribery charge. But with Flywheel on the bench, I oughta get off in a couple of hours.

SPIKE: What about that lawyer you got, that Ravelli? He don't look any too smart to me.

PLUNKETT: Oh, Ravelli's all right. Flywheel asked me to hire him. I guess they got the whole thing worked out between them.

SPIKE: Yeah?

PLUNKETT: Sure, I ain't even demandin' a jury—I'm leaving it all in Judge Flywheel's hands. Let's go in. The courtroom's filling up.
(*Buzz of voices, pounding of gavel.*)

BAILIFF: Hear ye, hear ye, hear ye. The district court is now in session and stands until adjournment. Everybody rise. His honor, Judge Flywheel. Good morning, your honor.

GROUCHO: Aw, lay down, bailiff. Don't come boot-licking around just because I'm a *judge* now. You never called me "your honor" *before* I became a judge.

BAILIFF: But your honor—

GROUCHO: Never mind that. Where's the court stenographer? I want him to take a letter to my wife.

BAILIFF: Why, *he* can't take a letter to your wife.

GROUCHO: He can't? Hmm. *Some* stenographer. Better look around for a *new* stenographer. And while you're at it, look around for someone to take *your* place too. What's the first case?

BAILIFF: It's the case of Harry Hillbert, charged with operating a poolroom within three hundred feet of a schoolhouse.

GROUCHO: A poolroom three hundred feet from a schoolhouse? That's a disgrace. Have them move the schoolhouse. I don't want those little kiddies walking that far. Bailiff, what day is this?

BAILIFF: Thursday, your honor.

GROUCHO: *Thursday* already? Then it's time I went out for lunch.

BAILIFF: But Judge Flywheel, you haven't tried any cases yet.

GROUCHO: All right, bring one on. I'll try anything once.

BAILIFF: Next case on the calendar is the trial of John H. Plunkett, charged with bribing public officials.

The Freedonian High Court in all its glory in *Duck Soup*, which recycled many of the courtroom shenanigans from Episodes 12 and 16 of *Flywheel*.

GROUCHO: Where's your lawyer, Plunkett?

PLUNKETT: You mean Mr. *Ravelli?* He isn't here yet, judge.

CHICO *(away):* Here I am, Flywheel.

GROUCHO: Look here, Ravelli! Call me *judge*!

CHICO: What'sa matter? You changed your name?

GROUCHO: Ravelli, are you the lawyer for the defendant?

CHICO: Naw, I'm da lawyer for dis *crook*, Plunkett.

PLUNKETT: Say! What do you mean by saying I'm a crook?

CHICO: Awright, awright. *I* didn't know it was a secret.

DISTRICT ATTORNEY: Your honor!

GROUCHO: What is it, district attorney?

DISTRICT ATTORNEY: The state is prepared to proceed with the trial of John H. Plunkett. Our first witness is Leo Greenbury.

GROUCHO: Oh, no. Greenbury can't be a witness in *this* court.

DISTRICT ATTORNEY *(astonished):*   *Why not,* your honor?

GROUCHO: Well, he told my wife's butcher that he didn't vote for me. The sneak!

DISTRICT ATTORNEY: Why, I have never heard a judge say anything so undignified.

GROUCHO: Oh, you're a *wise* guy! Just for that I fine you twenty bucks for contempt of court—

DISTRICT ATTORNEY: But your honor—

GROUCHO: That's allright. You can pay off in scrip. I can use it at my house tonight. We're going to play scrip poker.

DISTRICT ATTORNEY: I regret to say, your honor, that I consider your remark most unbecoming to a judge.

GROUCHO: *What did you say?*

DISTRICT ATTORNEY: I said your remark was most unbecoming to a judge.

GROUCHO: Hey, that's the *second* time you said that. Just for that I fine you a *hundred* bucks. I dare you to insult me again.

DISTRICT ATTORNEY: Oh, never mind.

GROUCHO *(coaxing):*   Oh, come on. I'll let you have this insult for *fifty* bucks.

DISTRICT ATTORNEY: Your honor, these proceedings have been most unjudicial. I move for a new trial.

CHICO: Hey, where you gonna move to?

DISTRICT ATTORNEY: *Please* don't interrupt, Mr. Ravelli. I don't know what right you have to appear in this case. You're not even a member of the bar.

CHICO: Oh, so you wanna get fresh wit me? Awright, joosta for dat *I* fine you twenty bucks for contempt of court.

GROUCHO: Ravelli, how can I charge a *hundred* bucks if you're going to let him insult you for twenty?

CHICO: Shut up, judge, or I fine *you* twenty bucks.

GROUCHO: In that case, I'll fine *you* twenty bucks, so we'll be even. Plunkett, you keep score, and if you let him win, I'll fine you twenty bucks, too.

CHICO: Another fine? At'sa *fine.*

DISTRICT ATTORNEY: *Your honor,* I don't think the state can get a fair trial in this court. I demand a change of venue.

GROUCHO: I'm sorry, old boy, but we're all out of them. Could you use a nice habeas corpus instead?

CHICO: Habeas corpus? You crazy, boss. You mean a Habeas Irish Rose . . . Come on, Plunkett, you get on da witness stand, I aska you questions.

PLUNKETT: Awright, Mister Ravelli.

BAILIFF: You promise to tell the truth, the whole truth and nothing but the truth.

PLUNKETT: I do.

BAILIFF: What's your name?

PLUNKETT: John H. Plunkett.

BAILIFF *(announcing):*   John Plunkett sworn in—

PLUNKETT: John *H.* Plunkett. You forgot the H.

CHICO: The aitch? Awright, I take your *aitch.* How old are you?

PLUNKETT: I'm forty-five.

CHICO: Hey, Judge, I object.

GROUCHO: You object to your own witness's answer? On what grounds?

CHICO: I don't know. I couldn't tink of anytin else to say.

GROUCHO: Objection sustained.

DISTRICT ATTORNEY: Your honor, you *sustain* the objection. On what grounds?

GROUCHO: *I* couldn't think of anything else to say either. Ravelli, proceed with your questioning.

CHICO: Okay, boss. Mister Plunkett, what is it dat has a trunk but no clothes and is in a circus?

DISTRICT ATTORNEY: Your honor, that's irrelevant!

CHICO: A relephant? Hey! Dat's de *answer.* Dere's a whole buncher elephants in a circus.

DISTRICT ATTORNEY: Please, Mr. Ravelli. Why don't you question Plunkett on the incidents mentioned in the indictment? Why don't you ask him about the part he played in that hotel episode?

CHICO: You crazy? Dere *ain't* no hotel episode. You mean da Hotel *Ritzmore?*

DISTRICT ATTORNEY: Mr. Ravelli, I would like to remind you that Plunkett is accused of having paid a thousand dollars to the mayor for a promise to let him run a gambling house. Fortunately for the people of the city, the major did *not keep his promise.*

CHICO: Oh, is *dat* so? Well, den we gonna sue da mayor for breach of promise, eh Plunkett?

DISTRICT ATTORNEY: *If your honor pleases,* the state wishes to—

GROUCHO: Aw, pipe down and give somebody else a chance. You talk more than my wife. That's why I never got married. Now, after hearing both sides of the case, I'm clearly convinced that there's too much divorce in this country. How does divorce start?

CHICO: I know, boss! It starts wit a *d—*

GROUCHO: Shut up, Ravelli! Folks, I'll tell you how divorce starts. The husband goes to Paris, the wife goes to Japan, and then they gradually drift apart.

DISTRICT ATTORNEY: The state objects, your honor. This is not a divorce case! John H. Plunkett is charged with *bribery!*

GROUCHO: Bribery? Why wasn't I told about that? I don't count, do I? Oh, no. I'm just the judge here, that's all. Plunkett, I'm going to give you your choice of sentences: ten years in Leavenworth, or eleven years in twelveworth.

PLUNKETT: What?

GROUCHO: All right. We'll make it five and ten in *Woolworth*.

PLUNKETT: Wait a minute, your honor. I'm on *trial* here. The state ain't *proved* that I'm guilty of bribery.

GROUCHO: The state doesn't have to. I know you're guilty.

PLUNKETT: Say, how do you *know* I'm guilty?

GROUCHO: Are you *kidding*, Plunkett? Don't you remember? You bribed *me*. That's how I became a judge.

PLUNKETT: You doublecrosser! I'll take this to a higher court.

CHICO: Okay, Plunkett, dere's a nicea court upstairs.

(*Buzz in court.*)

MAXWELL (*away*): Right this way. Right this way.

CHICO: Boss, here comes Judge Maxwell.

MAXWELL: Mr. Flywheel, we have just come from the election board. Your sitting on the bench is absolutely illegal. We've just discovered that Emmanuel Ravelli voted more than once.

GROUCHO (*excited*): Is that *right*, Ravelli? Did you vote more than once?

CHICO: Well, let me see. (*Thoughtfully.*) Mmm, maybe I did.

GROUCHO (*excitedly*): Well, did you or didn't you? Think, man, think!

CHICO (*slowly*): I voted one . . . two . . . tree . . . YEP, I voted *tree tousand times*.

(*Signature music.*)

FIVE STAR THEATER
PRESENTS

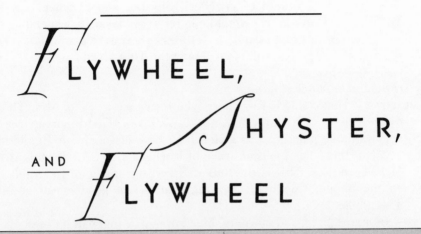

FLYWHEEL,

SHYSTER,

AND FLYWHEEL

EPISODE NO. 17   *MARCH 20, 1933*

CAST

Groucho Marx as Waldorf T. Flywheel
Chico Marx as Emmanuel Ravelli
Miss Dimple
Mrs. Thorndyke
Meadows, the butler
Reporter

(Typewriting heard; phone rings.)

MISS DIMPLE: Law offices of Flywheel, Shyster, and Flywheel . . . No, Mr. Flywheel isn't in. He won't be in for a few days. He's spending the weekend out in Long Island . . . at Mrs. Thorndyke's home . . . Yes, his assistant, Mr. Ravelli, is visiting at the Thorndykes' too . . . *(Fade out.)* Goodbye . . .

(Fade in on phone ringing.)

MEADOWS: Hello, this is the Thorndyke residence . . . No, Mrs. Thorndyke declines to be interviewed . . . Well, yes. That report is true. A very valuable painting was stolen from here last night. A Rembrandt . . . No, there has been no trace of it whatsoever . . . No, this is not Mr. Thorndyke. This is the butler. Sorry, but that's all I can tell you on the phone. Goodbye. *(Turning away.)* Oh, good morning, Mrs. Thorndyke.

MRS. THORNDYKE: Good morning, Meadows. Was that call for me?

MEADOWS: It was another newspaperman.

MRS. THORNDYKE: Did he have any news about the stolen painting?

MEADOWS: No, that's what he was after, madam.

MRS. THORNDYKE: Oh dear, that Rembrandt was the finest picture in my collection. Why, it cost over a hundred thousand dollars.

MEADOWS: Yes, madam.

MRS. THORNDYKE: And the humiliation! Being robbed when I'm entertaining so many prominent guests.

MEADOWS: Have the police found any clues at all, madam?

MRS. THORNDYKE: No, they seem completely baffled.

MEADOWS: May I suggest, madam, that you ask Mr. Flywheel and his assistant, Mr. Ravelli, to take over the case? They are lawyers, and surely they must have some understanding of the criminal mind and its workings.

MRS. THORNDYKE: A splendid suggestion, Meadows. I think I'll speak to Mr. Flywheel. Have you seen him this morning?

MEADOWS: Yes, he went horseback riding. Say, I believe he's coming in.

MRS. THORNDYKE: Why yes. *(Calling out.)* Oh, good morning, Mr. Flywheel . . . Why, what in the world are you looking for?

GROUCHO: I lost my horse. He slipped right out from between me. I had my feet in the syrups too. I don't know how he got away. I didn't care about that. But I lost the bit you loaned me.

MRS. THORNDYKE: Oh, that's all right. I'll get you another bit.

GROUCHO: Well, that'll be *two* bits I owe you.

MRS. THORNDYKE: Mr. Flywheel, I hope you've not been distressed by last night's unfortunate occurrence.

Groucho defends the honor of Margaret Dumont (Mrs. Rittenhouse) in this scene from *Animal Crackers* [1930]. Episode 17 lifts the movie's plot device of a stolen painting as well as its Long Island setting.

GROUCHO: You mean the dinner you served? It wasn't much worse than the lunch.

MRS. THORNDYKE: No, I mean the painting that was stolen.

GROUCHO: Was there a painting stolen? I haven't seen a paper in three weeks. Are you sure you're in the right house? Where's my assistant, Ravelli?

CHICO *(entering):*   Hey, here I am, boss!

GROUCHO: Ravelli, why didn't you inform me that there was a painting stolen? What do you think I hired you for?

CHICO: But boss, I didn't know it.

GROUCHO: You should have asked me. I didn't know it either.

CHICO: Well, I'm sorry.

GROUCHO: Sorry, are you? Well, you're a contemptible cur. I repeat, sir, you're a contemptible cur. Oh, if I were a man, you'd resent that . . . I can get along without you, you know. I got along without your father, didn't I? Yes, and your grandfather. Yes, and your uncle. Yes, Mrs. Thorndyke, and your uncle too. And my uncle as well.

MEADOWS *(away):* I beg pardon, madam.

MRS. THORNDYKE: What is it, Meadows?

MEADOWS: The police are here.

MRS. THORNDYKE: The police? Have them come in.

MEADOWS *(receding):* Very good, madam.

GROUCHO: Oh, that's your game, Mrs. Thorndyke! Well, you can't shut *me* up.

MRS. THORNDYKE: But, Mr. Flywheel—

GROUCHO: Never mind, your attorney will hear about this. Ravelli, take a letter. I'll show this dame a thing or three. Ravelli, take dictation.

CHICO: I am takin it, boss.

GROUCHO: Read me what you have . . . Never mind. Take this: "Honorable Charles D. Vasserschlogel, c/o Vasserschlagel, Vasserschlegel, Vasserschlugel, and McCormick, semicolon."

CHICO: How do you spell semicolon?

GROUCHO: Make it a comma. Hmmm. "Dear Elsie:". . . No, never mind Elsie.

CHICO: Oh, you wanna I should scratch Elsie?

GROUCHO: Well, if you enjoy that sort of thing, it's quite all right with me. However, you'd better take it up with Elsie. Begin this way, Ravelli: "Honorable Charles D. Vasserschlogel, c/o Vasserschlagel, Vasserschlegel, Vasserschlugel, and McCormick. Gentlemen, question mark. In re yours of the fifth inst. yours to hand and in reply, I wish to state that the judiciary expenditures of this year, i.e., have not exceeded the fiscal year—brackets—this procedure is problematical. Quotes, unquotes, and quotes. Hoping this finds you, I beg to remain"—

CHICO: Hoping dis finds him where?

GROUCHO: Well, let him worry about that. Hang it all, don't be insolent, Ravelli . . . Sneak. "Hoping this finds you, I beg to remain as of March twentieth, Cordially, respectfully, regards." Ah, that's all, Ravelli. Well, Mrs. Thorndyke, this will show you where I get off. Now, Ravelli, read me what you have.

CHICO *(reading):* "Honorable Charles D. Vasserschlogel, c/o Vasserschlagel, Vasserschlegel, and McCormick"—

GROUCHO: You left out a Vasserschlugel. Thought you could slip one over on me, didn't you, eh? All right, leave it out, and put in a windshield wiper instead. No, make it three windshield wipers and one Vasserschlugel. Go on with the reading.

CHICO: "Dear Elsie, scratch"—

GROUCHO: That won't do at all, Ravelli. That won't do at all. The way you've got it, you've got McCormick scratching Elsie. Turn that around and have Elsie scratch McCormick. You'd better turn McCormick around too, Ravelli. And see what you can do for me.

CHICO: Awright, I read some more. "Gentlemen, question mark . . ."

GROUCHO: Well, go on.

CHICO: After dat, boss, you said a lot of tings I don't tink was important, so I joosta left dem out.

GROUCHO: So you just left them out, eh? You just left them out? You left out the body of the letter, that's all. Yours not to reason why, Ravelli. You left out the body of the letter. All right, send it that way and tell them the body will follow. Closely followed by yours.

CHICO: Hey, boss, you want da body in brackets?

GROUCHO: No, it'll never get there in brackets. Put it in a box. Put it in a box and mark it *fragile.*

CHICO: Mark it what?

GROUCHO: Mark it *fragile.* F-r-a-g—look it up, Ravelli. Look under *fragile.*

CHICO: Lemme see. Ah . . ."quotes, unquotes, quotes."

GROUCHO: That's three quotes.

CHICO: Yeah, I add another quote and make it a gallon.

GROUCHO: That's fine, Ravelli. That's going to make a dandy letter. I want you to make two carbon copies of that and throw the original away. And when you get through with that, throw the carbon copies away. Just send a stamp, airmail. That's all.

MRS. THORNDYKE *(approaching):* Mr. Flywheel—

GROUCHO: Now, what's the matter, Mrs. Thorndyke?

MRS. THORNDYKE: I'm sorry, you're so upset. I guess that stolen picture has upset everybody in the house.

CHICO: Picture stolen? Hey, you don't gotta worry, lady, everytin's gonna be all right. You just let me and my boss work on dis case for twenty-four hours, and den we'll call in somebody else.

GROUCHO: Madam, you think it's a mystery now. Wait till you see it tomorrow! Remember the Charley Ross disappearance? We worked on that case for twenty-four hours and they never did find him.

CHICO: Yeah. Dey couldn't find *us* for five years.

(Music in strong.)

. . .

(*Doorbell rings.*)

MRS. THORNDYKE: Meadows, answer the door.

MEADOWS: Yes, Mrs. Thorndyke.

(*He walks to door; opens it.*)

REPORTER: Is Mrs. Thorndyke in?

MEADOWS: Who shall I say is calling?

REPORTER: I'm a reporter from the *Morning Dispatch*. I'd like to talk to Mrs. Thorndyke about the robbery.

MRS. THORNDYKE: I'll speak to the gentleman, Meadows. Mr. Reporter, you may say in your paper that I have every confidence that the picture will be returned and the mystery solved.

REPORTER: Have the police found any clues?

MRS. THORNDYKE: No, but that eminent criminal lawyer, Waldorf T. Flywheel, is one of my houseguests, and he has very kindly offered to aid in the investigation.

REPORTER: Could I talk to Mr. Flywheel?

MRS. THORNDYKE: Oh, no. He has taken over the case and he is very much absorbed in it. I wouldn't want to disturb him.

REPORTER: I just wanted to know what he's doing about finding the picture.

MRS. THORNDYKE: Well, he hasn't talked to me about his activities, but I do know that he has sent for a copy—an exact duplicate—of the stolen painting. He says it will be useful in his investigation.

GROUCHO (*away*): Mrs. Thorndyke, Mrs. Thorndyke!

MRS. THORNDYKE: That's Mr. Flywheel calling me. If there's any more news, I'll phone your paper.

REPORTER: Thank you. Goodbye.

(*Door closes.*)

GROUCHO (*near*): Hey, Mrs. Thorndyke!

MRS. THORNDYKE: Here I am, Mr. Flywheel. Have you found any trace of the picture thieves?

GROUCHO: You've nothing to worry about, madam. I hadn't been on the case five minutes and they stole my watch. It wasn't going, and now it's gone. Wait a minute! The watch fob's gone now, too. Well, I've still got the pocket. Anything I retain now is velvet, except the coat, and that's Prince Albert.

MEADOWS (*approaching*): Pardon me, Mrs. Thorndyke.

MRS. THORNDYKE: Yes, Meadows.

MEADOWS: Here's that copy of the stolen painting, the duplicate that Mr. Flywheel asked me to get.

GROUCHO: Yes, Mrs. Thorndyke, the copy may help me solve the mystery. Let me take a look at that picture.

MEADOWS: There you are, sir.

GROUCHO *(examines it):*   Hmm. Hmm. Say, it's signed Rembrandt. There's the criminal—Rembrandt.

MRS. THORNDYKE: Why, Mr. Flywheel! Rembrandt is dead!

GROUCHO: What! Rembrandt is dead? Then it's murder. Now we've got something. Ravelli, Ravelli!

CHICO: Whatta you want, boss?

GROUCHO: Come over here, Ravelli! Isn't there something that strikes you very funny about this picture?

CHICO: Yeah. *(Laughs heartily.)*

GROUCHO: Come, come! It isn't as funny as all that. Did you ever see a tree like the one in this picture?

CHICO: Dat'sa no tree, dat's spinach.

GROUCHO: It can't be spinach, where's the egg?

CHICO: Well, it could be spinach. Look at all da sand around dere. Nope, you're right, boss, dat'sa cole slaw.

GROUCHO: Cole slaw? Did you ever see cole slaw like that?

CHICO: Sure, I got a cole slaw on my mout'.

GROUCHO: I don't want any of your lip. Say, this is a left-handed painting. Look at the signature.

CHICO: You're right. It's in da right-hand corner.

GROUCHO: This is either a left-handed painting or a vegetable dinner. Now, in order to solve the mystery, all we got to do is to find the left-handed person who painted it. In a case like this, the first thing we got to do is to find a motive. Now, what could have been the motive of the guys who swiped the Rembrandt?

CHICO: I got it, boss. Robbery!

(Music in strong.)

CHICO: Boss. Boss!

GROUCHO: What is it, Ravelli?

CHICO: Mrs. Thorndyke is givin a five-tousand-dollar reward for anybody who finds dat paintin.

GROUCHO: Well?

CHICO: I got an idea how to find it. Of course, in a case like dis, what's so mysterious—you gotta to do like a Sherlock Holmes. You gotta get whatta dey calla da clues. Now you go about it lika dis—you say to yourself, What have you? And de answer come right back, Someting was stolen. Den you say to yourself, What was stolen? And de answer come right back, A painting.

GROUCHO: Say, what are you, a ventriloquist?

CHICO: Now, you say to yourself, Who stola da painting? And de answer come right back, Somebody in dis house. So far I'm right, eh boss?

GROUCHO: Well, it's pretty hard to be wrong if you keep answering yourself all the time.

CHICO: Now, you take da clue, and you put 'em together. And whatta we got? A painting was stolen. Where was it stolen? In dis house. Who stole it? Somebody in dis house. Now, to find de painting, all we got to do is to go to everybody in dis house, and we ask dem if dey took it. Dat's what you call a brain—eh, boss?

GROUCHO: You know, I could rent you out as a decoy for duck hunters. You say you're going to go to everybody in this house and ask them if they took it, eh? Suppose nobody in the house took the painting?

CHICO: Den we go to da house next door.

GROUCHO: Well, suppose there isn't any house next door?

CHICO: Well, den of course, we got to build one.

GROUCHO: Well now, you're talking. What kind of a house do you think we ought to put up?

CHICO: Well, I tell you what my idea is. I tink we builda someting nice and small and comfortable.

GROUCHO: That's the way I feel about it. I don't want anything elaborate. Just a little place that I can call home and tell the wife I won't be home for dinner.

CHICO: Look here, boss, I draw some plans on da table. What you say we build right about here?

GROUCHO: No, I think I'd like something over here, if I could get it. I don't like Junior crossing the tracks on his way to the reform school. As a matter of fact, I don't like Junior at all.

CHICO: All right, we gotta someting over here. And believe me, dat'sa very convenient. Oh, very convenient. Look, all you have to do is to open da door, step outside, and dere you are.

GROUCHO: There you are? There you are where?

CHICO: Outside.

GROUCHO: Well, suppose you want to get back in again?

CHICO: You had no right to go out.

GROUCHO: Well, that's a quarter I owe you. Now all we've got to do is to find the painting.

CHICO: Ah, dat's where my detective brain comes in. Now we gotta hurry up and build da house because I tink the painting is inside.

GROUCHO: Maybe it's me. Maybe I'm not getting enough sleep these days. Let me take a look at those plans. Say, maybe that's the painting down in the cellar.

CHICO: Dat's no cellar. Dat's da roof.

GROUCHO: That's the roof, way down there?

CHICO: Sure, you see we keep da roof in da basement, so when da rain comes, da chinemy he'sa no get wet. Now, what do you say? Are you ready to sign da lease?

GROUCHO: Well, it's a little abrupt. I'd like to discuss it with my husband. Could you come back this evening?

CHICO: Are you married?

GROUCHO: Didn't you see me sewing on little things? Why, I've got a girl as big as you are.

CHICO: Well, get me one.

GROUCHO: How about the painting, Ravelli?

CHICO: Oh, we take care of dat. I tink da kitchen should be white, da dining room should be green—

GROUCHO: No, no, the painting. The *painting.*

CHICO: Dat's what I say, da painting. Da kitchen should be white, da dining room—

GROUCHO: No, I'm not talking about the kitchen. I mean the painting. The painting that was stolen. Don't you remember there was a painting stolen? A valuable oil painting? Don't you remember that?

CHICO: No, I'm a stranger around here.

GROUCHO: Who do you think I am? One of the early settlers? Don't you remember that Mrs. Thorndyke lost a valuable Rembrandt oil painting worth a hundred thousand dollars? Don't you remember that?

CHICO: No. But I've seen you someplace before.

GROUCHO: Well, I don't know where I was, but I won't go there again.

CHICO: Hey, boss, it comes to me like a flash. You know what happened to dis painting? Dis painting wasn't stolen.

GROUCHO: No?

CHICO: Dis painting disappear. And you know what make it disappear? Moths. Moths eat it. Left-handed moths. Dat's my solution.

GROUCHO: Well, I wish you were in it. You say that left-handed moths ate the painting, eh? You know, I'd buy you a parachute if I thought it wouldn't open.

CHICO: I got a pair of shoes.

GROUCHO: Well, let's get out of here. I've taken an awful lacing here tonight. We solved it, though. You solved it. Let's go and get the reward. The painting was eaten by a left-handed moth. I don't know how I overlooked it.

CHICO: You know we did a good day's work.

GROUCHO: How do you feel, tired? Maybe you ought to lie down for a couple of years?

CHICO: Naw, I stick it out.

MRS. THORNDYKE *(away, excited):*   Oh, Mr. Flywheel, Mr. Flywheel!

CHICO: Hey, it'sa Mrs. Thorndyke. We ask her for da reward.

MRS. THORNDYKE: Gentlemen, something amazing has happened.

CHICO: We don't care about dat. We joosta found out what happened to da picture. Da moths ate your picture, so you can give us the five-tousand-dollar reward.

MRS. THORNDYKE: Give you five thousand dollars' reward! Why, the picture was just found under your bed. Mr. Ravelli, I hate to say this, but I suspect *you* stole the Rembrandt.

CHICO: Awright, den I take *tree* tousand dollars' reward.

(Music in strong.)

AFTERPIECE

CHICO: Ladies and gentlemens. Ladies and gentlemens.

GROUCHO: Chico, you said that twice.

CHICO: Well, da first time I said it I wasn't listenin.

GROUCHO: Chico, you've got the brain of a four-year-old boy. And I'll bet he was glad to get rid of it. Say, what's the matter with your eye? It looks bruised.

CHICO: Aw, dat's from overeatin.

GROUCHO: A black eye from overeating?

CHICO: Sure, I went in a restaurant and ate more dan I could pay for. *(Whispering.)* Hey, Grouch, you better go out da back way. Dat taxi driver is still waitin for da dollar and a half you didn't want to pay him.

GROUCHO: Is he a taxi driver? *(Laughs.)* That's a good one on him. I didn't want a taxi. I just wanted a lift. I was hitch-hiking. I could have walked, but I wanted to come early.

CHICO: Hey, a taxi don't come erly. You gotta erl it yourself . . . with Essolube, dat hydrofined motor erl.

GROUCHO: Yeah? How do you know?

CHICO: My garage man, he sez so.

GROUCHO: Not sez so. You mean Esso, which is more powerful than any gasoline.

BOTH *(singing):*   Good night, ladies. Good night, ladies.

(Signature music.)

FIVE STAR THEATER
PRESENTS

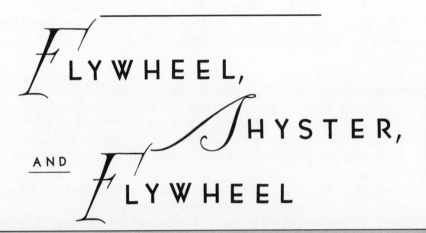

Flywheel, Shyster, and Flywheel

EPISODE NO. 18   MARCH 27, 1933

CAST

Groucho Marx as Waldorf T. Flywheel
Chico Marx as Emmanuel Ravelli
Miss Dimple
Colonel Thistledown
Barkers
Madame Zodiac
Zodiac
Spindello
Freaks
Man
Lady
Crowd voices

(*Phone rings.*)

MISS DIMPLE: Hello. Law offices of Flywheel, Shyster, and Flywheel . . . Oh, Alfred. I've told you not to phone me at the office . . . No, Alfred. Mr. Flywheel doesn't like me to talk to gentlemen on his phone . . . Goodbye.

(*Door opens.*)

GROUCHO: Miss Dimple, who was that on the phone?

MISS DIMPLE: Why . . . er . . . er, that was nobody, Mr. Flywheel.

GROUCHO: Come, come, Miss Dimple. If you want to fool me you'll have to get up pretty early in the morning. But there's no use your doing that, because I won't be awake anyhow. Miss Dimple, is that you snoring?

MISS DIMPLE: Why, no. I didn't want to say anything about it, but your assistant, Mr. Ravelli, is asleep under the desk.

GROUCHO: Ravelli, get off the floor. You'll catch cold sleeping there with nothing but that thin desk over you.

CHICO: Okay, boss. Trow on another desk.

GROUCHO: We haven't got another desk handy, but if you'll get up, I'll wrap this chair around your neck. Tell me, why didn't you come to work yesterday?

CHICO: Well, boss, my grandmotter died and I had to go to da ball game.

GROUCHO: Ball game? Why, the baseball season won't start for three weeks.

CHICO: Awright, I can wait.

GROUCHO: You can wait, eh? You can *wait?* Ravelli, I'd horsewhip you if I had a horse.

CHICO: Hey, don't be mad, boss. Here, I bring you a nice red apple. But you gotta give me half.

GROUCHO: Why, you've already eaten half.

CHICO: Yeah, but dat was your half I ate.

(*Knock on door.*)

MISS DIMPLE: Come in.

(*Door opens.*)

COLONEL: Good morning. My name is Thistledown.

GROUCHO: Say! Your face is familiar. Did anyone ever tell you that you look like a rat?

COLONEL: Sir, I want to hire a lawyer. Where's Mr. Flywheel?

GROUCHO: What's the difference where I am? How much is there in it for me?

COLONEL: Mr. Flywheel, I'm here on rather ticklish business.

GROUCHO: Well, you can tickle Miss Dimple. I've got more important things to do. Ravelli, where's my jigsaw puzzle?

COLONEL: Just a minute, Mr. Flywheel. I came to see you on legal business. I'm Colonel Oliver S. Thistledown.

CHICO: Hey, boss, what's da *colonel* for?

GROUCHO: That's obvious, Ravelli. The man's a nut.

COLONEL: Mr. Flywheel, let's not beat about the bush—

GROUCHO *(coaxing):*   Ah yes, *let's.* The last one around the bush is a cockeyed weasel.

COLONEL: *Please,* Mister Flywheel. I am the owner of Thistledown's famous emporium of human abnormalities, now on public display in the great amusement center of Coney Island. To be more explicit, sir, I operate a freak show.

GROUCHO: Sorry, colonel, we can't join your freak show. We're lawyers.

COLONEL: I know, sir, that's why I'm here. You see, last week an upstart who calls himself Cyrus Braxley opened a rival freak show right across the street from me. Up until that time, sir, my great show was the only one of its kind in Coney Island. But now . . . now I can tell you a different story.

GROUCHO: Why don't you stick to this story? It's pretty dull, but I'd like to know how it ends.

COLONEL: Ah . . . This Braxley has not only stolen my customers but has dared to slander my good name. Me—Oliver S. Thistledown!

CHICO: Hey, at'sa not such a good name.

COLONEL: To go on with my story. Braxley has said things about me that I would not even repeat in public. I intend to sue him for libel. Why, only yesterday he dared to call me a . . . dirty crook.

GROUCHO: He called you a dirty crook, eh? That settles it. We'll handle your case, colonel. Miss Dimple, take this dirty crook's telephone number.

COLONEL: Sir, I resent that.

GROUCHO: Oh, you do, eh? Then I'll wash my hands of this case. Miss Dimple, give him back his telephone number. *(Muttering.)* The dirty crook!

COLONEL: Sir, I'll thank you not to insult me.

GROUCHO: You're very welcome, colonel. I knew you'd see it our way. Now what's on your mind besides tickling Miss Dimple?

COLONEL: Well, sir, this Braxley has been using underhanded methods to steal away my business. He has tried to get my employees to break their contracts, and he has spread false reports about me. Now, as a lawyer, Mr. Flywheel, I feel that you are in a position to do something for me.

GROUCHO: If you'll turn around, colonel, I think I'm in a position to kick you out of the office.

COLONEL *(annoyed):*   What! Well, I've said all I'm going to say about the case. If you're interested, I'll expect you at Coney Island this afternoon. *(Receding.)* Good day! *(Slams door.)*

GROUCHO: Ravelli, get my lawbook. We're off to Coney Island.

CHICO: Okay, boss, you take da lawbook, I'll take da subway.

GROUCHO: We'll need some money. Run over to the bank and get that ten dollars you deposited for me.

CHICO: I didn't have time to go to da bank, boss, so I put da money in my wife's stocking. Here it is.

GROUCHO: Hold on. I gave you ten dollars and there are only four dollars here.

CHICO: I forgot to tell you, boss, but dere was a run on da stocking. *(Music in strong.)*

(Sound of calliope, loud voices, merrymaking. Fades down.)

CHICO: Some fun, eh, boss? Hey, I lika dis Coney Island.

GROUCHO: Come on, Ravelli, come on. We've got to find Colonel Thistledown and his aggregation of freaks.

BARKER 1 *(voice entering scene):*   In this tent, folks, Madame Zodiac, the world's greatest palm reader! From your hand she reads the past, the present, and the future. Only a quarter, folks.

CHICO: Come on in, boss. I wanna get my hand read.

GROUCHO: Look at those hands. Aren't you ashamed to show Madame Zodiac such dirty hands?

CHICO: She won't see 'em. I'll wear gloves.

ZODIAC *(approaching):*   Sit down, gentlemen. For twenty-five cents, I look at your palm.

GROUCHO: I've only got a dime. Just look at my tonsils.

CHICO: Here's my hand, lady. Read it out loud.

ZODIAC: Not this hand. The other hand.

GROUCHO: If you want his other hand, Madame, you'll find it in your pocketbook.

ZODIAC *(spiritually):*   Ah, in your hand I see a beautiful woman.

CHICO: Where? I don't see nuttin.

ZODIAC: Quiet. I see a beautiful woman.

GROUCHO: Take another look and see if she's got a friend for me.

ZODIAC: Ah, she is so sweet, so young, so charming—

GROUCHO: In that case, see if she has a friend for *Ravelli.* I'll take *her.*

ZODIAC: From the palm, gentlemen, I see all life—the past, the present, and the future. Have you any question to ask?

CHICO: Yeah, dere's sometin I'd like to find out. If it takes a hunnerd and eighty chipmunks to make a baby elephant a fur coat, how long will it take a cockroach wit a wooden leg to crawl through a bar of kitchen soap?

GROUCHO *(indignant):* Just a minute, Ravelli! This woman is a palm reader, and she hasn't time for your idiotic drivel. *I'll* ask her a question, a question I've been wanting to ask from the moment I came in. Madame Zodiac, have you been eating onions?

ZODIAC: What! Get out of here! Both of you. Insolent dogs! Get out! Get out!

(Calliope again; shots heard.)

CHICO: Hey boss! She's shootin at me! Do sometin! I'm too young to die.

GROUCHO: Nonsense, Ravelli. You're just the right age. Unfortunately, no one's shooting at you; it's only the shooting gallery next door.

(A few shots, then barker's voice; sound of shooting dies down.)

BARKER 2: Step right up, gentlemen. Ten shots for ten cents. Here ye are, gentlemen. Hit the target and get a cigar.

CHICO: Wait a minoots, boss. I want a cigar. Give me dat gun, mister.

GROUCHO: Take two guns, Ravelli, and get me a cigar too.

BARKER 2: Here you are, buddy. Aim at the bull's-eye.

CHICO: Bull's eye? I can't even see da bull.

BARKER 2: Here you are, sir. I'll show you how to do it. *(Shot followed by ringing bell.)* See, I hit the bull's-eye. Now you try it.

CHICO: At'sa fine. Hey boss, I'ma some shot. Watcha me ring da bell.

GROUCHO: Ravelli, why don't you try shooting off the gun instead of your mouth?

(Shot, glass crashes.)

CHICO: Hey, what did I hit?

GROUCHO: A plate-glass window in that house behind you. You're doing fine. Just a minute. Don't shoot.

CHICO: Why not?

GROUCHO: Wait till I get in front of you. When *you're* shooting, that's the safest place to stand. Now blaze away.

CHICO: Awright, joost watcha me. *(Series of shots.)* Hey, I'ma pretty good, eh, boss?

GROUCHO: What do you mean? You haven't hit anything yet.

CHICO: Well, I wasn't aimin at anyting.

GROUCHO: Well, aim at those ducks, and you might hit that heifer and get a prize.

CHICO: Okay, boss. You know, a heifer prize is better dan none. Awright. I aim at da ducks, joost lika you say.

GROUCHO: Thanks, Ravelli. You aim to please.

CHICO: Here I go, boss! *(Shot.)* Duck. *(Shot.)* Duck. *(Shot.)* Duck. *(Shot.)*

GROUCHO: Run, Ravelli, run. You hit three ducks.

CHICO: At'sa fine. But why should I run?

GROUCHO: You hit three ducks and the proprietor.

CHICO: I didn't know it was da proprietor.

GROUCHO: Well, I don't blame you for making a mistake. He had on duck pants.

CHICO: Hey, you crazy? Ducks don't wear pants.

(*Sound of merry-go-round and other noises; dies down.*)

GROUCHO: Hurry up, Ravelli. I think we're near the colonel's freak show.

BARKER 3 *(away):* Ladies and gentlemen. Right this way for Colonel Thistledown's big show . . .

CHICO: Hey, boss, look! Dere's da colonel standing on dat little platform over dere. Whata you tink he's up to?

GROUCHO: He's up to his knees in midgets. Ah, there, colonel!

COLONEL: Gentlemen, welcome to my emporium. See how my business is being ruined by that scoundrel Braxley? Just look at the crowds at his place.

GROUCHO: Never mind, colonel. We'll fix him. In the meantime, let's take a look at your freaks.

COLONEL: This way, Mr. Flywheel. Just step inside this tent. It gives me great pleasure to show you my aggregation of strange people. Now here is Bravura, the only living sword-swallower.

GROUCHO: That man's a sword-swallower? He's laying down on you, colonel. I just saw him swallow a penknife.

CHICO: Maybe he's on a diet.

COLONEL: And there's Spindello, the world's thinnest man. Just look at those ribs.

GROUCHO: Do you think I could get him to come over to my house next Monday? We're having spare ribs and sauerkraut, and we've only got the sauerkraut.

SPINDELLO *(approaching):* Colonel Thistledown.

COLONEL: What is it, Spindello?

SPINDELLO: We're quitting the show. You haven't paid us for weeks. And besides, Braxley has offered us more money to work across the street, and we're joining him.

COLONEL: You can't walk out on me, Spindello.

SPINDELLO: Yes, we're all going. The strongman, Bravura the sword-swallower, Almira the fat lady, the midgets, and all the rest. Come on, all of you, all over to Braxley's.

FREAKS: Okay. Right. We're with you.

GROUCHO: Just one big happy family, Ravelli. It makes me homesick.

CHICO: Hey boss. You ain't *home* sick. You're sick right here. *(Big laugh.)* Some joke, eh, boss?

COLONEL *(frantic):* They're going! They're walking out on me! Stop them, Mr. Flywheel! Stop them!

GROUCHO: Ravelli, this calls for action. We've got to stop them. You grab the strongman. I'll tackle a midget. *(Scuffle heard.)* Help, Ravelli! This midget's choking me!

CHICO: How can a little midget choke you?

GROUCHO: He's choking me around the knees.

CHICO *(big laugh):*   Some choke, eh, boss?

COLONEL: Oh, this is terrible. Terrible. What will I do?

(Sounds of scuffling and loud noises.)

GROUCHO: Ravelli, come out from behind the fat lady and fight like a man.

CHICO: I can't move, boss, she's sittin on me.

SPINDELLO: Come on. Come on, everybody. Leave 'em alone. Let's go over to Braxley's.

FREAKS: Come on. On to Braxley's. *(Receding.)* This'll teach Thistledown not to pay us.

COLONEL: Gentlemen, my freaks have quit me. I'm ruined. I'm crushed.

CHICO: You think you're crushed. Look what da fat lady did to me.

GROUCHO: Come, Ravelli, come. This is no time to cry over spilled milk.

CHICO: Hey, at'sa no milk. At'sa blood.

(Music in strong.)

COLONEL: Why, Mr. Ravelli, what are you doing out here in front of my tent with that little table?

CHICO: Hey, colonel, don't you worry. Da freaks, dey run away, but you still gotta me and Flywheel.

COLONEL: Well, what do you plan to do?

CHICO: Me, I joost learn a new game. I make us a lotta money.

COLONEL: A new game? What is it?

CHICO: It's called da confidence game. Da customer, she got da money, and I gotta confidence I can take it away.

COLONEL: How does it work?

CHICO: Look, I show you. Right here I got tree walnut shells. *(Sound of shells on table.)* Now here I gotta little ball. I putta da ball under da shell. I mova da shells around lika dis. Da hand she'sa quicker dan de eye. Now, I betcha you no can guess which shell da ball is under.

COLONEL: It's under the middle one.

CHICO *(laughs):*   You wrong. It's under disa one. Am I good?

COLONEL: Marvelous. Marvelous!

CHICO: You joost wait, colonel. We gonna clean up. You come back in a little while and watcha how much I got for you.

COLONEL: Well, I wish you luck. I'll see you later.

CHICO *(yelling):* Anybody wanna bet? Anybody wanna make a bet? Anybody wanna play da confidence game? Anybody wanna get trimmed? What you say dere, sucker?

MAN: Huh? What have you got there?

CHICO: You wanna play dis game wit me? I show you da hand she is quicker dan de eye. You see dis little ball? I betcha you can't tell which shell I gotta dis ball under.

MAN: Okay, I'll take that bet. I'll bet you a dollar.

CHICO: Awright, mister. You watcha close. I prove it da hand she is quicker dan de eye. *(Sound of moving shells.)* Now whicha one you guess it's under?

MAN: It's under the one on the left.

CHICO: Wait a minoot, I look. *(Slight pause, then plaintively:)* I tell you what. I give you one more guess.

MAN: I don't want another guess. I saw you put it under the one on the left.

CHICO: Hey, at'sa no fair. You peek.

MAN: Come on. Give me my dollar.

CHICO: Awright, awright.

MAN *(receding):* Thanks. Goodbye.

CHICO: At'sa funny. It no work. Well, maybe next time. Anybody wanna bet? Anybody else wanna lose at da confidence game? How about you, lady? I show you da hand she is quicker dan de eye.

LADY: Oh, what have you there?

CHICO: You never mind. Joosta betta me a dollar. I take no chances. I explain it to you after it's over. I pusha dis little ball under da shell. I move 'em around quick. *(Sound of moving shells.)* You know da hand she is quicker dan de eye. Now lady, I tell you what shell to pick. You say da ball she is under da middle one.

LADY: But it's not under the middle shell. It's under the shell on the right.

CHICO: Hey, lady, who's playing dis game, you or me? You picka da middle shell.

LADY: But I insist that it's under the shell on the right. Here, I'll pick it up myself. See, I told you.

CHICO: Well, maybe I got it wrong. Maybe the *eye* she is quicker dan da *hand.*

LADY: My dollar, please. Do you want to play again?

CHICO: No, lady, I no can afford it. I tink dis is a rich man's game.

LADY: Goodbye.

CHICO: Anybody want to buy a nice shell game? Anybody want a lawyer? Anybody want a lawyer?

GROUCHO *(approaching):* What are you doing, Ravelli? What sort of act are you putting on?

CHICO: Hey boss, I just lose two dollars puttin on a shell act.

GROUCHO: And you got shellacked, eh?

COLONEL *(approaching):* Mr. Flywheel, Mr. Flywheel!

GROUCHO: Now what are you beefing about, Colonel Thistledown?

COLONEL: Look at the crowds going into Braxley's tent. It's terrible. Terrible!

GROUCHO: Colonel, never let it be said that a Flywheel lay down on a job —unless there was a bed handy. The show must go on. Say! I've got an idea. Ravelli, you stand inside the tent and come out when I call you.

CHICO: What for, boss?

GROUCHO: Never mind. Just come out every time I call you. Colonel, in ten minutes I'll fill this tent to overflowing. You just watch.

COLONEL: If you only could, I'd be your debtor for life.

GROUCHO: Big boy, if you were any deader than you are now, they'd have to bury you. But don't worry. Flywheel, the live wire, will now electrify the public. Colonel, you stay here and set the chairs. Ravelli, be ready for my call.

CHICO: Okay, boss.

GROUCHO: I go. *(Sound of crowd murmur up for a moment.)* Hiya, hiya, hiya. Ladies and gentlemen. Don't waste your time and money on Braxley's show. Come in here and waste your money. *(Murmur of crowd swells up.)* My friends, within these canvas walls behind me are ensconced wonders of nature such as you have never dreamed of.

VOICE: Show us. I'm from Missouri.

GROUCHO: You're from Missouri? Say, that's very interesting. I have a brother in Missouri.

VOICES: Aw, cut the gab. What have you got to show us? Start the show.

GROUCHO: Very well. Ladies and gentlemen, out here I will give you but a sample of the miraculous sights you are about to see for the small cost of a dime, ten cents, a ninth part of a dollar. My first exhibit will be General Tom Thumb Ravelli, the midget. Ravelli, are you ready?

CHICO: Here I am, boss.

GROUCHO: My friends, here he stands. General Tom Thumb Ravelli, the midget.

The MARX BROTHERS

Directed by Norman McLeod

in "MONKEY BUSINESS"

Paramount  Pictures

Monkey Business, the Marx Brothers' first screen original, was credited to writers S. J. Perelman and Will B. Johnstone, but the boys were less than happy with the script and brought in Arthur Sheekman and Nat Perrin to rework it—the first Hollywood assignment for young Perrin.

VOICES: It's a gyp! That's no midget; he's a full-grown man! Why, he's bigger than I am.

GROUCHO: Ah, that is the miraculous part of it. General Tom Thumb Ravelli is the world's largest midget!

VOICES: Booo! Rotten! Terrible! Take him off! Get the hook!

GROUCHO: That will be all, general. You may step inside now. Next, ladies and gentlemen, I take great pleasure in presenting Goliath Ravelli, the giant. Goliath, stride out here.

CHICO: Hey boss, I just was out.

GROUCHO: Well, come out again.

CHICO *(laughs):*   Some fun, hey boss? Who am I now?

GROUCHO: Ladies and gentlemen, you see before you Goliath Ravelli, the world's smallest giant.

VOICES: It's the same man. That guy was just here! We saw him before.

GROUCHO: Ah, ladies and gentlemen, it may seem hard to believe, but this is Tom Thumb's twin brother. That will be all, Goliath.

VOICES: Booo! He's a faker! He's a phony! He's a ringer!

GROUCHO: Thank you, my friends. Now for the amazing, crowning, triumphant feature of our exhibit. I am about to show you something you wouldn't believe even if you saw it. In fact, I don't believe it myself. I am about to show you, ladies and gentlemen, the living picture gallery—Sailor Ravelli himself, the most-tattooed man in the world. To look at him is to gain a liberal education in art. A second look is like a trip around the world. Sailor, come out here.

VOICES: Booo!

CHICO: Hey boss, I no tink they like me.

VOICES: Booo!

GROUCHO: Ladies and gentlemen, kindly pipe down. Wait till you've seen what you are about to see. On Sailor Ravelli's chest is a picture of the battleship *Maine.* On one arm is an etching.

CHICO: Hey, boss, my *nose* etches too.

GROUCHO: Quiet, Ravelli. Running up and down his arm is an etching of Man o' War, the most famous racehorse of all time. The horse could go twice as fast, but the sailor's arm is muddy.

CHICO: Hey, boss, don't forget to tell 'em about da mole on my shoulder.

VOICES: Booo! You fooled us twice! We don't believe it—take off your shirt! Come on, strip!

GROUCHO: And now, my friends, on the sailor's back you'll see . . . ah . . . but seeing is believing. Ravelli, take off your shirt.

CHICO: Hey, I no take offa my shirt. I'll catch cold.

GROUCHO: If that's all you catch, you'll be in luck. Take off that shirt! *(Pause.)* There, ladies and gentlemen, feast your eyes on this human work of art. Covered from head to toe with pictures. Beautiful pictures! Every time he moves he makes a moving picture.

VOICES: I don't see anything. Where are the pictures? He's not tattooed!

GROUCHO: You are mistaken, ladies and gentlemen—don't jump to conclusions. Sailor Ravelli *is* tattooed. He is the only tattooed man in the world tattooed with invisible ink.

VOICES: Booo! It's a fake! Get him! Get the cheat! Kill him!

GROUCHO: Come on, Ravelli, into the tent, quick. They're after us. You were a flop.

CHICO: Hey, boss, I no can find my shirt. Where's my shirt?

GROUCHO: Forget about your shirt. Quick! Out of our way, Colonel Thistledown.

COLONEL: Gentlemen, where are you going?

GROUCHO: We're quitting this business. Ravelli doesn't like it.

COLONEL: But why not?

GROUCHO: He's only been in show business two hours, and he's already lost his shirt.

(*Music in strong.*)

AFTERPIECE

CHICO: Ladies and gentlemens of de unheard radio audience. Please keep quiet cause I gonna tell you a story. Once upon of a long time of ago . . . oh, it was a very long time of ago . . . dere was tree bears— Antonio, Salvador, and Angeles. Dis one bear Angeles he gets lost, so they call him *Los* Angeles—

GROUCHO: Just a minute, Chico. Just a minute! This is a *fine* time to be telling a story like that!

CHICO: No, Groucho, it's a bad time. It's a badtime story.

GROUCHO: I see. You know, that story ought to go very well at the surprise dinner party I'm giving tomorrow night.

CHICO: You givin a surprise dinner party? What's da surprise?

GROUCHO: There won't be any dinner. In fact, there won't even be a party.

CHICO: At'sa fine. I'll be dere.

GROUCHO: Well, if you're *sure* you're coming, I won't be home.

CHICO: At's awright. I can find de ice box. You gotta some nicea roasta biff?

GROUCHO: I think so, Chico. What kind do you like, fat or lean?

CHICO: Fat or lean? (*Big laugh.*) Hey, you maka mistake. It's *gas*erline.

GROUCHO: No, when I talk about gasoline, I say Esso, which is more powerful than any gasoline. Just as when I speak of motor oil, I always say Essolube.

CHICO: What do you say when you say good night?

GROUCHO: I say . . . (*singing:*) Good night, ladies.

BOTH (*harmony*): Good night, ladies. Good night, ladies.

(*Signature music.*)

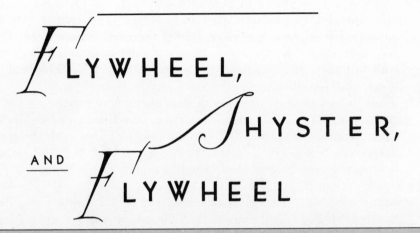

Flywheel, Shyster, and Flywheel

EPISODE NO. 19   *APRIL 3, 1933*

CAST

Groucho Marx as Waldorf T. Flywheel
Chico Marx as Emmanuel Ravelli
Miss Dimple
Assistant Manager
Bellboy
Bell Captain
Sheriff
Mrs. Morley
Squeaky Voice
Male Voice
Creditor

(Phone rings twice.)

MISS DIMPLE: Law offices of Flywheel, Shyster, and Flywheel . . . No, Mr. Flywheel isn't in town. He's in Florida. . . . Uh-huh . . . He was appointed receiver of a bankrupt hotel there—the Palm Tree Hotel. He's managing it for the creditors . . . No, his assistant, Mr. Ravelli, isn't in either. He's on his way to Florida to join Mr. Flywheel . . . *(Fade out.)* Goodbye.

(Fade in background voice paging Mr. Jones; phone ringing.)

ASSISTANT MANAGER: Hello, this is the Palm Tree Hotel . . . No, Mr. Flywheel, the new manager, isn't in right now. . . . This is Mr. Simpson, the assistant manager . . . Oh, you forgot a bag? Well, I'll send a bellhop right over. *(Rings bell.)* Front! Front! *(Pause.)* Bellboy.

BELLBOY: Yes, sir.

ASSISTANT MANAGER: The guest checking out of 422 forgot a bag here. Better get it and take it down to the railroad station.

BELLBOY: Sorry, sir, but the bellboys are walking out. We're through.

ASSISTANT MANAGER: What? Where's your captain?

CAPTAIN *(away):* Here I am, sir.

ASSISTANT MANAGER: What's the meaning of this?

CAPTAIN: We're quitting. Jim! Tony! Come on over here, fellows! We're going to settle this thing right now.

ASSISTANT MANAGER: Why—

CAPTAIN: We haven't been paid for weeks, and we want our money.

ASSISTANT MANAGER: Boys, don't get excited. You know what this hotel's been up against.

CAPTAIN: We don't care. We've got to get paid.

BELLBOYS: Yeah. We ain't gonna work for nothing.

ASSISTANT MANAGER: See here, boys. I'm just the assistant manager. Mr. Flywheel is the one to talk to. He's running the place now. Say, there's Mr. Flywheel. Oh, Mr. Flywheel!

GROUCHO *(approaching):* What's the trouble? Did somebody pay their bill?

BELLBOYS: Mr. Flywheel, we want our money.

CAPTAIN: Yes, we want our money.

GROUCHO: You want your money? You mean you want *my* money. Is that fair? Do I want *your* money? Suppose Washington's soldiers had asked for money, where would this country be today?

CAPTAIN: But they did ask.

GROUCHO: And where is Washington? No, my friends, no. Money will never make you happy, and happy will never make you money. That might be a wisecrack, but I doubt it.

BELLBOYS: We want our money.

GROUCHO: Well, I'll make you all a promise. If you'll all stick with me and work hard, we'll forget about money. Let's get together. We'll make a regular hotel out of this place. I'll put writing paper in the hotel, and next year maybe if business picks up I'll put in envelopes. I'll put extra blankets, free, in all your rooms. There'll be no cover charge. Think—think of the opportunities here in Florida! One week ago I came to Florida without a nickel in my pocket. And now I've got a nickel in my pocket.

CAPTAIN: We want our wages.

GROUCHO: Wages? Do you want to be wage slaves? Answer me that.

BELLBOYS: No.

GROUCHO: No. Well, what makes wage slaves? Wages. I want you to be free. Remember, there is nothing like Liberty. Except *Colliers* and the *Saturday Evening Post*. Be free, my friends. One for all, and all for me, me for you, and three for five. I feel hurt because you don't trust me.

Violence erupts in the Florida hotel run by Groucho in this scene from *The Cocoanuts*, the Marx Brothers' first film, adapted from their Broadway stage success. *Flywheel*'s Episode 19 borrows liberally from this source.

Now go back to work. Don't worry about your salary; you won't get it anyhow.

(*Muttering from bellboys.*)

CAPTAIN: Awright, but you can't stall us off much longer. (*Receding.*) Come on, fellows.

CHICO (*approaching jovially*): Hullo dere, boss!

GROUCHO (*surprised*): Why Ravelli, I didn't know you were coming here. Why didn't you send me a telegram?

CHICO: Well, boss, I knew I was coming here, so I brought da telegram wit me. Here it is. I read it to you. "Dear Flywheel. Having lots of trouble. Please send hunnerd dollars quick. Signed, Ravelli."

GROUCHO: You're having trouble?

CHICO: Yeah. I'ma having trouble getting da hunnerd dollars.

GROUCHO: Well, as long as you're here, I might as well get you a room. Hand me your suitcase. (*Pause.*) Say, this suitcase is empty.

CHICO: At's awright. I fill it up before I leave. What about my room? I wanna nice room and no bath.

GROUCHO: Oh, I see. You're just here for the winter. Well, how would you like a suite on the third floor?

CHICO: No, but I'll take a Polack in da basement.

GROUCHO: Ravelli, I can see what's wrong with this hotel. But I'm too lazy to throw you out.

CHICO: You crazy, boss. Wit me helpin, you'll soon be cleanin up.

GROUCHO: Yes, and making the beds, too. Ravelli, we've got to raise some cash. This hotel owns a lot of property here, and I'm going out to see if I can sell a few lots. You look after the desk, and if the lobby's missing when I get back (*receding*) I'll know who took it.

CHICO: Okay, boss. (*Phone rings.*) Hello . . . Ice water in Room 340 . . . Is dat so? Where you get it? . . . Oh, you *want* some. Dat's different . . . Have you got any ice? . . . No, I no got ice . . . Dis is Palm Tree Grove. No snow, no ice . . . You still wanna some ice water? I tell you what. Eat some onions. Dat'll make your icewater. (*Laughs.*) Oh boy, at'sa some joke! Goodbye. (*Hangs up receiver.*)

GROUCHO (*approaching*): Oh, Ravelli!

CHICO: Whatta you want, Mr. Flywheel?

GROUCHO: It's been reported to me that there's a poker game going on in Room 420. Go up there and knock on the door and see if you can get me a seat.

CHICO (*receding*): Okay, boss.

GROUCHO (*taps bell*): Front! (*Pause.*) Front! We haven't got the front around here we used to. Maybe the front isn't back yet.

MRS. MORLEY (*approaching*): Oh, Mr. Flywheel!

GROUCHO: What is it, babe?

MRS. MORLEY: Mr. Flywheel, as a guest of your hotel, I feel that you ought to know that your new clerk, Mr. Ravelli, has been insulting the guests.

GROUCHO: He has, has he? Well, he can't do that around here. That's my job. But we can discuss that later. Mrs. Morley, you're just the woman I'm looking for. And now, whether you like it or not, I'm going to tell you about Florida real estate.

MRS. MORLEY: I'm sorry, Mr. Flywheel, but—

GROUCHO: Do you know that Palm Tree Grove is the biggest development since Sophie Tucker? Do you know that Florida is the show spot of America, and that Palm Tree Grove is the sore spot of Florida?

MRS. MORLEY: But you told me about it yesterday.

GROUCHO: I know, but I left out a comma. Look, in a little while I'm going to hold an auction sale at Palm Tree Grove, the suburb terrible. I mean beautiful. Only sixteen hundred miles from New York as the crow flies, and eighteen hundred as the horse flies. Palm Tree Grove —glorifying the American sucker. It's the most exclusive residential section in Florida. Nobody lives there at all. And the climate. Ask me about the climate, I dare you.

MRS. MORLEY: Very well . . . How is the—

GROUCHO: I'm glad you brought it up. Our motto is, Palm Tree Grove, no snow, no ice, and no business. Do you know that Florida is the greatest state in the Union?

MRS. MORLEY: Is it?

GROUCHO: Take its climate. No, we took that. Take its fruits—take the alligator pears—take all the alligator pears and keep them, see if I care. Do you know how alligator pears are made?

MRS. MORLEY: I haven't the slightest idea.

GROUCHO: There you are, that's because you've never been an alligator, and don't let it happen again. Do you know that it sometimes requires years to bring the pear and the alligator together? They don't like each other.

MRS. MORLEY: No.

GROUCHO: Do you know how many alligator pears are sent out of this state every year and told not to come back?

MRS. MORLEY: I don't think I do.

GROUCHO: All they can get hold of. Florida feeds the nation, but nobody feeds me. And that's what I want to talk to you about.

MRS. MORLEY: Mr. Flywheel—

GROUCHO: And another thing. Take our cattle-raising—

MRS. MORLEY: Sir—

GROUCHO: Oh, I don't mean anything personal, but here is the ideal cattle-raising section.

MRS. MORLEY: Mr. Flywheel, will you let me say something, please—

GROUCHO: I hardly think so, and something else I want to bring to your mind—where will you be when you're sixty-five? Join the navy and see the world.

MRS. MORLEY: I'm sorry, but I'm afraid I must be going.

GROUCHO: Before you go, let me show you a sample of the sewer pipe we're going to lay.

MRS. MORLEY: Sewer? Sewer!

GROUCHO: Look at this piece of pipe. Isn't it beautiful? Nobody can fool you on a sewer, can they? A big woman like you. This is an eight-inch pipe. But of course, all property owners will be allowed to vote on the size of their pipe. In case of a tie, it goes to the supreme court, and I can slip you a little inside information in advance. Chief Justice Hughes is crazy about this type sewer. Here, put it in your pocket. (*Music in strong.*)

BELLBOY (*paging voice*):   Paging Mr. Ravelli. Paging Mr. Ravelli.

CHICO: Who'sa calling me, boy?

BELLBOY: Mr. Flywheel is looking for you.

CHICO: Yeah?

GROUCHO (*away*):   Over here, Ravelli, I want to see you.

CHICO: Here I am, boss.

GROUCHO: Ravelli, we can make a lot of money for this hotel. In about thirty minutes I'm going to auction off some lots at Palm Tree Grove. That's our new subdivision. Of course, you know what an auction is.

CHICO: Sure. I came from Italy on de Atlantic Auction.

GROUCHO: Well, let's go ahead as if nothing happened. I say I'm holding an auction at Palm Tree Grove. Now, when the crowd gathers around, I want you to mingle with them. Don't pick their pockets, just mingle with them and . . . stimulate the bidding.

CHICO: At's awright. I find time for both.

GROUCHO: Well, maybe we can cut out the auction. Here's what I mean: If somebody bids one hundred dollars, you say two hundred, if somebody says two, you say three. Now in case nobody says anything at all, then you start it off.

CHICO: Well, how will I know if nobody says anytin?

GROUCHO: They'll send you a postal card. You fool, if they don't say anything, you'll hear 'em, won't you?

CHICO: Well, maybe I won't be listenin.

GROUCHO: Well, in that case, don't answer. Now, if we're successful in selling these lots, I'll see that you get a nice commission.

CHICO: Yeah, and how about some money?

GROUCHO: You can have your choice. Now, in arranging these lots of course we use maps—blueprints. That's to determine the various locations of—you know what blueprints are, huh?

CHICO: Sure, oysters.

GROUCHO: The next time I see you, remind me not to talk to you. Do you know what a lot is? A lot?

CHICO: Yes. It's too much.

GROUCHO: Not a whole lot. I mean a little lot with nothing on it—a lot, a lot.

CHICO: Sure, anytime you got too much, you gotta lot. Look, I explain it for you. Sometimes you gotta little bit, and you no tink it's enough, it's a whole lot. Sometimes you got a little bit, you tink it'sa too much, somebody else maybe tink it's not enough—dat's a whole lot too. Sometimes you gotta nuttin, somebody else maybe tink dat'sa sometin—so dat's a whole lot, too. So, a lot is too much and too much is a whole lot. Now you unnerstan?

GROUCHO: I understood it until you explained it to me. Come here, Rand-McNally, and I'll make the whole thing clear to you. Here's a map and diagram of the whole Palm Tree section. This whole area is within a radius of approximately three-quarters of a mile . . . radius. Is there a remote possibility that you know what radius means?

CHICO: Sure. NBC.

GROUCHO: Well, I walked right into that one. It's going to be a cinch explaining the rest of this thing to you. That's a rodeo you're thinking of. Look, Einstein! Look at this blueprint. Now, this is Palm Tree Grove. No matter what you say, this is Palm Tree Grove. Here is Palm Tree Grove, and here is Coconut Heights. That's the swamp, and down here where the road forks—right where the road forks—that's Coconut Junction.

CHICO: Where you got coconut custard?

GROUCHO: Why, that's on one of the forks. You probably eat with your knife, so you wouldn't have to worry about that. Now, here is the main road I wish you were on. Now over on this site, we're going to build an eye-and-ear hospital. This is going to be a sight for sore eyes. Now here is the residential section.

CHICO: People live dere.

GROUCHO: No, it's the stockyards. People live there. Certainly people live there. That would be a good place for you to live. The only bad feature is, it's right near the chocolate factory. But if you don't like the odor from the chocolate factory, you could live over here, where the fertilizer plant is. That is, providing the fertilizer people don't object.

CHICO: Dey wouldn't object. Dey'll like me.

GROUCHO: Like you? They'll probably use you. Now, over here is the river front, and all along the river, those are all levees.

CHICO: Oh, dat's da Jewish neighborhood?

GROUCHO: Well, we'll Passover that. Now here is a little peninsula and here is a viaduct leading to the mainland.

CHICO: Why a duck?

GROUCHO: I'm all right. How are you? I say here is a little penounsular or peninsula, and here is a viaduct leading to the mainland.

CHICO: Awright. Why a duck?

GROUCHO: I'm not playing Ask-me-another. It's a viaduct.

CHICO: Awright. Why a duck? Why a duck? Whya no chicken?

GROUCHO: I don't know. I guess they never thought of it that way. This happens to be a viaduct, that's all. I never heard of a Via Chicken. You try to cross over there on a chicken, and you find out viaduct.

CHICO: Why a duck? Why a duck?

GROUCHO: It's a deep water. That's viaduct. Look, sap. Suppose you were out horseback riding and you came to that stream and you wanted to ford over? You couldn't make it. It's too deep.

CHICO: Well, whatta you want wit a Ford, if you gotta horse?

GROUCHO: Well, I'm sorry the matter ever came up. I don't care where you're from. It's a viaduct.

GROUCHO: Hey, look. I unnerstan why a horse, I unnerstan why a chicken. I unnerstan why a dis, why a dat. But I don't unnerstan why a duck.

GROUCHO: Well, I was only fooling. They're going to build a tunnel in the morning. Is that clear?

CHICO: Yeah, it's all clear, except why a duck.

GROUCHO: Now, if you'll come with me, I'll take you down and show you our cemetery. I've got a waiting list of fifty people at that cemetery just dying to get in. But I like you and I'm going to shove you in ahead of all of them. I'm going to get you a steady position, and I hope it's horizontal. Now, don't forget, when the auction starts, if somebody says one hundred dollars—

CHICO: I say two hunnerd.

GROUCHO: That's right. If somebody says two hundred—

CHICO: I say tree hunnerd.

GROUCHO: That's perfect. Ravelli, we're going to make a lot of money. Now are you sure you'll find the place?

CHICO: I no tink so.

GROUCHO: Now look. You walk right down that road until you come to the outskirts of the jungle. Now, right at the edge of the jungle is a clearing with a wire fence all around it.

CHICO: Why a fence?

GROUCHO: Oh, no, we're not going to start that thing all over again! (*Music in strong.*)

(*Buzz of voices from crowd, gavel pounds.*)

SHERIFF: Ladies and gentlemen! I, as sheriff, am here to announce the auctioning of some lots in Palm Tree Grove. These lots are the property of the bankrupt Palm Tree Hotel, and the proceeds will go to pay off the creditors. The auction will be conducted by the receiver in bankruptcy, Waldorf Tecumseh Flywheel. Ready, Mr. Flywheel?

GROUCHO: I'll be with you in a second, sheriff. (*Whispers.*) Oh, Ravelli!

CHICO (*whispers*): Whatta you want, boss?

GROUCHO (*whispers*): Now don't forget to bid 'em up. If I say one hundred dollars, you say two hundred. If I say two hundred, you say three hundred.

CHICO (*whispers*): Awright, don't worry. I bid 'em up.

GROUCHO (*whispers*): Okay. (*To crowd:*) All right, folks. Step right up for the big auction. My friends, you are now in Palm Tree Grove, one of the finest cities in Florida. Of course, we still need a few finishing touches. But who doesn't? This is the heart of the residential district. Every lot is a stone's throw from the station. As soon as they throw enough stones we're going to build a station. Eight hundred beautiful residences will be built right here. They're as good as up. Better—you can have any kind of a house you want to. You can even get stucco. Oh, how you can get stucco. Now is the time to buy—while the new boom is on. Remember the old saying, a new boom sweeps clean. And don't forget the guarantee. If the lots don't double themselves in a year, I don't know what you can do about it. Now then, we'll take lot number twenty, right at the corner of De Soto Avenue. Of course, you all know who De Soto was. He discovered a body of water. You've all heard of the water they named after him? De Soto water. This lot has a twenty-foot frontage, a fourteen-foot backage, and a mighty fine garbage. Now then, what am I offered for lot number twenty? Anything at all to start it. Anything at all.

CHICO: Awright, I make a bid. Two hunnerd dollar.

GROUCHO: Thanks, Ravelli. There you are, folks, a gentleman bids two hundred dollars. Who'll bid three?

CHICO: Awright, tree hunnerd dollars.

GROUCHO: Oh, another gentleman says three hundred dollars. Do I hear four?

CHICO: Awright. Four hunnerd dollars.

GROUCHO: Well, the auction is practically over. Yes, it's all over but the shooting. I'll attend to that later.

CHICO: Fiva hunnerd dollars.

GROUCHO: Who'll say six hundred?

CHICO: Awright. Six hunnerd dollars.

GROUCHO *(pounds gavel):*   Sold for six hundred dollars. Wrap up that lot for Mr. Ravelli, and put some poison ivy on it. Well, I came out even on that one. Now folks, we'll take lot number twenty-one. There it is, right over there, where those coconut trees are. What am I offered for lot number twenty-one?

CHICO: Awright. Two hunnerd dollars.

GROUCHO: Why, my friend, there's over two hundred dollars worth of milk in those coconuts, and what milk! Milk from contented coconuts. Who'll bid three hundred?

MRS. MORLEY: Three hundred.

CHICO: What? You say tree hunnerd? Then I say four hunnerd.

SQUEAKY VOICE: Five hundred.

CHICO: Six hunnerd, seven hunnerd, eight hunnerd. What da heck I care?

GROUCHO: Yes, what the heck do you care? How about me? *(Pounds gavel.)* Sold to what the heck he care for eight hundred dollars. Ravelli, I hope all your teeth have cavities. And don't forget, abscess makes the heart grow fonder. When you said viaduck, I should have smelled a rat. As a matter of fact, I did, but I didn't know who it was. Now, my friends, the next swindle—I mean the next lot—is number twenty-two. This is one of the finest lots in America. What am I offered for lot number twenty-two?

MRS. MORLEY: One hundred dollars.

GROUCHO: Sold for one hundred dollars.

CHICO: Oh no. Two hunnerd dollars.

GROUCHO: Well, I almost had you that time. Ravelli, what are you going to do with all these lots? Play lotto? Who'll say three hundred?

CHICO: Four hunnerd.

GROUCHO: Four hundred. Do I hear five?

SQUEAKY VOICE: Five hundred.

CHICO: Ravelli says six hunnerd.

SQUEAKY VOICE: Seven hundred.

CHICO: Awright. Eight hunnerd.

GROUCHO: Eight hundred dollars. Do I hear nine? Will the gentleman who said seven say nine?

SQUEAKY VOICE: No.

GROUCHO: Will the gentleman who said seven say seven again?

SQUEAKY VOICE: I think not.

GROUCHO: Will he say six?

CHICO: Awright. He say six. I say seven.

GROUCHO: Will the gentleman say five?

CHICO: He say five. I say six. He say six, I say seven. He say seven, I say eight. He say eight, I say nine. I got a lotta numbers left. When I start, I no stop for nuttin. I bid 'em up, I go higher, higher, higher.

GROUCHO: You'll go higher when I get hold of you. Sold to Ravelli for eight hundred dollars. Before you leave, cut yourself a piece of throat and get away from that tree before it does. Psst! Folks! Ravelli isn't looking. What am I offered for lot number twenty-four?

MRS. MORLEY: Fifty dollars.

GROUCHO: Sold for fifty dollars.

CHICO: Two hunnerd dollars.

GROUCHO (*in high-pitched voice*):   Too late. Too late.

CHICO: You bid 'em up yourself, boss. *(Receding.)* I go take a rest.

GROUCHO: That's fine. Now, folks, we'll take lot number twenty-five, right there where you're standing. Would you people mind taking your feet off that lot? You're getting it all dirty. Now, here is a lot. I know it doesn't look very big on top, but it's yours as far down as you want to go, and it's dirt cheap. Now then, what am I offered for lot number twenty-five? Anything at all to start it, anything at all. What am I offered for lot number twenty-five? Come, come, folks, you're all allowed to bid. What am I offered for lot number twenty-five and a year's subscription to *Youth's Companion*? Will somebody take a year's subscription? I'm trying to work my way through college. Will anybody take a six-month subscription? I'll go to high school. Does anybody want to buy a lead pencil? I'll wrestle anybody in the crowd for five dollars. I'll wrestle with Mrs. Morley for nothing. Well, if you're not going to do any bidding I might as well quit. What's the matter with you people? Can't you visualize bargains? Don't you want to make money? I'll try one more lot, and if I don't dispose of this one, I'm going to fold up. I tell you what I'll do. I'll throw in all the lots for the price of one. What am I offered for all the lots?

SQUEAKY VOICE: Four hundred dollars.

MRS. MORLEY: Five hundred.

GROUCHO: Five hundred. Who says six hundred?

SQUEAKY VOICE: Six hundred.

GROUCHO: Now, there is a gentleman with vision. Who says seven hundred?

MALE VOICE: Seven hundred.

GROUCHO: Now, *there* is a gentleman with television. Who'll say eight hundred?

SQUEAKY VOICE: Eight hundred dollars.

GROUCHO: There's a gentleman with astigmatism. *(Whistle blows.)* There's the whistle. Time for lunch. Sold to the gentleman with astigmatism for eight hundred dollars.

CREDITOR *(approaching indignantly):* Just a moment, Mr. Flywheel. I am one of the creditors of the Palm Tree Hotel. You deliberately put an end to the bidding. You can't sell all those lots for eight hundred dollars.

CHICO *(approaching):* Hey, boss. Boss!

GROUCHO: What is it, Ravelli?

CHICO: Did you sell the lots?

CREDITOR: Sell them? He practically gave them away.

CHICO: At'sa fine, boss. I just found out that the land around here is no good.

VOICE: No good?

CHICO: Yeah. You can't live on it.

VOICE: Why not?

CHICO: A man just dug a hole with a drill on one of the lots, and a lot of black oil came shooting up.

(Music in strong.)

AFTERPIECE

CHICO: Ladies and gentlemens of the radio audience, if you'll excuse it please, I tink I say hello to my friend Joe Tarentoola in Philadelphia. Hello crazy Joe, you no-good skunk.

GROUCHO: Chico, Chico! What's the matter with you? That's no way to talk to a friend, with all these people listening in. How do you suppose Joe feels, hearing you call him a skunk?

CHICO: He can't hear me. He ain't got a radio. Good night, crazy Joe.

GROUCHO: Chico, why don't you give your brain to the medical research society? You're not using it.

CHICO: Dey don't need it. Dey got more brains dan I have. But I'm better looking.

GROUCHO: Better looking than what?

CHICO: Well, what have you *got*?

GROUCHO: I've got rheumatism. What have you got?

CHICO: I got a new way of spelling automobile. S—

GROUCHO: Automobile doesn't start with an S.

CHICO: Well, it starts very quick with Esso, which is better than any gasoline, and it runsa very smooth with Essolube, dat hydrofined motor oil.

GROUCHO: Nice work, Chico. Now take a little bow, and what do you say to the nice people?

CHICO *(baby voice):*   Good night, ladies.

GROUCHO AND CHICO *(singing):*   Good night, ladies.

   (Signature Music.)

FIVE STAR THEATER
PRESENTS

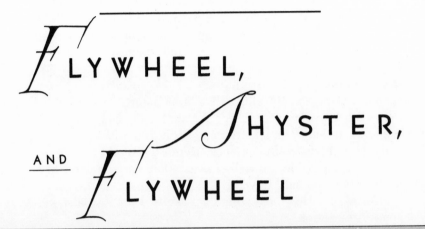

Flywheel, Shyster, and Flywheel

EPISODE NO. 20   *APRIL 10, 1933*

CAST

Groucho Marx as Waldorf T. Flywheel
Chico Marx as Emmanuel Ravelli
Miss Dimple
Woman
Farmer
Chairman
Mayor
Man
Ghost

(Phone rings.)

MISS DIMPLE: Hello. Law offices of Flywheel, Shyster, and Flywheel . . . No, I'm sorry, Mr. Flywheel and his assistant, Mr. Ravelli, have gone out of town . . . Yes, they're up in the country on a walking trip for Mr. Flywheel's health . . . I'll tell them you called. *(Fading.)* Goodbye.

(Rooster crows, birds chirp.)

GROUCHO: Come on, Ravelli, walk a little faster.

CHICO: What's your hurry, boss? We ain't going no place.

GROUCHO: In that case, let's run and get it over with.

CHICO: Hey, Flywheel! Look, look! Dere's a snake!

GROUCHO: Step aside, Ravelli. I'll get that stick and hit him with it. *(Screaming.)* Ravelli! Ravelli!

CHICO *(laughs):*   Hey, boss! Don't get skairt. I make a mistake. At'sa no snake, at'sa stick.

GROUCHO: I know, but the thing I picked up to hit him *isn't* a stick. It's a *snake.*

CHICO *(laughs):*   My motter was once skairt by a snake—

GROUCHO: I know the answer. It turned out to be your father.

CHICO: No, it was me. *(Pause.)* Hey! I no can walk anymore. I'ma hungry. Let's go to dat farmhouse and get sometin to eat.

GROUCHO: Okay.

CHICO: Say, looka dat old apple tree. I betcha dey don't get very much apples offa dat tree.

GROUCHO: I bet they don't either. That's no apple tree. It's a telegraph pole.

CHICO: How can dat be a telegraph pole? Dere's no *telegrams* on it. Hey, dat reminds me of a riddle. A couple got married in California. What company was it?

GROUCHO: A couple got married in California, and it was a *company*?

CHICO: Sure, it's da Western Union. *(Laughs.)* Oh, boy! At'sa some joke. I got even a better one. Da same couple gets a divorce in California. What company is *dat*?

GROUCHO: Go right ahead. I'm not listening.

CHICO: It's a milk company. Do you want to know why?

GROUCHO: I don't think so.

CHICO: It's a milk company because da wife was keeping company wit da milkman.

GROUCHO: Lucky for you I wasn't listening. Come on. Here's the farmhouse.

CHICO: Hey, boss. Looka through dis window. Looka all dose pies. Let's knock at da door and ask da lady of da house for some.

GROUCHO: You don't know the woman in the house. You can't ask her for pies. Just break through the window and steal a few pies.

CHICO: Okay, boss. What *you* gonna do?

GROUCHO: I'll stand on guard outside, and if I hear anybody coming I'll meet you in the next town.

CHICO: At'sa fine. Here, boss, help me up into da window.

GROUCHO: Keep very quiet. You don't want to scare the poor woman.
(Sound of window being raised.)

CHICO: Okay, boss. I'm in.
(Dog barks fiercely, away.)

CHICO: Hey, boss. Hey, boss! Help me out. Dere's a dog in here.

GROUCHO: Hold your ground, Ravelli. His bark is probably worse than his bite.

CHICO: No it ain't, boss. He just bit me.

WOMAN *(opens door):* What's going on here? What do you hoboes want?

CHICO: Hey, my uncle used to play one of dose.

WOMAN: Your uncle played *what?*

CHICO: A hobo. A hobo in de orchestra.

WOMAN: Well, get away from here or I'll sic the dog on you.

GROUCHO: You're too late, madam. The dog just bit Ravelli and he's probably sick already.

WOMAN: What do you want, anyway?

GROUCHO: We are hungry. Could you spare a piece of cake?

WOMAN: Cake? What's the matter? Isn't bread good enough for you?

GROUCHO: It usually is, madam, but today happens to be my birthday.

WOMAN: All right, here's a piece of cake.

GROUCHO: Oh, no you don't. Where are the candles?

WOMAN: Candles? What nerve! You should be ashamed of yourselves even asking for cake.

CHICO: We have to ask. Last time we took some cake witout asking, and we nearly got arrested.

WOMAN: I am sorry, but I can't give you anything. I'm having enough trouble trying to make both ends meet.

CHICO: All right, make one end meat and de odder end vegetables.

GROUCHO: Yes, madam, my assistant is somewhat of a vegetarian. He only eats meat when he can get it. And now, if you will let us have some of those pies, we will be very glad to clean the snow off your sidewalk.

WOMAN: Snow? Why, there *isn't* any snow on the sidewalk.

GROUCHO: Is that our fault? Now, how about dishing out the grub?

WOMAN: Sir! You are very impertinent. If you were a gentleman, you would at least take off your hat while talking to a lady.

GROUCHO: I can't, madam—my hat is full of sandwiches. But I'll take off my *coat*.

WOMAN: Why! You no-good *tramps*. Scat! *(Slams door.)*

GROUCHO: That settles it. We'll sleep elsewhere tonight. Come on. We've got to find a town. It'll be dark pretty soon.

(Wagon approaches.)

CHICO: Here comes a man on a wagon, boss. Maybe he'll tell us where da next town is.

GROUCHO: I'll talk to him. *(To* FARMER:*)* Say, farmer, do you know where we can find food and lodging hereabouts?

FARMER: Huh?

CHICO: And some cake, too?

FARMER: Well, the town nearest here is Witchville, but it's harvest time, and I reckon they're all full up there. Of course, there's the old Crexton mansion, but I don't think you'd want to sleep there. There's *ghosts* in that house.

CHICO: At's awright. We bring 'em some tin cans.

FARMER: Tin cans?

CHICO: Yeah! Dey like to eat tin cans.

GROUCHO: Ravelli, he said *ghosts*, not goats.

FARMER: The town board of Witchville is mighty anxious to have somebody sleep in that Crexton mansion to prove it ain't really haunted, because a haunted house hurts business in the whole neighborhood. They're offering a hundred dollars reward for anybody who'll sleep there.

CHICO: A hunnerd dollars a night joosta for sleeping? We'll take da job.

FARMER: Well, it won't be so easy as you think. Everybody that ever tried to sleep here has been found dead the next morning.

GROUCHO: In that case, we'll have to get the hundred dollars in advance. Where's this Crexton mansion?

FARMER: You just go down to the town hall and ask for the mayor. He'll see that you're taken to the Crexton mansion. But he'll warn you against it, I tell you.

CHICO: Never you mind. How we get dere?

FARMER: Just follow this road. You can't miss it. I got to hurry along. The pig in my wagon has been sick and I got to get him to a veterany.

CHICO: Your pig is sick? Dat'sa too bad. How's da rest of your family?

GROUCHO: Ravelli, you keep those cracks for the haunted house and there won't be a ghost left in the place.

FARMER: Well, I got to be going.

GROUCHO: Well, goodbye.

FARMER: Goodbye.

GROUCHO: I wasn't talking to you. I was talking to the pig.

FARMER *(lashes horse):*   Giddap.

(Wagon recedes.)

CHICO: Look, boss. Da road goes two ways. Which way do we go?

GROUCHO: I tell you what, Ravelli. You take the road on the left, and I'll take the one on the right. If you get there first, you make a chalk mark on the steps of the town hall.

CHICO: But, boss, suppose you get dere first?

GROUCHO: In that case, I'll rub the chalk mark out. I don't think we've got far to go, because we're on the outskirts now.

CHICO: Huh?

GROUCHO: Outskirts! Don't you know what that means?

CHICO: Sure! I know a chorus girl dat dances wit *outskirts.*

(Music in strong.)

CHAIRMAN *(pounding gavel):*   Mayor Watkins. I, as chairman of the town board, feel compelled to remind you that you are doing a very unwise thing in interfering with the board's decision regarding the Crexton haunted house.

MAYOR: But squire, you can't let those two men enter that house. It means certain death.

CHAIRMAN: See here, mayor, we've got to get at the bottom of this thing. A haunted house in a civilized town is a disgrace. The town board has offered a reward of a hundred dollars to anyone who'll sleep in the house. Mr. Flywheel and Mr. Ravelli, here, have accepted the board's offer. And the offer *stands!*

MAYOR: Very well, I shan't be responsible if anything happens to them. Mr. Flywheel and Mr. Ravelli—I hope you gentlemen have insurance against accidents.

CHICO: Hey, at'sa no good. My brudder, he took out insurance against accidents, and it no work. He had an accident da next day.

GROUCHO: That's fine, Ravelli. When we get back to the office we'll start a suit for damages.

CHICO: My brudder don't want no damages. He got damaged enough in da accident.

(Sound of approaching band, playing funeral march.)

CHICO: Hey, what'sa dat moosic?

MAYOR: Well, the villagers have heard that you men are foolhardy enough to sleep in the haunted house. They've come to get a last look at you. *(Music swells.)* You know, that's one of the finest bands in the whole county. Probably *the* finest. Great music, *isn't* it, Mr. Flywheel?

GROUCHO: What did you say?

MAYOR: I say, that band certainly does know how to play. It's probably the best band in the *entire* state.

GROUCHO: What's that?

MAYOR: I say the music is fine. I'll bet our Witchville Band has some of the best players in the whole country.

GROUCHO: I'm sorry, mayor. You'll have to speak louder. That confounded band is making so much noise I can't hear a word you're saying.

(*Music subsides.*)

MAYOR: Come outside, gentlemen, the town folk want to see you. (*Opens door; crowd cheers.*) Fellow citizens of Witchville, it is with great regret and fear in my heart that I present the two men who are going to risk their lives tonight in the Crexton haunted house. (*Crowd cheers.*) Mr. Ravelli, will you say a word?

CHICO: Sure.

MAYOR: Well, go ahead.

CHICO: I joosta said it. Sure.

GROUCHO: That was splendid, Ravelli. Now, I'll say a word. Scram.

MAYOR: Mr. Flywheel, suppose we hear from you.

(*Cries of "Speech!" "Speech!"*)

GROUCHO: Ladies and gentlemen, looking into your vacant and imbecilic faces I am reminded of a joke. Ha, ha, ha. It's some joke.

MAYOR: Well, what *is* the joke, Mr. Flywheel?

GROUCHO: You wouldn't like it, it's clean. Now, ladies and gentlemen, your mayor—your old gray mare—has told you that we're about to spend the night in the haunted house. Flywheel isn't afraid of adventure. Why, I can remember driving recklessly across the desert without food or water. On, on, on, I drove—till the car turned turtle. Was I frightened? No. I sat right down and had turtle soup.

MAYOR: Mr. Flywheel, excuse me, but here's a gentleman who wants to speak to you and Mr. Ravelli.

MAN: I'll start with you, Mr. Ravelli. If you don't mind, I'd like to take a few measurements so that we can have everything ready for you in the morning.

CHICO: At'sa fine. Go ahead and measure.

MAN: Thirty-two inches, sixty-three inches, forty-two inches. Say, this is fine. I think we can fit you out of stock.

CHICO: Hey, at'sa very nice, boss. Dey must like us. Dey're giving us new suits.

GROUCHO: Some reception, eh, Ravelli? Listen, stranger, what kind of material are you planning to make this out of?

MAN: White pine with silver handles. Just like we gave the others.

CHICO: Hey, what odders you giva dis to?

MAN: The last two who tried to spend the night in the haunted house.

CHICO: Hey, boss, I no feel so good.

GROUCHO: Nonsense, Ravelli, they're just trying to scare us.

CHICO: Well, dey can stop now. I'm scared already.

MAYOR: Come gentlemen, it's getting late. If you insist on going to the haunted house, you might as well start now. I'll drive you there myself. *(Band starts playing "Goodbye Forever"; voices join in.)*

MAYOR: Here's my car. Step right in.

(Car door closes, motor starts.)

CHICO: Hey, Mr. Mayor, dis sure is a nicea car you got here.

MAYOR: Yes, people like this car. They like it so much it's been stolen three times.

CHICO: Yeah? Who stole it da *first* two times?

MAYOR: Oh, look on your left, gentlemen. There's the Witchville golf course—one of the finest in the country.

CHICO: Golf? I play datta very good.

MAYOR: Really? What's your handicap?

GROUCHO: Ravelli's handicap is his face, and his golf isn't very good either, but that's only because he's never played.

MAYOR: There you are, Mr. Flywheel. Right ahead of you, up on that hill, is the Crexton mansion. Don't you want to change your mind about spending the night under that awful roof?

CHICO: What'sa matter wit da roof? Does she leak?

MAYOR: That house has been haunted for a hundred years—ever since Roderick Crexton murdered his wife and his six children and then killed himself.

CHICO: Who did he kill first, his wife or himself?

MAYOR: Since that terrible day, the ghost of Roderick Crexton has dwelt in that house. Every night, as the clock tolls three, the ghost of Roderick Crexton appears, and woe unto him who meets this apparition.

CHICO: Hey, did I ever tell you about *my* operation?

MAYOR: I tell you, gentlemen, you're risking your lives for a hundred dollars—a paltry sum.

GROUCHO: Yes, it is a poultry sum. Mere chickenfeed.

MAYOR: Well, you're braver than I am. I don't dare go any further. I'll leave you here at the gate. Goodbye, Mr. Ravelli. Farewell, Mr. Flywheel. *(Sound of car doors opening and shutting.)* Oh, one last thing. Where would you like your bodies shipped?

GROUCHO: You can send mine F.O.B. Detroit.

CHICO: Joosta leave mine here. I'll call for it sometime next week.

MAYOR: Very well, gentlemen. Here's the key. If you get out of this alive, I'll be mighty surprised. Goodbye.

(*Car starts up and recedes.*)

GROUCHO: Say, this is a pretty spooky-looking house. I don't like the key he gave us, either. It's a skeleton key.

(*Wind howls.*)

CHICO: Hey, boss. Boss! What'sa dat noise?

GROUCHO: That's nothing, Ravelli. Just the wind. Come on, I'll open the door.

(*Key turns in lock.*)

CHICO: Hey, I no lika dis.

(*Door creaks open.*)

CHICO: I no lika dis, boss, I tell you.

(*Sound of castanets.*)

GROUCHO: Ravelli, this is no time to be shaking dice.

CHICO: I ain't shakin dice, boss. At'sa my knees shakin.

GROUCHO: Now, keep cool. Keep cool.

CHICO: Don't worry, I'm cool. I'm cool. I'm so cool I'm shiverin.

(*Music in strong.*)

(*Sound of wind blowing.*)

GROUCHO: Wake up, Ravelli. Wake up!

CHICO (*drowsily*): Huh?

(*Clanking of chains.*)

GROUCHO: What's that noise? I think it's the ghost.

CHICO: Well, tell him to come back in an hour. I'm sleepy.

(*Clanking of chains.*)

GROUCHO: There it goes again. Ravelli, I hear chains clanking. However, it may be nothing but a fugitive from a chain gang.

CHICO: Well, it'sa time he was in bed. It musta be very late. What time is it?

GROUCHO: It's a quarter to three on my watch, but my watch is always a quarter to three. The ghost isn't due until three, but he might be ahead of schedule. Come on, Ravelli. Get up.

CHICO (*yawns*): Hey, boss. I lika dis house. I tink maybe I live here.

(*Wind howls.*)

GROUCHO: I think maybe you'll die here, too.

(*Another clank.*)

GROUCHO: Listen, I've got an idea.

CHICO (*sleepy*): Aw, whatta you want?

GROUCHO: That ghost isn't due until three o'clock. We're going to disguise ourselves. We'll take those sheets, dress up like ghosts—and the real ghost will think we're relatives.

CHICO: At'sa fine. But I rather sleep.

GROUCHO: Come on! Take this sheet and start haunting the house.

CHICO: We don't have to haunt for da house—we found it awready.

GROUCHO: Here. Put on the sheet.

CHICO: Awright. Awright.

(Door creaks open.)

CHICO: Hey, boss look! Da door to dat room is opening. Come on! I tink we better go into da hall.

(Clock strikes three.)

GROUCHO *(calls):* Ravelli, where are you going? Ravelli, where are you? It's dark here. Where *are* you? Come back, Ravelli! *(Relieved.)* Oh, there you are. I thought you had run out on me. Come in here and shut that door after you.

(Door slams.)

GROUCHO: Say, that sheet makes you look tall. You've grown, Ravelli, haven't you? Well, speak. Speak, man. Say something to me.

GHOST: Whooo.

GROUCHO: Who? To me.

GHOST: Whooo.

GROUCHO: To *me*, you fool. Flywheel. *Say* something to me.

GHOST *(hollow laughter):* Ha, ha, ha.

GROUCHO: Would you mind doing that again?

GHOST: Ha, ha, ha.

GROUCHO: Just as I thought. You're not Ravelli. You're an imposter. Pretending to be Ravelli, of all people. Why, you must be *crazy*. Now, beat it, if you want to go on living.

GHOST: I . . . am . . . dead.

GROUCHO: Well, that's what you get for not taking care of yourself— running around in this drafty house with nothing but a thin sheet over you.

GHOST: I . . . am . . . a . . . ghost.

GROUCHO: See here, ghost. If you take my advice, you'll send that sheet to the laundry. It's filthy. Of course, you could save money by having a woman come in once a week and do the flatwork for you.

GHOST: I am the spirit of Roderick Crexton. Ha, ha, ha.

GROUCHO: Say! Old Crexton must have died laughing.

GHOST: Flywheel, your doom is sealed. You are about to join your ancestors.

GROUCHO: Oh, no! You're not going to get *me* in the poorhouse.

(Terrific crash, away.)

GHOST: What . . . was . . . that?

GROUCHO: I don't know, unless it was a mortgage falling due.

GHOST: I go to see who dares disturb the tranquility of my ghostly sphere. As for you, if you are here when I return, you will die.

GROUCHO: Hmmm. Fine business. A hundred-year-old ghost, and you still think it's funny to go around scaring people.

GHOST: I go . . .

(Door opens.)

GROUCHO: Ravelli, Ravelli!

CHICO: Here I am, boss.

GROUCHO: Ravelli, come on, quick. I've got a special reason for wanting to get out of this house alive.

CHICO: What's da reason, boss?

GROUCHO: I wouldn't want to be seen dead with you.

CHICO: Hey, if we gonna die, I might as well pay you da twelve dollars I owe you.

GROUCHO: Ravelli, this is no time to discuss trifles. Besides you owe me *thirteen* dollars, not twelve.

CHICO: I know, but I'ma superstish.

GROUCHO: Where did you get that twelve dollars?

CHICO: I found it in de odder room. Lotsa money. Look. A hunnerd dollars! A tousand dollars! Ten tousand dollars! Money all over the house.

GROUCHO *(excited):* Let's see it, Ravelli. Let's see it.

CHICO: Here, take a look—but you gotta give it back.

GROUCHO: Say, the ink on this money isn't dry yet. You know, I think it's phony.

CHICO: It'sa phony? It'sa phony? *I* don't see da joke.

GROUCHO: Ravelli, even a ghost is better company that you are. It is obvious this money is counterfeit. I want to get some too. You stay here. *(Slams door.)*

(CHICO *whistles "Daffodils"; door creaks open.*)

GHOST: Whooo.

CHICO: Hey, you no scare me. I know it's you, boss.

GHOST: I am the ghost of Roderick Crexton.

CHICO: Aw, you crazy. Crexton, he'sa dead.

GHOST: I am his ghost. Is that clear?

CHICO: Sure, da ghost is clear, come on in.

GHOST: Who are you?

CHICO *(frightened):* Ah . . . ah . . . ah . . .

GHOST: Well, can't you talk?

CHICO: No, I can't talk. I'm from Can'ttalky. *(Laughs.)* Some joke, eh, Mr. Ghost?

GHOST *(fiendishly sneering):*   Ha, ha, ha.

CHICO: You lika dat joke, eh? Awright, I tell it to you again. Hey! You a nice fella. I like you better dan my boss, Flywheel. He always hollers at me.

GHOST *(laughs again):*   Ha, ha, ha.

CHICO *(laughs too):*   Oh, boy! We're having *some* fun.
   (Door opens.)

GROUCHO: Ravelli! Ravelli! Oh, pardon me, I didn't know you had company. I'll be back later.

CHICO: Hey, boss. Disa fella says he's a ghost.

GHOST: Whooo.

GROUCHO: A ghost, eh? That's fine. I've always wanted to play Hamlet.

GHOST: I am the ghost of Roderick Crexton.

GROUCHO: If he's a ghost, Ravelli, I'll eat your hat with ketchup.

GHOST: Whooo.

CHICO: Awright, boss. Here's my hat. I'm going.

GROUCHO: Where are you going?

CHICO: I'm going to da kitchen to get you da ketchup.

GHOST: Whooo.

GROUCHO: Make it two ketchups—one for the ghost.

GHOST: I am the ghost of Roderick Crexton.

GROUCHO: Say, I'm getting pretty sick of hearing you say that. You'll have to take off your sheet and prove it. Come, Ravelli, off with his sheet.

CHICO: Okay, boss. Grab him.
   (Sounds of scuffling and sheet ripping.)

GHOST *(during scuffle):*   Don't touch me. Let go of me.

CHICO: Look, boss! It's da mayor!

GROUCHO: So that's your game, Mr. Mayor? You thought you could run this joint as a haunted house and scare people away, while you made counterfeit money? Stick up your hands.

CHICO: Hey, boss, you no gotta gun.

GROUCHO: That's right, Ravelli. I never thought of that. All right, mayor, you can put your hands down.

MAYOR: Listen, boys, if you give me away, I'll be disgraced for life. Please give me another chance.

CHICO: You mean, you want to scare us again?

MAYOR: No, no, gentlemen. I offered you a hundred dollars if you'd sleep here. If you'll keep this whole thing hushed up, I'll give you a thousand dollars.

CHICO: Hey, a tousand ain't enough.

GROUCHO: Nonsense, Ravelli. We'll get this thousand, and we'll probably get another thousand as reward when we turn him over to the police.

MAYOR: No, no, gentlemen. You mustn't say anything to the police. I'll give you *two* thousand dollars.

GROUCHO: Who will say three thousand?

MAYOR: All right, I will give you three thousand dollars.

GROUCHO: Sold to the ghost for three thousand dollars.

MAYOR: You don't know what this means to me, gentlemen. Here, here is the money. Three thousand dollars. Thank you, thank you, I will never forget this.

GROUCHO: It's nothing at all, mayor. Come over and scare us again sometime.

MAYOR: Goodnight, gentlemen.

(*Door opens and closes.*)

CHICO: Tree tousand ain't bad, eh, boss?

GROUCHO: No, but we should have asked for more. We'd have gotten *five* thousand if we had asked for it.

CHICO: Yeah? What makes you tink so?

GROUCHO: Well, it's counterfeit money, anyway.

(*Music in strong.*)

AFTERPIECE

CHICO: Hey, Groucho?

GROUCHO: Yes, Chico?

CHICO: You know what I tink? I tink joosta because I play da part of a dumb fella like Ravelli, people tink I *really* gotta no brains.

GROUCHO: Frankly, Chico, I've always been under that impression myself.

CHICO: Well, maybe you could ask me a few questions. Den I'll come back wit some smart answers, and people'll say, "Dat Chico, he'sa pretty smart."

GROUCHO: All right, Chico. What's the shape of the world?

CHICO: It's ah . . . ah . . . ah . . .

GROUCHO (*whispers*):   Here, I'll give you a hint. Look at my cuff buttons. (*Louder.*) Now, what's the shape of the world.

CHICO: Square.

"That Chico, he'sa pretty smart." And he was. It was he who negotiated the brothers' lucrative contract with Irving Thalberg and MGM in 1934 after they had been without a movie deal for over a year.

GROUCHO *(whispers):* That's my mistake, Chico. Not these cuff buttons. I mean the cuff buttons I wear on Sunday.

CHICO: Oh, yeah!

GROUCHO: *Now* what's the shape of the world?

CHICO: Square on weekdays, round on Sundays.

GROUCHO: Well, that's pretty close. It's round, stupid.

CHICO: Awright, it's *round.* I don't wanna argue.

GROUCHO: Chico, what did Columbus find out when Queen Isabella sent him on her royal expedition?

CHICO: Royal? How was it?

GROUCHO: How was what?

CHICO: Her royal? Her *motor* oil? Did she use Essolube? Say, I wonder if da history book says so.

GROUCHO: Saysso? Don't you mean Esso, which is more powerful than any gasoline?

CHICO: I tink so.

GROUCHO: Then we can say good night.

BOTH *(singing):* Good night ladies, good night ladies . . .

(Signature music.)

FIVE STAR THEATER
PRESENTS

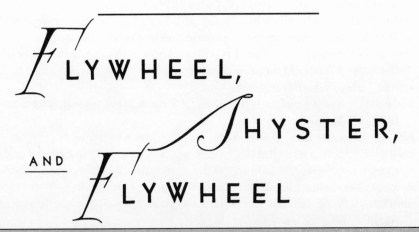

Flywheel, Shyster, and Flywheel

EPISODE NO. 22*   APRIL 24, 1933

CAST

Groucho Marx as Waldorf T. Flywheel
Chico Marx as Emmanuel Ravelli
Miss Dimple
Guide
Mounted Policeman
Stranger

* No, we haven't made a mistake. Episode 21, alas, was
not included in the Library of Congress collection.

(*Phone rings.*)

MISS DIMPLE: Law offices of Flywheel, Shyster, and Flywheel . . . No, I'm sorry, Mr. Flywheel's away . . . Yes, he and his assistant, Mr. Ravelli, have gone on their vacation. They're on a fishing trip in the Canadian woods . . . Yes, I'll tell them you called. (*Fading.*) Goodbye. (*Sounds of birds chirping, water splashing.*)

CHICO: Hey, Flywheel, I gotta bite.

GROUCHO: You've got a bite? Well, I itch a little myself, but I'm not bragging about it.

CHICO: Hey, da bite'sa gone now. I tink it was a fish bite.

GROUCHO: Nonsense, Ravelli, we've been sitting here five hours and not even a nibble. If the fish are biting, they must be biting each other.

CHICO: Maybe da fish no like da bait we got on our hooks.

GROUCHO: Well, if that potted ham's good enough for us, it certainly ought to be good enough for the fish.

CHICO: Yeah, but I tink dey like some fish cakes better. You know, if we catch a mackerel, we can make 'em some fish cakes.

GROUCHO: Ravelli, if we catch a fish around here, it won't be a mackerel —it'll be a miracle.

CHICO: A miracle? I never caught one. But I once caught a pickerel in a delicatessen store.

GROUCHO: A pickerel in a delicatessen store?

CHICO: Sure. A *dill* pickerel. (*Big laugh.*) At'sa some joke!

GROUCHO (*whispers*): Quiet! I feel a nibble. I think I've got a haddock.

CHICO: At'sa funny. I gotta haddock, too.

GROUCHO: Is that so? What do you take for a haddock?

CHICO: Well, sometimes I take a aspirin, sometimes I take a calomel.

GROUCHO: Say, I'd walk a mile for a calomel.

CHICO: Ah, you mean a *chocolate* calomel. I lika dat, too. You know, I'm getting tired of dese woods. Why we come all da way up here for, anyhow?

GROUCHO: What's the matter? Don't you like nature's handiwork? Do you realize what it means to be in these great Canadian woods miles and miles from civilization? Do you realize what it means?

CHICO: Sure, it means we can't go to da movies tonight.

GROUCHO: So that's what life means to you. Here you are in the great open spaces where the hand of man has never set foot. Where the sounds of civilization are never heard. Where the—

(*Sound: "Honk—Honk."*)

GROUCHO: What's that?

CHICO: I tink it's a taxicab.

GROUCHO: Look, you fool, it's a wild goose! Let's chase it!

CHICO: Aw, I no wanna go on a wild goose chase. Hey, boss. Boss! I got anodder bite. It's a great big bite. It must be a whale.

GROUCHO: Well, pull it in.

CHICO: She's a putting up some fight. I tinka dis fish is plenty mad. *(Sound of water splashing.)*

GROUCHO: If it's mad now, wait till it sees what caught it.

CHICO: I got her. I got her. Here she comes. *(Soggy plop.)* Oh, look boss. It ain't a fish at all. It's a rubber boot!

GROUCHO: That's fine. What size is it?

CHICO: I tink it's about nine and a half.

GROUCHO: Just my size. Throw in your line again and see if you can catch the other one.

CHICO: Hey, I no wanna fish for shoes anymore. Let's go back to da camp and eat.

GROUCHO: All right. Come on. Our Indian guide, Chief Pain-in-the-Face, ought to have supper ready by this time.

CHICO: At'sa fine. I can't catch no fish here.

GROUCHO: Well, to catch a fish, Ravelli, you've got to be smarter than the fish. Why don't you go over to the depot and try to catch a train?

CHICO: Hey! Here comes Chief Pain-in-da-Face. Hello, chief.

GUIDE *(approaching):* How!

GROUCHO: Terrible. And how are you, Pain-in-the-Face? Say, do you mind if I call you Neuralgia for short?

GUIDE: Humph.

CHICO: Hey, Pain-in-da-Face! You gotta supper ready for us?

GUIDE: You no bring fish, me no can cook supper. Me no have anything to cook.

GROUCHO: Hmm. Nothing to eat, eh? A fine thing to tell us after we're out slaving all day to provide you with a good home and fine feathers for your ugly head. I suppose you've been standing in front of that cigar store all afternoon.

GUIDE: Me no savvy.

GROUCHO: You no savvy, and me no dinner. Is your face red!

GUIDE: You no catchem fish?

GROUCHO: No, we didn't catch any fish, but we certainly gave them a good scare.

GUIDE: You heap better catchem some food.

CHICO: Hey, boss, maybe we could shoot some game.

GROUCHO: Well, we could shoot a little pool if we had a table.

CHICO: We gotta table, but dere'sa nuttin to eat on it.

GROUCHO: I'll take care of that. Oh, Pain-in-the-Face. Here. You take this gun and bring back some dinner.

GUIDE: Humph. I go.

GROUCHO: And don't come back until you've caught something, even if it's only a smallpox. A smallpox of sardines will do. Now, Ravelli, get busy and make a fire.

CHICO: How can I make a fire? I no gotta any wood.

GROUCHO: Well, take the axe and get busy.

CHICO: I'm sorry, boss, but I already burned de axe. Anyway, I no got matches.

GROUCHO: No matches? That's bad.

CHICO: Hey! I could use my cigar lighter, but I no gotta cigar.

(*Crashing of bushes.*)

CHICO: Boss! I tink I hear someone coming.

GROUCHO: Say, that's marvelous. Ravelli, you must know the woods.

CHICO: Sure I know da woods. I know both—da woods *and* da music.

(*Another crash of underbrush.*)

MOUNTED POLICEMAN: Say, are you guys Ravelli and Flywheel?

GROUCHO: That's right, stranger.

MOUNTED POLICEMAN: What are you doing here?

GROUCHO: We're just feeding the fish. Get in the water and we'll throw you a worm.

MOUNTED POLICEMAN: Never mind that. I just met your guide, Chief Pain-in-the-Face, and he told me to tell you he shot two rabbits and a wild turkey.

CHICO: At'sa fine. Maybe we eat soon. When is he coming back?

MOUNTED POLICEMAN: He's not coming back. He also told me to tell you that he's quitting.

GROUCHO: So he's *quitting* on us. Hmmm. After we invited him to a nice turkey dinner. All *he* had to do was to bring the turkey. There's breeding for you.

CHICO: What do you expect, boss? He's only a half-breed.

MOUNTED POLICEMAN: Well, I don't think you'll see him again. He was beating it hotfoot to his tribe.

GROUCHO: Back to his tribe, eh? Well, I hope he has a reservation. Now, stranger, who are *you?*

MOUNTED POLICEMAN: I am Reginald Fitzgerald of the Northwest Mounted Police.

CHICO: Is dat so? Where's your horse?

GROUCHO: A mounted policeman, eh? Say, that's an idea. My uncle once killed a policeman, but we never thought of having him mounted.

MOUNTED POLICEMAN: Have either of you men seen a tall, fat, prosperous-looking man with a bald head anywhere around these woods?

GROUCHO: Was he a little thin fellow with red hair who played the piano like a fool?

MOUNTED POLICEMAN: Certainly not. This man I'm looking for is a desperate character. There's a reward for him, dead or alive.

CHICO: Hey, if he'sa dead, da reward won't do him much good.

MOUNTED POLICEMAN: Listen, you. I've got to catch this man. He's one of the most dangerous criminals in Canada. There's no crime that he wouldn't stoop to!

CHICO: Well, he couldn't stoop to *porch climbing. (Big laugh.)* Some joke, eh, boss?

MOUNTED POLICEMAN: I've got to go on. There's a big reward for this man. One thousand dollars alive, five hundred dollars dead.

CHICO: Hey, how mucha you get if he's joost a little bit unconscious?

MOUNTED POLICEMAN: Well, if you see him, you'd better look out for yourselves. This man's a killer. They call him the Laughing Hyena. You'll know him because he laughs at everything.

GROUCHO: Ravelli, there's just the man for your jokes.

MOUNTED POLICEMAN: Well, gentlemen, I'm going. I've got to find him. We Northwest Mounted always get our man.

GROUCHO: Well, I guess it's all a matter of taste. Personally, I think a woman is *much* better company.

MOUNTED POLICEMAN *(receding):* Goodbye.

(Crashing in underbrush.)

CHICO: Hey, boss, I hope dat Laughing Hyena ain't around here.

GROUCHO: I don't like it here, either. Come on, Ravelli. Let's get our canoe and beat it.

CHICO: Okay.

(Sound of walking in woods.)

GROUCHO: We'll paddle downstream and shoot the rapids.

CHICO: Hey, at'sa no good. We can't shoot da rapids.

GROUCHO: Because Pain-in-the-Face ran away with our gun!

(Music in Strong.)

(Sound of paddle splashing.)

GROUCHO: Faster, Ravelli, faster. We're getting nowhere.

CHICO: Hey, I no can paddle any harder. Why don't you get up off your back and *help* me for a while.

GROUCHO: I'm sorry, Ravelli. I didn't mean to be critical. You're doing fine, but I wish you'd get past that tree on the bank there. I'm getting sick of looking at it.

CHICO: Hey, boss, look! I work and I work and I work, but da canoe she stand still.

GROUCHO: I've got an idea. Maybe if you untied the rope it might help. You know, we're fastened to that tree.

CHICO *(stops paddling):* Ha, ha. And I tought I couldn't paddle because I didn't have a *paddler's* license. *(Starts paddling again.)* Here we go. I'ma pretty good, eh, boss?

(Splash.)

GROUCHO: Ravelli. Ravelli! A little easier with that paddle. You've got me all wet!

CHICO *(big laugh):* You're always all wet!

GROUCHO: Look, sap! I'm sitting in three inches of water. There's a hole in this canoe. The water's coming in!

CHICO: Don't worry. I'll fix dat, boss.

(Paddling stops, hammering begins.)

GROUCHO: *Now* what are you doing?

CHICO: It's awright. I'ma joost making anodder hole to let da water run out.

GROUCHO: Well, make the hole big enough so you can let yourself out, too.

CHICO *(excited):* Hey, look! Now da water's coming in from two holes!

GROUCHO: In that case, you'll have to dig two holes to let the water out.

CHICO: No, I gotta better idea. I'll stick my fists through the holes. *Dat'll* stop it.

GROUCHO: Why not stick your head through? It might be good bait for the fish.

(Roar of approaching waterfall.)

CHICO: Hey, Flywheel! Look ahead of us! Da river stops. I thinka dis is whata you call a blind alley.

GROUCHO *(excited):* Turn around, Ravelli. Turn around! We're coming to a waterfall!

CHICO: I no need to turn around. I can see it from *here.* It'sa very pretty.

GROUCHO *(excited):* Quick! Put it in reverse, or we'll be swept over the falls!

(Sound of heavy paddling.)

CHICO *(excited):* Hey, boss, da current's too strong. I no can go back again. We joost stay in da same place.

GROUCHO: Keep paddling, Ravelli. Keep paddling! *We're headed for the falls!* It's a drop of fifty feet. *Keep paddling!*

CHICO: Leave it to me, boss. *(Softer tone.)* But first I gotta blow my nose.

(Paddling stops, waterfall grows louder.)

GROUCHO *(bleating):* Ravelli! Ravelli!!

(Roar of water; "Blub, blub, blub" from GROUCHO. *Heavy splashing continues about five seconds then fades.)*

GROUCHO: Ravelli! Ravelli! Where are you?

CHICO: I'ma right here under da shower.

GROUCHO: Well, pass the soap and let's get out of here. The hot water is all gone. Come on, get out of that whirlpool and swim ashore.

CHICO: Okay.

(Sound of splashing.)

GROUCHO *(ad libs grunts):* This is a fine mess. All our equipment gone, and us nearly drowned just because you had to *blow your nose.* Do you realize you blew the canoe and all our clothes at the same time?

CHICO: At's awright. Look! Dere's our stuff right over dere on dat beach. It musta washed ashore.

GROUCHO: Well, that's more than *you* ever did. Come on, we'll camp here. Pitch the tent.

CHICO: Okay.

(Heavy splash.)

GROUCHO: *Now* what are you doing?

CHICO: You told me to pitch da tent.

GROUCHO: Well, I didn't tell you to pitch it back in the river. Come on, pull that tent out . . . *(splashing sounds)* and bring it here under this tree . . . that's right. Now pass me that rope . . . now push up on that side.

(Flapping of canvas, ad lib grunting.)

CHICO: I tinka next time we better take along a house. At'sa not so much work.

GROUCHO: What are you *kicking* about? Look—the tent's up, all ready for a nice night's rest. *(Yawns.)* Boy, am I tired.

(Crashing through bushes.)

CHICO: Look, boss. Look. Over dat bush—a face!

GROUCHO: Why, Ravelli. It's my Uncle Julius. I'd know that face anywhere. *(Calls.)* Hello, Uncle!

(Moose bleats.)

CHICO: Hey, at'sa not your uncle. At's a elk.

GROUCHO: Well, so is Uncle Julius.

(More crashing through bushes.)

CHICO: No, I make a mistake. It'sa no elk either. It's a *moose.*

GROUCHO: You're right, Ravelli. That isn't Uncle Julius. Uncle Julius wears glasses. *(Louder.)* Hey, moose, next time blow one of your horns! Do you want to run us over?

CHICO: Hey, boss, he's walking all over our tings. Hey, moose, go home. Go away. Shoo. Scat!

GROUCHO: If we could only catch him, Ravelli, we could have moose steak for dinner.

(Moose bleats.)

CHICO: I tinka da whole ting's a moosetake. Now he'sa going in our tent.

GROUCHO: Come on, moose, don't make a fool of yourself. You can't get in that tent. It's not big enough.

CHICO: Boss. Stop him. Moose . . . moose. Please. You mustn't! *(Rip of canvas, crashing and clattering.)* Hey, boss, looka what he do. He'sa walked right through our tent. Our tent is hanging around his neck.

GROUCHO: Well, it looks rather well on him. There he *goes! (Crashing through underbrush diminishes.)* And there goes our tent with him, too. Well, tonight I guess we'll have to sleep in the river bed.

CHICO: Oh! I'ma glad da moose is gone.

(Crashing through underbrush.)

GROUCHO: Say, he's coming back again.

CHICO: Aww! At'sa no *moose!*

GROUCHO: Well, as far as I'm concerned, no moose is good moose.

CHICO: Look! At'sa *man.*

GROUCHO: No, it's a moose. I can see his moosetache. *(Whispers.)* Say! He's tall and fat and has a bald head. Maybe it's the Laughing Hyena.

CHICO *(whispers):* At'sa fine. Remember da reward—one tousand dollars alive, five hunnerd dollars dead.

STRANGER *(away):* Hallooo.

GROUCHO: If that's the Laughing Hyena, we'd better get out of here.

CHICO: I find out if he laughs easy. You watch.

STRANGER *(approaching):* Good evening, gentlemen. I am—

CHICO: Don't tell us! Don't tell us who you are, we find out. I ask you a riddle. What is yellow, has nine noses, and catches flies?

STRANGER: What is yellow, has nine noses, and catches flies?

CHICO: A Japanese baseball team!

STRANGER *(laughs heartily):* Ha, ha, ha, ha.

GROUCHO *(whispers):* Ravelli, it's him. It must be him. Only a hyena would laugh at a gag like that.

STRANGER: Ha, ha, ha, that's a good one . . .

GROUCHO: Come, now. It's not *that* good. Ravelli! He's dangerous. Run for your life.

STRANGER: Well, stranger, that certainly is funny. Your little partner here kills me. Ha, ha, yes sir, he certainly kills me.

GROUCHO: Well, he'd better not.

CHICO: Why shouldn't I, boss?

GROUCHO: Well, if you kill him, we'll lose five hundred dollars.

(Music in strong.)

. . .

(Chirping of birds.)

CHICO: Hey, boss, can't we sit down for a while? We've been walking through da woods for tree days and my dogs are tired.

GROUCHO: I'm dog tired, too. Listen, we've got to get this Laughing Hyena back to civilization and claim the reward before he suspects we've captured him.

CHICO: Hey, not so loud. Da hyena, he's right behind us.

GROUCHO: Well, maybe we ought to walk faster. I don't like that fellow.

CHICO: Aw, what'sa matter. He's a *nice* killer. He laughs at all your jokes.

GROUCHO: I know, but he's probably crazy, because he laughs at *your* jokes, too. Say, he must be sleeping. I haven't heard him laugh in two minutes.

CHICO: Boss. Boss! Look behind us. He's *gone!*

GROUCHO: Trying to escape, eh? Ravelli, we've got to trap him. Quick. Ask me a riddle—and ask it out loud.

CHICO: Okay. *(Yells.)* Who was dat lady I seen you wit last night?

GROUCHO *(also yelling):* That was no lady, that was YOUR wife!

STRANGER *(away):* Ha, ha, ha.

GROUCHO: There he is. Ravelli, over that way. Quick, after him!

(Crashing through bushes.)

CHICO: I no see him. Look! Here's *footprints.*

GROUCHO: You're right. Say, this is strange. Four footprints. He's either found a friend, or he's walking on all fours.

CHICO: Maybe he joosta lost his collar button. Look. Da footprints, dey go right into dis cave. I'll go inside and take a look around.

GROUCHO *(outside):* Say, is there any light in there?

CHICO: I don't know. It's so dark I can't tell. I'll light a match and see.

GROUCHO: Never mind. Is that guy in there? Come out, come out, wherever you are!

CHICO: He ain't coming, boss. I'll go in a little farther.

(Pause as RAVELLI enters.)

GROUCHO: I'm right with you, Ravelli!

CHICO: Hey . . . look . . . look. I see him. He's over in dat corner of da cave.

GROUCHO: Yeah . . . that's him all right. But where did he get that fur coat? Tell him a joke, Ravelli. Get him in a good humor.

CHICO: Okay, boss. *(Calls:)* Hey, hyena. What is da difference between a Scotchman and a coconut?

GROUCHO *(whispers):* Keep it up, Ravelli, he's interested.

CHICO *(calls):* Give up? You can get a drink out of a coconut. *(Big laugh.)* Some joke, eh, hyena?

(Bear snarls.)

CHICO: Hey, boss, he ain'ta laughing. He'sa growling.

GROUCHO: Maybe he's not such a fool after all. There's a limit to even a hyena's endurance.

(Snarling becomes louder.)

CHICO: Boss, it's a bear . . . it's a bear . . . it's a bear!

GROUCHO: Ravelli, cut out the old-fashioned ragtime singing. Jumping Jupiter! It really *is* a bear. Why didn't you *tell* me?

CHICO *(excited):* Come on! Let's get out of dis cave. *(Sound of running.)* Quick! Let's climb dis tree. *(Sound of climbing.)* Hey, Flywheel! Where are you?

GROUCHO: I'm way ahead of you . . . on the top branch. Climb, Ravelli, climb!

CHICO *(breathless):* I'ma coming, boss. But it joosta come to me like a flash—*bears* can climb trees *too!*

GROUCHO: Not so loud. You'll put ideas in his head.

CHICO: Hey, Flywheel, look! He'sa coming up. *He'sa coming up!*

GROUCHO: Eight million trees in these woods and he has to pick *this* one to climb.

CHICO: Boss, I got a idea. We can catch him wit a trap.

GROUCHO: That's fine. All we need is the trap. We could buy one if there were a trap drummer in town.

CHICO: I got a trap right in my pocket. Here it is.

GROUCHO: You can't catch a bear with that. That's a *mouse*trap.

CHICO: Aw, da bear won't know da difference.

(Snarling becomes louder.)

GROUCHO: Besides, there's no cheese in that trap.

CHICO: Well, da store didn't have any bear cheese.

GROUCHO: *Bear* cheese?

CHICO: Sure, Camembert cheese.

GROUCHO: Ravelli, I wish you'd shut your trap.

CHICO *(whispering):* Oh no, boss. I put da trap right here. Come on, bear. Jump right in.

GROUCHO: Say, that's no way to get him. Put the trap where he can't *see* it.

CHICO: Well, if he can't see it, how will he find it to get trapped?

GROUCHO: Let *him* worry about that.

(Snarl gets even louder.)

CHICO: Hey, Flywheel, Flywheel! Dere's a mouse in dis trap!

GROUCHO: That's no mouse, stupid! It's your finger.

(Snarl again.)

CHICO: Da bear'sa comin! What are you gonna do?

GROUCHO: I'll wait and see what you do. He'll come to you first.

STRANGER *(away):* Ha, ha, ha!

CHICO: Hey, boss, it's da Laughing Hyena again.

STRANGER *(closer):* Ha, ha, ha!

CHICO: Look—da bear's going downstairs after him!

STRANGER *(close):* Ha, ha, ha! My, you fellows look funny up in that tree!

GROUCHO: Ravelli, if the bear gets him we'll be out five hundred dollars. *(Calls:)* Run, stranger, run. Look out for the bear!

STRANGER: Bear? Say, I'm not afraid of that bear.

CHICO: Boy, is dat hyena tough!

STRANGER: Come down out of that tree. The bear won't hurt you. He's only climbing up there to *play* with you.

GROUCHO: I see. Just a social climber.

STRANGER: Look. I put my arm around its neck. It's just a honey bear.

GROUCHO: Come on, Ravelli. Maybe those two would like to be left alone. Say, if we had a hand organ we could make some money—if we had a crowd.

STRANGER: Ha, ha, ha! That's a good one.

(Bear growls.)

CHICO: Da bear, he don't tink so. Look! He'sa going home.

GROUCHO: That gives me an idea. Which way is home?

STRANGER: Well, we ought to head due south.

GROUCHO: Yes, but how do you know which way is south?

STRANGER: Ha, ha. That's easy. Just look at the moss on the rocks. The moss only grows on the north side of the rocks. You can always tell the north that way.

CHICO: North? At'sa no good. We want to know which is south.

STRANGER: Well, if you want to go south, you look at the other side of the rock.

CHICO: Yeah, but de other side ain't got any moss. Hey, *dis* stone ain't got any moss on *either* side.

GROUCHO: Ignore it, Ravelli. It's probably just a rolling stone.

STRANGER: That's funny. Ha, ha, ha!

GROUCHO: Now, I'm sorry I said it.

CHICO: But boss, we don't know where south is yet.

GROUCHO: Look, Ravelli. It's all very simple. Right in front of you is north. North bids two spades. Heart doubles and redoubles. On your left is west. On your right is east. Now, what have you in back of you?

CHICO: A patch on my pants.

STRANGER: Ha, ha, ha!

CHICO: Now which way we go?

GROUCHO: I don't know. Ask Laughing Gas.

STRANGER: To tell the truth, gentlemen, I don't know which way to go myself. I'm afraid we're lost.

GROUCHO: Lost? Where are we?

STRANGER: I don't know.

GROUCHO: Then how do you know we're lost?

STRANGER: Ha, ha, ha! Brother, you're rich.

GROUCHO: Rich? Not until I get *you* back to civilization. And I'm not sure it's worth it.

CHICO: Hey, boss, maybe we could yell for help.

GROUCHO: Not a bad idea, Ravelli. Go ahead and yell.

CHICO: Okay. *(Yells:)* Hellooo.

MOUNTED POLICEMAN *(far away):*   Hellooo.

CHICO: Hey. Somebody answered.

STRANGER: I hate to disappoint you, boys, but that was an echo.

GROUCHO: An echo? That's my cue. *(Burlesques singing:)* Just an echo, oo-ooo, in the valley, oo-ooo—

CHICO: You keep quiet, boss. You scare de echo away. I try it again. *(Yells:)* Where are you?

MOUNTED POLICEMAN *(away):*   Where are you?

GROUCHO: Well, echo or no echo, that's the dullest conversation I ever listened to.

CHICO: Wait a minoot, boss. *(Yells:)* Can you hear me?

MOUNTED POLICEMAN *(away):*   Can you hear me?

STRANGER: You're wasting your breath. I tell you it's an echo.

GROUCHO: I'll settle this once and for all. Let me try. *(Yells:)* Would you like a drink?

MOUNTED POLICEMAN: I'll be right over!

GROUCHO: That's the thirstiest echo I ever heard.

CHICO: He's going to be awful mad when he finds we got nuttin to drink.

GROUCHO: Well, it's your echo, not mine.
   (Crashing through bushes.)

CHICO: Look, boss, it's da mounted policeman.

GROUCHO: Quick, Ravelli, grab the hyena before he gets away.

CHICO: I got him.
   (Scuffle.)

STRANGER: What's the meaning of this? Let go of me!

MOUNTED POLICEMAN *(away):*   Hello, there. Where's that drink?

GROUCHO: Listen, officer. I've got something better than a drink for you. Look! We've captured the Laughing Hyena. Flywheel always gets his man.

CHICO: And Ravelli helps him. Hey, Mr. officer—how about dat tousand dollars? I tink he's still alive.

STRANGER: Ha, ha, ha!

MOUNTED POLICEMAN: Ha, ha, ha!

GROUCHO: Gentlemen, gentlemen! This is no laughing matter. You can't laugh us out of the reward.

MOUNTED POLICEMAN: Say, that's good. Do you know who this man is? This gentleman is one of the leading bankers in Canada. Why, we captured the real Laughing Hyena this morning.

GROUCHO: Never mind that. How about our thousand dollars?

MOUNTED POLICEMAN: But I tell you, this man is a banker. He's worth over a million dollars.

GROUCHO: Well, if he's worth a million dollars, you certainly ought to be willing to give us a *thousand* for him.

(*Music in strong.*)

AFTERPIECE

CHICO: Ladies and gentlemens. I wanna tell you dat it wasa very nice to go to an Esso station and get what you call a jigsaw puzzle. Oh, it was a whole lotsa fun.

GROUCHO: Chico, did you really get one?

CHICO: Oh, sure I get one. But when I come home, I see dat da man, he made a mistake. He gimme a jigsaw puzzle dat was all broke. It was broke up in about a hunnerd and fifty pieces.

GROUCHO: That's the whole point of the puzzle. Did you put it together?

CHICO: No, de Esso man, he wasa very nice. If I bring it back, I tink maybe he'll give me a *whole* puzzle dat's all in one piece.

GROUCHO: Jiggo, I'd make a jigsaw puzzle out of you, if I were sure I couldn't put you together again. Now will you *listen* while I explain?

CHICO: I will if you will.

GROUCHO: What do you mean, "if you will"?

CHICO: *Any* fuel. If you want motor fuel, Esso motor fuel is very good. It'sa more powerful dan any gasoline. If you want—

GROUCHO: I'll tell you what I want. I want you to say good night.

BOTH: Good night ladies.

(*Signature Music.*)

FIVE STAR THEATER
PRESENTS

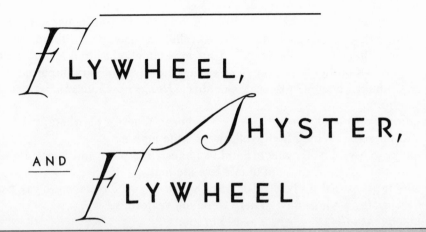

FLYWHEEL, SHYSTER, AND FLYWHEEL

EPISODE NO. 23   *MAY 1, 1933*

CAST

Groucho Marx as Waldorf T. Flywheel
Chico Marx as Emmanuel Ravelli
Miss Dimple
Mrs. Vandergraff
Maid
Roscoe Baldwin

(Typing, phone rings.)

MISS DIMPLE: Law offices of Flywheel, Shyster, and Flywheel . . . Oh, it's *you*, Mr. Flywheel . . . No, you didn't leave your house slippers in the office. Your assistant, Mr. Ravelli, was looking for them too . . . Yes, there *was* a phone call. Your new client, that rich Mrs. Vandergraff, is on her way over to see you. She says it's very important . . . Uh huh, I'll ask her to wait. Goodbye. *(Hangs up phone, hums, resumes typing.)*

CHICO *(opens door; away):*   Where'sa boss? Where's Flywheel?

MISS DIMPLE: Why, Mr. Ravelli, what's the matter?

CHICO: Aw, dat Flywheel, he ain't honest. He went and cheat a client out of forty dollars, and didn't give me half.

MISS DIMPLE: Mr. Flywheel is very angry at you for staying away from work for a whole day. Where were you yesterday?

CHICO *(casually):*   Me? I was in Europe.

MISS DIMPLE: You went to Europe and you came back in *one day?*

CHICO: Yeah, I didn't like it over dere.

MISS DIMPLE: But Mr. Ravelli! Don't you realize that Europe is over three thousand miles away?

CHICO: Yeah, it's too far. I don't tink I'll go any more. But it wasa nice to see my grandpop, my Uncle Pasquale and—

MISS DIMPLE: That's preposterous, You *couldn't* have gone to Europe.

CHICO: Hey! Whatta you talk? I know I see my Uncle Pasquale yesterday. *(Dawning on him:)* Say. Maybe . . . he . . . he came over to *dis* country.

MISS DIMPLE: That's what I thought. You know, it takes five days to cross the ocean in even the fastest vessel.

CHICO *(bewildered):*   Huh?

MISS DIMPLE: You know what a vessel is, don't you?

CHICO: Sure, I can vessel. Look. *(Whistles a few bars of "Daffodils.")* *(Knock on door.)*

MISS DIMPLE: Shhh! Someone's at the door. *(Knock heard again.)* Come in. *(Door opens; whispers.)* It's that rich Mrs. Vandergraff.

MRS. VANDERGRAFF *(away):*   Ah . . . Good morning.

CHICO *(expansively):*   Hullooo, Mrs. Grafter.

MRS. VANDERGRAFF: My name is *Vandergraff!*

CHICO: Awright, awright. You knew I meant you. I was lookin right *at* you—

MRS. VANDERGRAFF: Why, I—

CHICO: Well, tell me, kid, how's tings? You workin?

MRS. VANDERGRAFF: Working? Why, of course not. I don't have to work.

CHICO: Hey, I gotta brudder who don't have to work.

MRS. VANDERGRAFF: Is he wealthy?

CHICO: No. He can't find a job, either, poor fella! He look for a job for twenty years. He look and he look and he look, and den when he finds a job, he no feel like taking it.

MRS. VANDERGRAFF: No?

CHICO: No, he no like dat kind of job, where you joosta gotta sit around all day. He like to *lay* around. Me, I'm different. I like to lay around, too.

MRS. VANDERGRAFF: Why, that's laziness!

CHICO: Laziness? At'sa my brudder, awright. He laziness bed all day. Hey, catch on? Hey, maybe you can give him a job at your house.

MRS. VANDERGRAFF: Just what does your brother do?

CHICO: He don't do nuttin. Dat's why he got fired from his last job. But I tink he'll be very good for trimming da hedges.

MRS. VANDERGRAFF: Trimming *what* hedges?

CHICO: Da hedges of his beard. *(Big laugh.)* At'sa some joke, eh, Mrs. Grafter?

MRS. VANDERGRAFF: I came to see Mr. Flywheel! Who are you?

CHICO: I'm fine. How are you?

MRS. VANDERGRAFF: Why I . . . *Where* is Mr. Flywheel?

(Door opens.)

CHICO: Hey, here he comes.

MRS. VANDERGRAFF: Oh, good morning, Mr. Flywheel.

GROUCHO *(closes door):*   Ah, it's you, Mrs. Vandergraff. You haven't changed a bit—and it's a pity you haven't.

MRS. VANDERGRAFF: Mr. Flywheel, your assistant here has been insulting me.

GROUCHO *(dramatic):*   Oh, he has, has he? See here, Ravelli. I'll teach you to insult my clients.

CHICO: You don't have to teach me. I was doing awright until you came in.

GROUCHO: You'll do a lot better by getting out. Scram!

CHICO *(sulking):*   Awright. Some office. I can't even have any fun. *(Opens and closes door.)*

MRS. VANDERGRAFF: Now, Mr. Flywheel—

GROUCHO *(whispers):*   Ravelli's gone. You can call me Snooky now.

MRS. VANDERGRAFF: Mr. Flywheel! You forget that I'm here on *business*!

GROUCHO: No, I didn't forget. *(Coyly.)* But I'm willing to.

MRS. VANDERGRAFF: Sir! Just what kind of woman do you think I am?

GROUCHO: Frankly, that's what I'm trying to find out. Ah, if we could only find a little bungalow! Oh, of course I know where we could find one. But maybe the people wouldn't get out. But if we could find a nice

"Your eyes, your throat, your lips—everything about you reminds me of you. Except you. How do you account for that?" Groucho romances Margaret Dumont in the opening scene of *A Night at the Opera*, the Marx Brothers' first film for MGM.

empty bungalow just for you and me, where we could bill and cow . . . no . . . I mean bull and cow.

MRS. VANDERGRAFF: Do you know what you are trying to say?

GROUCHO: Yes, but it's not what I'm thinking. What I mean is, if we had a nice little bungalow, and you were on the inside—and I was on the outside trying to get in—and you'd be upstairs and I'd be in the kitchen . . . and you . . . I don't know where I'd be. Maybe I wouldn't be there at all. I'll tell you what. If you don't hear from me by next Wednesday, the whole thing is off.

MRS. VANDERGRAFF: I don't think I understand.

GROUCHO: I mean it's you—your eyes. Your eyes, they shine like the pants of a blue serge suit.

MRS. VANDERGRAFF: What! The very idea. That's an insult.

GROUCHO: That's no reflection on you. It's on the pants. What I mean is, if we had a nice little place and I came home from work—that is, if *you* came home from work . . . that's more like it. And we met at the gate and sort of . . . say, are you sure your husband is dead?

MRS. VANDERGRAFF: Why, yes.

GROUCHO: When will you know definitely? You know, a yes like that was once responsible for me jumping out of a window. I'm not the jumper I used to be. I'm five pounds overweight now. That's with buckshot. But what I was going to say was, I realize I'm no Don Quixoxie, but why don't you marry me until you can make other arrangements?

MRS. VANDERGRAFF: Just what is the *matter* with you?

GROUCHO *(dramatically):*   Oh, I'm not myself today. Maybe that's why I love you.

MRS. VANDERGRAFF: I don't think you'd love me if I were poor.

GROUCHO: I might, but I'd keep my mouth shut.

MRS. VANDERGRAFF: Mr. Flywheel! You're my lawyer. Are you or are you not going to listen to my case?

GROUCHO: A law case? Say, maybe I can get your money *without* marrying you. Now, what's the case?

MRS. VANDERGRAFF: Mr. Flywheel, I suppose you know that the famous Kimberly diamond has been in our family for generations?

GROUCHO: Yep.

MRS. VANDERGRAFF: Well, it was stolen last night.

GROUCHO: Well, I've got an alibi. I was home taking a bath—

MRS. VANDERGRAFF: I haven't told the police about it, because I don't want it in the papers. You see, I have as my guest Roscoe Baldwin, the famous philanthropist, art connoisseur, and globetrotter.

GROUCHO: Does he play pinochle too?

MRS. VANDERGRAFF: I haven't told the police because the scandal would be very embarrassing to Mr. Baldwin—

GROUCHO: Well, what are you coming to me for? Why don't you go to the guy who stole the diamond?

MRS. VANDERGRAFF: What I want you to do is to help me get the insurance. The diamond is insured for fifty thousand dollars.

GROUCHO: Fifty thousand dollars? Say, let me take a look at that diamond!

MRS. VANDERGRAFF: But the diamond is lost. It's gone!

GROUCHO: Well, how do you expect me to find it if I don't know what it looks like. Why didn't you come to me *before* it was stolen? What you're trying to do is lock the barn door after the horse is stolen. When did you last see your horse?

MRS. VANDERGRAFF: But I didn't lose a horse. I lost a diamond!

GROUCHO: Well, that was your first mistake. You should have lost a horse. A horse would be much easier to find.

MRS. VANDERGRAFF: Now what about the *diamond*?

GROUCHO: Don't change the subject. You go home and lock all the doors. See that no one leaves the house unless you think they stole the diamond.

MRS. VANDERGRAFF: Why, how strange!

GROUCHO: Not at all! You wouldn't want any crooks in your house, would you? Now, honey, just what did you want to see me about?

MRS. VANDERGRAFF: Well, I want you to help me get either the insurance or the diamond back.

GROUCHO: Madam, Flywheel doesn't compromise. I'll get both or nothing. And now, cookie, how about a little plain and fancy necking?

MRS. VANDERGRAFF: Well, I'm not going to stay here and be insulted. I'm going.

GROUCHO: No, no. Don't go away and leave me here alone. You stay here and I'll go away.

MRS. VANDERGRAFF: Why, I don't know what to say.

GROUCHO: Well, say that you'll be truly mine, or truly yours, or yours truly. Life is short, let's live while we may, for tomorrow the landlord may be here for the rent.

MRS. VANDERGRAFF: All right, then I'll put the case in your hands. We've got to act quickly. Remember, Mr. Flywheel, a stitch in time saves nine.

GROUCHO: And change your oil every five hundred miles. And make sure it's Essolube.

MRS. VANDERGRAFF: Well, I'll expect you at my house tonight.

GROUCHO *(dramatic):* Ah, tonight. Tonight! When the moon is sneaking around the clouds, I'll be sneaking around you. I'll meet you tonight under the moon. Oh, I can just see you now, you and the moon. You wear a necktie so I'll know you. I'll meet you tonight by the bungalow under the moon. If the moon isn't out, I'll meet you under the bungalow.

MRS. VANDERGRAFF: Mr. Flywheel! I don't like your innuendo.

GROUCHO: Well, that's what I always say. Love flies out the door when money comes innuendo.

(Music in strong.)

(Phone rings.)

MAID: Hello. This is Mrs. Vandergraff's residence . . . No, this is the maid speaking . . . I'm sorry, but Mrs. Vandergraff doesn't want you newspapers to have any information . . . No, the Kimberly diamond has *not* been found . . . *(Moved.)* Yes, it's true. Mrs. Vandergraff's chauffeur was arrested this morning. But only on *suspicion*, I tell you. Alfred's a fine boy. I'm *sure* he didn't do it. For any more information you'll have to talk to Mrs. Vandergraff's lawyers . . . Mr. Flywheel, or his assistant, Mr. Ravelli . . . Yes, they've been here since this morning. Goodbye. *(Hangs up; door opens.)* Oh, Mr. Ravelli, the newspaper just called.

CHICO: Awright. Tell 'em I'll buy one.

MAID: But they wanted *news*.

CHICO: Tell 'em to read da papers. Dey're full of news.

MAID *(dramatic):* Oh, Mr. Ravelli! Mrs. Vandergraff should never have let the police take Alfred away. I'm *sure* he's innocent . . . and I love him so much. But there's nothing I can do. I'm only the maid. Won't you help me?

CHICO: Awright. I help you. Get me a dishtowel.

MAID: No, help me get Alfred out of jail. I tell you he's innocent.

CHICO: Hey! It joosta come to me like a flash. If he's innocent, den he ain't guilty. But if he ain't guilty, what did he take da diamond for?

MAID: But he *didn't* take the diamond.

CHICO: Den he must be crazy. It's a very nicea diamond.

MAID: Oh, they've *got* to let him out of jail.

CHICO: Yeah, jail she's a very bad place. Yesterday I meet a friend—he was in jail two years. He looka very bad. He look so different his own motter wouldn't know him.

MAID: Then how did you know him?

CHICO: Well, *I* ain't his motter.

(Door opens.)

MAID: Oh, there's Mr. Flywheel. Maybe he can help me.

GROUCHO *(away):* Oh, Ravelli! *(Closer.)* Mrs. Vandergraff is playing bridge in the library and needs another hand.

CHICO: I tink she could use anodder face.

GROUCHO: Go on, Ravelli. They're only playing for small stakes.

CHICO: Small steaks and French-fried potatoes?

GROUCHO: Ravelli, why don't you stand at the wrong end of a shooting gallery?

MAID: Oh, Mr. Flywheel! You *know* that Alfred—Mrs. Vandergraff's chauffeur—didn't steal her diamond.

GROUCHO: No, I didn't know it.

MAID: Well, they're holding Alfred under two-thousand-dollar bail. And they've got him in a dingy little cell.

GROUCHO: Don't worry. I've got influence in this town. I'll have him put in a bigger cell.

MAID: Oh, Mr. Ravelli, could you lend me two thousand dollars?

CHICO *(big laugh):*   Goodbye.

MAID: Mr. Flywheel, will *you* lend me two thousand dollars?

GROUCHO: Sorry, but I've got all my money tied up in blondes.

MAID: Don't you mean bonds?

GROUCHO: No, I mean blondes.

MAID: Oh, I must find help somewhere. I've just *got* to get two thousand dollars.

CHICO: Boss, she's a nicea girl. We gotta get dat boy out of jail. Where are we gonna get two tousand dollars for bail?

GROUCHO: That's the question. Where are we going to get two thousand dollars? I'll tell you what. If you two will each put up a thousand dollars, I'll put up the balance.

CHICO: Aw, no. You gotta put up a tousand, too.

GROUCHO: Then we'd have three thousand. That's too much. Now the question is, how are we going to get rid of the extra thousand?

CHICO: Hey, maybe we can get dem to raise da bail to tree tousand dollars.

GROUCHO: I doubt it. They're very particular. Ravelli, have you got a thousand dollars with you?

CHICO: Let's see . . . I got sixty cents.

GROUCHO: Sixty cents. Well, we're still short. We've got to get the money. Each one has got to raise his quota.

CHICO: Hey, I gotta nickel *and* a quarter.

GROUCHO *(dramatically):*   Ravelli, this is no time for dilly-dallying. This poor little maid is in love. We've got to get her chauffeur out of jail.

CHICO: Well, if we can't get him out, she can use *my* chauffeur.

GROUCHO: Oh, have you got a chauffeur? What kind of car have you got?

CHICO: I no gotta car. I joosta gotta chauffeur.

GROUCHO: Maybe I'm crazy, but when you have a chauffeur, aren't you supposed to have a car?

CHICO: I had one, but it cost too much money to keep a car and a chauffeur, so I sold da car.

GROUCHO: That shows you how little I know. I would have kept the car and sold the chauffeur.

CHICO: At'sa no good. I gotta have a chauffeur to take me home to see my wife.

GROUCHO: If you've got no car, how can he take you home to see your wife?

CHICO: Well, he don't have to. My wife ain't home anyway. She went to Reno for her health.

GROUCHO: Reno for her *health?*

CHICO: Yeah. She said she's sick of me.

GROUCHO: Well, I can understand that. If I thought I could get rid of you, I'd leave for Reno myself.

CHICO: At'sa fine. I'll go wit you.

(MRS. VANDERGRAFF's *voice heard away.*)

MAID *(whispers):* Mrs. Vandergraff is coming in. *(Receding.)* I'd better get back to the kitchen.

(Door opens.)

MRS. VANDERGRAFF: Oh, Mr. Flywheel! I do hope something can be done about getting back the Kimberly diamond. It's worth over a hundred thousand dollars. I'll give a thousand dollars reward for its return.

CHICO: I'll give you two tousand.

GROUCHO: Hm! I'll give three thousand, and the stone isn't even mine. *(Mutters.)* She offers a thousand. The piker.

MRS. VANDERGRAFF: I said I'd give a *thousand* dollars.

CHICO: We never find a diamond for less dan two tousand dollars.

GROUCHO: That's the standard price all over.

MRS. VANDERGRAFF: Gentlemen, we've got to find the diamond. And I want to thank you for keeping your activities secret. You see, none of my guests suspect that there has been a robbery. I'm particularly concerned about Mr. Baldwin, the philanthropist. I wanted to make his visit here a very happy one.

GROUCHO: Then I've got an idea.

MRS. VANDERGRAFF: You have?

GROUCHO: Yes. If you want to make his visit happy, why don't you clear out of the joint until he leaves?

(Music in strong.)

BALDWIN *(opens door):* Oh, good morning, Mrs. Vandergraff.

MRS. VANDERGRAFF: Why, good morning, Mr. Baldwin. I trust you slept well last night? But I suppose with all your vast interests—art, philanthropy and whatnot—on your mind, you never rest any too well.

BALDWIN: Yes, yes. That is quite true. Right now my mind is occupied with a new opera house which I may donate to the city.

MRS. VANDERGRAFF: Splendid, splendid, Mr. Baldwin.

BALDWIN: Oh, Mrs. Vandergraff. If you don't mind my asking, I would like to know who are those rather strange-looking gentlemen you have here as guests. Mr . . . er . . . Flywheel, and I think . . . a Mr. Ravelli.

MRS. VANDERGRAFF: Mr. Flywheel is my attorney—*(Door opens.)* Here's Mr. Flywheel. I do want you to meet him. Oh, Mr. Flywheel, shake hands with Mr. Baldwin.

GROUCHO: Is that necessary?

MRS. VANDERGRAFF: You two gentlemen have a lot in common, so I'll leave you alone for a little chat. *(Receding.)* See you later. *(Opens and closes door.)*

GROUCHO: Well, Baldwin, I'm certainly glad I ran into you. I'm only sorry it wasn't an automobile instead.

BALDWIN: I've heard of you, Mr. Flywheel.

GROUCHO: Well, that's fine. You've heard of me, and I've heard of you. Now, have you ever heard the one about the two Irishmen?

BALDWIN *(laughing heartily):* Yes, yes.

GROUCHO: Well, now that I've got you in hysterics, let's get down to business. My name's Flywheel.

BALDWIN: And I am Roscoe W. Baldwin.

GROUCHO: I am Waldorf T. Flywheel. I'll bet you don't know what the T. stands for.

BALDWIN: Thomas?

GROUCHO: No, Edgar. You were close, though. You were close, and you still are, I'll bet. Now, Mr. Baldwin, this is what I wanted to talk to you about. How would you like to finance the building of a new law school?

BALDWIN: Well, that's a question.

GROUCHO: Yes, that is a question. You certainly know a question when you see it. I congratulate you, Mr. Baldwin. And that brings us right back to where we were. How would you like to finance the building of a new law school?

BALDWIN: Well, is there any particular kind of law school you have in mind?

GROUCHO: Well, I'll tell you. I'm getting along in years now, and there's one thing I've always wanted to do before I quit.

BALDWIN: What is that?

GROUCHO: Retire. Now, would you be interested in a proposition of that kind? I've always felt that my retirement would be the greatest contribution to the legal profession that the world has ever known. This is your chance, Mr. Baldwin. When I think of what you've done for this country—and, by the way, just what *have* you done for this country?

BALDWIN: Well, I've tried to do what I could. Especially in the world of art.

GROUCHO: Well, I don't know how we got around to that, but what is your opinion of art?

BALDWIN: I'm glad you asked me.

GROUCHO: I withdraw the question. Tell me, Mr. Baldwin, where do you plan on putting your new opera house?

BALDWIN: I thought I would put it somewhere near Central Park.

GROUCHO: Why not put it right *in* Central Park?

BALDWIN: Could we do that?

GROUCHO: Sure. Do it at night when no one is looking. Why not put it in the reservoir and get the whole thing over with? Of course, that might interfere with the water supply. But after all, we must remember that art is art. Still, on the other hand, water is water, isn't it? And East is East and West is West. And if you take cranberries and stew them like applesauce, they taste much more like prunes than rhubarb does. Now you tell me what you know.

BALDWIN: Well, I would be very glad to give you my opinions.

GROUCHO: That's fine. I'll ask you for them sometime. Remind me, will you. I'll tell you what, can you come to my office at ten o'clock tomorrow morning? If I'm not there, ask for Mr. Ravelli—that's my assistant. And if he talks to you, I'll discharge him. That's a date now, Tuesday at three. No, you'd better make it Friday. I'm going to Europe on Thursday. Pardon me, my name is Flywheel. I've always wanted to meet you, Mr. Baldwin. Tell me, Mr. Baldwin, what do you think of the stock market?

BALDWIN: Well, you see, last year, after all, was a presidential year.

GROUCHO: Wasn't it though? Everybody was complaining. Remember the year we had the locusts? I voted for them, too. And what did I get? A lot of promises before election, and a lot of locusts after. What do you think of the traffic problem? What do you think of the marriage problem? What do you think of at night before you go to bed? You beast.

BALDWIN: Well, I'll tell you—

GROUCHO: I'd rather not hear any more about it. Remember, there may be traveling men present.

BALDWIN: Well, Flywheel, in the last analysis, it's a question of money. You see, the nickel is not what is used to be ten years ago.

GROUCHO: I'll go further than that. I'll get off at Philadelphia. It's not what it was fifteen years ago. Do you know what this country needs today?

BALDWIN: What?

GROUCHO: A seven-cent nickel. We've been using the five-cent nickel in this country since 1492. That's pretty near a hundred years daylight saving. Why not give the seven-cent nickel a chance? If that works out, next year we can have an eight-cent nickel. Think what that would mean. You could go to a newsstand, buy a three-cent paper, and get the same nickel back again. One nickel carefully used would last a family a lifetime.

BALDWIN: Mr. Flywheel, I think that is a wonderful idea.

GROUCHO: You do, eh?

BALDWIN: Yes.

GROUCHO: Well, then there can't be much to it. Forget about it. Where's my assistant? Where's Ravelli?

BALDWIN: Why do you want him?

GROUCHO: Maybe *he* won't mind listening to you.

CHICO *(door opens, away):* Did you call me, boss?

GROUCHO: Yes, Ravelli. You stay here and talk to this windbag for me. I can't get a word in edgewise. *(Receding.)* I'm going out in the kitchen to try and help the maid forget about her chauffeur. *(Closes door.)*

BALDWIN: Mr. Ravelli, my name is Baldwin. Roscoe W. Baldwin.

CHICO: And my name is Emmanuel T. Ravelli. You know what da T. stands for?

BALDWIN: Ha, ha! I can't be fooled again. It stands for Edgar.

CHICO: No, Thomas. You know, I got a feeling I met you someplace before.

BALDWIN: After all, I am one of the best-known men in America. The newspapers will insist on running my photographs.

CHICO: You're not Krazy Kat?

BALDWIN: No, no.

CHICO: Let me see. I met you someplace. Were you ever in Sing-Sing . . . Joliet?

BALDWIN: Please—

CHICO: Don't tell me. Let me guess—San Quentin? Leavenworth?

BALDWIN: No, you are entirely wrong. I spent most of my life in Europe.

CHICO: Europe? I got it. Ah, Czechoslovakia.

BALDWIN: You are wrong. I was never there. You are mistaken.

CHICO: I tell you you're from Czechoslovakia!

BALDWIN: No, no, no.

CHICO: Ah, I know! It comes to me joosta like a flash. You're Peter Palooky, da fish peddler!

BALDWIN: I am *not* Peter Palooky!

CHICO: Yes, Peter Palooky. Wait, da birthmark! Peter Palooky had a birthmark on his arm—
(Scuffle starts.)

BALDWIN: Please! What are you trying to do to me? Let go of me! Stop pulling up my sleeve!

CHICO: Ah-ha! Dere it is. Da birthmark. You see? I was right.

BALDWIN: All right, all right, I confess. I was Peter Palooky. But please —don't tell anyone. If you'll keep quiet, I'll make it worth your while. I'll give you, shall we say, five hundred dollars?

CHICO: Cheapskate! Five hunnerd dollars!

BALDWIN: Here. It is all the cash I have with me.

CHICO: Awright, I take your IOU.

BALDWIN: I'm sorry, but that is my best offer. That is all you will get.

CHICO: Dat's all you'll give? Awright, I tell everybody. *(Sings out:)* He's Peter da horsethief . . . Peter da fish peddler!

BALDWIN: Keep quiet. Please, please. Just a minute. I have a check with me for a thousand dollars. Here, I will give it to you. Yes?

CHICO: Is it good?

BALDWIN: Of course, it's good. Who would give me a bad check?

CHICO: I would.

BALDWIN: All right. If you won't take this check, then that is all you will get.

CHICO: Awright. *(Loudly:)* He's Peter da fish peddler, Peter da horse-thief—

BALDWIN: Shhh. *Please!*

CHICO: Hey, *now* I know who took da Kimberly diamond.

BALDWIN: Please, please. Don't say anything, and I'll give you five thousand dollars.

CHICO: Aw, now! Mrs. Vandergraff is my pal. You tink I double-cross her for five tousand dollars? You got to make it six tousand.

BALDWIN: All right, here is all the money I have with me now. I'll go to the bank for the rest. But remember, you promise to say nothing about this to Mrs. Vandergraff.

CHICO: Okay, horsethief. I promise.

(Voices of GROUCHO *and* MRS. VANDERGRAFF *away.)*

BALDWIN: Shhh. That sounds like Mrs. Vandergraff and Mr. Flywheel.

(MRS. VANDERGRAFF's *laughter is heard.)*

MRS. VANDERGRAFF: Ha, ha, ha! Oh, Mr. Flywheel!

GROUCHO *(pleading):* Oh, come on. Just one kiss.

MRS. VANDERGRAFF *(coyly):* Why, Mr. Flywheel!

GROUCHO: Oh, I don't want it for myself. It's for an old blind man.

MRS. VANDERGRAFF: A blind man?

GROUCHO: Certainly. If he could see your face, he wouldn't take the kiss. Come on, don't be an old meany.

CHICO *(away):* Hey, I know a song about a meany. Meany da Moocher. *(Big laugh.)* Some joke!

GROUCHO: Never mind that, Ravelli. Have you got any news of the Kimberly diamond?

CHICO: Oh, yeah, boss. I was joosta gonna tell you. Oh, boy, are you gonna laugh! You know who stole da diamond?

BALDWIN *(terrified):* Please, Mr. Ravelli. Remember your promise.

CHICO: Joosta you leave it to me, Peter. Joosta you leave it to me.

GROUCHO: Talk, man, talk! Who stole the diamond?

CHICO: Dis guy here. Peter da horsethief.

MRS. VANDERGRAFF: Peter, the *horsethief?*

CHICO: At'sa right. Eh, horsethief?

BALDWIN: You . . . you *double-crossing rat.* You promised me you wouldn't tell Mrs. Vandergraff.

CHICO: Well, I didn't tell Mrs. Vandergraff. I told my boss, Flywheel. (*Music in strong.*)

AFTERPIECE

GROUCHO: Ladies and gentlemen. My brother Chico and I just flew into New York from Hollywood. The weather was great for flying.

CHICO: Hey, wait a minoots, Groucho! I saw you on da train wit me. You wasn't *flying!*

GROUCHO: I certainly was. I was flying a kite from the observation platform. You know, Benjamin Franklin did just that, and he discovered electricity.

CHICO: He coulda saved time if he joost turned on a switch.

GROUCHO: You fool! He was getting electricity from lightning, and lightning *never* strikes twice in the same place!

CHICO: My fadder was different. He always kept striking me in da same place—in da log carbon, where I used to play.

GROUCHO: Log carbon? Don't you mean cabin?

CHICO: No, a cabin is a fellow who runs a ship. I used to play in a carbon —da place where dey keeps cars.

GROUCHO: Chico! You don't find cars in a carbon. You find carbon in cars, that is, in cars that don't use good fuel like Esso, which is more powerful than any gasoline.

(*Signature music.*)

FIVE STAR THEATER
PRESENTS

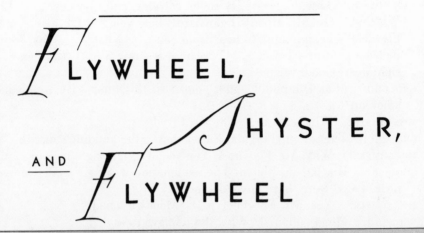

Flywheel, Shyster, and Flywheel

EPISODE NO. 24   MAY 8, 1933

CAST

Groucho Marx as Waldorf T. Flywheel
Chico Marx as Emmanuel Ravelli
Miss Dimple
Mr. Moody
Cop
Various voices
Woman

(Phone rings.)

MISS DIMPLE: Law offices of Flywheel, Shyster, and Flywheel . . . Who? Who? . . . Oh, Mr. Moody. I can hardly hear you . . . Oh, yes . . . Mr. Flywheel's been hoping to hear from you . . . What? . . . Yes, I know he'll be glad to see you . . . Yes, he just came in . . . You can come right over. Goodbye.

GROUCHO: Miss Dimple, I smell smoke in this office. Have you been smoking?

MISS DIMPLE: Why, of course not, Mr. Flywheel.

GROUCHO: Then it must be me. Either that or the building's on fire.

MISS DIMPLE: Why, Mr. Flywheel. You've got a cigar right in your mouth.

GROUCHO: Ha, ha! So I have. The explanation was right under my very nose. I say, were there any calls for me?

MISS DIMPLE: Yes, Mr. Flywheel, a Mr. Moody phoned.

GROUCHO: Moody phoned? What did he have to say?

MISS DIMPLE: I think he said he was coming over here. I couldn't understand him very well. He seemed to have a cough.

GROUCHO: He has a bad cough? Well, maybe he'll cough up that money he owes me.

(Door opens.)

MISS DIMPLE: Good morning, Mr. Ravelli.

CHICO: Hello, Miss Dimp. Hey, boss. You shoulda come outside. Whatta day! Da birds is singing, da spring she is coming . . . da flowers, da trees. *(Kiss.)* Oh baby, whatta day.

GROUCHO: Well, Ravelli, if it's so beautiful outside, what did you come in here for?

CHICO: I come in because it wasa snowing.

GROUCHO: Well, I'm glad you didn't come in on my account.

CHICO: Say, dat joost reminds me. Your account, she'sa no good. I go to da bank to get some money, and dey tella me you write too many checks. You gotta no money left.

GROUCHO: What do you mean, no money left? Look at all the checks left in this checkbook.

CHICO: At'sa what I tell him. I tella your banker you gotta money in da bank. I saw you put some in dere lasta year.

GROUCHO: Yes, but the interest has eaten it all up. By the way, did you see an envelope lying around here marked "Confidential"?

CHICO: Sure, boss. I mailed it.

GROUCHO: You mailed it? Why, you sap! It didn't have any address on it.

CHICO: At'sa right. I see on da envelope it says "Confidential," and I tought you didn't want anybody to know where it was going.

(*Knock on door.*)

MISS DIMPLE: Come in.

MOODY *(opens door):*   Howdy, Flywheel.

GROUCHO: Well, what can I do for you?

MOODY: Now, about that three-hundred-dollar debt.

GROUCHO: See here, my good man. I don't like your attitude. I can't pay you the three hundred dollars. Why didn't you come in yesterday? Yesterday I was out of town.

MOODY: Why, I—

GROUCHO: When I say I can't pay, I can't pay. In these times a creditor must be lenient.

MOODY: Flywheel, you took the words right out of my mouth. My name's Moody. I owe you the three hundred dollars, and I can't pay it. Ha, ha! Yes, sir, when you said that a creditor must be lenient, you took the words right out of my mouth.

GROUCHO: In that case, I'll put 'em right back in again! Come on, fork over that three hundred or I'll throw you in jail, you crook!

MOODY: But Mr. Flywheel, I haven't got the money, and that's the truth.

GROUCHO: Well, I've always heard that the truth hurts, and it's killing me now.

MOODY: Gentlemen, I'm broke, and you know the old saying—you can't get blood out of a turnip.

CHICO: Hey, we no wanna blood. We wanna da tree hunnerd bucks.

GROUCHO: If I had three hundred dollars, I wouldn't eat turnips.

MOODY: Well, gentlemen, I am a man of honor. I don't intend to see you cheated. As you know, I'm in the automobile business, and I'm going to leave you one of my little buses as security until I raise the necessary cash.

CHICO: Hey, you mean you giving us an automobile? At'sa fine!

GROUCHO: Keep out of this, Ravelli. Listen, Moody. What sort of car is it?

MOODY: You'll find it right downstairs. The license number is X-13. Here are the keys. I've got to dash now. Good luck with the bus. So long.

(*Slams door.*)

GROUCHO *(calls):*   Hey Moody. Moody! *(Opens door.)* Hey, wait a minute!

CHICO: Hey, boss. Let's go down and take a look at our new car.

GROUCHO: Well, I'll go look at it. I'm not very crazy about this proposition. I've had a strong prejudice against autos ever since you were struck by one.

CHICO: At'sa awright. I wasn't hurt very bad.

GROUCHO: Well, here's the street and here's the building. See, Ravelli, I knew that guy Moody was a phony. There's no car parked in front of this building. Just that big sightseeing bus.

CHICO: Hey, Flywheel. Look at the license on that bus—X-13.

GROUCHO: What! That can't be Moody's car. That bus is an imposter.

CHICO: But look at the license, boss, it says X-13.

GROUCHO: Well, this bus is a great disappointment to me. I visualized a coupe. Why, that boat is as big as a house.

CHICO: Maybe it's a houseboat.

GROUCHO: It can't be as houseboat, there's no water under it. Anyway, it hasn't even got a roof. Oh, I see they've got the top down.

CHICO: Hey, here comes a policeman.

COP *(approaching):*   Say, do you guys own this sightseeing bus here?

CHICO: Sure, you want to buy it?

COP: Listen. You got it parked right here so nobody can get at that hydrant.

CHICO: That's all right, Mr. Policeman, we're not thirsty.

COP: Get in that bus and get it out of my sight. You're blocking traffic. Come on, get in there!

GROUCHO: All right, all right, we'll get in.

COP: Come on. Step on it!

GROUCHO: Ravelli. Drive on!

CHICO: Drive on what?

GROUCHO: Preferably on the street.

CHICO: Some fun, eh, boss? Watch me make it go. Hey, I'll give you a race.

GROUCHO: How can we race when we're both in the same car?

CHICO: It's easy, boss. You sit on one side and I sit on da odder. *(Starts bus.)* I like driving dis car.

GROUCHO: Watch where you're going. Ravelli, slow down until the back of the bus catches up with us. It's a block behind.

CHICO: Don't worry, boss. This is joost as easy for me like riding a bicycle.

GROUCHO: Can you ride a bicycle?

CHICO: I could if I didn't always fall off.

GROUCHO: Nice work, nitwit. Look out! That's a red light ahead of us!

CHICO: At'sa awright, boss. We won't hit it. It'sa hanging up in air. *(Pause.)* See? We went right *under* it.
(Bus stops.)

GROUCHO: What's the big idea of passing the red light and *then* stopping?

CHICO: It joosta came to me. Da red light, she means danger. I wanna to get past it quick.

GROUCHO: Well, all right, when you passed it what did you stop for?

CHICO: Dis bus, she don't ride so good.

GROUCHO: I think maybe we ought to get some new tires—balloon tires.

CHICO: At'sa no good. We ain't got a balloon.

(Honking of horns.)

VOICE: Hey, move on out of here.

CHICO: Hey, Flywheel, what's all dat noise about?

VOICES: You're blocking the whole street. Where do you think you're going?

GROUCHO: Where would you suggest? Do you know any good places?

VOICES: Go on! Get going! Move on!

CHICO: Hey, boss, what'll I do?

GROUCHO: Well, Noah, I think we'd better get this ark out of here. I think I see land.

(Bus starts, honking of horns subsides.)

CHICO: Well, we're off again. Oh boy, am I a driver!

GROUCHO: I wish I knew, Ravelli. I'd feel much safer.

CHICO: Look. Looka dat lady crossing da street. Some pip!

GROUCHO: Look out, Ravelli! Look out. *(Sotto voce.)* That's no good. *(Yells.)* Look out, lady!

CHICO: Hey, we missed her!

GROUCHO: I think you can still get her, Ravelli. Quick, up on the sidewalk before she gets in that building.

CHICO: I drive dis bus. Hey, boss, where you wanna go? Where you like to be?

GROUCHO: Well, with you driving, I'd like to be home in bed.

CHICO: Okay. Let's turn off da road and go to bed.

GROUCHO: Don't turn down this street. See that sign? It says "Look out for schoolchildren!"

CHICO: Ah, who's scared of little schoolchildren?

(Music in strong.)

(Street noises.)

CHICO: Hey, boss. I can hardly drive anymore. If da cops don't let us park dis bus someplace, I'm gonna be pretty sick. Maybe a cop let us park here.

GROUCHO: I like your optimism. Say, look. Look! Head in there, quick. We can stop here. They're expecting us.

CHICO: What you mean, dey expecting us?

GROUCHO: There's a sign there says, "Bus Stop."

CHICO: Hey, boss, look at all dose ladies standing dere and waiting. Whatta dey waiting for?

GROUCHO: It's probably a welcoming committee. I think we broke the record for a nonstop flight.

CHICO: Whatta you say, should we stop here?

GROUCHO: Pull into the curb. *(Pause.)* I said *into* it, not *over* it.

CHICO: Okay. *(Stops bus.)* Hello, ladies! How's dat for a landing?

WOMAN: Well, driver, it's about time you got here. Come on, girls, get in.

(Loud babble of women's voices.)

GROUCHO: Ladies . . . ladies!

CHICO: Hey, boss, we certainly make a hit. All dose old warhorses is getting in da bus with us.

WOMAN: Well . . . well . . . Driver, why don't you get going?

CHICO: Hey, lady, we not going. We joost got here.

WOMAN: Nonsense. I engaged this bus for the afternoon, for an outing of our teachers' association. Girls, have you all got your basket luncheons?

GROUCHO: Yes, girls, I hope you brought a couple of extra baskets for Ravelli and me.

CHICO: Hey, boss, I no want any. I no like to eat baskets.

WOMAN: Well, driver, what are you going to show us?

GROUCHO: How would you like to see a couple of card tricks? Have any of you old crows got a deck of cards?

WOMAN: Well, why don't we start?

GROUCHO: I'll bite. Why don't we? Ravelli, why don't we start?

CHICO: I can't finda da little ting you step on.

(Terrible explosion.)

CHICO: Dat can't be it.

GROUCHO: That's quick thinking, Ravelli! Step on something else. No, not that—that's a teacher.

CHICO: I tink I got it, boss.

(Bus starts.)

WOMAN: Stop. Stop!

CHICO: Stop? Hey, you joost say you wanna start.

WOMAN: You're going too fast!

GROUCHO: Aren't you ever satisfied?

WOMAN: Well, I certainly hope this bus has four-wheel brakes!

CHICO: I don't even tink it got four wheels.

WOMAN: Well, aren't you going to point out anything to us?

GROUCHO: Certainly, madam. If you look out on your left you'll see a dog. Now leave me alone.

WOMAN: We agreed to pay you for this trip, but the man told us that there'd be a lecture along the way.

CHICO: A lecture? Awright, lady, you look out for it and when you see it, we stop.

WOMAN: We insist upon having a lecture! That's what we're paying you for!

GROUCHO: All right, madam, you'll have your lecture and you'll be the first to regret it. Ladies and Ravelli, unaccustomed as I am to public speaking—

CHICO: Hey, boss, sit down.

GROUCHO: How can I sit down and lecture? Shut up! Ladies, unaccustomed as I am to public speaking . . . Well, I'm getting more accustomed to it.

CHICO: Hey, boss, sit down.

GROUCHO: Ravelli, you may not like my lecture, but there are those who appreciate the finer things in life. Ladies, accustomed as I am to public . . .

(*Thud, bump, screams.*)

GROUCHO: Who hit me? Who hit me? Who threw that brick? Ravelli, we've been attacked!

CHICO: I told you to sit down, boss. It was a low bridge.

GROUCHO: I'll say it was a low bridge! One of the lowest bridges I've ever seen. Sneaking up on me when my back was turned! Hereafter, back up when I'm lecturing. Now, where was I?

CHICO: You were standing on da seat right beside me.

GROUCHO: Well, I'll have to go back to where I started.

CHICO: You wanna me to turn around and go under da bridge again?

GROUCHO: Listen, you, we've had enough bridge for one afternoon. Besides, I'm vulnerable now, and I don't want to go down again.

WOMAN: What's that big building we just went by?

CHICO: Which building?

GROUCHO: You'll have to speak faster, madam, it's gone already.

WOMAN: Well, then, what's that building we're coming to?

GROUCHO: You'll have to speak slower, we haven't got there yet.

WOMAN: Well . . . now, what are we passing?

GROUCHO: Why . . . ah . . . that's the tomb of General Grant.

WOMAN: Nonsense. Grant's tomb is on Riverside Drive in upper New York.

GROUCHO: Well, he got wiped out in the market and he had to move to a cheaper neighborhood. Any more idiotic questions?

WOMAN: What's that funny-looking thing on your right?

GROUCHO: Don't be alarmed, that's Ravelli.

WOMAN: I'm not interested in your stupid-looking friend.

GROUCHO: Well, that'll take a load off his mind.

CHICO: Lady, you gotta stoppa your complaining.

WOMAN: I don't like the way you're driving this car, young man! Have you got a driver's license?

CHICO: Well, dey said dey'd give me one.

WOMAN: Haven't you got one now?

CHICO: No, I don't know how to drive yet.

WOMAN: I never heard of such a thing!

CHICO: Lady, you talka too much.

GROUCHO: Is that a way to talk to a lady? Don't you know that you must always be polite to the inferior sex?

WOMAN: I never was so insulted in my life.

GROUCHO: Please shut your mouth, madam, you talk too much.

CHICO: At'sa joosta what I said, boss.

GROUCHO: I know you did, Ravelli, but you didn't say please.

WOMAN: Well, I'm getting sick and tired of this. We came out on this trip to go sightseeing and you haven't told us a thing.

CHICO: Hey, we joosta told you to shut up. What more do you want?

GROUCHO: All right, madam. Anything to keep you quiet. Do you see that big building over there?

WOMAN: No, where?

GROUCHO: The one on your left with the tall chimneys and the big doorway.

WOMAN: Oh yes, I see it now. What is it?

GROUCHO: I haven't the faintest idea. I imagine it's a building.

WOMAN: You're a fine guide. I know more about this town than you do.

CHICO: Sure, lady, but you been here before.

WOMAN: I *knew* he didn't know this town!

GROUCHO: Oh, you think I don't know this town? Well, I'll have you understand that this is the finest residential section of this city. On your right is the municipal gas works. On your left is the city dump, where we will stop on the return trip for a picnic lunch. And while we're there we'll drop Ravelli.

WOMAN: Driver! Driver, where are we going? We seem to be leaving town.

GROUCHO: Why, so we are. What's the big idea, Ravelli? Stop and turn around.

CHICO *(whispers)*: Hey, boss, I no can stop.

GROUCHO *(whispers)*: What do you mean, you can't stop?

CHICO: *I* can stop, but I can't stop da car. I forgot to tella you before, but da brakes on dis car are no good. I tink they are broke.

GROUCHO: Well, it might help if you took your foot off the gas.

CHICO: Da gas, she'sa broke too.

GROUCHO: Is there anything on this car that isn't busted?

CHICO: Sure, boss, da steering wheel, but dat doesn't work.

GROUCHO: Now, ladies, to resume our travel talk. We are now leaving the city for the open country. As we pass into the great unknown, we approach one of the last signs of civilization—a coal truck.

WOMAN: Careful, driver, you almost ran into that load of coal.

CHICO: Don't worry, lady, it wouldn't hurt us. It's only soft coal.

(Music in strong.)

(Sound of bus.)

WOMAN: Driver. Driver. Are we going back to the city or aren't we? We've been driving through the country for hours, and the girls and I have to catch a train.

CHICO: Awright, lady, you find a train, and I'll chase it.

WOMAN: And I *insist* upon being taken back to the city. Why, we must be miles out in the country! What's the name of that town we just went through?

GROUCHO: Never mind the details, madam. What I want to know is, what state are we in?

WOMAN: This is outrageous! Why, the sun's setting. It'll be dark in another hour.

GROUCHO: I suppose that's our fault, too! Ravelli, I'm getting sick of these women. Can't you stop this bus and dump 'em out?

CHICO: No. Dere's a sign over dere dat says "No Dumping."

WOMAN: Driver, driver! We're coming to a railroad crossing. It says, "Stop, Look, and Listen."

CHICO: Well, ladies, you can look and listen as much as you want, but we no can stop.

GROUCHO: Ravelli, look out for that bump. We're going over the rails.

(Bus stops.)

CHICO: Hey, boss, at'sa wonderful! I make da car stop. I'ma pretty good, huh?

WOMAN: You've stopped right on the railroad tracks. Back up! Get off! Move on! You're on the track!

GROUCHO: One thing at a time, madam. He has a one-track mind.

(Train whistle in distance.)

WOMAN: Quick. Quick, there's a train coming! Get off the tracks.

(Bus starts, train rushes by.)

GROUCHO: Well, we gave that engineer a scare he won't soon forget.

CHICO: It woulda serve him right if we hadn't got off da track at all.

WOMAN: Good heavens, what a fright!

GROUCHO: That wasn't a fright. That was a freight.

WOMAN: That little incident just added ten years to my age.

CHICO: At'sa impossible, lady. Nobody could be dat old.

GROUCHO: Well, Ravelli, how about stopping now and turning around?

CHICO: I no can do it.

GROUCHO: What do you mean? You just stopped a minute ago.

CHICO: Yes, boss, but I don't know how I did it.

WOMAN: This is intolerable! We can't go on like this. First you drive us in the country, and then you risk our lives.

GROUCHO: Madam, if we could stop either the car or your squawking, I'd be happy.

WOMAN: Why, look at this woods we're coming to. This is awful!

CHICO: I wisha I could remember what to step on to stoppa dis bus.

WOMAN: Why, we're *in* the forest. It's all dark. Look in back of us, girls, there's a storm coming up!

CHICO: Where, lady? Where?

GROUCHO: Ravelli, Ravelli! Don't look around. Watch where you're going! *(Wham, crash.)* Well, Ravelli, that's one way of stopping.

CHICO: Hey, boss. I no like to say anything, because you always get mad. But I tink we hit a telegraph pole and I tink we do some damage.

GROUCHO: That's all right. It isn't *our* pole.

WOMAN: Can't you be careful? Why don't you look where you're going?

GROUCHO: Ravelli, I think I know what the trouble is, We've got flat tires.

CHICO: Wait a minoots, boss, I look . . . Hey, we gotta no flat tires.

GROUCHO: Oh, you don't think so? Well, what do you call those dames?

WOMAN: Well, what are we waiting for? You take us out in this car, you rush us out of the city, you drive like a maniac, and then stop in this lonely spot with a storm coming up. What are you going to do about it?

GROUCHO: Say, I'm just as sick of it as you are. Come on, Ravelli. We've got to get out of here. Hurry up. Throw out the clutch.

CHICO: Okay, boss.

(Clank of metal, crash of glass, thud.)

GROUCHO: Hey, fathead, what's the big idea?

CHICO: You tolda me to trow out da clutch.

GROUCHO: I know, but I didn't tell you to throw it through the windshield!

(Sound of thunder.)

WOMAN: It's going to rain any minute.

GROUCHO: Well, you'd look cleaner after a rain.

WOMAN: I think we're lost.

GROUCHO: Pipe down, madam. We won't be lost long. There's a signpost right here beside the car. Get out and see what it says, Ravelli.

CHICO: I no can see it, boss, It's too dark.

GROUCHO: Come, come, if you can't see it down there, then climb up on it and read it.

CHICO: Okay, boss. Here I go.

(Pause.)

GROUCHO: Well, Balboa, what does it say?

CHICO *(away):* I got it, boss. I tink it says West Point.

GROUCHO: West Point? How's the game coming out?

CHICO: Aw, I make a mistake. It says *wet paint.*

GROUCHO: Nice work, Ravelli. You stay up there till you dry off.

(Clap of thunder.)

WOMAN: Goodness, look at him. He's got paint all over him. He's a sight!

CHICO: Well, you wanted to go sightseeing, didn't you?

(Rain starts.)

WOMAN: Oh, it's raining. This is terrible. Miles from home and it's raining.

CHICO: What's da difference? I bet it's raining home, too.

WOMAN: We're getting soaked, driver.

GROUCHO: If you think you're getting soaked now, wait till you get our bill.

WOMAN: You can at least put up the top. Hurry.

GROUCHO: Come on, Ravelli. You take that side, and this side . . . and the back, and I'll supervise.

CHICO: At'sa fine, I'll help you supervise, but you gotta help me put up da top.

GROUCHO: I'd just love to, but I'm afraid it's a one-man top.

CHICO: Okay, I push.

GROUCHO: That's it, now . . . push it up. Careful of the side. Go slow. Don't strain yourself. Remember my operation.

WOMAN: Hurry, hurry. We're getting wetter and wetter.

CHICO: Yeah, it'sa *very* wet wetter. Some joke, huh?

GROUCHO: There it goes . . . there it goes.

(Sound of terrific ripping, flop of heavy canvas, women's muffled screams.)

WOMAN *(muffled):* Help! Help, we're suffocating! The top fell on us. Take it off.

GROUCHO: Say, there's no way of satisfying you buzzards. I have a good mind to give up the whole business.

CHICO: Hey, boss, where did all dose old ladies go?

GROUCHO: They're under the big top, Ravelli. Say, this is turning into a circus. Run out and get me some peanuts.

WOMAN: Get this thing off us. Quick. Quick!

GROUCHO: All right, all right.

(Sound of canvas flopping.)

GROUCHO: How do you feel now, ladies?

WOMAN: What are you trying to do, smother us?

CHICO: Boss, at'sa swell idea! How did you happen to tink of it?

GROUCHO: That's the smother instinct in me.

BOTH *(simultaneously):*   Some joke, huh?

CHICO: Look at da water in da road. She's rising.

GROUCHO: She certainly is, Ravelli. Throw out the anchor before we start to drift.

CHICO: We gotta no anchor. I'll trow out one of da ladies instead.

WOMAN: I insist that you start this car right away!

GROUCHO: Very well, madam. Then the only thing to do is for everybody to get out and push. Come on! No shirking! Everybody out! We'll get you back to town in no time. *(Women's voices protesting.)* Come on Ravelli, get in. You and I have to steer this car and get it back on the road.

(Women grunting and groaning.)

CHICO: Hey, boss, she'sa moving. She'sa moving.

GROUCHO: Come on, girls, heave-ho. You can do better than this.

WOMAN *(panting):*   Driver, how far do we have to push this bus?

GROUCHO: With luck, madam, we ought to hit a town within ten or fifteen miles. And I wish you'd hurry. Ravelli and I are getting all wet up here in this seat.

WOMAN: What! Do you mean to say that you can't start this car?

CHICO: No, lady, you better go back dere and push some more.

WOMAN: We won't push you brutes another foot!

GROUCHO: Okay, madam, then I'm afraid you'll have to walk.

WOMAN: Walk from here? I never heard of such a thing! You take us out in your bus, and expect us to walk home?

GROUCHO: What are you kicking about? I bet it's the first chance any of you battle-axes ever had to walk home from an automobile ride.

(Music in strong.)

AFTERPIECE

GROUCHO: Ladies and gentlemen. My brother, Chico, has prepared a few remarks on farm problems. Oh, Chico, are you ready to give your address?

CHICO: Sure, my address is Six Seventy-one Main Street.

GROUCHO: There's my argument. Restrict immigration. Look, stupid! You were supposed to talk about farming—about machinery, cows, hogs . . .

CHICO *(suddenly recalling):* Oh, yeah, Hogs! You know, ladies and gentlemens, da guy dat first named hogs *hogs* sure knew what he was doing. Because hogs sure are *hogs*.

GROUCHO: Well, I guess that covers everything. Except your mouth. But my foot can take care of that.

CHICO: Aw, don't get mad, Groucho. Here I was going to take you wit me to a surprise party a fella on our block is giving.

GROUCHO: You can't take me to that surprise party. I wasn't invited.

CHICO: Hey! At'sa awright. If you show up, it'll be a *bigger* surprise. You'll lika dis fella dey're giving da party for. He's been around da world on a ship, and dey tell me he's got a gal in every port.

GROUCHO: I'm not interested in a gal in every port. What *I'm* interested in is a gallon of Esso, which is more powerful than any gasoline. Or Essolube, that hydrofined motor oil.

CHICO: What *I'm* interested in is saying good night.

BOTH *(singing):* Good night, ladies . . .

(Signature music.)

FIVE STAR THEATER
PRESENTS

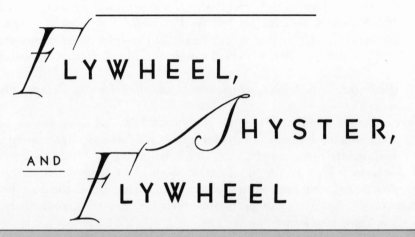

Flywheel,
Shyster,
AND *Flywheel*

EPISODE NO. 25   *MAY 15, 1933*

CAST

Groucho Marx as Waldorf T. Flywheel
Chico Marx as Emmanuel Ravelli
Miss Dimple
Receptionist
Information Clerk
Reginald Princeley, movie star
Blitzen
Cutthroat Evans
Killer Martin
Officer
Voices
Cameraman
Miss Winsome

(Phone rings.)

MISS DIMPLE: Law offices of Flywheel, Shyster, and Flywheel . . . No, Mr. Flywheel isn't in. He left for Hollywood last week . . . Yes, on business . . . He's attorney for Reginald Princeley, the famous movie star . . . Uh-huh, Mr. Flywheel's assistant, Mr. Ravelli, went with him . . . Goodbye.

(Fade into train effect, which swells and dies down to silence. Phone rings.)

RECEPTIONIST: Hello, this is the Hollywood Film Art Company . . . No, you can't see Reginald Princeley unless you have an appointment . . . Visitors are not allowed . . . That's a strict rule . . . No, this isn't the operator. This is the information desk . . . Goodbye. *(Banging on door.)* Say, what are you two fellows trying to do? Break the door down?

GROUCHO: Not if we can get in any other way. See here, young lady, do you know who I am?

CHICO: Hey, boss, you don't have to ask *her.* I can tell you who you are. You're Flywheel.

RECEPTIONIST: Oh, Mr. Flywheel? Why, Mr. Princeley was expecting you here yesterday.

GROUCHO: I know, but this numbskull, Ravelli, made me miss the train.

CHICO: What'sa matter, you always holler. We only missed it by a minoots. If it wasn't for me taking care of da baggage, we'da missed da train by an hour. *Fifty-four* pieces of baggage!

GROUCHO: *Fifty-four* pieces?

CHICO: Sure. Two socks and a deck of cards.

GROUCHO: Ravelli, you knew we were going to be here a *week.* You should have brought *two* decks of cards.

RECEPTIONIST: See here, gentlemen—you can't stand here. This is the information desk.

GROUCHO: Good, then maybe you can give me some information. Tell me, do girls think less of boys who let themselves be kissed? I mean, don't you think that although girls go out with boys like me, they always marry the other kind?

RECEPTIONIST *(impatient):*   I'm here to answer *sensible* questions!

CHICO: Awright, den I ask you sometin. What is it dat is very wide, but very tin, too?

RECEPTIONIST: Wide and thin?

CHICO: Sure! Da wide of an egg. *(Big laugh.)* Oh boy, dat's some joke!

GROUCHO: Ravelli, when I said you had the brain of a mosquito, I was wrong. You have no brain at all.

RECEPTIONIST: If you want to see Mr. Princeley, go right through this door. His dressing room is down the hall, first door to the left.

GROUCHO: Okay, toots. *(Opens door.)* Come on, stupid. *(Closes door.)*

CHICO *(mutters):*   Hmmm. You calla me stoopid. Well, sticks and stones can breaka my bones, but names won't ever hurt me.

GROUCHO: All right. After a while, I'll get a stick. Here's Princeley's door.

(They knock.)

PRINCELEY *(inside):*   Come in . . . Come in, there. *(Door opens. Hammy:)* Ah, gentlemen! Welcome to sunny California. Did you ever see a spring so warm as this?

CHICO: Sure. Last summer.

GROUCHO: See here, Princeley, we didn't travel three thousand miles to talk about the weather. Let's get down to business. How about introducing us to a couple of Hollywood blondes?

PRINCELEY: Please, Mr. Flywheel. That isn't important.

GROUCHO *(sneers):*   Oh, it isn't, eh? Romance isn't important? Well, what about Romeo and Juliet? What about Dante and Beatrice? What about Amos and Andy? And you—the great lover of the screen? Do you know what your public expects of you, Princeley?

PRINCELEY: Why, what *do* they expect?

GROUCHO *(quickly):*   Oh no, I asked you first.

PRINCELEY: Mr. Flywheel, I've been in motion pictures for ten years. Ten years of struggle . . . ten years of battling . . . ten years of heartaches.

GROUCHO: That makes thirty years in all. You must have started when you were a baby.

CHICO: Hey! You ain't Baby Peggy, are you?

PRINCELEY: Mr. Flywheel, I cannot give my public the best that is in me, with conditions as they are in this studio. They give me bad stories, unsuitable roles, incompetent directors. And now they want me—*me*, the screen's greatest lover—to play the part of a gangster! I refuse to do it. I must think of my position.

CHICO: Don't worry. We get you anodder position. We get you a job selling peanuts.

PRINCELEY *(going right on):*   Not only are my pictures mismanaged; I work for months and months without getting paid.

GROUCHO: You worked for months and months without getting paid? I'll attend to that. Ravelli, get Months and Months on the phone.

PRINCELEY: But I'm not worried about the money. My main reason for bringing you out here is to look over my contract and see if I can force the producer here to let me pick my own stories.

(Knock on door.)

BLITZEN: Oh, Reggie, my boy.

PRINCELEY *(hoarse whisper):*　That's the producer. *(Aloud.)* Come in.

BLITZEN *(opens door):*　Oh, Reggie—pardon me, I didn't know you had callers.

CHICO:　I've got two shirts and tree collars.

PRINCELEY:　Gentlemen, Mr. Blitzen is our producer. Mr. Blitzen, I want you to meet my attorneys, Mr. Flywheel and Mr. Ravelli. They want to talk to you about my next picture. I'm going out for a bit of air. *(Receding.)* See you later.

BLITZEN:　Mr. Flywheel, Reggie's friends have been giving him a lot of bad advice.

CHICO:　Well, from now on, tings is gonna be different. He'll get his bad advice from us.

BLITZEN:　Gentlemen, between you and me, Reggie is through as a great lover.

GROUCHO:　Hold on, Blitzen. There are some things that *gentlemen* don't gossip about. But go right ahead. I'm listening.

BLITZEN:　You know, Princeley isn't the star he used to be.

CHICO:　No? What star did he used to be? Tony da Wonder Horse?

BLITZEN:　Gentlemen, we must consider the public. Do you know what people want to see when they go to the movie theatres?

GROUCHO:　Yes, movies.

BLITZEN:　Well, yes, yes—

GROUCHO:　Oh, don't be a yes-man, Blitzen. What you ought to do is make more sex pictures.

BLITZEN:　But I *have* been making sex pictures, and they're losing money.

GROUCHO:　In that case, you ought to *stop* making more sex pictures. How about a couple of gangster pictures?

BLITZEN *(enthusiastic):*　Ah, Mr. Flywheel, that is just it! I want to make a gangster picture, but my star, Reggie Princeley, refuses to play the part of a gangster.

GROUCHO:　Yes, and that's what he wanted us to see you about. It seems to me, Blitzen—and I'm talking now as Princeley's attorney—if my client doesn't want to play a gangster role, you ought to throw him out of the studio. The conceited ham! Doesn't he think I get tired of seeing him in those silly love stories?

CHICO:　Sure—me, too. I saw him in *Da Virtuous Horse*—

GROUCHO:　Ravelli, don't you mean *The Virtuous* Hussy?

CHICO:　Sure, Hossie. But dey didn't have one horse in da whole picture. And dey had anodder picture. It was crazy altogedder. I couldn't even follow da story.

BLITZEN:　What was the name of the picture?

CHICO:　Da name was *News Reels*.

BLITZEN: If Princeley remains in my company, gentlemen, he's got to play a gangster's part. Not a Don Juan.

CHICO: Well, he Don Juana play da gangster's part.

GROUCHO: Why should he? Let the gangster play his own part.

BLITZEN *(repeating):*   A gangster to play the part . . . I get it—a real gangster to play the part! Flywheel, do you realize you have said something colossal?

GROUCHO: No, I wasn't listening.

BLITZEN: A real gangster! It's sure-fire box office. It's dynamite. I tell you, it's terrific. Stupendous!

GROUCHO: Well, you can say what you like about it, Blitzen, but I *still* think it's a good idea. I've got just the gangster for you. I defended him on a highway-robbery charge just a few days ago.

BLITZEN: Good. Where can I reach him?

GROUCHO: In the penitentiary.

BLITZEN: No, we must get a gangster right away.

CHICO: Hey, maybe you could give my brudder dat job. Dey put him in jail because a friend loaned him some money.

BLITZEN: They jailed him because a friend loaned him money?

CHICO: Well, you see, before dis friend would lend him da money, my brudder had to hit him wit a blackjack.

BLITZEN: No, no, we must get a well-known gangster for the role. Mr. Flywheel, I'll leave it in your hands. What publicity we'll get! *(Door opens.)* Ah, it's Princeley.

PRINCELEY *(approaching):*   Well, Flywheel, did you make Blitzen see things my way?

GROUCHO: I should say I did.

PRINCELEY: Then I won't have to play in the gangster picture?

GROUCHO: Not you, old boy.

PRINCELEY: That's superb. What part will I play?

GROUCHO: Blitzen and I didn't discuss that. We had a long talk and came to only one decision.

PRINCELEY: What was that?

GROUCHO: You're fired.

(Music in strong.)

(Phone rings.)

RECEPTIONIST: Hollywood Film Art Company . . . Yes, this is Mr. Flywheel's office. Yes, Mr. Flywheel and Mr. Ravelli have been placed in complete charge of Mr. Blitzen's new super-special, *Blood and Bullets* . . . No, there has been no selection made for the leading role yet, but Mr. Flywheel will interview some more gangsters this morning . . .

Yes, I'm sure he'll see you. Goodbye. *(Door opens.)* Good morning, Mr. Blitzen.

BLITZEN *(excited):*   Where's Mr. Flywheel?

RECEPTIONIST: He's not in yet.

BLITZEN: I can't understand it. Rockliffe, the author of *Blood and Bullets*, telephoned that Flywheel sent his script back. And I made it very clear to Flywheel that I wanted to buy that story. And *produce* it.

RECEPTIONIST: But you can get it back, can't you?

BLITZEN: That's the whole trouble. The author sold the story to another studio. After I spent twenty thousand dollars for advance publicity! *(Door opens.)*

RECEPTIONIST: Mr. Flywheel's coming in.

BLITZEN: Mr. Flywheel! I—

GROUCHO: Just a minute, Blitz. Oh, Miss Jones.

RECEPTIONIST: Yes?

GROUCHO: Did any dames call?

BLITZEN: Look here, Flywheel, you *knew* I wanted to produce *Blood and Bullets*, and you sent the script back.

GROUCHO: I know, but the author wanted fifteen thousand for that script.

BLITZEN: But it was worth it!

GROUCHO: Blitzen, you're crazy. Why do we have to use *his* script for fifteen thousand dollars? I had a stenographer make an exact copy for only four dollars.

BLITZEN: Why, I have never—

GROUCHO: That's the thanks I get for saving you fifteen thousand dollars. No wonder your business is flat on its back. The last business I managed—things were slightly different. *I* was flat on my back. But Ravelli and I put our shoulders to the wheel and it wasn't long before we were *both* flat on our backs. What the movies need is new faces. *(Door opens.)* Here's Ravelli. Certainly *he* could use a new face.

CHICO: Hullo, boss.

GROUCHO: A fine time to be coming in. *(Menacingly:)* Ravelli, what did I tell you I'd do if you came in late again?

CHICO *(laughs):*   Dat's funny. I forgot, too.

BLITZEN: Gentlemen, we have *got* to get a story for a gangster picture!

CHICO: Hey, I got a swell story. Listen, there's a littla girl. Her name is Opium.

BLITZEN: Opium?

CHICO: Sure. Opium comes from a wild poppy, and this girl's poppy is plenty wild. *(Excited.)* Da story opens up and a whole bunch of people is having dinner. When dis Opium comes in, dey all get up and leave da table. Well, two years later—

BLITZEN: Just a second, not so fast. Why do they leave the table?

CHICO: Because dey're through eating.

GROUCHO (*snapping fingers*): I see it, Ravelli. It's terrific. She is about to marry a rich broker, but she breaks her engagement with him because, in the first place, he hasn't any money and he talks too much. And in the second place, he doesn't want to marry *her* because he's already married, and very happily too. So she takes her friends' advice and throws him over.

CHICO: Yeah, over a fence.

GROUCHO: What do you mean, over a fence?

CHICO: Awright, den she pushes him in a mud puddle.

BLITZEN: But where is the drama? Where is the *pathos*?

GROUCHO: I was getting to that. She marries a poor, blind musician. Are you following me, Blitzen?

BLITZEN: Yes . . . yes.

GROUCHO: Good. In case you lose me, I'll meet you at the corner drugstore. Well, after marrying the blind musician, Opium works her fingers to the bone to save up enough money to have his eyesight restored. And finally—get this, Blitzen, this'll tear your heart out. It might even remove your appendix, but that will cost a hundred dollars extra. Well, in our big scene, the boy recovers his eyesight, and when he takes one look at his wife, he commits suicide.

CHICO: Boss, da rest of da story comes to me like a flash. Da wife, she feelsa very bad. She goes into mourning. She sits in da house all day long playing da piano.

BLITZEN: In mourning and she plays the piano?

CHICO: Well, she plays only on da dark keys.

GROUCHO: Certainly. That's why dark keys were born.

BLITZEN: Gentlemen, that story seems familiar. It's something like the story of *Fools in Love*.

CHICO: *Sometin* like it? You crazy! It's *exactly* like it. Flywheel and me see it yesterday, and oh boy was it a great picture. We gonna see it again.

BLITZEN: Again?

CHICO: Sure, we fell asleep during da second half.

BLITZEN: How was the first half?

GROUCHO: We don't know. We came in during the middle.

BLITZEN: This situation is serious. Here we are ready for the production and we have no story!

(*Phone rings.*)

RECEPTIONIST: Hello . . . I'll tell him. Mr. Flywheel, the author of *Blood and Bullets* is on the phone. He says he has another gangster story.

BLITZEN: That's wonderful!

RECEPTIONIST: He says you can have it for fifteen thousand dollars.

GROUCHO: Fifty thousand dollars? Tell him we'll give him thirty-five thousand dollars.

RECEPTIONIST: He said *fifteen* thousand.

GROUCHO: All right. Then tell him we'll give him six.

BLITZEN: Wait a minute. Wait a minute. He won't take six thousand. We ought to offer—let's say, nine thousand dollars.

CHICO: Awright. Let's *say* nine tousand, but we'll *offer* him six.

BLITZEN: We *must* get that story. Miss Jones, switch the call to my office. I'll talk to him there.

RECEPTIONIST: Very well.

(Phone rings.)

RECEPTIONIST: Hello . . . Yes, send them up. *(To* BLITZEN.) Some gangsters are coming up for that part in the gangster picture.

BLITZEN: You talk to them, Flywheel. I'll be in my office. I *must get that story.*

(Knock on door, door opens.)

CUTTHROAT: You looking for some gangsters?

BLITZEN *(excited):* Talk to Mr. Flywheel. *(Receding.)* I am very busy. *(Opens and closes door.)*

GROUCHO: All right, gorilla. Sit down. What's your name?

CUTTHROAT: My name is Cutthroat Evans.

CHICO: At'sa very pretty name.

GROUCHO: Come on, Cutthroat. Let's see how tough you are. Take a sock at Ravelli.

CUTTHROAT: Sure, lemme at him. I'll knock him through dat winderpane.

CHICO: Hey, wait a minoot! You break dat window and Blitzen'll get mad.

GROUCHO: Ravelli's right, Cutthroat. I'll open the window.

CUTTHROAT: Aw, cut da stallin'! Do I get dat actin' job or not?

GROUCHO: Well, first we've got to see if you can act. I'll try you on a couple of lines. Ravelli, hand me that play.

CHICO: Hey! Dis ain't a play. It's a cookbook. It says omelet on it.

GROUCHO: Omelet! It's *Hamlet*, stupid. Never mind. Here's another script. Read this, Cutthroat. Begin here.

CUTTHROAT: Awright. Er . . . "ah, sweet, sweet, my heart cries out for your bitter, sweet love."

GROUCHO: Wait a minute. That isn't the way a gangster talks. I don't think he's the type. Ravelli, throw him out.

CHICO: Okay, boss. Get out, bum.

CUTTHROAT *(receding):* Aw, you guys! *(Ad libs exit.)*

Groucho tangles with a gangster in *Horse Feathers.*

(*Door opens and closes.*)

CHICO (*calling out*):   Next!

KILLER MARTIN (*approaching*):   Dat's me. I'll take da job.

CHICO: What's your name, tough guy?

MARTIN: My name is Joe Martin, but dey call me da Killer.

CHICO: At'sa fine. Sit down, Killer.

GROUCHO: I'm sorry, Killer, you're not the type. You look too old with your mustache.

CHICO: Don't worry, boss. I got a razor, I fix dat. Come on, Killer, I shave it off.

(*Ad lib struggle.*)

MARTIN: Hey, hey . . . wait a minute! Let go of me!

CHICO: Don't move. Don't move. I get 'em off.

MARTIN: Ouch!

CHICO: Hey, Killer—have you been eating ketchup?

MARTIN: No . . . no.

CHICO: Well, den I must have cut you. Dere you are—no mustache. You look fifteen years younger.

GROUCHO: Let me take a look at him. No, Killer, you still won't do for the part. Now you look too young. Throw him out, Ravelli.

CHICO: Okay, boss. Come on, dope!

KILLER MARTIN (*menacingly*): Take it easy, you guys. I came here to get a job as an actor. And if I don't get it, dere's only one guy walkin' out of dis room alive. And dat guy's me.

GROUCHO: Well, in that case, Ravelli, give him back his mustache. He's hired.

(*Music in strong.*)

(*Knock on door.*)

GROUCHO (*inside*): Come in.

(*Door opens.*)

RECEPTIONIST: Mr. Flywheel, Mr. Blitzen wants to see you in his office.

GROUCHO: *I* should go to *his* office? Why can't he come here? I'll tell you what I'll do. I'll meet him halfway. I'll meet him in the hall, near the staircase.

RECEPTIONIST: He said . . . ah . . . oh, he's coming in.

BLITZEN (*opens door*): Flywheel! Flywheel! That gangster will be the ruination of this studio. I would drop the whole production if we had not shot thirty thousand feet of film. The director tries to tell that murderer what to do, and he smashes the camera over the director's head. I try to interfere, and now he says he'll *kill* me. What shall I do?

GROUCHO: If I were you, Blitzen, I'd take out some life insurance.

BLITZEN: You don't seem to understand. He said if I go out on the set, he'll put a bullet through me.

GROUCHO: He did, eh? Well, he can't scare me. You go right out on that set. If he kills you, I'll have him thrown out of the studio.

BLITZEN: Maybe I ought to get some bodyguards.

GROUCHO: I'd do more than that. I'd get some mudguards, too.

BLITZEN: Yes, I think I'll hire a bodyguard.

GROUCHO: No, that wouldn't do. In that case you'd have one fellow trying to attack you and one fellow trying to defend you. That's a waste of fifty percent. Why couldn't you be attacked by your own bodyguard? Your life would be saved and that would be a one-hundred-percent waste.

BLITZEN: Just what are you getting at?

GROUCHO: I anticipated that question. How does an army travel? On its stomach. How do you travel? In an automobile. You see? You're saving your stomach. But the movie industry is too important for us to sit here and talk about your stomach. Now run along. I want to see if my picture is in any of the movie magazines.

BLITZEN: Why aren't you out on location? I pay five thousand dollars a day for the right to use that big jewelry store, just so we can get some realism in our holdup scene. Why aren't you there supervising?

GROUCHO: Well, I'm waiting for Ravelli. He went out to borrow a broom. (*Door opens.*)

CHICO: Hullo, boss. How you feel, Blitz?

GROUCHO: Where's the broom? Didn't they lend it to you?

CHICO: Sure, da lady next door lend me one, but she say I have to use it right dere. So I stay dere and sweep up her floor.

BLITZEN: That's a fine thing for a movie executive—sweeping a floor.

CHICO: Yeah, I like it fine. I always sweep up for my wife. I treat her like an angel.

GROUCHO: Like an angel? You haven't bought her any clothes in five years.

CHICO: Well, angels don't wear clothes. Anyway, last week I buy her a new dress, but it don't fit.

GROUCHO: Well, what are you going to do about it?

CHICO: I tink I get a different wife.

BLITZEN (*incensed*):   Mr. Ravelli, I have something to say to you. Please tell me why you hired *twenty-eight girls* for the part of the cabaret dancer, when I told you I wanted *just one* girl? Nice, sweet, demure—

CHICO: Well, demure de merrier! (*Big laugh.*) Some joke, eh, Blitz?

BLITZEN: My name is *not* Blitz. It's Blitzen.

CHICO: Well, I was in a hurry.

BLITZEN: Why do you gentlemen stand here idling? I have a mob of five hundred people waiting at the jewelry store on the corner for our big holdup scene.

GROUCHO: Ravelli, he's right. Let's get going.

BLITZEN: I'll stay here. I don't feel safe around that Killer Martin.

CHICO: Hey, Blitz! If a nicea-looking girl calls up and asks for Sweetsy-Eatsy Daddy, don't you talk to her. She means me. (*Door opens and closes; footsteps on pavement, street noises.*)

GROUCHO: Come on, Ravelli! And stop drooling. There's work to be done.

CHICO: Work? Den I stay here.

GROUCHO: You're coming with me. And remember, all I'm asking from you is a little common sense.

CHICO: You could use some, boss.

GROUCHO: There's the jewelry store down the street.

CHICO: Boss, I'm too tired to walk. I tink I'll take a streetcar. Does it make any difference which car I take?

GROUCHO: Not to me, it doesn't.
(*Buzzing of crowds.*)

GROUCHO: Here we are, let's get through these ropes.

OFFICER: Hey, you fellows, you can't go through those ropes. This block is roped off for the Hollywood Film Art Company.

GROUCHO: See here, officer. You're a public servant, aren't you?

OFFICER: Er . . . yes.

GROUCHO: Well, brush my coat and get out of my way, or I'll get another servant. I gotta get through this crowd.

VOICE *(away):* Say, officer, that's Mr. Flywheel. You'd better let him through.

OFFICER: All right. Go ahead.

CAMERAMAN: Oh, Mr. Flywheel! It's a good thing you got here. The director just quit. Killer Martin just broke another camera over his head.

GROUCHO: Oh, he did, did he? Where's Martin? Martin! Martin!

MARTIN: Whadda you want?

GROUCHO: Killer, we've stood for about enough of your horseplay around here. From now on, I'm directing this picture.

MARTIN: Oh, yeah?

GROUCHO: Yeah. Now remember, I'm not afraid of you. It'll take *three* guys like you to lick me.

MARTIN: Tree guys, eh?

GROUCHO: Well, in a pinch, I guess you could do it alone. But it would be much easier if you had three.

MARTIN: Get dis, Flywheel, and get dis straight. Nobody tells Killer Martin what to do. One peep outta you, and I'll break every bone in your body and trow you right down dat sewer! *Now* you got anyting to say?

GROUCHO: No, I think you covered about everything. Let's get going.

CHICO: Sure, let's go, boss. I'm sick of dis picture anyway.

MARTIN: Another ting, Flywheel. Dat's a fine dame you put in dis pitcher —she won't even let me kiss her.

GROUCHO: Well, you can hardly blame her. Did you ever get a look at that kisser of yours? Ravelli, get Martin a hand mirror.

CHICO: We ain't got no hand mirror, boss. But I can get him one for his face.

GROUCHO: He wants to be a lover! Look at that scar on his forehead.

CHICO: I tink he bit himself, boss.

GROUCHO: Nonsense, how could he bite himself way up on his own forehead?

CHICO: Maybe he stood on a chair.

MARTIN: Come on, quit da stallin'!

GROUCHO: Ravelli, you work the camera. I'm going to rehearse the love scene with Miss Winsome.

MARTIN: Hey! Whadda ya mean *you* gonna rehearse it? Ain't I gonna play it in da pitcher?

GROUCHO: That's the whole point. You get your chance later. Why can't *I* have a little fun now? Don't you think I'm human? *(Calling out.)* Oh, Miss Winsome!

MISS WINSOME *(away):*   Yes, Mr. Flywheel.

GROUCHO *(coyly):*   Just to get you in a romantic mood, how about your making a little fuss over me? Sort of a rehearsal.

MISS WINSOME: But, Mr. Flywheel—there's no love scene in the picture.

GROUCHO: We don't have to put it in the picture. We can just *rehearse* it. However, if you're going to be snooty about it, I can get along without you. I've got a wife almost as nice as you.

CHICO *(approaching):*   Hey, boss. We better get anodder camera.

GROUCHO: Why?

CHICO: The Killer wants to hit you wit this one.

GROUCHO: He does?

CHICO: Yeah, but I'll talk him out of it. I'll tell him to use a club instead.

GROUCHO: Ravelli, get the cameras ready. I've got to take this scene.

CHICO *(receding):*   Okay, boss. I'll go.

GROUCHO *(quietly):*   All right, Miss Winsome, you stand right by the window here. Killer, you run into the store, grab the jewelry, smash the glass door, and dash out. When Miss Winsome sees you, she screams and you start choking her. But you get away. Ready! *(Whistle.)* Lights . . . camera . . . action!

(Sound of footsteps, cameras turning, glass smashing.)

MISS WINSOME: He's choking me. Help! Help!

CHICO: Okay, lady, I help you.

(Crash.)

MARTIN: Who hit me? What hit me?

CHICO: I got him, boss. I got him.

GROUCHO: Ravelli, what's the idea? Smashing the camera over Martin's head! You spoiled the whole scene.

CHICO: Well, it serves him right, da liar. He hits a weak lady after he promises to hit you.

GROUCHO: Ravelli, this studio isn't big enough for both of us.

CHICO: Dat's awright, boss. We can make da studio bigger.

GROUCHO: Come on, everybody. We've got to take this scene again. Property man! Put the jewelry back. And handle it carefully. It's real jewelry and it cost a lot of dough. And you, Ravelli, no matter what happens, you stick with the camera. Understand?

CHICO: Leave it to me, boss.

GROUCHO: Ready? *(Whistle.)* Lights . . . camera . . . action!
(Sound of cameras turning, footsteps, glass smashes.)

GROUCHO: Hey, Martin! Where are you going? You forgot to choke the dame! *(Yelling:)* Killer! Where you running to? Come back with that jewelry! Stop him, Ravelli. Stop him!

CHICO *(laughs):* Dis time I no get fooled, boss. I stick to da cameras.

GROUCHO: He's running away with the jewelry! He's getting into a car. *(Motor starts.)*

CHICO: Oh, boy! Dis is gonna be some picture!

GROUCHO: You idiot! Martin just got away with thirty thousand dollars' worth of the jewelry store's diamonds. *That wasn't part of the picture!*

CHICO: Dat wasn't part of da picture? . . . At'sa fine, den. Everytin's aw right. Dere's nuttin to worry about.

GROUCHO: Nothing to worry about?

CHICO: Cause I forgot to put film in da camera.
(Music in strong.)

AFTERPIECE

CHICO: Ladies and gentlemens. I wanna tell you about a little huntin trip I was on last week. I taka some worms and—

GROUCHO: Take some worms? Just a minute, Chico. Didn't you say you went hunting?

CHICO: Sure. I went huntin for a place to fish. But it wasa no use. I no catch nuttin.

GROUCHO: No?

CHICO: No. I don't tink dose worms was tryin.

GROUCHO: Keep on talking, Chico. It's great for my insomnia.

CHICO: You got insomnia? Why don't you go home and sleep it off?

GROUCHO: Chico, your mind's wandering.

CHICO: Yeah, I'm wanderin what dat new product is de Esso stations are gonna bring out next month. It couldn't be sardines, huh?

GROUCHO: No, it's probably something you put in your automobile.

CHICO: Well, when I went fishin I put two cans of sardines in my automobile.

GROUCHO: Well, I'm different. The only things I put in my car are Essolube, that hydrofined motor oil, and Esso, which is more powerful than any gasoline.

CHICO: You said it.

GROUCHO: No, I'm going to say it now. Good night, ladies.

BOTH *(singing):*   Good night, ladies.

(Signature music.)

FIVE STAR THEATER
PRESENTS

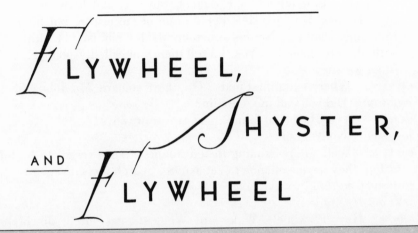

Flywheel, Shyster, and Flywheel

EPISODE NO. 26   MAY 22, 1933

CAST

Groucho Marx as Waldorf T. Flywheel
Chico Marx as Emmanuel Ravelli
Miss Dimple
Captain
First Mate Johnson
Steward
Bos'n's Mate
Mrs. Rivington
Customs Officer
Meadows, the butler
Reporters
Officers
Various voices

(Phone rings.)

MISS DIMPLE: Law offices of Flywheel, Shyster, and Flywheel . . . No, Mr. Flywheel isn't in. He's been on an ocean cruise, but his boat is returning today . . . No, his assistant, Mr. Ravelli, isn't in, either. He's with Mr. Flywheel . . . Yes, I'll tell them you called. Goodbye.
(Boat whistle.)

CAPTAIN: Where's that first mate? Oh, there you are, Mr. Johnson!

JOHNSON: Did you call me, captain?

CAPTAIN: Yes. Have you found those two stowaways?

JOHNSON: Not yet, sir.

CAPTAIN: Well, we're landing in ten minutes. They've got to be found before they have a chance to get ashore. Search the ship again.

JOHNSON *(receding):*   Aye, aye, sir!
(Footsteps fade.)

CHICO: Hey, Flywheel—Wake up! We gotta get out of dis lifeboat. Dey're still lookin for us! *(Snores from* GROUCHO.*)* Boss. Boss! Get up!

GROUCHO *(sneering):*   That's fine! Here I am dreaming that I'm having a nice two-dollar dinner and you have to wake me up!

CHICO: But Flywheel, da boat's landin.

GROUCHO: Never mind. Go away till I finish my dream. *(Sighs.)* Now, where did I leave off?

CHICO: But we're at da dock—da pier.

GROUCHO: Dock pier? I'd rather have light beer. Let me go back to sleep —my dinner's getting cold.

CHICO: Maybe you can dream me a ham sandwich. I haven't eaten in tree days.

GROUCHO: *Three* days? Why, you've only been on the boat *two* days.

CHICO: Well, I didn't eat yesterday. I didn't eat today. And I ain't gonna eat tomorrow. Dat makes tree days. *(Voices away.)* Quick! Duck down in da lifeboat. Dere's somebody coming!

OFFICER *(approaching):*   Steward, what are you doing with those bags up here on this deck?

STEWARD: Beg pardon, sir. They belong to Sir Roderick Mortimer.

OFFICER: Oh, he's that African explorer. Where's he been the whole voyage? I haven't seen him once.

STEWARD: Oh, 'e keeps to 'is cabin, sir. 'E's very shy. 'E wants to be the last one off the boat to avoid the reporters on the dock. 'E awsked me to put 'is luggage up 'ere out of the way till 'e's ready to get off.

OFFICER: All right. Pile it over by that lifeboat there, out of the way.

STEWARD: Beg pardon, sir? 'Ave they laid 'ands on those two stowaways, sir?

OFFICER: No, but we'll get them when they try to get ashore. *(Fading.)* When we do, I'll see that they get their deserts!

CHICO: Hey, Flywheel! Dey said we'll get desserts! I tink I'll take prunes.

GROUCHO: I wouldn't, Ravelli. Prunes aren't what they used to be.

CHICO: No?

GROUCHO: No. They used to be plums. But that's neither here nor there. We've got to figure how to get ashore.

CHICO: I know how to get ashore, boss!

GROUCHO: You do?

GROUCHO: Shore. I say to myself, "How we get on dis boat?" I answer myself, "We walk on." Den I say to myself, "How we get off dis boat?" Quick as a flash, de answer come: "We walk off."

GROUCHO: Nice work, Ravelli! Now ask yourself, "How are we going to get by all the ship's officers that'll be guarding the gangplank looking for us?"

CHICO: Oh, no. I only ask myself easy questions. Hey, dere's nobody around. Let's get outta da lifeboat.

GROUCHO: Okay.

(Sounds of clambering out.)

CHICO: Look, dere's an officer. He's seen us!

GROUCHO: I'll talk to him. You pick up six or eight of those bags lying over there and try to look like a passenger. *(Raises voice.)* Oh, captain.

BOS'N'S MATE *(rough):*   I'm not the captain, I'm the bos'n's mate.

GROUCHO: You're his mate. I hope you are very happy together. Give my regards to the bos'n. Come, Ravelli, bring that luggage.

BOS'N'S MATE *(suspiciously):*   D'you know you fellows look just like a couple of stowaways we're looking for?

CHICO: Well, we heard joosta de opposite. We heard da stoways look joosta like us.

BOS'N'S MATE: One is a little fellow with an Italian accent—

GROUCHO: Well, it can't be me. No one ever said Flywheel was a little fellow with an Italian accent.

BOS'N'S MATE: And the other is a tall guy with a black mustache who talks a lot.

CHICO: Well, cap, I no talka so much.

GROUCHO: Say, captain, how do we know you're not the stowaways? You've got a black mustache, and you talk too much.

BOS'N'S MATE: Have you seen any suspicious-looking characters around here?

GROUCHO: Nobody but you. Why don't you throw yourself in irons?

Come, Ravelli, bring that luggage. Unless I'm very much mistaken, and I usually am, the gangplank is down this way.

BOS'N'S MATE: Things don't look right around here. *(Receding.)* I'm gonna see the captain.

CHICO *(whispers):*   Hey, Flywheel, I tink he's gotta suspicious.

GROUCHO: Well, hang on to those bags and shut up.

(Murmur of voices growing louder.)

BOS'N'S MATE *(away):*   Passengers line up by the gangplank. One at a time. Single file, please.

GROUCHO *(approaching):*   Gangway. Gangway!

Groucho trips the light fantastic aboard ship with Thelma Todd. Zeppo provides the helping hand and Harry Woods gives the disapproving stare in this scene from *Monkey Business*.

CAPTAIN: Wait a minute, wait a minute. May I ask what your rush is?

GROUCHO: You may ask, but I bet we won't know the answer. Keep moving, Ravelli.

CAPTAIN: Hey, who are you pushing?

CHICO: I don't know. Who are you?

CAPTAIN: I'm the captain.

GROUCHO: Well, I don't speak to underlings. Get me the general. If he isn't around, I'll talk to two colonels.

CAPTAIN: There's something fishy about this. How did you tramps get on this boat?

CHICO: We tought it was a tramp steamer.

CAPTAIN: Oh, you did, did you? Well, you're not going to find it so easy to get off. Stand away from this gangplank until the passengers leave. I'll attend to you later.

MRS. RIVINGTON (approaching): Why, I do believe it's Sir Roderick Mortimer.

GROUCHO: If you'd believe that, you'd believe anything.

MRS. RIVINGTON: Now, now, Sir Roderick. I know you have a reputation for a retiring nature, but you can't fool me. I see your name on your luggage.

GROUCHO: Oh, stop your snooping.

MRS. RIVINGTON: But I'm Mrs. Rivington, and you're coming down to my Long Island home for the weekend.

GROUCHO: Don't be a piker, madam. Make it a month or we can't do business.

MRS. RIVINGTON: Oh, Sir Roderick. This honor overwhelms me. Well, aren't you going to get off the boat? My car is waiting for us on the dock.

GROUCHO: Lead the way, Goldilocks. And would you mind carrying some of these bags? Ravelli's tired. On second thought, never mind the bags. Carry *me*. You take my shoulders and Ravelli will bring up the rear.

CAPTAIN: Pardon me—

GROUCHO: Now what are you going to beef about, captain?

CAPTAIN: I want to apologize, sir. I had no idea you were Sir Roderick Mortimer, the explorer.

GROUCHO: Well, it came as a surprise to me, too. Come on, Ravelli. You too, Cluck.

MRS. RIVINGTON: *Cluck?* Sir Roderick! Did you call me a *cluck*?

CHICO: Sure. Dat's because you're cuckoo. You're a cuckoo cluck.

GROUCHO: Sir Ravelli, that's no way to talk to a lady.

CHICO: Well, show me a lady, and I'll talk different.

BOS'N'S MATE *(away):*   Watch your step, please . . . one at a time on the gangplank.

MRS. RIVINGTON: Well, here we are on the dock. My car is right over this way.

CUSTOMS OFFICER *(approaching):*   I beg your pardon, sir. I'm from the customs. I'll have to examine you.

GROUCHO: Anything to oblige. What do you want me to take off? Did you ever hear me take off Maurice Chevalier? I'm going to *seeng* for you *raht* now.

CHICO: Hey, boss, don't you remember? We traded in our Chevalier for a Buick.

CUSTOMS OFFICER: I mean, have you got anything to declare?

GROUCHO: Ah declayah ah'm gettin' pretty sick of this. Any mo' questions?

CUSTOMS OFFICER: Open up that big bag.

GROUCHO: Very well. Sir Ravelli, open that big bag.

CHICO: Awright, I open it.

(Bag snaps open.)

CHICO: Hey, look!

GROUCHO: What's in there?

CHICO: I don't know, boss. It's green and looks like big spaghetti. It must be green spaghetti. Hey, it's moving. Look, it's alive! It's a snake! Look out! Say, boss, dat big one dere almost bit me!

GROUCHO: Quick, find out which end is its face and slap it.

CUSTOMS OFFICER: Hurry! Shut the bag before those snakes escape all over the deck.

CHICO: Dat's awright. We don't want 'em anyway.

CUSTOMS OFFICER: But they're dangerous!

GROUCHO: Then I'm *sure* we don't want them. However, I haven't time for this idle chatter. Close the bag for this pest, Sir Ravelli. And let's scram.

CHICO: Okay, Sir Watchamacallit.

(Bag snaps closed.)

MRS. RIVINGTON: Aren't you coming, Sir Roderick? My car is waiting.

GROUCHO: That's fine, babe. We'll hop in your car. You can follow on foot.

VOICE: Sir Roderick! Sir Roderick! Three of your elephants are loose on the boat.

GROUCHO: The elephants are loose? Well, am I responsible for their morals?

(Music in strong.)

.   .   .

(Phone rings.)

MEADOWS: This is Mrs. Rivington's residence . . . The butler speaking . . . No, Mrs. Rivington is now showing the mansion and the grounds to Sir Roderick Mortimer and . . . I believe, Sir Ravelli . . . Yes . . . Goodbye.

MRS. RIVINGTON *(approaching):* Oh, Meadows, have you seen Sir Roderick?

MEADOWS: Why, madam, I thought you were showing him the estate.

MRS. RIVINGTON: I was, but . . . never mind, he's coming in. Well, Sir Roderick, how do you like my little home?

GROUCHO: Oh, it's not so bad. Wait a minute. Come to think of it, it's pretty bad. As a matter of fact, it's one of the frowsiest looking dumps I've ever seen.

MRS. RIVINGTON: Why, Sir Roderick!

GROUCHO: You're letting the place run down. What's the result? You're not getting the class of people you used to. You're getting people like yourself now. I'll tell you what we'll do. We'll put a sign up, "Place under new management." We'll set up a seventy-five-cent meal that'll knock their eyes out. After we've knocked their eyes out we can charge them anything we want. Now sign here and give me your check for fifteen hundred dollars. And I want to tell you, madam, with this insurance policy you've provided for your little ones and your old age, which will be here any day now, if I'm any judge of horseflesh.

CHICO *(away):* Hey, boss. Boss!

MRS. RIVINGTON: Sir Roderick, there's one question I'd like to ask you. What is that little man to you?

GROUCHO: If you must know, he's a pain in the neck.

CHICO: Boss. Boss! You tell dis old warhorse I gotta have a new room.

MRS. RIVINGTON: A new room? What's the matter with the one I assigned you? It's the best room in the house.

CHICO: Sure, but da snakes are running around up dere.

MRS. RIVINGTON: What! Snakes in your room?

GROUCHO: Say, Mrs. Rivington. Maybe the snakes can stay in *your* room.

CHICO: Aw, no. Dese snakes would never stand for dat.

GROUCHO: Well, madam, you can see that he's nobody's fool. Possibly because nobody wants him. And see here, Ravelli, what's the idea of going around looking as if you slept in your clothes?

CHICO: Well, I *do* sleep in dem.

GROUCHO: Well, the least you can do is have my shoes repaired. I can see your toes sticking through them.

CHICO: What you repair shoes wit?

GROUCHO: With cowhide.

CHICO: Huh?

GROUCHO: Cowhide. Hide! You know what hide is—a cow's outside.

CHICO: A cow's outside? Well, let her come in. I'm not afraid.

MEADOWS: I beg pardon, madam—

MRS. RIVINGTON: What is it, Meadows?

MEADOWS: The gentlemen from the press are here.

MRS. RIVINGTON: Show them in.

MEADOWS: Yes, madam.

MRS. RIVINGTON: Sir Roderick, you wouldn't mind making a small statement to the press, would you?

GROUCHO: No. As a matter of fact, I've prepared a small statement. Ravelli, where's that statement?

CHICO: Here it is, boss. She owes us fourteen dollars. Dat's for our time. If we had a good time, we coulda done it cheaper.

MEADOWS: The gentlemen from the press.

GROUCHO: Is the reporter from the *Star* here?

REPORTER 1:   I'm from the *Star*.

GROUCHO: Well, I want you to go back and tell your editor I don't like your paper. It's no good. Every time I sleep under it in the park, it gets all torn.

REPORTER 2:   Sir Roderick, I'd like to ask you a question.

CHICO: Hey, first *I* ask a question. Why does an Indian sleep wit his head toward da fire?

GROUCHO: All right, Mr. Bones, why does an Indian sleep with his head towards the fire?

CHICO: To keep his wigwam. Ha, ha. Some joke, eh, boss?

REPORTER 3:   Sir Roderick, what do you think of marriage?

GROUCHO: I think marriage is a noble institution. It's the foundation of the American home. But you can't enforce it. It was put over on the American people while our boys were over there. You've been asking a lot of questions. Now let me ask you one. When are you dopes going to get out of here and let me go to sleep?

MEADOWS: Mrs. Rivington, your guests are assembling in the drawing room.

MRS. RIVINGTON: I'm afraid I'll have to ask you gentlemen of the press to excuse us.

REPORTER 3:   Ah, Sir Roderick, one question before you go. Do you believe in clubs for women?

GROUCHO: Only in self-defense.

MRS. RIVINGTON: Come, Sir Roderick. (*Door opens, murmur of voices.*) After you.

GROUCHO: Oh, no you don't—you go first. I've had that one pulled before. You're not going to kick *me*.

MRS. RIVINGTON: All right, just as you say. *(Door closes.)* Why look . . . All my guests are seated and waiting for the lecture to begin.

CHICO: Dat's funny, I can't wait till it's over.

MRS. RIVINGTON: Oh, Sir Roderick. I thought before dinner you wouldn't mind telling us a few of your African experiences.

GROUCHO: Why can't we skip Africa and get right down to dinner?

MRS. RIVINGTON: Now, Sir Roderick! You wouldn't throw me down, would you?

GROUCHO: Well, I couldn't do it alone, but if Ravelli helped I might try.

MRS. RIVINGTON: Wait a minute, I'll introduce you. *(Raises her voice.)* Now I would like to introduce Sir Roderick Mortimer, the famed African explorer, who has kindly consented to tell us about his latest trip to Africa. Sir Roderick.

(Heavy applause.)

GROUCHO: My friends, I'm here to tell you about the great and mysterious continent known as Africa. Africa belongs to the hunter. And he can have it. Well, we left New York drunk and early on the morning of February thirtieth. After fifteen days on the water and six on the boat, we finally arrived in Africa. We at once proceeded into the heart of the jungle, where I shot a polar bear.

MRS. RIVINGTON: But, Sir Roderick, I thought polar bears lived in the frozen north.

GROUCHO: They do, usually. But this one was anemic and couldn't stand the climate.

CHICO: Anyway, he was a rich bear and could afford to go away in da winter.

GROUCHO: See here, Ravelli, you take care of your animals and I'll take care of mine. From the day of our arrival we led an active life. The first morning saw us up at six, breakfasted, and back in bed at seven. This was our routine for the first three months. Then we finally got so we were back in bed at six-thirty.

MRS. RIVINGTON: But Sir Roderick, you promised to tell us about the wildlife in Africa.

GROUCHO: So I did. One day we were out prospecting. We got wind of a herd of goats. Let me tell you that it's an ill wind that passes a herd of goats. And then the next day while standing in front of the cabin, I bagged six lions.

MRS. RIVINGTON: Bagged six lions?

CHICO: Sure, he bagged dem to go away, but dey kept hangin around all day.

GROUCHO: Now children, the principal animals inhabiting the African jungles are moose, elks, and Knights of Pythias. That's big game. The first day I shot two bucks. That was the biggest game we had. Of course you all know what a moose is.

CHICO: Sure, I know what a moose is. A moose runs around da floor, eats cheese, and gets chased by da cat.

GROUCHO: Now, as I was saying, the elks are different from the moose. The elks stay up in the hills most of the year. But in the spring they come down for their annual convention. It is very interesting to watch them come to the waterhole—and you should see them run when they find that it's only a waterhole.

CHICO: Sure, boss. What dose elks are lookin for is an elkohol.

GROUCHO: One morning I shot an elephant in my pajamas. How he got in my pajamas I don't know. Then we tried to remove the tusks, but they were embedded so firmly we couldn't budge them. Of course, in Alabama the Tuskaloosa. We took some pictures of the native girls, but they were not developed. But we're going back again. Now, I'd like to pass around my hat, but I'm afraid I wouldn't get it back.

MRS. RIVINGTON: A very enlightening speech, Sir Roderick.

(*Applause.*)

GROUCHO (*over applause*): Would you like me to run through it again or would you like my ape man, Mr. Ravelli, to play some African folk songs on the piano? Or maybe you'd like to see him swing from the chandelier. Personally I'd like to see him swing. Is there a piece of rope in the house?

MEADOWS: Mrs. Rivington. Mrs. Rivington.

MRS. RIVINGTON: Not now, Meadows. Can't you see we're being entertained?

GROUCHO: You old flatterer.

MEADOWS: But Mrs. Rivington, I just heard that a lion has escaped from the circus down the road. When last seen it was heading in this direction.

CHICO: What—da circus?

MEADOWS: No, the lion, sir!

(*Screams, comments. "What are we going to do?" "A lion is loose." "Isn't it terrible?"*)

MRS. RIVINGTON: A lion is loose? How fortunate it is we have Sir Roderick Mortimer, the most famous lion hunter in the world, with us! He'll know what to do—won't you, Sir Roderick?

GROUCHO: Absolutely. But I don't think there's room under my bed for all of us!

(*Music in strong.*)

. . .

(Comments: "This suspense is terrible!" "Are they going to keep us locked up in the living room all night?" "Why don't they get through searching the grounds?" "Do you suppose they've caught the lion?")

MRS. RIVINGTON: Be calm, be calm, everybody! There's no danger. Even if the lion *is* out on the grounds, he can't get in here. Besides, Sir Roderick Mortimer is here.

GROUCHO: You bet I'm here. If you think I'd go out, you're crazy.

(Door opens.)

MRS. RIVINGTON: Oh, Meadows, is the lion captured?

MEADOWS: Madam, we have searched the grounds thoroughly. We find no trace of it anywhere. No doubt the circus people have captured it by this time.

(Murmur of relief.)

MRS. RIVINGTON *(loudly):*   I hope you won't let this silly scare spoil the party for you. Come, come, there's no danger. Let's all go out in da garden. The roses are lovely in the moonlight.

(Laughter and voices receding, fade out.)

CHICO: Hey, Flywheel. Flywheel, where are you?

GROUCHO: Shh. Have they all gone?

CHICO: Yeah, boss, dey all went out in da garden.

GROUCHO: Come on, Ravelli, through this window. We won't be safe till we get away from this place. *(Slides window open.)* We'd better scram before the real Sir Roderick shows up. Or that Rivington dame finds a rhinoceros for us to play with. Well, here I go.

(Loud bump.)

CHICO: Hey, boss. Boss, where are you?

GROUCHO *(away):*   Jump, you fool!

CHICO: Here I come!

(Loud bump; GROUCHO grunts loudly.)

CHICO: Hey, Flywheel, I tink I land on somebody.

GROUCHO *(gasping):*   I know you did, nitwit! It's me!

CHICO: Hey, Flywheel, sometin's comin.

GROUCHO: It can't be us. We're going. Quick, down behind this bush.

(Sound of crashing through bushes.)

CHICO: Dere it is, boss. I tink it's a hippopotamus.

GROUCHO: No, but you're close. It's Mrs. Rivington.

MRS. RIVINGTON: Who's there?

GROUCHO: Where?

MRS. RIVINGTON: Why, Sir Roderick. Why are you over on *this* side of the house? All my other guests are in the rose garden.

GROUCHO: Well, madam, Ravelli and I weren't satisfied that the house was safe, so we thought we'd reconnoiter the shrubbery looking for lions. Reconnoiter. Say, that's not so easy to say. You try it sometime.

MRS. RIVINGTON: Did you find anything?

GROUCHO: Sure we did. We found three dozen hair pins and five empty gin bottles. But don't be discouraged, madam, we're on the job. We'll find a full gin bottle if it takes all night.

MRS. RIVINGTON: Wouldn't you like to come and tell my guests some more of your African experiences?

GROUCHO: No, I want to talk to you here. Oh, Mrs. Rivington, you're just the kind of girl I crave. You've got beauty, charm, money. You *have* got money, haven't you? Because if you haven't got money, we can quit right now.

MRS. RIVINGTON: Oh, Sir Roderick, I'm fascinated.

CHICO: I was fascinated last year—right on de arm.

GROUCHO: Ravelli, I'll thank you to mind your own business. Thank you. *(Softly.)* Mrs. Rivington, ever since I met you, I've swept you off my feet. There's something on my mind. There's something burning in my brain. Something I must ask you.

MRS. RIVINGTON: What is it, Sir Roderick?

GROUCHO: Will you wash out a pair of socks for me?

MRS. RIVINGTON: Why, Sir Roderick! I'm surprised!

GROUCHO: It may be a surprise to you, but it's been on my mind for months. It's just my way of telling you that Ravelli and I love you. We want to marry you. How about it, my shrinking violet?

CHICO: Shrinking violet? Say, it wouldn't hurt her to shrink tirty or forty pounds.

MRS. RIVINGTON: Why, gentlemen, you leave me speechless.

GROUCHO: Well, see that you remain that way. Now, after we three are married—

MRS. RIVINGTON: Why, Sir Roderick! I can't marry you. I've got a husband already.

GROUCHO: There you go, always thinking of yourself. And what a dreary subject that is!

MRS. RIVINGTON: But you don't understand. If I married you, it would be bigamy.

GROUCHO: Yes, and that would be big o' me, too. It's big of all of us. Let's be big for a change. I'm sick of all these conventional marriages. One woman and one man was good enough for your grandmother, but who wants to marry your grandmother? Nobody—not even your grandfather!

MRS. RIVINGTON: This is all perfect nonsense. Take me back to my guests.

GROUCHO: Well, I'll take you back to your guests. But they're probably just as sick of you as I am. Ravelli, you wait here. *(Recedes.)* I'll be right back.

CHICO *(yawns)*:   I tink I lay down. *(Noise in bushes.)* Who's dere? *(More noise in bushes.)* Maybe dat'sa Flywheel comin back. Hey, Flywheel! *(Lion snarls away.)* What'sa da matter, Flywheel? You gotta sore troat? *(Lion snarls nearer.)* It no sound like Flywheel. It moost be a rabbit. *(Crashing through bushes, lion roars close.)* Dat'sa da biggest rabbit I ever saw. Why, dat ain't a rabbit at all. It's a big yellow dog! *(Lion snarls very close.)* Hey, I never saw a dog wit a fur collar before. Hey, dog, what'sa you name? *(Snarl.)* Come on now, no back talk! Say, maybe he'sa lost. You lost, doggie? Say, I tink I taka him back to Miss Dimp for a present. She always wanted a lapdog. I betta dis dog got da biggest lap she ever saw. Here doggie, doggie, doggie. Come here. *(Snarl.)* Don't be afraid, I ain'ta gonna hurt you. Come here. Nice doggie, nice doggie. *(Terrific roar.)* Oh, you're gonna get tough, are you? *(Wham! Lion grunts as if wind knocked out of him.)* Now, Rover, you gonna be good? At'sa fine. Sometime when I ain't hungry myself, I give you a piece of liver. *(Lions snarls.)* Hey, I'ma tired of sittin here. Come on, Rover, I taka you up to da house and show you to Flywheel. I bet he like it. *(Another snarl.)* Come on, I'ma tellin you! At'sa fine. You walk right behind me. Awright, now, Rover—march!

GROUCHO *(away)*:   Ravelli! Ravelli! Where are you? It's important.

CHICO: Here I am, boss!

GROUCHO *(approaching)*:   Quick, we've got to run for our lives. The real Sir Roderick has arrived. Mrs. Rivington is making a fuss over him. Is she fickle!

CHICO: Okay, boss, lead da way. I run wit you. *(Whistles.)* Come on, Rover.

(Lion roars.)

GROUCHO: Wh-wh-what's that?

CHICO: Flywheel, I gotta big surprise for you. We gotta new dog. Come here, pooch!

(Lion snarls close.)

GROUCHO: Dog, nothing! *That's* the *lion!* Run! *(Lion snarls.)* Look out, Ravelli! *He's coming after us!*

CHICO: Da lion? *Come on!* Whatta we waitin for? *(Running footsteps and panting.)* Faster, boss, faster!

GROUCHO: Are we getting away from him? You look—I haven't got the heart!

CHICO: Flywheel . . . he's runnin after us! *(Lion roars.)* Go home, Rover! Go home! Hey . . . he's stilla comin!

GROUCHO: He must . . . like you . . . Ravelli. I don't know what . . . h-h-he sees in you.

CHICO: Maybe he sees his dinner.

(*Lions roars close.*)

GROUCHO: I can feel his . . . hot . . . breath . . . on my . . . pants!

CHICO: Hey, look . . . Flywheel! On . . . on da driveway. A kind of a cage . . . on a automobile. It must . . . must be where da lion lives. I guess dey brought . . . it over from da circus.

(*Lion roars.*)

GROUCHO: The door of the cage is open, Ravelli. If we . . . can get in there . . . we're safe.

CHICO: Okay, boss. Jump!

(*Thump, thump.*)

GROUCHO: Quick, Ravelli . . . slam the door!

(*Slam of iron door. Lion roars.*)

CHICO: Ooo . . . we joosta made it. We're safe.

GROUCHO: Whew! What a narrow escape! They're certainly building escapes narrow these days.

(*Lion roars recede.*)

CHICO: Dere goes da lion, boss, down da driveway, over da gate.

GROUCHO: All right. Now, we've gotta get out of *here*. Open this cage door.

(*Rattling of door knob.*)

CHICO: I can't, boss! It's locked. Hey, Flywheel, here comes Mrs. Rivington wit a coupla men. Maybe dey could help us out.

MRS. RIVINGTON (*approaching*):   Well, I'm afraid he got away.

OFFICER 1 (*gruff*):   I wonder which way he went, the rat!

CHICO (*shouting*):   It wasn't a rat, it was a lion! He went out da gate.

MRS. RIVINGTON: Look! There they are. Both of them. In there!

OFFICER 1 (*laughs*):   Ha, ha, ha! Well, I'll be darned! What a break! Come on, Mike, get up in the driver's seat. Let's get going!

OFFICER 2:   Okay.

(*Motor starts.*)

GROUCHO: Hey, where are you taking us? We don't want to go back to the circus!

OFFICER 1:   Circus? Ha, ha, ha! Say, buddy, this is a patrol wagon. You guys are going to jail!

CHICO: Jail? Hey, I wonder if we'll get our old room back.

GROUCHO: Say, officer, do you happen to know if there's any mail there for Waldorf Tecumseh Flywheel?

(*Music in strong.*)

CLOSING ANNOUNCEMENT

ANNOUNCER: You have been entertained tonight in the Five Star Theatre by Groucho and Chico Marx in their three-act comedy, "Flywheel, Shyster, and Flywheel, Attorneys at Law." *(Applause.)*

Keep your seats, ladies and gentlemen, for Groucho and Chico will be back in just a moment.

The Five Star Theatre is sponsored by the Standard Oil Companies of New Jersey, Pennsylvania, and Louisiana, and the Colonial Beacon Oil Company.

Do not forget. On June second the sponsors of this program will place a new product on the market, which will be an important milestone in motor-fuel history. This new motor fuel is a challenge to *all* gasolines. It is a product of the world's largest oil laboratories.

Watch for announcements of this new product in the newspapers, or better still, go to your nearest Esso—spelled E-S-S-O—station or dealer on June second and find out for yourself.

With tonight's program we bring to a close, for the season, the Monday feature in the Five Star Theatre. Throughout the winter the sponsors have been presenting for your pleasure a wide variety of the best radio entertainment it is possible to assemble. The world's leading comedians, great opera and concert singers, stories from the pens of America's leading short-story and mystery writers, symphony, and popular music have all appeared in the Five Star Theatre. If you have enjoyed these programs and would like to have the Five Star Theatre back on the air in the fall, we would appreciate hearing from you.

(Orchestra and chorus: "Auld Lang Syne"; applause.)

ANNOUNCER: Well, I see Groucho and Chico are out on the platform again . . .

AFTERPIECE

CHICO: Ladies and gentlemens. Da broadcast season is over, and I wanna say we was havin some fun here every week.

GROUCHO: Just a minute, Chico. Don't say *havin* some fun. Say *having*. Pronounce the *g*.

CHICO: Awright. *Gee!* We was havin some fun. And now, radio audience, I want you all to coma to my house for dinner tonight.

GROUCHO: Chico! Do you know what you're doing? You're inviting millions of people, and your house is only big enough to hold ten or fifteen.

CHICO: Well, maybe some of 'em can't come. Hey, Groucho, how about you comin over to dinner tonight?

GROUCHO: Dinner tonight? You couldn't make that tomorrow night, could you?

CHICO: Why tomorrow night?

GROUCHO: Because your wife had already invited me over to your house for dinner tonight.

CHICO: Yeah, she like parties and tings, but I'm different. I'd go far away on a ranch. If I had the money.

GROUCHO: Well, if the ranch were far enough away, I'd *give* you the money.

CHICO: At'sa fine. I can go on a ranch, and ride a horse wit a littla lasso.

GROUCHO: Ride a horse with a little Esso? You're crazy. You ride in a car with Esso, which is more powerful than any gasoline.

CHICO: I didn't say Esso. I said lasso, da rope you make in a loop.

GROUCHO: You mean lassolube.

BOTH *(quickly):* That hydrofined motor oil.

GROUCHO: Well, we came out even on that one. Good night, ladies.

BOTH *(singing):* Good night, ladies.

(*Signature music.*)